VIA BOURNEMOUTH HUMANISTS

# Yours Faithfully, Bertrand Russell

*Bertrand Russell in 1916*

# Yours Faithfully, Bertrand Russell

---

## A Lifelong Fight for Peace, Justice, and Truth in Letters to the Editor

BERTRAND RUSSELL

Edited by Ray Perkins, Jr.

OPEN COURT

Chicago and La Salle, Illinois

**To order books from Open Court, call toll free 1-800-815-2280.**

Permission is gratefully acknowledged from: the Bertrand Russell Peace Foundation, for many of the documents reproduced in this book; McMaster University, for the frontispiece photograph; the London *Daily Mail,* for the cartoon by Emmwood; the London *Evening Standard,* for the cartoon by JAK.

Open Court Publishing Company is a division of Carus Publishing Company.



First printing 2002



Printed and bound in the United States of America

**Library of Congress Cataloging-in-Publication Data**

Russell, Bertrand, 1872–1970.
[Correspondence. Selections]
Yours faithfully, Bertrand Russell : a lifelong fight for peace, justice, and truth in letters to the editor / Bertrand Russell ; edited by Ray Perkins, Jr.
p. cm.
Includes bibliographical references and index.
ISBN 0-8126-9449-X — ISBN 0-8126-9450-3 (pbk.)
1. Russell, Bertrand 1872–1970—Views on peace. 2. Russell, Bertrand 1872–1970—Political and social views. I. Perkins, Ray, Jr. II. Title.

B1649.R94 A4 2001
192—dc21

2001036228

*In memory of*
*Frank Birmingham,*
*philosopher, friend*

# Contents

# Preface

Bertrand Russell's letters to the editor give us a unique look at one of the most important philosophers, and one of the most oustanding fighters for justice and peace, of the past one hundred years.

Russell was a great and prodigious writer, penning some 80 books and thousands of articles during his long and active life and receiving the Nobel Prize for Literature in 1950. He made special use of the letter to the editor as a principal means of connection with, and persuasion of, the body politic. This is especially true of his anti-nuclear campaign of the late 1950s and early 1960s; it is true as well of his revelatory criticisms of the American intervention in Vietnam in the mid-1960s.

*Yours Faithfully, Bertrand Russell* is a collection of Russell's letters to the editor between 1904 and 1969. (A few other documents, not strictly letters, are included, but the great majority are letters to the editor.) All of Russell's known letters to the editor, about 400 *in toto*, were carefully read and culled for duplication, leaving nearly 300 letters which are presented here. The letters, on a wide variety of topics, are arranged chronologically in six Parts representing six historical periods. Since Russell's public life was largely focused on the prevention of war and the preservation of humanity, these six historical periods are very naturally demarcated according to the chronology of World War I, World War II, and the Cold War, with the Cold War being divided at the end of 1962, after the Cuban Missile Crisis. Although the theme of war and peace largely defined Russell's public life, many other topics are also covered in these letters.

I have provided a brief introduction to each Part to give the reader a sense of the historical context of Russell's life and an overview of his activity during that period, and I have given each letter a brief introduction where additional information is needed.

To help the reader navigate among a plethora of letters, Parts III–VI have been organized into topics, including human rights and civil liberties, war and peace, education, and philosophy and religion. In some of the letters, Russell refers to people, places, and events that some readers—especially those unfamiliar with British politics and history—may not recognize. In these cases I have provided informative footnotes.

A few of the documents contain more than one letter (for reasons which will be clear on reading them). Each document in the book is numbered consecutively, from [1] to [290]. Because some of the chronological Parts are divided by topic, this numbering order does not always strictly follow the chronological dating of the letters.

In my research, collection, and editing of these letters, I have been helped immensely by Ken Blackwell's and Harry Ruja's remarkable work, *A Bibliography of Bertrand Russell*, Volume II, Part C, which includes detailed bibliographical information for nearly all of Russell's published letters to the editor. Throughout *Yours Faithfully, Bertrand Russell*, I have given the Blackwell and Ruja indexical code for each document. For example, document [1], Russell's earliest letter to the editor, has the indexical code C04.05, showing that this is the fifth published item listed for the year 1904.

Each document is also headed by the original title or description as found in the journal in which it appeared (except for a few where I have supplied a title, given in brackets). In the letter titles, as in the letters themselves, I have allowed the original vagaries of punctuation, spelling, style, and grammar to remain.

The completion of this collection of letters gives me a welcome opportunity to thank those who have helped in matters great and small.

I wish to thank Plymouth State College for their financial support and for granting me time, in the fall of 1999, to work on the letters. Thanks also to my students and colleagues at Plymouth State.

Thanks to my students and colleagues at Plymouth State College: Ben Porter, Deb Naro, David Haight, Dan Kervick, Robin Bowers, Leo Sandy, Joann Guilmett, Jeannie Poterucha, Gary McCool, and especially to Charlene McLaughlin, through whose hard work and word-processing skill 290 documents were typed onto disk.

To the folks at Open Court: Marc Aronson, Kerri Mommer, Jennifer Asmuth, and my editor, David Ramsay Steele, whose good eye and good sense have effected many improvements.

To my friends and associates who provided ideas, information, and encouragement: Jack M. Clontz, Steve Manning, Nancy Needham, Kendall Perkins, John Roberts, Alan Brady, and Stefan Andersson.

To the folks at McMaster University and its Bertrand Russell Archives: Sheila Turcon, Carl Spadoni, Nick Griffin, and Louis Greenspan, and of course, Ken Blackwell, who has provided much assistance and inspiration.

To Ken Coates, Tony Simpson, and the Bertrand Russell Peace Foundation for their generous permission to reprint Russell's letters.

And a special thanks to my family—my wife Karen and my daughter Candice—whose encouragement (and tolerance) I could not have done without.

# Bibliographical Notes

I have used several sources for my brief history of Russell's life and work including Russell's own three-volume *Autobiography of Bertrand Russell* (Little, Brown, 1967–69) as well as his philosophical autobiography, *My Philosophical Development* (Unwin Hyman, 1985; first published in 1959). Another important source of information about Russell's philosophy is the old, but good, *Philosophy of Bertrand Russell*, edited by P.A. Schilpp (Open Court, 1971; first published in 1944). A very readable and succinct account of Russell's philosophy may be found in A.C. Grayling's little book, *Russell* (Oxford University Press, 1996).

Ronald Clark's *The Life of Bertrand Russell* (New York: Knopf, 1976) has been valuable, as has Ray Monk's two-part biography, *Bertrand Russell, 1872–1921: The Spirit of Solitude* (Jonathan Cape, 1996) and *Bertrand Russell, 1921–70: The Ghost of Madness* (Jonathan Cape, 2000). Monk's works are especially good on Russell's philosophical doctrines, and they provide much new material on his life, despite some inattention to its public aspect and, in my judgment, a thinly-disguised antipathy to their subject. Nicholas Griffin's epistolary biography, *The Selected Letters of Bertrand Russell: The Public Years, 1914-1970* (Routledge, 2001), appeared too late to be of use here, but provides a wealth of fascinating detail concerning Russell's life after the First World War.

I have derived much pleasure and help from Barry Feinberg and Ronald Kasrils' two volumes, *Bertrand Russell's America*, Volumes 1 and 2, published by Viking Press (1973) and South End Press (1983), respectively.

In providing historical background for Russell's letters to the editor from 1904 to 1922, I have relied heavily on the marvelous and on-going series, *The Collected Papers of Bertrand Russell: Volume 12, Contemplation and Action 1902–14*, edited by R. Rempel, A. Brink, and M. Moran (Allen and Unwin, 1985), *Volume 13, Prophecy and Dissent 1914–16*, edited by R. Rempel, B. Frohmann, M. Lippincott, and M. Moran (Unwin, 1988), and *Volume 15, Uncertain Paths to Freedom: China and*

*Russia 1919-22*, edited by R. Rempel, B. Haslam, A. Bone, and A. Lewis (Routledge, 2000).

The remarkable and exhaustive work of Ken Blackwell and Harry Ruja, *A Bibliography of Bertrand Russell*, Volume II (Routledge, 1994) has been indispensable for this collection of letters. It has enabled me to identify and obtain virtually all of Russell's published letters to the editor and has enormously facilitated my research.

In the last few years, the Russell email list, owned and managed by the Bertrand Russell Research Centre at McMaster University, has been a much-appreciated source of information, as has the excellent journal, *Russell: The Journal of the Bertrand Russell Archives* (now called *Russell: The Journal of Bertrand Russell Studies*), edited by Ken Blackwell.

# Introduction
## Russell, the Public Gadfly

Bertrand Russell was one of the twentieth century's greatest intellects and one of the world's greatest philosophers. His contributions to technical philosophy and mathematics were enormous. His long, astonishingly productive life spanned nearly a hundred years (1872–1970), but his reputation as one of the century's profoundest thinkers had already been secured by 1910 with the publication of the first volume of *Principia Mathematica*, ranked by some with the theory of relativity as among the very greatest achievements in the domain of human thought.

Russell was more than a great intellect. From almost the beginning of his long professional life, he emphasized the importance of practical, as well as theoretical, wisdom, and, profoundly sensitive to suffering of humankind, he engaged in a life-long battle with the forces of injustice and cruelty. "The good life", as he once put it, "is one inspired by love and guided by knowledge."[1] His unique brand of impassioned logic and political action in defense of reason and human happiness often infuriated conventional opinion and caused him to be opposed by the powers that be, including, at times, his own British government which twice imprisoned him.

These letters to the editor afford us a clear vision of Russell come down from the ivory tower of academia, of Russell in his role of public conscience and gadfly. When the times posed serious threats to human freedom and happiness—British conscription in the First World War, Fascism, McCarthyism, the Cold War and the threat of nuclear annihilation—Russell readily resorted to the letter to the editor as an important tool of communication to challenge the Establishment and to inform public debate.

1. *What I Believe*, a 1925 booklet reprinted in *Why I Am Not a Christian* (Allen and Unwin, 1957), p. 56.

Russell wrote about 400 letters to the editor between 1904 and 1969, approximately 300 of which have been selected for this volume. Most of these letters deal with issues of war and peace; many concern matters of social justice. A few of the omitted letters are of trivial content, but the vast majority are either duplicates or abridged versions of the letters included. Russell, it seems, saved almost everything he wrote, and he wrote much indeed. In 1967, when he sold his papers to McMaster University in Hamilton Ontario, some of his letters to the editor were among the mix, but many required an assiduous search. I obtained copies of most of the letters from the Bertrand Russell Archives about ten years ago. All the letters have been referenced (along with thousands of articles and statements) in the prodigious *Bibliography of Bertrand Russell*, Volume 2, by Ken Blackwell and Harry Ruja (Routledge, 1994).

In volume, the letters amount to no more than a small fraction of the 80 books and several thousand articles in newspapers and journals that Russell published over the course of his long life, but they are an important complement to them. Certainly Russell found them a useful device when he urgently wanted to reach large numbers of the public. This was especially true during the late 1960s when Russell's controversial stance on the Vietnam War made it difficult for him to get his views published as articles in the popular press, his status as renowned philosopher, Nobel Laureate, and recipient of the Order of Merit notwithstanding.

The letters are also important because they help us—professionals and non-professionals alike—to fill in the gaps in our knowledge of the evolution of Russell's political and philosophical ideas, and thereby help us to understand this extraordinary man more completely. For one thing, these letters vividly reveal Russell as a man of almost life-long public concern and conscience. This important aspect of Russell has sometimes been less than fully appreciated. For example, Ray Monk's recent biography of Russell suffers, in part, from inattention to these letters. One of Monk's criticisms is that after 1921 Russell largely stopped doing "serious" work and took to writing "second rate" articles and books just to make money to support his family. Quite apart from the existence of at least four "serious" philosophical works[2] between 1921 and 1948, the view of Russell as a concerned citizen attempting to contribute to public policy through public dialogue on matters of peace and justice provides an important counterweight to Monk's unflattering and incomplete portrayal. Surprisingly, Monk has

2. *The Analysis of Mind* (1921), *The Analysis of Matter* (1927), *An Inquiry into Meaning and Truth* (1940), and *Human Knowledge: Its Scope and Limits* (1948).

almost nothing to say about Russell's extensive work on behalf of human rights in the 1950s and 1960s—work which becomes quite apparent on even a cursory reading of his public letters.

Moreover, Russell's letters to the editor frequently offer clarification of his published views, as well as rebuttals of criticisms of those views. So inattention to the letters can easily result in a kind of straw man criticism of the form: "Russell is unclear about . . ." or "Russell has nothing to say about . . ." Monk, on more than one occasion, inadvertently indulges in this form of criticism—for example, in his claim that Russell defended Soviet missiles in Cuba at the time of the Missile Crisis, even though Russell denies the charge and explains its origin in his letters.[3] The point isn't, of course, that Russell's explanation was right or wrong, but rather that Monk completely failed to consider it.

Even worse, such inattention can lead to unwarranted inferences about Russell's official views, such as Monk's speculations about the radicalizing influence of Russell's young American secretary, Ralph Schoenman, on Russell's political views in the 1960s. Thus, Monk notices that Russell's anti-nuclear writings had not, in the late 1950s, included a demand for British withdrawal from NATO, but did include such a demand in the early 1960s, soon after he met Schoenman.[4] The implication drawn is that Schoenman caused Russell to abandon the earlier position that was "still undeniably his and not Schoenman's." But the anti-NATO position was undeniably his too, inasmuch as he had publicly advocated that position, in a letter to the editor of the *Manchester Guardian*, at least a month before he met Schoenman (see document [139] below).

It's not just confirmatory details about his other writings that the public letters can supply. Indeed, they can also be a source of information about aspects of Russell's career otherwise wholly unknown. None of Russell's biographers has had anything to say about his concern with Gandhi's movement in India in the 1930s, despite the fact that Russell served as Chairman of The India League in the U.K. and penned seven letters to the *Manchester Guardian* on Indian politics.

Although his letters to the editor are largely concerned with issues of peace and justice, they should be of interest to students of Russell's technical philosophy as well. To take just one example, Russell was a pioneer in the formulation of a metaethical theory known as subjectivism or emotivism—the doctrine that ethical judgments have no cognitive meaning

3. For example, in his response to Paul Johnson, "Labour and the Intellectuals," *New Statesman* (8th March, 1963), p. 336. See below, document [224].

4. Ray Monk, *Bertrand Russell: The Ghost of Madness* (London: Cape, 2000), p. 406.

and lack truth-value. This view finds one of its earliest expressions in Russell's *Religion and Science* (1935). But a nascent form of the doctrine appears as early as 1916 in one of Russell's letters to the editor concerning the ethics of the First World War.[5] Other examples include letters dealing with his theory of neutral monism, the status of sense-data, the nature of mathematical induction and reflections on the speed of light.

Russell's public letters allow us to see Russell at his polemical best, dueling wittily and wisely with some of the most important political leaders of the day. They tell us much about the social and political history of the last century. But most of all, they tell an inspiring story of one remarkable man's protracted battle to infuse public policy with reason and compassion.

## Russell's Life and Work

Bertrand Russell begins his autobiography with this sentence: "Three passions, simple but overwhelmingly strong, have governed my life: the longing for love, the search for knowledge, and unbearable pity for the suffering of mankind" (*The Autobiography of Bertrand Russell* [Little, Brown, 1967], Volume 1, p. 3). Most of Russell's letters to the editor—certainly those on war and peace—fall under the governance of the third passion. But no account of his life and work can fail to notice the other two as well.

Bertrand Russell was born in Wales in 1872 to John and Catherine Russell (Lord and Lady Amberley). His godfather (a secular godfather—his parents were free-thinkers) was John Stuart Mill, the famed English philosopher and arch-advocate of liberty and justice. His grandfather was Lord John Russell (1804–1874), twice Prime Minister of Great Britain. Russell's parents and his younger sister died when he was three, and he and his older brother Frank were left in the care of their paternal grandparents in England. When his grandfather died two years later, young Bertrand ('Bertie', as he was called) was raised in the dour Victorian household of his grandmother. Russell was tutored at home and showed special talent for mathematics at a very early age. He entered Trinity College of Cambridge University in 1890 where he studied mathematics and philosophy. At Cambridge he met and befriended many who would become important contributors to twentieth-century thought, including Alfred North Whitehead, J.M.E. McTaggart, Ludwig

5. "North Staffs' Praise of War." *The Cambridge Magazine* (11th March, 1916), p. 386. See below. The importance of this letter is duly noted by Charles Pigden in his excellent book, *Russell on Ethics* (London: Routledge, 1999), p. 17.

Wittgenstein, G.E. Moore, and John Maynard Keynes. It was with Moore that Russell broke away from the influence of Hegelian Idealism, then in vogue at Cambridge, and took philosophy in the direction of logical and linguistic analysis. In 1894 he married Alys Pearsall Smith.

Russell's early fame was for his seminal work in the foundations of mathematics. His pioneering *Principles of Mathematics* (1903)—which some experts mark as the beginning of contemporary philosophy—and the later three-volume *Principia Mathematica* (1910–13), written with his friend and teacher Alfred North Whitehead, established the thesis of logicism, according to which all of mathematics is reducible to a few basic ideas and principles of logic.

While working on *Principles of Mathematics* in 1901, Russell discovered the famous paradox that bears his name. Russell's Paradox concerns the class of classes that are not members of themselves. Some classes are apparently members of themselves, for instance: the class of abstract objects is itself an abstract object. Some classes are not members of themselves, for instance: the class of men is not itself a man. But what about the class of classes that are not members of themselves? Is it a member of itself? If it is, it isn't; and if it isn't, it is—a contradiction! To Russell in 1901 this seemed to mean that the concept of class—and therefore of arithmetic which he took to be built on the concept of class—was logically defective. When Russell reported his discovery to the great German mathematician-logician Gottlob Frege, the latter remarked that the paradox "shook the foundations of arithmetic." Russell spent the next seven years searching for a satisfactory solution of this paradox—his theory of types—and finally incorporated it into *Principia Mathematica*.

Along this intellectual trek he also discovered, in 1905, his famous theory of descriptions—"that paradigm of philosophy" as Frank Ramsey described it. The theory of descriptions was an instrument of linguistic analysis that helped to solve many ancient puzzles about meaning and existence. We all manage to talk about non-existent things, and even to make true assertions about them, for example that the round square does not exist. Some philosophers, including apparently even Russell in his 1903 *Principles of Mathematics*, thought that non-existent objects had to have some kind of Being in order to be thought about. The theory of descriptions helped to explain, among other things, how it's possible to talk—and make true assertions—about such things without supposing that there really are such strange entities. His main idea was that descriptions (phrases of the form 'the so and so'), don't function like proper names for objects or people that we are acquainted with, even if they grammatically appear to. Rather, they pick out their objects indirectly through universal words and what Russell called propositional functions (for example, 'x is round and square'). Thus, when we say that the round square does not exist, we are really saying something like 'Nothing fulfills the description (satisfies the propositional function) of being round and square.' In so doing we speak truly without having to assume the reality of some such object named by the descriptive phrase.

His early genius in the philosophy of mathematics notwithstanding, Russell expressed a strong interest in politics and political theory. His first book, published in 1896, was *German Social Democracy.* This work defended democratic socialism, but criticized Karl Marx's ideas regarding violent revolution and the primacy of economic motive as the determinant of history. Regarding these criticisms Russell said more than a half-century later, "I have had no reason to change."

In 1903–04, at the same time that he was struggling with the Paradox, Russell's concerns also focused on politics, and he took up defense of the free trade issue in opposition to official government policy. In the watershed 1906 general election, in which the Liberals came to power, Russell ran (or, in British parlance, 'stood') for Parliament as a member of the Liberal Party on behalf of women's suffrage. He was unsuccessful.

The next seven years were years of intense intellectual labor and great philosophical production. About the time that Russell was winding up the third and last volume of *Principia Mathematica*, he published his popular *Problems of Philosophy* (1912). This little book has been widely read throughout the world since its appearance, and many still regard it as one of the very best introductions to philosophy. It was at this time that he met Lady Ottoline Morrell who became his lover for several years and a confidante until her death in 1938.

In the spring of 1914, a few months before the outbreak of the First World War, Russell went to Harvard University to teach and lecture. One of his pupils was the poet T.S. Eliot who became a close friend and even wrote a poem about him. At Harvard, Russell gave the Lowell Lectures which were published as *Our Knowledge of the External World* (1914), a brilliant book combining the empiricism of Berkeley and Hume with mathematical logic to solve the problem of how we know the physical world and how we bridge the philosophical gulf between appearance and reality. It was a highly influential work which set forth the outline of Russell's special brand of analysis known as Logical Atomism, and it inspired the related philosophical school of Logical Positivism which developed and thrived in the 1930s.

During the First World War Russell continued to produce important technical work in philosophy. This is remarkable given the fact that Russell was almost immediately swept up in the politics connected with the war. He became a principal spokesman for the pacifist cause and one of the most ardent opponents of military conscription in England. In this capacity he wrote much and lectured widely until the government forbade him to travel abroad (he was prevented from going to Harvard to lecture in 1917) and restricted his movements within Great Britain. He was fined in 1916 for his pamphleteering on behalf of conscientious objection, and he was consequently dismissed from his lectureship at Cambridge.

In 1918, Russell was sentenced to six months in prison for writing an anti-war essay which the government said violated the Defense of the Realm Act by insulting the United States, a wartime British ally. Many of Russell's wartime lectures and speeches appeared as two books during the war: *The Principles of Social Reconstruction* (1916)—also published in America as *Why Men Fight*—and *Justice in War Time* (1917). By this time Russell had spent virtually all of his inheritance (most of it given away to needy friends, including his most famous pupil, Ludwig Wittgenstein) and was fully dependent on his pen to support himself.

Prison was not wholly an unpleasant experience for Russell and provided him with something of a respite from what had been an exhausting schedule. In his *Autobiography*, he recounts an early event that helped to sustain his spirits.

> I was much cheered in my arrival by the warder at the gate who had to take particulars about me. He asked my religion and I replied "agnostic." He asked how to spell it, and remarked with a sigh: "Well, there are many religions, but I suppose they all worship the same God." (*Autobiography*, vol. 2, p. 30)

The war was a radicalizing experience for Russell, and afterwards he gave much attention to the task of reorganizing society along the lines of internationalism and socialism sketched in his *Principles of Social Reconstruction*. In 1920 he went to Russia with a delegation of trade unionists for the purpose of seeing first hand how the Russian society was faring under Bolshevism. His visit—which included a meeting with Lenin—resulted in *The Theory and Practice of Bolshevism* (1920), a book which angered many British socialists and conservatives alike: the former because it was forthright about the brutality and repression that Russell found in the new Soviet society; the latter because it equally denounced the evils of capitalism and espoused a form of evolutionary democratic socialism as a goal for the West.

In 1920, shortly after his trip to the U.S.S.R., Russell and his secretary (soon to be his second wife) Dora Black went off for a year-long visit to China. Russell lectured at the University of Peking, where his audiences included Chou En-lai. Russell fell in love with China and criticized western imperialist interference with Chinese civilization. His impressions and outlook were recorded in *The Problem of China* (1922) and, jointly with Dora Black, *Prospects for Industrial Civilization* (1923). When he returned from China he divorced Alys and married Dora with whom he produced two children, John (1921) and Kate (1923).

In addition to travels in Russia and China, the 1920s were a full and fascinating decade for Russell—including two more unsuccessful runs for Parliament, as a Labour Party candidate (1922 and 1923); a third visit to America lecturing on world peace and socialism; and the founding, with Dora, of a progressive school for children (Beacon Hill) in southern England, an undertaking which built on his ideas in education as set forth in his earlier *Principles of Social Reconstruction* and *On Education* (1926).

Russell also ventured into the realm of science, writing *The ABC of Atoms* (1923), *Icarus, or the Future of Science* (1924) and *The ABC of Relativity* (1925), one of the best popular accounts of Einstein's theories ever written.

But perhaps his most popular work at the time—certainly his most controversial—was *Marriage and Morals* (1929). This little book, in which Russell advocated a more humane and tolerant sexual ethic, shocked conventional moralists who cited it a decade later at City College New York—usually out of context—as evidence of Russell's moral depravity and unfitness to teach.

When Russell's older brother Frank died in 1931, the earldom passed over to Bertrand. He officially became Lord Russell, although he was indifferent to the title—usually signing his public letters as 'Bertrand Russell' and only rarely using the correct aristocratic form of simply 'Russell'—and he never became an active member of the House of Lords. "The House of Lords," as he once said with characteristic directness, "is not a body whose deliberations affect events."[6] He did appear before that august body on one rare occasion in 1945 to warn against the dangers of a nuclear arms race.

In the years leading up to World War Two, Russell foresaw the approaching calamity in Europe. But he advocated pacifism and non-violent resistance should war come. His reasons were carefully set forth in *Which Way to Peace?* (1936). His ideas about the nature and origins of power, then assuming totalitarian proportions in Europe, soon appeared as *Power: A New Social Analysis* in 1938, a highly original work in which Russell analyzes the various kinds of power and the prospects for taming them. As in his earlier *Religion and Science* (1935), he frequently compares the ideological fanaticism of communism and fascism with the religious fanaticism that retarded the progress of science for 300 years after Copernicus. For fanaticism of both kinds, Russell's antidote is an open,

6. Ronald Clark, *The Life of Bertrand Russell* (Knopf, 1976), p. 594.

liberal society in which individual free thought has attained a proper blend of scientific rationality and kindly feeling—a formula not so different from that proffered in his delightfully profound 1925 essay 'What I Believe'.

The approaching war in Europe and hopes of getting a teaching position in America brought Russell to the United States once again where he and his family remained until their return to England in 1944. Shortly after the beginning of the Second World War, Russell came to doubt that pacifism was a satisfactory response to the Nazis, and he repudiated his earlier position of non-violent resistance and supported the armed struggle against Fascism. He performed this *volte-face* publicly in a long letter to the *New York Times*. Russell was then living in California with his three children and his third wife, Patricia Spence, whom he had married in 1936 after a bitter divorce from Dora.

After teaching briefly at the University of Chicago and UCLA, Russell accepted an appointment at City College of New York. But the position was blocked by Russell's detractors, who carried on an extensive campaign of personal vilification. In the spring of 1940, he found himself with his family cut off from England by the war, unable to get a job or publish his work. Even Harvard, feeling the heat generated by the CCNY controversy, nearly canceled his William James Lectures scheduled for that spring. These lectures became his *An Inquiry Into Meaning and Truth* (1940)—an important work in the philosophy of language and in his on-going attempts to solve the problem of the connection between language and reality.

Despite Russell's troubles at City College and the controversy surrounding his name, the Barnes Foundation of Philadelphia hired him to give a series of lectures in the history of philosophy. These lectures eventually became Russell's very popular *A History of Western Philosophy* (1945), a best-seller which sustained him financially for several years, and which was probably instrumental in his receiving the Nobel Prize for literature (there is none for philosophy) in 1950.

After the war, Russell returned to England and was reinstated as a Fellow at Cambridge. Even though he produced an important technical work in the theory of knowledge in 1948 at the age of 76—*Human Knowledge: Its Scope and Limits*—it was the Bomb and Cold War politics that dominated his writing and thinking for the rest of his days.

Russell was one of the first to see clearly the threat to human civilization in the nuclear age if war were not abolished. In his mind the need for world government had never been greater. In the early post-war years, Russell proposed that the West might use its temporary nuclear monopoly to coerce Stalinist Russia to agree to world government and to international controls on the instruments of war. Soon after the Russians got their own bomb in 1949, Russell emphasized the idea that it was nuclear war—not the victory of this or that ideology—which posed the gravest dangers to all human beings, capitalist and communist alike. Only a policy of East-West co-operation, not confrontation, held hope, he thought, for averting nuclear annihilation.

For a while after the war, Russell was afforded the status of the venerated grand old citizen and resident sage, a status of 'respectability' with which he was not altogether comfortable. He received the prestigious Order of Merit in 1949 and the Nobel Prize in 1950. These accolades enhanced his already considerable international reputation. The BBC invited him to do radio broadcasts on politics and philosophy, and the British Foreign Office even made him a spokesman for NATO policy. He was frequently quoted for his wit and wisdom in *Reader's Digest*. In 1952 he married his fourth wife, Edith Finch, an American professor he had met at Bryn Mawr and with whom he would remain happily married until his death in 1970.

In 1955, Russell and Albert Einstein proclaimed the Russell-Einstein Manifesto—a document signed by some of the world's most distinguished scientists, and which appealed to human beings as human beings to renounce war and nuclear weapons as instruments of policy. In the memorable words of the Manifesto (borrowed from an earlier essay by Russell), the great philosopher urges us to "Remember your humanity, and forget the the rest. If you can do so, the way lies open to a new Paradise; if you cannot, nothing lies before you but universal death."

At this time, Russell's anti-nuclear campaign had begun to irritate official Western Cold War policy makers. He criticized both superpowers for their brinkmanship, and he urged the British government not to become a nuclear power. After Britain tested the H-bomb, he publicly urged that it give up its nuclear weapons unilaterally, withdraw from NATO, and assume a neutralist role to help defuse East-West hostilities. Many of his ideas at this time were set forth in his *Common Sense and Nuclear Warfare* (1959).

For several years he served as President of the Campaign for Nuclear Disarmament, and when he thought it had become less than effective, he, along with his young American secretary, Ralph Schoenman, organized the 'Committee of 100', which advocated and practiced civil disobedience. In 1961, at the age of 89, Russell (with his wife Edith) was, for a second time in his life, sentenced to prison for disobeying his nation's laws in the cause of peace.

During October of 1962, Russell received world-wide notoriety when, in the midst of the Cuban Missile Crisis, he exchanged telegrams with Khrushchev and Kennedy, beseeching both to step back from the brink of nuclear war and find a political solution to the standoff. Many hailed Russell as a hero who had helped resolve the Crisis and spare the world by providing Khrushchev with a face-saving way out. But his opponents never forgot, or forgave, his own assessment that it was Khrushchev, not Kennedy, who had practiced proper restraint and to whom the world should be grateful.

In 1963, at the age of 91, he founded the Bertrand Russell Peace Foundation to carry on, institutionally, work for world peace and human rights. Among its sponsors were nine heads of state, including Nehru of India and Ayub Khan of Pakistan. Although the Foundation's mission was wide-ranging (it launched 'The British Who Killed Kennedy? Committee' which denounced the Warren Commission Report as a cover-up), Russell and his Foundation soon became primarily focused on the expanding U.S. war in Vietnam, which he characterized as one of "imperialist aggression." Russell came under severe criticism at this time for what many said was his failure to contain Ralph Schoenman's excesses, including the latter's extension of the Foundation's peace functions to include support for indigenous rebellions in the Third World on the models of Cuba and Vietnam. In 1969, a few months before his death, Russell formally repudiated Schoenman.

Many of Russell's writings against the war were published as *War Crimes In Vietnam* (1967). At that time, with the help of his Foundation, he initiated the International War Crimes Tribunal to expose and condemn U.S. war crimes in Vietnam in accordance with the principles set down by the Allies at Nuremberg at the end of World War Two. Although his criticisms of U.S. foreign policy were often harsh, even strident, and many accused him of rabid anti-Americanism, he was never blind to Soviet transgressions, domestic or foreign. Despite his advanced age (96), he unequivocally and repeatedly condemned the 1968 Soviet invasion of Czechoslovakia.

By the end of his life his fame had become global. In the course of ten decades he had dined with nearly a dozen prime ministers, written more than 80 books, corresponded with eminent world leaders, organized scientists from East and West to dialogue on ending the nuclear arms race, and served as an inspiration for the cause of peace and justice across the planet.

Socrates is reputed to have said: "The unexamined life is not worth living." Russell certainly agreed; and, perhaps even more than Socrates, he was convinced that rational inquiry could lead to genuine understanding about the world. But he also put a premium on action in the pursuit of justice rationally revealed. And the role that he played out in his public life was a role not unlike that described by Socrates when pressed to defend himself against Athenian charges of political and religious heresy: that his relationship to the state was like that of a gadfly to a large horse "which because of its great size is inclined to be lazy and needs the stimulation of some stinging fly." Russell was a twentieth-century Socrates. And, like that great teacher, he too was a public gadfly—not only for his native Britain, but for the world and the human family.

PART I

# Early Letters

(1904–1913)

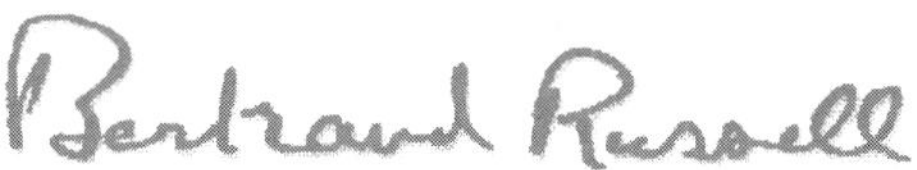

There are only nine known public letters to the editor from the nine years before World War I.[1] Seven of these are reprinted below. By contrast, in the last decade of his life Russell produced ten times as many letters, dealing mainly with the Cold War.

This early period was one of enormous achievement in technical philosophy. These were the years in which Russell produced his famous theory of descriptions, worked out several solutions to Russell's Paradox, wrote his perennial primer *The Problems of Philosophy*, and, with Alfred North Whitehead, published three volumes of *Principia Mathematica*. Yet, Russell manages to find time to join in the public debate on some of the most controversial topics of the day, and even to stand for Parliament.

Russell himself was something of a paradox, a curious combination of an intellectual need to understand the world and a practical desire to change it. Part of this, no doubt, was due to his grandmother's upbringing which was designed to produce a sense of public duty befitting the grandson of a Prime Minister. But it also had to do with a quasi-religious experience that Russell underwent in 1901 when he witnessed a close friend (Evelyn Whitehead) suffering a severe bout of pain from an apparent heart attack:

> She seemed cut off from everyone and everything by walls of agony, and the sense of solitude of each human soul suddenly overwhelmed me. . . . Suddenly the ground seemed to give way beneath me, and I found myself in quite another region. Within five minutes I went through some such reflections as the following: the loneliness of the human soul is unendurable; nothing can penetrate it except the highest intensity of the sort of love that religious teachers have preached; whatever does not spring from this motive is harmful, . . . it follows that war is wrong, that a public school education is abominable, that the use of force is to be deprecated, and that in human relations one should penetrate to the core of loneliness in each person and speak to that. . . . At the end of those five minutes, I had become a completely different person. . . . Having been an imperialist, I became during those five minutes a pro-Boer and a pacifist. Having for years cared only for exact analysis I found myself filled with semi-mystical feelings about beauty, with an intense interest in children, and with a desire almost as profound as that of the Buddha to find some philosophy which should make human life endurable. (*Autobiography*, Volume I, pp. 220–21)

1. All of these letters have been reprinted in *The Collected Papers of Bertrand Russell*, Volume 12.

Russell's rational and analytic side would reassert itself in the decades ahead, but he was indelibly marked by that experience, and an undeniable empathy for the welfare of humankind became a passion as great as his love of knowledge.

In 1902 Russell joined the Coefficients—a political discussion club organized by Sidney and Beatrice Webb, the economists and social reformers—where he frequently met with influencial political people, including H.G. Wells, Edward Grey (Foreign Secretary 1905–1916) and Arthur Balfour (Prime Minister 1902–1905). The group proved to be too imperialistic and militaristic for Russell's pacifist sentiments. On one occasion, Edward Grey introduced the idea of the Entente, soon to become Government policy. Russell objected, arguing that it would lead to war. Nobody would agree with him, and he resigned from the club.

In 1904, he took up the defense of free trade which was then under attack by the Conservative government of Arthur Balfour and his Colonial Secretary, Joseph Chamberlain. He gave many free trade speeches and wrote a substantial piece for the *Edinburgh Review* criticizing the government's ideas on protectionism and tariff reform, especially those of Chamberlain. Russell saw abandonment of free trade as bad for England, but especially bad for international relations.

The Conservatives were defeated in 1905, largely because of their stand on the free trade question, and the Liberals took control of British politics until a coalition government under David Lloyd George was formed in 1915. With the free trade issue cooled, Russell took up the cause of women's suffrage. Like his 'radical' parents, he favored the franchise for women, and stood for Parliament as a Liberal Party candidate in a Wimbledon by-election (an election to fill a vacant seat) in 1907. This was a bitter campaign in which he was assisted by his American Quaker wife, Alys Pearsall Smith, who had long been involved in feminist causes.

Russell, after a deeply religious adolescence, became a life-long agnostic. And though he frequently revealed quasi-religious emotion toward both humanity and the physical universe, he was very critical of organized religion. In 1910, Russell felt an urge to go into politics, but he made it clear to the Liberal Party Selection Committee that he was an agnostic and would not be willing to attend church for the sake of appearance. The Party chose another candidate. We get a hint of Russell's disapproval of organized religion, as well as his puckish delight in riling Church authorities, in his 1913 letter on the "The Proposed Changes in the Ordination Service" within the Church of England.

[1]

## Mr. Charles Booth on Fiscal Reform

*The Spectator* (16th January, 1904), pp. 83–84 | C04.05

*This is Russell's earliest known letter to the editor. It concerns the issue of free trade which the Conservative government—under Arthur Balfour and his Colonial Secretary, Joseph Chamberlain—wanted to curtail with various protectionist measures. It is best understood in the context of a lengthy article, 'The Tariff Controversy',[2] that Russell published at that time.*

*Free trade had been part of British fiscal policy since 1846, and it was very much part of Russell's Liberal heritage according to which free trade promoted class harmony, prosperity at home, and peace abroad. In a letter to a friend he wrote, "We are all wildly excited about Free Trade; it is to me the last piece of sane internationalism left, and if it went I should feel inclined to cut my throat."[3]*

*Here Russell defends free trade against the proposals of Charles Booth, a social critic, poverty expert, and friend of Secretary Chamberlain.*

Sir, —The great weight justly attaching to the opinions of Mr. Charles Booth renders it important to examine the proposals for fiscal reform which he has set forth in the current number of the National Review. These proposals are:—(1) To place a tax upon all imports from foreign countries to the extent of 5 per cent. ad valorem when we have a commercial treaty with the country concerned, or of 10 per cent. when we have no treaty. (2) To give an export drawback to those who manufacture for export from imported materials. His defence of this scheme begins by a somewhat unfair criticism of the Free-trade case, which is said to be "cosmopolitan in its ideal, laissez-faire in its philosophy, and individualist in its principles." It is impossible to see how such a description can apply to the contention that a nation is impoverished by the imposition of Protective import-duties or export-bounties. This contention is purely scientific, and is wholly independent of any particular philosophy. And it has no cosmopolitan element, except a refusal to admit without evidence that the prosperity of one nation requires the poverty of others. Mr. Booth next contends that it is desirable to receive the payment on our foreign investments in the shape of raw materials rather than finished manufactures, in order that employment may be given to British labour by such imports. It is not necesary to examine whether this is desirable,

2. *The Edinburgh Review*, 199 (January, 1904), pp. 169–196.
3. *Autobiography*, Volume I, p. 258.

since no reason is given for supposing that a uniform tariff would have this effect. On the contrary, the export policy of foreign Trusts, by giving us half-finished goods more cheaply than they can be obtained in the countries where they are produced, tends to give us an advantage, in all the later stages of manufacture, which we should lose by abandoning Free-trade. How real this advantage is may be seen in any account of those doings of those German Cartels that control the production of half-finished goods. One of the objects aimed at by Mr. Booth is to increase the regularity of employment. He gives no grounds for supposing that this result will follow, and it is hard to guess what his grounds are. Unemployment does not depend upon whether we import much or little, but upon the fluctuations of trade. A sudden increase or a sudden diminution of imports of any kind of goods will alike cause unemployment. The imposition of a tariff is likely at first to cause unemployment in those trades not directly benefited by it; later, through over production, it causes unemployment also in the protected trades. And theory and experience alike show that the fluctuations in protected countries, such as Germany and the United States, are more violent than in the United Kingdom.

Mr. Booth desires a uniform scheme, both as a safeguard against corruption and as a guarantee of finality. In both respects there is reason to think his scheme would fail. Taxation of raw cotton and wool, for example, is not within practical politics; thus some exceptions become inevitable. In regard to other commodities, 5 per cent. would soon be declared insufficient; it would be found that a uniform rate for different stages of some particular manufacture was too unscientific and must be modified. Ad valorem duties, again, are well-known causes of fraud; this would doubtless lead to their abandonment, in many cases, in favour of specific duties aiming at a 5 per cent. average; and in fixing these duties there would be endless opportunities for corrupt influence. Another cause of divergence from uniformity would be commercial wars. Is it likely that we should remain content with a beggarly 10 per cent. if we were met by an embargo on our shipping and prohibitive duties on all our exports? The difficulties of export drawbacks are also very great, as experience has shown in Germany; and in any case they cannot compensate a manufacturer for the increased cost of all his tools and machinery, even assuming (as we legitimately may) that Mr. Chamberlain's promise of higher wages is groundless. On the effect of Protection on prices Mr. Booth is strangely inconsistent. He maintains in a single paragraph (p. 697) both that competition among home producers prevents Protection from raising prices, and that the formation of Trusts and Cartels resulting from Protection leads to the policy of selling dear at home and cheap abroad. The latter is, of course, the truth in regard to all goods of which the production can be monopolised, and this includes almost all finished manufactures as well as (in America) a very large proportion of the food supply. One might have supposed that the gibe of being "friends of every country but their own" would have applied to those who advocate the policy of making presents to the foreigner which are refused to the home consumer, especially when, as in such a case as steel, the commodity concerned is vital to many of the greatest industries. And it is very important to note that Mr. Booth speaks of the "absolute need" of Trusts and Cartels in Protective countries. Such organisations have been sometimes supposed to aim chiefly at economy of production. In a Free-trade country, if they exist, this must be their motive; and in any case they are powerless for harm. But in Protective countries their chief motive has always been the exaction of monopoly prices, and economies, when they have occurred, have only swelled profits without lowering prices; and it has been customary, at least in America, to devote part of such profits to "educating" the Legislature, the Executive, and the electorate. It is hard to believe that Mr. Booth views these results with equanimity. Yet if he does not, it is strange that he should have joined Mr. Chamberlain's Commission, where a uniform tariff is the very thing not desired.

—I am, Sir, &c., Bertrand Russell

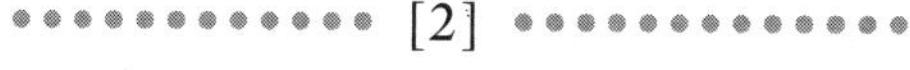

## International Competition

*The Spectator* (30th January, 1904), p. 180 | C04.07

*This is Russell's reply to the new Colonial Secretary, Alfred Lyttelton, who had recently claimed in a speech before the House of Commons, that under free trade, British industries could not compete with those of other countries which had the advantage of cheaper labor—an argument still very often heard today.*

Sir, —Mr. Alfred Lyttelton in a recent speech is reported by the *Times* of January 27th as having said that it was amazing that "people who were absolutely convinced of the necessity that in England industry should be carried on under humane conditions to the worker were wholly unable to derive from that principle the obvious corollary that, if you allow these conditions to prevail in England, which of course make the production of commodities more expensive, and permit to be be freely imported into this country commodities from countries abroad where those conditions of humanity do not prevail, you are obviously subjecting the workers of this country to the competition of men of lower standards, which must tend either to pull down the standard in England, or if it did not pull it down, cause the greatest friction and inconvenience." May I inquire on what terms Mr. Lyttelton would propose to admit the produce of India to compete with that of our own fields and factories? It is well known that the standard of life in India is much lower than that of any of our competitors in Europe or America. Will Mr. Lyttelton, when a tariff comes to be framed, admit American goods free for the reason—a reason constantly urged by Protectionists for other purposes—that American labour is more highly paid than ours? Of course Free-traders deny Mr. Lyttelton's premises. Apart from all objections to his argument that might be based upon the theory of international trade, it has been proved in innumerable instances that high wages and good conditions, by increasing efficiency, lower the cost of production instead of raising it. Does Mr. Lyttelton think that the low-paid Russians or the highly paid Americans are our more formidable industrial competitors? Perhaps, too, the new Colonial Secretary will conduct a cable controversy with Mr. Seddon as to whether the latter was right in describing protectionist countries as heaven and England as hell for workmen,—a statement which appears inconvemient for Mr. Lyttelton's argument. What is "amazing" is not the supposed blindness of Free-traders, but the fact that a man holding high office should, on the main question of the day, permit himself to repeat an argument which has been a thousand times refuted, and which he himself, by half an hour's conversation with any well-informed person, would have found to be wholly fallacious. The whole question of conditions of labour in connection with international competition is clearly and ably discussed in the first chapter of "The Case for the Factory Acts," edited by Mrs. Sidney Webb. If Mr. Lyttelton will read this discussion, perhaps his "amazement" will cease.

—I am, Sir, &c., Bertrand Russell

[3]

## M. Poincaré's Science and Hypothesis

*Mind* (15th January, 1906), p. 143. | C06.01

*In 1905 Russell had written two reviews of Henri Poincaré's famous* Science and Hypothesis *(1902). The second review, in which Russell gives Poincaré a lesson in the foundations of mathematics, annoyed Poincaré and he replied to Russell in the journal* Mind. *The following letter, reprinted here for the first time, is Russell's reply and attempt to clarify the main issue of disagreement between them.*

*Henri Poincaré (1854–1912) was a French mathematician and theoretical scientist, and one of the most influential philosophers of science of his day. His theory that truth in mathematics and science is largely a matter of convention was a view not shared by Russell in 1906, but one toward which he would move after World War I.*

M. Poincaré's reply to my review in MIND, July, 1905, calls for a few words of explanation.

On the subject of mathematical induction I await his forthcoming article in the *Révue de Métaphysique et de Morale*. But I should like to clear up a misunderstanding as to the sense in which, as I hold, mathematical induction does not proceed from the particular to the general. (Mathematical induction, by the way, does not define integers, but finite integers.) The principle may be stated as follows: "A number n is said to obey mathematical induction if it possesses every property which (1) belongs to 0, and (2) belongs to m + 1 whenever it belongs to m". Here the principle itself is doubly general, since (a) it makes a statement about all properties, (b) it makes a statement about all numbers. The statement about all numbers occurs in (2) above. And when we have taken a particular property, and thus ceased to concern ourselves with the general principle of induction, we still have a general statement about all numbers. Let us take an instance: Suppose we wish to prove that if n obeys mathematical induction, then n is not equal to n + 1. We prove (a) that 0 is not equal to 1, (b) that if m is not equal to m + 1, then m + 1 is not equal to m + 2. Here (b) is a statement about all numbers. It is only from (a) and (b) together that we reach the desired conclusion. The generality of (b) is not the kind of generality that M. Poincaré supposes me to mean when he suggests that I wish to adduce the principle of mathematical induction itself as a necessary premiss in all its applications.

As regards geometry, I do not think it is necessary to my point to decide what is meant by perception. My point is that relations of order, as opposed to metrical relations, are in some sense given in experience, and that this appears to show that spatial relations are to some extent empirically determined.

I regret that my remark about "Abracadabra" appeared to be a mere epigram. I meant to suggest that what it is convenient to suppose must have some meaning, and I did not suppose that I was "profiting by an ambiguity," which I should be most unwilling to do consciously.

B. RUSSELL

•••••••••••••• [4] ••••••••••••••

## To the Electors

3rd May, 1907 (CPBR, Volume 12, p. 268) | C06.01

*This one is not a letter to the editor. After the Liberal victory in the election of 1906, Russell stood for Parliament in the Wimbledon by-election the next year as a Liberal on behalf of women's suffrage.*[4] *Russell's loss was expected inasmuch as Wimbledon was a Unionist*[5] *stronghold. The following public message comes from Russell's election pamphlet.*

Gentlemen

I come before you primarily as a supporter of the proposal to GRANT THE SUFFRAGE TO WOMEN on the same terms as to men. I consider that the exclusion of women from direct political action is unjust and inexpedient, and that no reason exists for prolonging this exclusion. If elected, I should urge the claims of womem to enfranchisement at every opportunity.

Subject to the paramount claims of this question, I shall, if elected, be a supporter of the present Government. In particular, I consider the **maintenance of Free Trade** essential to the prosperity of the United Kingdom, and I believe that the imposition of preferential duties in favour of Colonial produce must raise the cost of living and tend to the disruption of the Empire, while a protective tariff must foster trusts and promote political corruption.

The proper complement of Free Trade is, in my opinion, the

TAXATION OF LAND VALUES

which would, I believe, affect very beneficially the development of suburbs, and remove the heavy burden on industry which is caused by the present rates. As a preliminary to this measure, **I should strongly urge**

4. The women's movement for the vote had split into two camps, the militant Women's Social and Political Union (WSPU, popularly known as 'suffragettes') and the more moderate National Union of Suffrage Societies (NUSS, popularly known as 'suffragists'). Russell represented the latter.

5. Unionism was the view that Ireland should remain united with Britain. Later, after the partition of Ireland, it became the view that Northern Ireland should remain united with Britain. 'Unionist' can mean Conservative or it can refer to that segment of Liberals which agreed with the Conservatives in opposing the Liberal Party's plans for Irish Home Rule.

LORD RUSSELL

*All earthly knowledge finally explored,*
*Man feels himself from doubt and dogma free.*
*There are more things in Heaven, though, my lord,*
*Than are dreamed of in your philosophy.*

Ronald Searle's cartoon and poem appeared in *Punch* (March 1957). Searle alludes to the line in *Hamlet* that "There are more things in heaven and earth, Horatio, than are dreamt of in your philosophy." Russell replied wittily, pointing out that, in contemplating for many years the class of classes that are not members of themselves, an object that turned out to be logically impossible, he had "dreamt" of a thing that was in neither heaven nor earth.

**the passing of a Valuation Bill,** by which the value of land should be estimated apart from that of houses or other improvements.

I am in favour of a **UNIVERSAL SCHEME OF OLD AGE PENSIONS**

which I hope to see carried out by the present Government.

I am, Yours faithfully, Bertrand Russell

[5]

## Last Message to Wimbledon Electors: "I am a Liberal."

*The Daily News* (14th May, 1907), p. 8 | C07.06

*Russell's opponent in the Wimbledon by-election was Henry Chaplin, a Conservative (Unionist Party) candidate who opposed women's suffrage and free trade. It was a bitter campaign and frequently rowdy. On one occasion Russell's wife, Alys Pearsall Smith, was struck in the face by an egg thrown by a Chaplin supporter. In his* Autobiography *Russell writes: "When, in later years, I campaigned against the First World War [which got him a six-month prison sentence], the popular opposition I encountered was not comparable to that which the suffragists met in 1907."*[6]

Last Message to the Electors

I ask for the Liberal vote because I am a Liberal through and through. I am just as much a Liberal as dozens of the Ministerialists in the House, who are as keen as ever I can be upon the women's suffrage question. To those who waver about giving me their vote because they have doubts on the women's question I would say: Do you prefer Mr. Chaplin, the Protectionist and crusted Tory, to one who is at least a Free Trader and a Progressive?

Such persons should remember that every vote not given to me is a vote given to my opponent.

6. *Autobiography*, Volume I, pp. 153, 231.

[6]

## A Protest From the Voteless

*The Common Cause* (28th April, 1910), p. 43 | C10.02

*Russell's letter here underscores the injustice of the disenfranchisement of women in Great Britain before World War I. Not until 1918 did reform come, and then only partial reform which gave the vote only to women aged thirty and over. Russell supports Dora Edgell's suggestion, and has an even more 'catchy' slogan to offer.*

Madam, —The suggestion of your correspondent, Dora Edgell, in this week's "Common Cause," entitled "A Protest from the Voteless," appears to me deserving of all possible support. A great effect could be produced by a placard bearing some such words as—

NOT ABLE TO VOTE.

Paupers, Lunatics, Criminals, and WOMEN HAVE NO VOTE.

I hope the N.U.[7] will consider the suggestion in time for the next election.

—Yours, Bertrand Russell
Bagley Wood, Oxford, April 21, 1910.

[7]

## A Protest Against the Prosecutions

*The Times* (27th March, 1912), p. 14 | C12.03a

*Between 1910 and 1914 Britain saw a great deal of labour unrest related in part to the syndicalists who advocated worker control of industry. After the war, Russell favored a form of syndicalism called guild socialism. Some, like the anarchist Guy Bowman, believed that such control required full-scale revolution.* The Syndicalist *newspaper was founded in January 1912 and published in its first issue an 'Open Letter to British Soldiers' which urged them to disobey should they be ordered to shoot strikers. (The issue foreshadows Russell's own free speech problems a few years later when he was sent to prison for suggesting that the United States government would use troops against strikers.) The government arrested and sentenced the editor and others to*

7. The N.U. was the N.U.S.S. (National Union of Suffrage Societies).

*prison. Russell and eleven other prominent intellectuals sent the following letter of protest to the* Times. *The list includes Christian Socialist Barnett, the historians Fisher and Trevelyan, the composer Vaughan Williams, the poet John Masefield and the novelist Israel Zangwill. Philip Morrell was a Member of Parliament and married to Ottoline Morrell, Russell's lover (1910–1916) and confidante until her death in 1938.*

Sir, —We, the undersigned, have read with the gravest alarm the reports of the trial of the editor and printers of the *Syndicalist* newspaper, and the sentences passed upon them. The offense was that the newspaper contained as one of its articles an "Open Letter to British Soldiers", of which the most incriminating sentences ran as follows:—

When we go on strike to better our lot, which is the lot of your fathers, mothers, brothers, and sisters, you are called upon by your officers to murder us. Don't do it . . . Boys, don't do it. "Thou shalt not kill", says the Book. Don't forget that. It does not say—unless you have a uniform on. No: murder is murder, whether committed in the heat of anger on one who has wronged a loved one or by pipe-clayed Tommies with rifles.

For publishing and printing this letter in his newspaper, the editor, Mr. Bowman, was sentenced to nine months' hard labour, and the printers, the brothers Buck, to six months' hard labour. The printers, by their counsel, "contended that they were merely the printers of the paper and had nothing to do with the article, the views of which they did not share." This was not denied, but they had the same measure meted out to them as the little printers and booksellers who supplied the public with Paine's works during the anti-Jacobin terror in England. The sentences the brothers Buck are now undergoing are cruelly severe, as well as impolitic.

These proceedings against the *Syndicalist* were taken under an Act of 1797, under which there has been no prosecution since 1804. The Act was passed in the year of the mutiny at the Nore, when the loyalty of the armed forces of the Crown was most seriously in question, in time of a dangerous European war. Today we have peace abroad, and at the date of the trial the strike had been remarkably orderly at home. The troops were nowhere in collision with the strikers or the mob. Above all, the loyalty of Army and Navy was never less in question than it is to-day. What soldier cared about the *Syndicalist* and how many had heard of it before this ill-advised prosecution?

Now, as the first result of these proceedings, there is perhaps not a soldier but has heard that it is a moot question under what circumstances he is justified in refusing to fire on a mob. And the civilian population has been set on to discuss the question with heat and mutual recrimination. In this way the prosecution has done, on a mild calculation, about ten thousand times as much to advertise the question as the *Syndicalist* could have done by itself. It has, moreover, compelled many who completely disagree with the *Syndicalist* to stand up at its side for the right of free speech.

If the Government adopts the course of prosecuting every one who expresses publicly the view that the soldiers should not fire on a mob of their fellow-citizens they will be issuing a challenge to the leaders of working-class opinion to take up that attitude.

The opinion that soldiers should refuse to shoot their fellow-citizens, whether true or not, is very prevalent and will not be put down by State prosecutions, but only fostered a hundredfold. If the expression of this opinion is persecuted, it will become more and more the shibboleth of the whole Labour movement. The view was held only by the Quakers in old time, but in our own day was taught to all Europe by Tolstoy in works which have been broadly circulated in translation and highly honoured by all classes and parties in this island, however much they may disagree with him.

There is another serious aspect of the matter—namely, the very different treatment accorded to the rich and powerful men who incite the Protestants of Ulster to prepare for armed rebellion, and who by threats of violence have actually prevented a meeting from being held in a certain hall in Belfast.

To Liberals and Conservatives in the House of Commons this is a subject of good-natured banter, but in the working man, who sees one of his own class thrown into prison for six months' hard labour for doing less, as he imagines, than some highly-placed politicians, feelings of fierce indignation against injustice are aroused. This is not an era when we can afford to have one law for the rich and another for the poor in political cases.

The methods by which Pitt crushed the premature Radicalism of his day will not serve to crush the Labour movement now, but they may serve to render it revolutionary and to enlist it under the banners of the more extreme leaders. These methods of State prosecution will certainly embitter the social strife which it is the object of all of us, whatever view we take of the questions at issue, to keep within peaceful channels.

We are, &c.,
Samuel A. Barnett.
H.A.L. Fisher
John Masefield.
Philip Morrell.
Arthur Ponsonby.
Joseph Rowntree.

Bertrand Russell.
G.M. Trevelyan.
J.C. Wedgwood.
Ralph Vaughan Williams.
J.H. Whitehouse.
Israel Zangwill.
House of Commons, March 26.

[8]

## The Proposed Change in the Ordination Service

*The Cambridge Magazine* (22nd November, 1913), p. 173 | C13.09

*This letter involves the relatively minor issue of the Church of England's ordination service. Russell thought that the practice of requiring "unfeigned belief" in the Bible would either prevent many good people from clerical service, or would make hypocrites of them. But it does mark the beginning of a life-long public criticism of organized religion. Russell's letter provoked many angry responses. Russell seemed to enjoy the controversy. As he wrote to Ottoline at the time, "The row with the parsons . . . [has] cheered me wonderfully."*

Sir, —A letter from seventeen Examining Chaplains in this University appeared in the *Church Times* for October 31st, which raises an issue interesting not only to Churchmen, but to all who desire an improvement in the national standard of honesty. As every one knows, the existing service for the ordination of deacons contains the following question and answer:

"The Bishop. Do you unfeignedly believe all the Canonical Scriptures of the Old and New Testament?.

"Answer. I do believe them."

Every educated person knows that, except in a very few instances, this answer is a lie. A small number of clergymen have expressed the opinion that a public and solemn falsehood ought not to be demanded of those who wish to enter a profession supposed to be specially concerned in upholding the moral standard. While carefully repudiating this extreme view (though not of course in set terms), the signatories to the letter in the *Church Times* propose, as a concession to the weaker brethren, that a change should be made in the question, in order to meet the scruples which they recognise but do not share.

But what is the change which they propose? It is, that the Bishop shall ask:

"Do you believe in the Holy Scriptures as given by inspiration of God?"

I cannot think that those who drew up this form of question can have realized the implications of their own suggestion. It must be remembered that the change is to be made for the sake of those who do not believe the whole of the Scriptures. Yet these very men are to be asked to say that what they do not believe is given by Divine inspiration. The only men, therefore, who will be admitted by the new formula and not by the old will be those who believe that falsehoods may be divinely inspired. Except for the authority of the Examining Chaplains, I should not have supposed that these were a large class among ordinandi.

It may, of course, be said that the word "all", does not occur in the proposed question. But anywhere except in a clerical formula such a question would be unhesitatingly regarded as impliying "all." And it is a natural (though no doubt an erroneous) supposition, that the formula is intended to suggest "all," while yet leaving a controversial loophole. If not, the question should be: "Do you believe in parts of the Holy Scriptures as given by inspiration of God?" Such a question, which would make explicit the limitations in what is required, would, I imagine, be at once rejected by the signatories. Either, therefore, the question is intended to deceive some, and to be understood by others in a non-natural sense, or else it must be supposed to apply to the whole of the Bible. But, I would ask, does any one of the signatories believe that such a passage as Genesis xix. is "given by inspiration of God"?

It may seem that the question is a purely domestic one for the Church, with which no outsider ought to concern himself. But those within the Church, for the most part, have completely ceased to understand the effect which is produced on ordinary people by their forced interpretations and by their amazing reluctance to abandon formulas now universally disbelieved. It is not only that this practice excludes from the Church most young men who do not fall below the average level of intellectual honesty, but that it tends to degrade those whom it does not exclude. Hypocrisy and indifference to truth are our national defects, and it is regrettable that so large and important a body as the Church should devote its influence to increasing and justifying them. Now, when a change is being proposed, something might be done to remove this reproach. Is it too late to hope that a better form of question will be found?

Bertrand Russell
Trinity College, November 16th, 1913

PART II

# Against the First World War

(1914–1918)

Bertrand Russell

The First World War had a profound effect on Russell. The loss of life and the great suffering caused by the War were deeply disturbing. But equally shocking was the widespread enthusiasm for the war that Russell perceived among his countrymen—including some of his friends like Gilbert Murray and Alfred North Whitehead—and it caused him to rethink some of his basic beliefs about human nature. As he reflected years later:

> [The War] shook me out of my prejudices and made me think afresh on a number of fundamental questions. . . . I had supposed until that time that it was quite common for parents to love their children, but the War persuaded me that it is a rare exception. I had supposed that most people like money better than almost anything else, but I discovered that they liked destruction even better. I had supposed that intellectuals frequently loved truth, but I found here again that not ten percent of them prefer truth to popularity. (*Autobiography*, Volume 2, pp. 3, 6)

Russell says in his autobiography that he became filled with "despairing tenderness" towards the young men who were to be killed, and with rage towards the politicians. "For several weeks I felt that if I should happen to meet Asquith [Prime Minister] or Grey [Foreign Secretary] I should be unable to refrain from murder."[1] Although he was tortured by a personal patriotism, he never doubted that he must actively oppose the war:

> I have at times been paralyzed by scepticism, at times I have been cynical, at other times indifferent, but when the war came I felt as if I heard the voice of God. I knew that it was my business to protest, however futile protest might be. My whole nature was involved. As a lover of truth, the national propaganda of all the belligerent nations sickened me. As a lover of civilization, the return to barbarism appalled me. As a man of thwarted parental feeling, the massacre of the young wrung my heart. I hardly supposed much good would come of opposing the War, but I felt that for the honour of human nature those who were not swept off their feet should show that they stood firm. (*Autobiography*, p. 7)

1. *Autobiography*, pp. 6–7.

Russell threw himself into the anti-war effort, and when conscription became official policy, he took the side of the NCF (No Conscription Fellowship) against the government. He wrote numerous articles and gave numerous lectures in opposition to the war. Many of these articles and lectures prompted public dialogue through the "Letters to the Editor" section of various journals and newspapers. He criticized the secretive, undemocratic dealings of the British government which had unwisely immersed his country in war; he denounced the inhumanity of the international killing; he exposed the underlying psychology of war which he attributed largely to mutual fear and suspicion; and he defended the plight of Britain's conscientious objectors. These efforts against the war were not without consequences for Russell. In 1916, for writing a leaflet on behalf of a conscientious objector, he was fined, and dismissed from his Fellowship at Cambridge. (If he hadn't been dismissed he likely would have taken a leave of absence anyway, since he was becoming less and less comfortable with the academic climate at Cambridge and longed for a more politically active role in opposing the war.) In 1918 he was sentenced to six months in prison for a article that insulted a British ally (the United States).

The 30 letters in this section are representative of some 35 known letters to the editor during this period, all of which have been reprinted in the *Collected Papers of Bertrand Russell*, Volumes 13–14, a remarkable collection of which I have made extensive use.

[9]

## The Rights of War

*The Nation* (15th August, 1914), pp. 737–38 C14.07

*This, Russell's first public letter against the war, is one of his longer letters to the editor. But it's one of his best—a masterpiece of prose and psychopolitical analysis.*

*Europe in 1914 had become a system of military alliances, made ready for war by a decade of arms races. Germany under Wilhelm II sought a political and imperial role appropriate to its industrial power, thus challenging Britain and threatening France which was still chaffing from the loss of Alsace-Loraine to Germany in 1871. Austria feared an expanded Serbia, and Russia feared Austrian and German influence in the Balkans and Turkey. The assassination of the Austrian Archduke Franz Ferdinand by a Serbian on 28th June, 1914, sparked a chain of events which engulfed Europe in war within weeks. Austria, with German support, declared war on Serbia on 28th July. When Russia mobilized forces to defend Serbia,*

*Germany declared war on Russia and attacked France and neutral Belgium. On August 4th Britain entered the war against Germany and Austria on grounds of the violation of Belgium neutrality.*

Sir, —Against the vast majority of my countrymen, even at this moment, in the name of humanity and civilization, I protest against our share in the destruction of Germany.

A month ago, Europe was a peaceful comity of nations; if an Englishman killed a German, he was hanged. Now, if an Englishman kills a German, or if a German kills an Englishman, he is a patriot, who has deserved well of his country. We scan the newspapers with greedy eyes for news of slaughter, and rejoice when we read of innocent young men, blindly obedient to the word of command, mown down in thousands by the machine-guns of Liège. Those who saw the London crowds, during the nights leading up to the Declaration of War, saw a whole population, hitherto peaceable and humane, precipitated in a few days down the steep slope to primitive barbarism, letting loose, in a moment, the instincts of hatred and blood-lust against which the whole fabric of society has been raised. "Patriots" in all countries acclaim this brutal orgy as a noble determination to vindicate the right; reason and mercy are swept away in one great flood of hatred; dim abstractions of unimaginable wickedness—Germany to us and the French, Russia to the Germans—conceal the simple fact that the enemy are men, like ourselves, neither better nor worse—men who love their homes and the sunshine, and all the simple pleasures of common lives; men now mad with terror in the thought of their wives, their sisters, their children, exposed, with our help, to the tender mercies of the conquering Cossack.

And all this madness, all this rage, all this flaming death of our civilization and our hopes, has been brought about because a set of official gentlemen, living luxurious lives, mostly stupid, and all without imagination or heart, have chosen that it should occur rather than that anyone of them should suffer some infinitesimal rebuff to his country's pride. No literary tragedy can approach the futile horror of the White Paper. The diplomatists, seeing from the first the inevitable end, mostly wishing to avoid it, yet drifted from hour to hour of the swift crisis, restrained by punctilio from making or accepting the small concessions that might have saved the world, hurried on at last by blind fear to loose the armies for the work of mutual butchery.

And behind the diplomatists, dimly heard in the official documents, stand vast forces of national greed and national hatred—atavistic instincts, harmful to mankind at its present level, but transmitted from savage and half-animal ancestors, concentrated and directed by Governments and the Press, fostered by the upper class as a distraction from social discontent, artificially nourished by the sinister influence of the makers of armaments, encouraged by a whole foul literature of "glory," and by every text-book of history with which the minds of children are polluted.

England, no more than other nations which participate in this war, can be absolved either as regards its national passions or as regards its diplomacy.

For the past ten years, under the fostering care of the Government and a portion of the Press, a hatred of Germany has been cultivated and a fear of the German navy. I do not suggest that Germany has been guiltless; I do not deny that the crimes of Germany have been greater than our own. But I do say that whatever defensive measures were necessary should have been taken in a spirit of calm foresight, not in a wholly needless turmoil of panic and suspicion. It is this deliberately created panic and suspicion that produced the public opinion by which our participation in the war has been rendered possible.

Our diplomacy, also, has not been guiltless. Secret arrangements, concealed from Parliament and even (at first) from almost all the Cabinet, created, in spite of reiterated denials, an obligation suddenly revealed when the war fever had reached the point which rendered public opinion tolerant of the discovery that the lives of many, and the livelihood of all, had been pledged by one man's irresponsible decisions. Yet, though France knew our obligations, Sir E. Grey[2] refused, down to the last moment, to inform Germany of the conditions of our neutrality or of our intervention. On August 1st, he reports as follows a conversation with the German Ambassador (No. 123):—

"He asked me whether, if Germany gave a promise not to violate Belgian neutrality, we would engage to remain neutral. I replied that I could not say that; our hands were still free, and we were considering what our attitude should be. All I could say was that our attitude would be determined largely by public opinion here, and that the neutrality of Belgium would appeal very strongly to public opinion here. I did not think that we could give a promise of neutrality on that condition alone. The Ambassador pressed me as to whether I could not formulate conditions on which we would remain neutral. He even suggested that the integrity of France and her colonies might be guaranteed. I said I felt obliged to refuse definitely any promise to remain neutral on similar terms, and I could only say that we must keep our hands free."

It thus appears that the neutrality of Belgium, the integrity of France and her colonies, and the naval defence of the northern and western coasts

2. Sir Edward Grey was British Foreign Secretary from 1905 to 1916.

of France, were all mere pretexts. If Germany had agreed to our demands in all these respects, we should still not have promised neutrality.

I cannot resist the conclusion that the Government has failed in its duty to the nation by not revealing long-standing arrangements with the French, until, at the last moment, it made them the basis of an appeal to honor; that it has failed in its duty to Europe by not declaring its attitude at the beginning of the crisis; and that it has failed in its duty to humanity by not informing Germany of conditions which would ensure its non-participation in a war which, whatever its outcome, must cause untold hardship and the loss of many thousands of our bravest and noblest citizens.

—Yours, &c., Bertrand Russell
August 12th, 1914

[10]

## Fear as the Ultimate Cause of War

*The Cambridge Magazine* (24th October, 1914), p. 54 | C14.14

*Here Russell responds to comments from W.E. Heitland, a Cambridge classicist, on Russell's article ("War: The Cause and the Cure"), part of which had appeared in* The Cambridge Magazine *two weeks earlier. In that article Russell had criticized the secretive foreign policy of an elite few as undemocratic and a major cause of the war. Heitland disagreed, claiming that democratic control of foreign policy was unworkable. In this letter Russell stresses one of his central ideas concerning war and peace: the importance of seeking to understand the situation from the other side's perspective. As he says, "I do not think we shall discover how to avert future wars so long as belligerent nations regard each other as simply wicked."*

Sir, —Mr. Heitland's comments on my views about the war call for a few words of reply. In the first place, the headings "*the* cause and *the* cure" were those of the Editor of *The Labour Leader*, and were more sweeping than any I should have chosen. I agree entirely that "a change in the habits and spirits of nations" is called for; I think, however, that forms of government not only embody, but also foster and perpetuate, good or bad national habits of mind. The Western nations are distinguished from Germany and Austria by a greater measure of democracy, and I wish to see this superiority recognized as worthy of extension to diplomacy. Mr. Heitland will hardly wish to deny that, in the present instance, the Governments resting on democracy have shown themselves less warlike than the two Kaisers; and I think any one who knows Germany will agree that if it were more democratic it would be less militarist. I agree also with Mr. Heitland that there is "need of addressing certain gentlemen in Berlin". But at the present moment, there is some difficulty in doing so effectively. I have, ever since I began to know Germany, consistently thought ill of the Kaiser and all his ways, even at times when many in England admired him. But I am afraid that criticism of the Kaiser by an Englishman is not likely to do much to lessen his influence in Germany.

The problem which I was considering was the problem why nations follow their Governments willingly into warlike adventures. The sacrifices demanded from individuals—in Germany and Austria just as much as here—are so great they cannot be attributed wholly to desire for conquest; and I think fear is the principal motive with ordinary citizens, though of course not the sole motive. Certainly fear operated powerfully in the case of Austria-Hungary, which believed—I do not know with what justice—that the Serbs were trying to stir up revolution, and were likely to receive the support of Russia. This fear may seem strange to Englishmen, yet we have entertained much more groundless fears in the past. Mr. Heitland will remember that in the early days of the Home Rule controversy one of the most popular arguments against the Nationalists was that Irish self-government would enable the French to effect a landing in Ireland in the event of war with us. I cannot think that it is undesirable to try to understand the reasons which make the German and Austrian people believe—quite mistakenly, as we are convinced—that they have a good case in this war. No nation is wholly devilish or wholly angelic; where there is a national unanimity, there must be some general belief which seems to afford justification. I do not think we shall discover how to avert future wars so long as belligerent nations regard each other as simply wicked, and I cannot think that a good case suffers from justice and fair-mindedness.

B. Russell.
Trinity College.

●●●●●●●●●●●●● [11] ●●●●●●●●●●●●●

## "Possible Guarantees of Peace."

The Economist (12th December, 1914) | C14.16

*Russell applauded United States neutrality as crafted by Woodrow Wilson and saw a coalition of neutral nations as providing a model for peace in the post-war world. Here is one of the earliest public statements of Russell's internationalism; it anticipates the League of Nations which Wilson proposed after the war, and it foreshadows Russell's later ideas about world government as a guarantor of world peace.*

Sir, —President Wilson's message to Congress encourages the friends of humanity and reason throughout the world to look to him as the one man able and willing to use, when the time comes, "an opportunity," as he justly says, "such as had seldom been vouchsafed to any nation—an opportunity to counsel and obtain peace in the world, and the reconciliation and healing settlement of many matters that have cooled and interrupted the friendship of nations."

Many men, in all the belligerent countries, have expressed the hope that, when this war ends, it will end with some stronger guarantee of permanent peace than any that has been obtained after previous wars. If the belligerents alone participate in the Peace Conference, it may be feared that the atmosphere of passion engendered by the conflict will be unfavourable to large and impartial statesmanship. There is reason to hope, however, that America, at least, will take part to represent the interests of neutrals, and will contribute—what is feasible, without insuperable difficulties—a measure of organisation of neutrals such as shall ensure future peace among the Great Powers.

It cannot be said that neutrals are unconcerned, and therefore have no right to be represented. Belgium was neutral in the original dispute, and through Belgium's misfortunes all neutrals are concerned. Holland has suffered economically as much as any of the great nations involved, through paralysis of trade, the expenses of mobilisation, shortage of food, and the influx of destitute refugees. Italy's finances are completely disorganised as a result of the war. Even the United States suffers heavily in loss of trade, and has a vital interest in securing peace at the earliest possible moment. The neutral nations have therefore a right to be heard when terms of peace come to be discussed. It is important that they should be heard, for their interests are simply the interests of mankind: to bring the war to a close, and to prevent the recurrence of any such war in the future. In these circumstances, the thoughts of all who desire a really stable peace turn naturally to President Wilson, who, if he shows that combination of boldness and wisdom of which he has given repeated proof in other directions, may render to mankind as great a service as has ever been rendered by any statesman.

There can be no doubt that, when this war comes to an end, and the imperious need of victory no longer fills men's whole horizon, the immense majority of the citizens of all the countries involved will ardently desire to be saved from a recurrence of such a disaster, and will welcome any safeguard to peace which is not obviously proposed in the interests of their enemies. Although Governments may cherish ambitious designs, the average man does not desire to be plunged into a life and death struggle, and only acquiesces in war because he believes it to be necessary as a protection against wanton aggression. If safety were obviously assured, it would become impossible for Governments to drag their countries into such a war as that in which they are now involved.

But there is only one way of insuring safety against attack, and that is to make an aggressive war obviously disastrous to those who embark upon it. At present the question who is the aggressor is decided by each side in its own favour, and there is no neutral tribunal which has an authoritative right to pronounce a verdict. If neutrals made it known in advance that, provided one side was clearly the aggressor, they would give support to the other side, it would become to the interest of both parties to avoid even a hint of aggression. In most cases, probably, diplomatic and economic support would suffice. In this way time would be secured for diplomatic adjustment, and resort to arms would always be disastrous to the attacking side.

All that is required in order to make wars between Great Powers for ever impossible is the combination of two policies both emanating from the United States—the one from Mr. Bryan,[3] the other from Col. Roosevelt.[4] Since the present Administration came into power Mr. Bryan has concluded with many countries unlimited arbitration treaties, providing for settlement of all possible disputes, with a year's delay in case of failure to agree. Such treaties are admirable as an expression of genuinely pacific intentions on the part of the nations concerned, and it is greatly to be hoped that other countries will follow the example of the United States. England, France, and Russia might well conclude such treaties with each other at the present moment, in order to demonstrate to the world the reluctance with which they resort to war. By a network of such

3. William Jennings Bryan (1860–1925) was an American political leader and Secretary of State from 1912 to 1915.

4. Theodore Roosevelt (1858–1919) was President of the United States from 1901 to 1909. He was popularly known by his nickname, 'the Colonel', after his exploits in Cuba in the Spanish-American War of 1898.

treaties the Powers which are genuinely willing to abandon possibilities of unjust conquest in the future for the sake of avoiding war might embody their willingness in mutual undertakings.

But such treaties will be useless, except as an expression of good intentions, unless they have some sanction making it obviously disastrous to any Power to treat them as mere "scraps of paper." For this purpose, it is necessary that they should all be guaranteed by all the contracting Powers, not only by the two immediately concerned, so that any offending Power incurs the hostility not only of the Power directly offended, but of all Powers which recognise the maintenance of peace as their supreme interest. If such a state of things existed, it would bring with it as an inevitable corollary the international tribunal advocated by Col. Roosevelt—at the end, curiously enough, of a series of articles urging the United States to join in the competition of armaments. Few genuine lovers of peace will wish to see the United States cursed with the military burdens which afflict Europe: but some policy like that of Col. Roosevelt seems the best, though the boldest, means of escaping from such a necessity. If every Power which used its armaments in an appeal to force found itself faced by the hostility of all the other Great Powers, armaments would be everywhere reduced owing to their obvious uselessness. But unless some such means is adopted, it is hard to see how America is to avoid the necessity of arming in defense of the Monroe Doctrine.

By the time the present conflict drags to its ending nations of Europe will be weary of war as they have never been before, and will be ready to welcome with acclamation any neutral suggestion which frees them from the nightmare terror of hostile aggression. The first essential for permanent peace is the recognition that the preservation of peace is, in the modern world, a vital interest of all neutrals, and the consequent undertaking by the Powers to intervene against the aggressor in any dispute in which they are not directly concerned. Such an undertaking would necessarily lead to a council of the Powers for the peaceful settlement of all disputes, and would, if neutrals displayed courage and fidelity, make the occurrence of another, war among Great Powers ever impossible.

Bertrand Russell
Cambridge, December 10th, 1914.

[12]

# The Policy of the Allies

*The Nation* (13th February, 1915) | C15.04

*Arthur Cecil Pigou (1877–1959) was a Cambridge economist whom Russell greatly admired from the earlier controversy concerning free trade. In an article in* The Nation *of 6th February, Pigou lamented the lack of a British government statement on the aims of the war and provision of conditions for its conclusion.*

*Russell reminds us of the mutual fear and suspicion making it difficult to secure a just peace without loss of honor. And he warns against retribution and the belief that German militarism can be expunged with force of arms. Pigou's article and Russell's letter of support helped to launch a campaign to get the Government to seek a negotiated peace.*

Sir, —Professor Pigou's letter, in your last number, must command the warm support of all who hope to see this war ended with wisdom and justice rather than in a spirit of blind vengeance. The ordinary German soldier, we may be sure, believes, not without ground, in the utterances of our public men and journalists, that we intend, if we can, to crush, devastate, and dismember his country. His great courage on the battlefield, to which all our soldiers bear witness, is not inspired by the desire to annex Belgium, whatever his Government may intend; he is inspired by a belief that he is defending his own territory. Nations misunderstand each other through mutual contempt—the Germans imagine we can only learn from "frightfulness" and we believe they can only become peaceful through humiliation. It is safer to judge others by ourselves; and we know that defeat is the one thing which could make us remain warlike after the war.

If the Allies now made it known that they would accept honorable terms, such terms as reason and justice would suggest, they would not only rivet to their side the wavering sympathy of neutrals, but they would rob the militarists in Germany of the chief means by which they have secured the almost unanimous support of their compatriots. If it were known that at any moment peace could be secured without loss of honor or of genuinely German territory, the losses and sacrifices entailed by the war would soon seem no longer worth enduring. The destruction of German militarism, however desirable—and no one desires it more ardently than I do—is a work which only the Germans themselves can perform. If we endeavor to effect it by force of arms, we shall experience the same disillusionment as befell Napoleon after 1806; but we may effect it by persuasion if we show that we do not intend to exact an eye for an eye or a tooth for a tooth.

For not now declaring the terms on which we are prepared to make peace, there can be only one or two adequate reasons—either that we fear our power is insufficient to obtain as much as is just, or that we hope it is sufficient to obtain more. There can be no ground whatever for the first of these reasons; probably, even now, Germany would be willing to evacuate Belgium and North-Eastern France, and to come to terms with Russia about the Balkans. We are left with the second alternative—that we will not now declare our terms, because we hope, by victory, to obtain concessions which would as yet appear preposterous. But in actual fact, probably the only motive is pride; we will not be the first to show a willingness to stop. But a willingness to stop when all legitimate objects have been attained does not prove weakness. It proves rather the strength which is not afraid to be just.

—Yours, &c., Bertrand Russell.
Trinity College, Cambridge. February 10th, 1915.

[13]

## "Mr. Russell's Reply to His Critics"

*The Cambridge Review* (24th February, 1915), pp. 218–19 | C15.05

*An article by Russell in* The Cambridge Review *two weeks earlier ('Can England and Germany Be Reconciled After the War?') initiated a bitter public controversy concerning his suggestion that after the war the British fleet should be replaced by an international navy. He wrote to Ottoline Morrell, "All the old fogies in the place [Cambridge University] have been tumbling over each other to attack me about my article in the Cambridge Review—but they are easy to answer."*

*In this letter we see Russell defending his internationalist approach to peace against five Cambridge academics, and criticizing the narrow nationalism that distorts perception, feeds pride, and promotes arms races.*

Sir, —A number of letters having appeared in criticism of my suggestion in the *Review* of February 10, I wish to make a brief reply to their chief points.

Professor Sorley's[5] main argument is that, though we do not hate the Germans, we ought not to attempt a reconciliation after the war, because

5. William R. Sorley (1855–1935) was an ethics professor at Cambridge. Russell had a poor opinion of Sorley whom he had described to Ottoline Morrell a few years earlier as "dull, pompous, hypocritical and stupid and Scotch" (CPBR, Volume 13, p. 532).

they are in the habit of bayoneting children in trenches. If Professor Sorley believes this, it seems surprising that he should not hate them; but it is not surprising that they should hate us, if we believe such things. That German atrocities have occurred is undeniable. Among millions of men forming an average sample, such as are to be found in any European army, there are bound to be a certain proportion of criminals. But this, Professor Sorley tells us, will not account for what the Germans have done. I must ask him, therefore: How many instances does he know of 'bayoneted children found in the German trenches,' established on such evidence as would convince him if alleged against English soldiers? If he cannot answer this question, he must admit that bias has helped to produce his certainty. Professor Sorley, like the rest of us, must have read the accounts of the Christmas truce, and of the great difficulty found by the officers on both sides in compelling the soldiers to cease fraternizing. Does he really think that our soldiers would have been so ready to be friends with men who bayoneted children? Apparently he has a lower opinion than I have of our soldiers' humanity.

I have no word to say in defence of the violation of Belgian neutrality. It was a great crime; but it was the kind of crime of which no great nation is guiltless. Though many here have forgotten, the Danes still remember that we did the same to Denmark in the Napoleonic war, and when I was a boy the young were still made to learn by heart a poem celebrating our prowess in treacherously defeating 'all the might of Denmark's crown.' Within the last few years, we and the Russians together behaved in Persia in a manner which seems to me quite as inhuman, without the excuse of imminent national danger. The facts were largely suppressed in the newspapers, but may be ascertained from Professor Browne's pamphlets[6] published by the Persia Committee. If Professor Sorley will read these, I shall be glad to know in what respect he considers the Germans worse.

Self-righteousness is no new vice, and it has been condemned authoritatively long ago. All of us, nationally and individually, have need of charity. To say that, because the Germans have sinned, we are not even to attempt friendly relations with them after the war, is un-Christian and vindictive, and shows that those who take this view 'have reverted to a barbaric morality in their attitude to questions between their own and other States.'

---

6. Edward Granvile Browne (1862–1926) was a professor of Arabic and Persian studies at Cambridge. He supported Persian Constitutionalists against the autocratic Shah by his writing and lecturing.

Professor Sorley and Mr. Mozley[7] argue that an international navy would be very good for Germany, but utterly unjust to us. Mr. Clapham[8] argues that it would be very good for us, but utterly unjust to Germany. On this point, I leave these writers to each other's criticisms. In reply to Mr. Mozley, however, I ought to add that I had never supposed any one could imagine I was speaking of what might happen 'at the end of the war' when I advocated an international navy. I spoke of the 'period of weariness and sanity which is likely to follow the conclusion of peace' as that in which such a proposal might begin to get a hearing: it is not a proposal for to-morrow, but for the time when people begin to have a serious desire to prevent wars.

The only reasons why I did not mention an international army were, because it is less directly concerned in the relations of England and Germany, and because an army, unlike a navy, may have great effectiveness without being the strongest in the world. But many arguments would apply to both equally.

I am surprised to find Mr. Clapham unaware of the fact, which I supposed universally known, that many prominent men have money in armament firms, which are generally considered as legitimate a field for investment as railways or consols. I have not myself verified at Somerset House the statements (uncontradicted, so far as I know) which are to be found in books on such subjects, but there seems no reason to doubt them. The following, from Brailsford's 'War of Steel and Gold,' published in the first half of last year, may serve as a sample:

'The share-list of Armstrong's alone includes the names of sixty noblemen or their wives, sons or daughters, fifteen baronets, twenty knights, eight Members of Parliament, five bishops, twenty military and naval officers, and eight journalists. Among those interested in these [armament] firms there were last summer two Liberal Cabinet Ministers, a Law Officer of the Crown, and two members of the Front Opposition Bench. There is an amusing correspondence between these share-lists and the membership rolls of the Navy League and the National Service League' (p. 90).

Both Mr. Clapham and Mr. Gaselee[9] strongly object to the suggestion that there is anything improper in these facts, although Mr. Clapham does not believe that they are facts. I know it is vulgar to suggest that pri-

---

7. John K. Mozley (1883–1946) was Dean of Pembroke College of Cambridge University.

8. John H. Clapham (1873–1946) was an economic historian and Fellow of King's College, Cambridge.

9. Stephen Gaselee (1882–1943) was librarian at Magdalene College, Cambridge.

vate interest ever warps the action of a public man, unless he is a Liberal Minister defending the interests of the working classes, in which case it becomes a patriotic duty. But I fail, myself, to see any difference between Marconi and Kynoch's.[10] Mr. Chamberlain was interested in Kynoch's; Mr. Chamberlain made the Boer War; Kynoch's profited. I agree with Mr. Gaselee in thinking that he made the war, not for pecuniary profit, but from a disinterested pleasure in bullying; but that does not make his connection with Kynoch's proper or desirable. I also agree that to say many prominent men are interested in armaments is like saying that the Union of Democratic Control[11] is financed by German money—except that the one is true and the other false.

Miss Jones[12] takes exception to my statement that the failure of governments is now evident as never before. I had supposed this was a platitude. I cannot but think it regrettable that a large proportion of the best young men of Europe should be killed, many others crippled for life, and many rendered insane. This has been brought about by governments, through their desire for territory and their pride of power. My chief object in suggesting an international navy was not any immediate hope of its being adopted, since obviously for a long time to come it will not be, but to make evident to readers, through their instinctive recoil, that England, like Germany, is fighting for what no nation ought to desire or achieve: dominion. Our navy serves two purposes: to prevent others from injuring us, and to enable us to injure others. An international navy would serve only one of these purposes, and would therefore be less delightful.

B. Russell

---

10. Marconi and Kynoch refer to two British political scandals. Kynoch was an armaments firm that the Colonial Secretary, Joseph Chamberlain, was accused of securing special favors for during the Boer War (1899–1902). Marconi was the Marconi Wireless Telegraph Company. In 1912–13 several prominent liberals were accused of using privileged information to buy and sell stock for personal gain. Both scandals were taken as examples of public officials abusing the public trust.

11. The Union of Democratic Control was an ad hoc organization made up of prominent people, including Russell, to oppose the war and to put foreign policy under parliamentary control. Unsubstantiated rumors in the jingoist press charged that it was funded with German money.

12. E.E. Constance Jones (1848–1922) was a logician and Principal of Girton College.

[14]

## "The Reconciliation Question"

*The Cambridge Review* (10th March, 1915) | C15.07

*Here Russell responds to letters printed the previous week in* The Cambridge Review i*n response to his February 24th letter. Hobson challenged Russell's claim that Germany's treatment of neutral Belgium was comparable to England's past treatment of smaller countries; Sorley cited his source regarding German atrocities; and Clapham demanded additional "proof" that statesmen and clergy were profiting from armaments investments.*

Sir, —The letters of Professor Hobson,[13] Professor Sorley, and Dr. Clapham, in the *Review* of March 3, call for a few words of reply.

With what Professor Hobson says on the subject of Denmark I am in entire agreement. I do not for one moment believe that England is as culpable as Germany, and I should be sorry to be thought to maintain such a view. In regard to Persia, the responsibility of our Government was much less than that of Russia. The conduct of Russia was, in my deliberate opinion, as bad as that of Germany in Belgium, and I believe that if Professor Hobson will study the case he will come to the same conclusion. Our responsibility arose through the following facts:—(1) We solemnly assured the Persians, through our Minister in Teheran, that we were determined to uphold the integrity and independence of Persia, and that to secure this end was one of the objects of our Agreement with Russia in 1907. (2) As a result of that Agreement, Russia occupied a large part of the North of Persia and we occupied a smaller portion of the South. (3) The Russian occupation was effected by means of incredible barbarity and perfidy. (4) Our Government used its utmost endeavours, even to denying all knowledge of events of which only the most culpable negligence could have left it ignorant, to prevent the British public from ascertaining the truth about what had happened in Persia. How successful it was is apparent from the fact that even now the events of that time can only be ascertained by special research.

When I say that the war has been brought about by Governments, I do not mean that it has been brought about without the participation of popular passions. What I mean is that those passions, which are capable of lying dormant if not aroused, have been incited by Governments and the newspapers which support them, partly by means of professed opinions, but still more by carefully selecting the information which was given

13. E.W. Hobson (1856–1933) was a professor of mathematics at Cambridge.

to the public. I do not deny that, by these means, the instinct of group-hostility has been aroused; but I maintain that in each nation a comparatively small number of men are responsible for arousing it.

Professor Sorley, in his original letter, spoke of 'bayoneted children in trenches.' I challenged him on this particular atrocity, because, while every one knows that atrocities have occurred, everyone capable of weighing evidence knows also that there has been much exaggeration. He now implicitly acknowledges that this phrase was merely rhetorical, and that the evidence upon which he relies concerns other kinds of atrocities. We all know that the narratives of wounded soldiers are not wholly reliable. I myself heard a wounded soldier relate to a full railway carriage abominable atrocities on the part of French soldiers. I did not believe him, but every one else laughed delightedly. As the *Times* remarked in a leading article on March 1:

'A man, who does not ordinarily tell the truth, will not tell it any the more because has been in Flanders. On the contrary, the very fact that he is eagerly listened to, and believed, will encourage him to depart farther from the truth than usual. He may be as brave as a lion, and as honest as the day; there are people who have all the virtues of action, and who yet cannot tell the truth when they see the chance of inventing an exciting story . . . Remember always the Russian Rumour; none that you hear is likely to be so universal or so circumstantial as that.'

I quote this because, so far as I can gather, Professor Sorley's only evidence for 'bayoneted children in trenches' is that soldiers' faces grow stern when they think of them.

Professor Sorley says: 'It seems to me an irony of fate that thus brings Mr. Russell on the side of Germany.' These words show a complete misunderstanding. No one is less 'on the side of Germany' than I am. I am, or try to be, on the side of justice, and I have seen very little indication of any sense of justice in Germany since the war broke out. The writings of Treitschke seem to me the ravings of a criminal lunatic. But when I find precisely similar opinions expressed by Seeley or Lord Rosebery, I dislike them equally. Ask any ordinary citizen what it is in the Germans that makes it necessary to resist them. He will enumerate various characteristics: militarism, love of dominion, perfidy, and so on. These characteristics are detestable, and are to be resisted wherever they are found. I think at this moment the Germans are the worst offenders in these respects, and, therefore I should regard it as a misfortune for mankind if they were victorious. But the same characteristics, in a less degree, exist among ourselves, and will be, unless we are on our guard, very greatly intensified by success, as they were in Germany by the Franco-Prussian war. If the senses which we detest in Germany are not merely to be transferred to the Allies, if any real good is to result from the war, it is of the utmost importance that we should not suppose ourselves ex officio impeccable. Professor Sorley is right in saying that there is no 'sympathy of spirit' between me and Germany. Can he truthfully say the same of himself? The Germans, like Professor Sorley, believe their enemies to be so wicked that, on the highest ground, they deserve to be punished. What they lack is the sense of justice that would enable them to see facts truly; and in that respect I find many in this country who resemble them.

Dr. Clapham is hard to satisfy. With regard to England, I supplied him with the evidence which his challenge demanded; without denying this evidence, he therefore now demands 'further proof.' I am accustomed to regarding one proof of a proposition as sufficient when it is valid; I have really not the time to produce a series of other proofs. But Dr. Clapham can easily obtain them for himself by a visit to Somerset House.

His other demand—which I must regard as a mere rhetorical device—is that I should produce similar evidence in regard to other countries. I really cannot accept the assumption, implied in this challenge, that England, in this respect, has a lower moral standard than the other civilized nations.

My suggestion was not that the men concerned would be 'base enough to put dividends before humanity.' It is not in this crude way that financial interest operates. Very few beliefs in practical matters are wholly free from unconscious bias: what is in fact to a man's private interest appears to him to be to the national interest or to the interest of mankind. Take for example the Tariff Reform question. Most of the well-to-do desired taxes on the necessaries of life; and they believe this desire to be based on the highest Imperial grounds. Most working men objected to such taxes. These facts do not prove that the greater part of the population of the United Kingdom 'put dividends before humanity.' They prove only that unbiased thought is rare and difficult. Illustrations are so frequent and universal that I feel sure Dr. Clapham, except in the heat of controversy, would never have allowed himself to put so crude and unreal an alternative as is implied in his letter.

Yours faithfully, B. Russell

[15]

# Mr. Bertrand Russell and the Ethics of War

*The Westminster Gazette* (27th March, 1915), p. 2 | C15.09

*Russell published an article, 'The Ethics of War', in* The International Journal of Ethics *in January, 1915. In that article he defended a non-absolute pacifism: war is usually (but not always) wrong, and pacifism and non-resistance are to be preferred to war on utilitarian grounds: their consequences generally involve more good or less evil than resorting to war. An anonymous criticism of Russell's article appeared in the* Westminster Gazette, *probably written by the editor J.A. Spender.*

Sir, —May I be allowed a few lines of your space to reply to "S." in your issue of March 25? He asks, first what we ought to have done last August. I own that we could not then, in view of our commitments, honourably adopt the line of non-resistance. We might honourably have adopted either of two courses: (1) We might have declared at once that we should stand by France and Russia; this would probably have prevented the war, as M. Sazonov urged. (2) We might have promised neutrality on condition that Germany refrained from invading either France or Belgium, remaining merely on the defensive in the West. As regards non-resistance, it could only be adopted as a national policy if it were accompanied by great faith and courage: it would have to be clear that it did not spring from cowardice, and that passive resistance, even to the point of enduring death, would be opposed to all acts of tyranny or injustice. "S." fails to grasp the point of the distinction between wars of principle and wars of self-defence when he says that my line of argument leads to abolishing the police. The essence of the police is that they are neutral, and that they act, not in their own quarrel, but in obedience to law. It is this method which ought to be adopted in international relations; there ought to be only one neutral army and navy, intervening only according to some recognized code. So long as each nation is the judge in its own quarrel, injustice and conflict are unavoidable.

Yours faithfully, Bertrand Russell.
Trinity College, Cambridge.

[16]

## Letter from Bertrand Russell [on sense-data]

*The Journal of Philosophy, Psychology, and Scientific Methods* (8th July, 1915), pp 391–92 | C15.16

*On April 12th, the Aristotelian Society held a meeting at which Russell responded to a paper presented by the philosopher C.D. Broad (formerly a student of Russell's) dealing, in part, with Russell's book* Our Knowledge of the External World. *Russell was misquoted in a report of the Society's meeting in the* Athenaeum.

*The letter is important, not only because its technical metaphysics contrasts sharply with the politics of the war with which Russell had become passionately engaged, but also because it provides a clear, succinct statement of his changing ideas about the nature of sense-data, the objects of immediate sensory experience such as patches of color, sounds, smells, and so forth. The notion of the sense-datum was central to Russell's metaphysics and epistemology from 1912 to 1918.*

*In this letter to the* Journal of Philosophy, Psychology, and Scientific Methods, *he attempts to set the record straight: sense-data are particulars which are physical, not mental; only facts involving certain sorts of relations are mental.*

To the Editors of "The Journal of Philosophy, Psychology, and Scientific Methods":

In a quotation from the *Athenaeum* printed in this Journal, I am represented as having said, "there may be perspectives where there are no minds; but we can not know anything of what sort of perspectives they may be, for the sense-datum is mental." I did not see the *Athenaeum* and do not remember what I said, but it can not have been what I am reported as having said, for I hold strongly that the sense-datum is not mental—indeed my whole philosophy of physics rests upon the view that the sense-datum is purely physical. The fact of being a datum is mental, but a particular which is a datum is not logically dependent upon being a datum. A particular which is a datum does, however, appear to be causally dependent upon sense-organs and nerves and brain. Since we carry those about with us, we can not discover what sensibilia, if any, belong to perspectives from places where there is no brain. And since a particular of which we are aware is a sense-datum, we can not be aware of particulars which are not sense-data, and can, therefore, have no empirical evidence as to their nature. This is merely the "egocentric predicament"; it is a tautology, not a "great truth". It is for this reason, and not because "sense-data are mental", that we can not know the nature of perspectives (if any) which belong to places where there are no minds.

I do not know what is the definition of "mental". In order to obtain a definition, I should first inquire what would necessarily be removed from the world if it were what one would naturally call a world without mind. I see no reason why colours or noises should be removed, but facts which involve such relations as perceiving, remembering, desiring, enjoying, believing would necessarily be removed. This suggests that no particulars of which we have experience are to be called "mental", but that certain facts, involving certain relations, constitute what is essentially mental in the world of our experience. (I use the word "fact" to designate that which makes a proposition true or false; it includes, I think, everything in the world except what is simple.) The term "mental", therefore, will be applicable to all facts involving such relations as those enumerated above. This is not yet a definition, since obviously these relations all have some common characteristic, and it must be this characteristic which will yield the proper definition of the term "mental". But I do not know what this characteristic is.

—Very truly yours, B. Russell.
Trinity College, Cambridge, June 7, 1915

[17]

## "The International Review"

*The Times* (20th September, 1915), p. 9 | C15.19

*In an article 'On Justice in War-Time' in* The International Review *(10th August–1st September), Russell denounced those intellectuals throughout Europe who had abandoned internationalism in favor of national militarism. The article offended many including A.E. Taylor, professor of philosophy at the University of St. Andrews and eminent Plato scholar, who asked "Why does the British Post Office . . . lend its services to the enemy by distributing this pestiferous and mendacious stuff?" He also criticizes Russell for not mentioning the Bryce Report, an independent investigation (later found to have relied heavily on hearsay) which claimed evidence of German atrocities in Belgium. Russell responds to Taylor.*

Sir, —In *The Times* of September 17 Professor A.E. Taylor complains that he has been pestered by my writing, and expresses a hope that I shall be sent to prison; he also finds fault with me for not mentioning the

Bryce Report. The article he criticizes, as he would have seen if he had read it through, was written before the Bryce Report appeared. I sent it off at the end of April or the beginning of May, and received no proofs from the *International Review.* (Proofs in these days are not an easy matter when they come from a neutral country.) At the same time, I do not see that the Bryce Report makes any difference to my argument. What it establishes is far less than what was believed in the early days of the war, and exactly bears out the conclusion I reach in the article in question, namely:— "No doubt atrocities have occurred on both sides. But it is certain that they have been far less numerous, and (for the most part) less unnatural, than they are almost universally believed to have been." The German Government has brought out reports as to the behaviour of the Russians, which I have not seen; but I have no doubt they similarly fall short of previous popular belief in Germany. In any case, I do not follow Professor Taylor's argument. His premiss is that the effect of war on human nature is even worse than I suppose. His conclusion is that therefore we ought to have more war than I desire. But if he is right, war is an even greater evil than I had supposed. I am not a Fellow of Trinity.

Yours faithfully, Bertrand Russell,
Trinity College, Cambridge, Sept. 18.

[18]

## "Two Letters"

*The Cambridge Magazine* (30th October, 1915) | C15.22

*The first of two letters to William R. Sorley, Professor of Philosophy at Cambridge, was addressed to Sorley personally. In it Russell defends himself against the charge of being unpatriotic, and he explains his opposition to the war. Russell's letter was written on 8th October, less than a week before Sorley's son was killed in the war. The editor provided the following introduction.*

By the courtesy of the Hon. Bertrand Russell and Professor Sorley we are enabled to print the following letters, which, though not originally intended for publication, seem to have a more than private interest. Editor.

Trinity College, Cambridge.
8th October, 1915.

Dear Sorley, —I am told, I do not know with what truth, that you believe I hate England, and am moved by hatred in what I have written about the war. If you and others believe this, I have failed most lamentably to make clear what I care for. I cannot sit down under such a misconception without doing my best to remove it, and I beg of you to read this letter, not in a controversial spirit, but as the expression of a sincere and painful conviction.

So far from hating England, I care for England more than for anything else except truth. News of defeats or successes raises in me exactly the same feelings as in you. But I do not desire for England only, or chiefly, the outward success of victory in war, any more than I desire for myself only or chiefly the outward success which is to be achieved through worldly advancement. The same things which I most wish to see England achieve are the same as the things which I most wish to achieve myself; and among these I do not include great possessions, or vast power based on force. I do not believe that our material existence as a nation is at stake in this war: so long as our Navy remains invincible, our material existence is safe. But I do believe that our spiritual existence, as a source of freedom and justice and humane dealing, is very gravely imperiled, and can only be preserved if we realise that we are not wholly and in all things above reproach. The spirit of the German Government is hateful to me, but I see much of the same spirit in many Englishmen, and in them I mind it more, because the honour of England is more important to me than that of Germany. And although many acts of the German Government and of individual German soldiers are hateful, I cannot believe that there is wisdom, or hope for the welfare of Europe, in hatred of the German nation. I think it is wholesome to realise that our Government, likewise, has done many hateful things, that all men have need of charity, and that a merely punitive justice is apt to make the judge as cruel as the criminal.

I think it is probable that, if our policy since 1904 had been wiser, the present war would never have occurred. I am convinced that we ought to have shaped our policy so as not to be obliged to participate in it, and that our participation has been a terrible misfortune for England, for Europe, and for the future of civilisation. While others are sacrificing their lives for their ideals, I cannot seek a cowardly and ignoble comfort in silence. It is very little that one man can do, but that little I must do towards persuading England and the world to adopt other principles and other ideals than those which have led to the present horror. I honour profoundly the men whose sense of duty leads them to face death on the battlefield. But, believe me, what I do is inspired by the same sincerity, the same earnestness, the same love of England, and perhaps an even greater hope for mankind. The sacrifice entailed is less, but if it were greater, I should only meet it the more gladly.

Yours very truly, Bertrand Russell.

•••••••••••••• [19] ••••••••••••••

## "Mr. Russell Replies"

*The Cambridge Magazine* (6th November, 1915) | C15.23

*Sorley's response to Russell's letter of 30th October in* The Cambridge Magazine *criticized his proposal for an international navy claiming that it would leave Britain with inadequate defenses. And he posed two questions for Russell: "Have you ever written anything which tends to encourage our fellow-countrymen . . . ?" and "Have you ever written or done anything which is likely to weaken their effort to achieve victory . . . ?" By this time Russell had become aware of the death of Sorley's son.*

Sir, —Professor Sorley's letter in your last number calls for a few words of reply, though I do not propose to deal with his points seriatim. What he says on the subject of my letters to the *Cambridge Review* rests partly upon insufficient recollection, partly upon interpreting very literally some remarks not intended to be taken quite *au pied de la lettre*. And as for the *International Review*, my article (as I have already pointed out in the Times) was written before the Bryce Report appeared. I was at that time very sceptical about atrocities, particularly as it appeared that the Germans were believing shocking things about the Belgians and Russians. I was mistaken, and I now admit that war is even more horrible than I thought it was. The Germans in Belgium, doubtless, behaved worse than we should have behaved in similar circumstances. I attribute this to militarism, and I think that if we adopt an equally severe military discipline we shall in time become equally cruel.

As for the two questions with which Professor Sorley ends his letter, he can hardly suppose that I have not asked myself those questions. But I may perhaps state generally what my attitude is. I do not consider, as Professor Sorley does, that this war is for England a life-and-death struggle; I do not think our national independence is in danger. Although I think there would be very great harm in a partial victory for the Germans, the harm done by the continuance of the war seems to me still greater. I see the nations incited to mutual hatred by what seem to me very misleading statements as to the facts, and I cannot believe that any good cause is served by misrepresentation. To mitigate bitterness and hatred, to promote a sense of truth and justice, has seemed to me as great a service as I personally could do for my country while the war continues.

Yours faithfully, Bertrand Russell

[20]

## "Mr. Russell's Reply"

*The Cambridge Magazine* (12th February, 1916) | C16.02

*Early in 1916 Russell gave a series of lectures that were published as his* Principles of Social Reconstruction. *T.E. Hulme*[14] *contributed essays on the war to* The Cambridge Magazine, *under the pen-name "North Staffs" (because he came from the north of Staffordshire). Hulme attended some of Russell's lectures and criticized Russell's pacifism and his theory of "impulse," according to which impulse is fundamental to human life, and the good society is one in which the individual's impulses are helped to grow in positive, creative ways. In a private note to the editor (C.K. Ogden) Russell described Hulme as "able but nasty." Hulme returned to the war in March 1916 and was killed the next year.*

*This reply to Hulme, and the following, are especially notable because they mark the beginning of a gradual change in Russell's ethical theory from the objectivism of his 'Elements of Ethics' (1910), written when he was under the influence of G.E. Moore's* Principia Ethica, *to a more subjectivist and emotivist position that would reach full maturity in his* Religion and Science *(1935).*

Sir, —Your correspondent "North Staffs" has contributed to the *Magazine* a criticism of a recent lecture by me, with the courteous title "The kind of rubbish we oppose." This criticism shows such profound misunderstanding of the lecture that I suspect "North Staffs" of being

14. T.E. Hulme (1883–1917) was an intellectual precursor of fascism. His ideas were a formative influence on Yeats, Eliot, and Pound; he wrote *Speculations* (a still widely-read book of literary essays) and translated Georges Sorel's *Reflections on Violence*.

the gentleman who ostentatiously read the *Daily Express* during the greater part of the hour.

He begins by suggesting that I regard the bellicose as moved by impulse and the pacifists as moved by reason. My whole lecture on the contrary, was concerned to represent both sides as moved by impulse, and to show that impulse is essential to all vigorous action, whether good or bad. "Blind impulses," so I contended, "sometimes lead to destruction and death, but at other times they lead to the best things the world contains. Blind impulse is the source of war, but it is also the source of science and art and love. It is not the weakening of impulse that is to be desired, but the direction of impulse towards life and growth rather than towards death and decay." And again: "It is not the act of a passionless man to throw himself athwart the whole movement of the national life, to urge an outwardly hopeless cause, to incur obloquy and to resist the contagion of collective emotion. The impulse to avoid the hostility of public opinion is one of the strongest in human nature, and can only be overcome by an unusual force of direct and uncalculating impulse; it is not cold reason alone that can prompt such an act."

Having misrepresented my thesis, he continues: "There is no doubt that this provides a happy method of controversy for general use by pacifists. They thus avoid the necessity for any tedious examination of the actual arguments used by their opponents, by depriving these arguments at one stroke of all validity." If "North Staffs" has such a love of "tedious examination" as he suggests, I would refer him to *The Policy of the Entente* and *Justice in War-Time* (both published by the Labour Press), where he will find that I have set forth the detailed discussion which I presupposed in the lecture.

He proceeds to suggest that the difference between him and me is one of the ethical valuation. No doubt this is true on the surface. But ethical differences usually spring from differences of impulse. "Whole philosophies, whole systems of ethical valuation, spring up in this way: they are the embodiment of a kind of thought which is subservient to impulse, which aims at providing a quasi-rational ground for the indulgence of impulse." "This difference of opinion will seem to be ethical or intellectual, whereas its real basis is a difference of impulse. No genuine agreement will be reached, in such a case, so long as the differences of impulse persists." (These again are quotations from the lecture.)

I cannot imagine what led "North Staffs" to his final exhortation not to "falsely simplify matters by assuming that it is a struggle between the assailants and the defenders of privilege. It is not Democracy against Privilege." There was not a syllable in my lecture to suggest to any one who listened to it that I regarded the matter in this light. It is not democracy, but liberty, that is in danger. The persecutions of early Christians, the massacre of St. Bartholomew,[15] the Press Gang, and Conscription for the Unmarried, have none of them been contrary to democracy. But the tyrannous power of the state, whether wielded by a monarch or by a majority, is an evil against which I will protest no matter how "negligible" may be the minority on whom it is exercised.

Yours etc., Bertrand Russell.

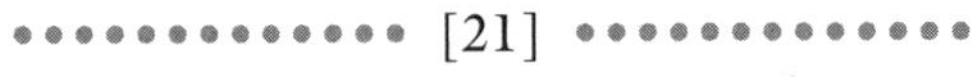

[21]

## "North Staffs' Praise of War"

*The Cambridge Magazine* (11th March, 1916), p. 386 | C16.05

*In his rejoinder to Russell's reply of February 12th, Hulme had complained that Russell had not proved that war is not ethically justifiable, and he noted that the absence of objectivity in Russell's current thinking about ethics was at odds with his pre-war view.*

*In Russell's reply, he criticizes Hulme's "praise of war" and outlines his own new view regarding the subjectivity of ethics and the nature of ethical argument.*

Sir, —In the *Cambridge Magazine* for February 26 North Staffs does something to bring to a clear issue the differences between him and me. These differences are rooted in character and disposition, and will not be dispelled by argument; but I will do my best towards helping to make them explicit.

North Staffs distinguishes two types of reasons: "(1) Those dealing with facts; (2) those concerned with ethics." I referred him to two pamphlets, one dealing with the one, the other with the other. He bought one of these pamphlets, and complains that it does not deal with the topics discussed in the other. This seems unreasonable.

As regards ethical reasons, he says that I "consistently refuse to admit that any such reasons can possibly exist." The reception given to Bernhardi's works[16] in this country, and the determination to maintain that Germany is wholly responsible for the war, had led me to think that

15. The massacre of French Protestants by Catholics beginning on the Feast of St. Bartholomew, 24th August, 1572.

16. Friedrick Bernhardi (1849–1930) was a German cavalry general and author whose published views preached Pan-Germanism and the glory of war.

this was common ground so far as Englishmen's explicit opinions were concerned. Does North Staffs wish to associate himself with Bernhardi in the praise of war as a good in itself? If so, he will find himself in an even smaller minority than that in which I find myself. If not, I must suppose that he wishes to praise only defensive wars. To this I would reply (1) that this war is less purely defensive than most of us believe; (2) that even defensive wars are less justifiable, on the grounds of their effects, than men usually suppose them to be. Both these points have been argued at length in the pamphlets referred to.

On the abstract question of ethics which North Staffs proceeds to raise, I do certainly mean to maintain that all ethics is subjective, and that ethical agreement can only arise through similarity of desires and impulses. It is true that I did not hold this view formerly, but I have been led to it by a number of reasons, some logical, some derived from observation. Occam's Razor, or the principle that constructions are to be substituted for inferred entities whenever possible, leads me to discard the notion of absolute good if ethics can be accounted for without it. Observation of ethical valuations leads me to think that all ethical valuations can be so accounted for, and that the claim of universality which men associate with their ethical judgments embodies merely the impulse to persecution or tyranny.

An ethical argument can only have practical efficacy in one of two ways: (1) By showing that the effects of some kind of action are different from what the opponent supposes: this is really a scientific not an ethical argument; (2) by altering the desires or impulses of the opponent, not merely his intellectual judgments. I cannot imagine any argument by which it could be shown that something is intrinsically bad; for this reason, ethical valuations not embodying desires or impulses cannot have any importance.

For my part, I should wish to see in the world less cruelty, persecution, punishment, and moral reprobation than exists at present; to this end I believe that a recognition of the subjectivity of ethics might conduce. But if North Staffs likes these things, and judges them to be in themselves good, I cannot prove by argument that he is mistaken: I can only say his desires and mine are different. If his belief in the intrinsic excellence of war has some other basis, I hope he will set it forth.

Bertrand Russell.

P.S. —Since writing the above I have seen North Staffs' continuation in the *Magazine* for March 4. Most of what he says in this continuation I said in my lecture on Religion on February 29. But the antithesis between heroic ethics and ethics devoted to life, which he draws, is quite baseless. An ethic is rendered heroic, not by the values which it recognises, but by the intensity of its recognition and the sacrifices it is willing to make to realise them. In that sense my ethic is as "heroic" as his; and I do not condemn all wars, as I stated in "The Ethics of War," and again in my lecture on war. But the things which I value are very seldom promoted by war. I value the kind of life which seems to me "heroic," the kind which is devoted to certain ends that are in one sense above life, but that only acquire actual existence when they are embodied in life. I find that it is not pursuit of these ends that leads to modern wars, and that modern wars are the greatest obstacle to the achievement of these ends. I wish North Staffs would tell us explicitly what are the things which he values: for so long as he keeps silence about this, the controversy remains indefinite.

[22]

## "A Clash of Consciences"

*The Nation* (15th April, 1916), p. 76 | C16.07

*Russell joined the No Conscription Fellowship (NCF) in 1916 soon after the British government established military conscription as law. The NCF was the only British organization which opposed the war and conscription. Russell had just attended a London conference of the NCF and addressed a crowd of some two thousand people.*

*Russell's letter on behalf of the NCF is a powerful plea for conscientious objection. His remark that it is "only through actual suffering that they will convince ordinary men of their inflexible courage" is reminiscent of Martin Luther King, Jr., and Mohandas Gandhi. Here he's especially concerned to challenge the stereotype of C.O.s as 'shirkers', and he insists that their "readiness for sacrifice [is] at least as great as that of the soldier who dies for his country."*

Sir, —To the great majority of Englishmen, at this time, it seems clear that duty requires the sacrifice of everything, even life, to the cause of victory in the war. To a small minority, it seems, on the contrary, that participation in war is wicked, and that duty requires the sacrifice of everything, even life, to the cause of peace and human brotherhood.

Both sides have the same moral integrity, the same determination, the same courage. Which side has the greater insight, time will show.

Is it really necessary that the majority should continue to misunderstand the minority? For their sakes, I cannot bring myself wholly to regret the persecution to which the conscientious objectors are being subjected, for I think it is only through actual suffering that they will convince ordinary men of their inflexible courage. But for the sake of the others, the majority, the men in power, the military authorities, the clergy, (with honorable exceptions), and the men above military age—for the sake of their souls, and for the sake of religious liberty, I could wish that it was not thought a mark of courage to join in the universal assault upon these few, or a mark of cowardice to stand upright against an angry nation because of a burning moral conviction.

The No-Conscription Fellowship is a spontaneous association of those who believe in the sacredness of human life and the brotherhood of man, and who are prepared to abide by this faith, even to the death. Last Saturday and Sunday, they held a large Convention, composed of delegates from all parts of Great Britain. An assembly of some 2,000, representing a scattered membership of many thousands, gave proof, to all who saw it, of the spirit by which these young men are actuated. The public imagines the conscientious objector as a pale, anemic, nervous youth, too lifeless and bloodless to feel the call of honor, too selfish to be willing to make sacrifices for his country. Nothing could be more unlike the reality. There were pugnacious Scotsmen, with the broad accent of Glasgow; brawny miners from the pit; impetuous Welshmen, full of Celtic fire, whom one could see in imagination leading a cavalry charge in some desperate battle of former days. From London, from the southern ports, from the Universities, even from the Northern Highlands, the delegates had been sent to the Convention. They had all the qualities of the best type of Briton: good humor, capacity for dispatching business, immense determination, and inflexible will. But, added to these things, they had something more, something more rare and more precious. Like Blake, they had seen a vision; they wished to "build Jerusalem in England's green and pleasant land." No one with any knowledge can doubt that Blake would have been with them, and Shelley, if these men were now alive, and subject to the Military service act (No. 2), the Tribunals would have told them to stop talking such sickening rubbish, and they would be at this moment undergoing arrest or solitary confinement in a military prison.

Let the authorities make no mistake. The men in that Convention were filled with a profound faith, and with a readiness for sacrifice at least as great as that of the soldier who dies for his country. If persecution is to be meted out to them, they will joyfully become martyrs. Public opinion is against them now, because it believes them to be "shirkers"; that stigma is in process of being removed by the military authorities. When it has been removed, public opinion will undergo a revulsion. Does the Government wish to bring about this result?

Many schemes of "alternative service" have been proposed as a possible means of compromise. But compromise is difficult for these men; if they are asked to change their occupation, they feel that it is in order to facilitate the prosecution of the war. They have a far stronger desire than most men to be of service to the community; but it is their belief that a stand for peace is the greatest service they can render to the community. For this reason every hint of compromise was rejected by the Convention with the utmost determination. Their belief may be wrong, or it may be right; but no one who has seen them can doubt that it is sincere and unshakeable. Persecution will sully the persecutors and smirch the fair fame of Britain; but it will only advance the cause for which its victims will have triumphed.

—Yours, &c., Bertrand Russell.
April 12, 1916.

[23]

## "Practical War Economy."

*The Labour Leader* (20th April, 1916), p. 6 | C16.08

*This letter, signed "F.R.S.", has been attributed to Russell by Kenneth Blackwell and Fenner Brockway (life-long British peace activist, friend of Russell, and leader of the NCF).*

*Russell had been elected a Fellow of the Royal Society (F.R.S.) in 1908. Students of British literature will find it hard to miss the Swiftian irony in Russell's proposal.*

Sir, —The Government having now decided to fall in with the Continental practice of automatic Conscription for boys as they reach the age of eighteen, a little clear thinking shows that it has become possible to simplify enormously the means of achieving all that is to be hoped for from Mr. Asquith's noble pledge never to sheathe the sword until the military domination of Prussia has been wholly and finally destroyed.

My plan, which all will agree to be enormously more humane and economical than the present mode of conducting the war, is this: Let all the Great Powers of Europe agree that boys, when they reach the age of eighteen, shall be divided by lot into three classes, one containing the half of them, the other two each containing a quarter. The class containing one half shall be painlessly executed in a lethal chamber. Of the other two classes, the members of the one shall be deprived of an arm, a leg, or an eye at the discretion of the surgeon; the members of the other shall be exposed day and night to deafening noises, until they acquire some nervous affliction—madness, speechlessness, mental blindness, or deafness—after which they shall be liberated to form the future manhood of the country.

Sir, in the name of science and economy, but still more in the name of humanity, I call upon the Government to propose these terms at once to all the belligerents, and thus avoid an immense mass of preventible suffering caused by the lack of science in our present methods of killing.

—Yours, etc., F.R.S.

[24]

## "Will They Be Shot?"

*The Herald* (6th May, 1916), p. 10 | C16.10

*At the time of this letter, the British government had not clarified its policy regarding conscientious objectors and military obligation. Russell and others in the NCF feared that some five thousand C.O.s—those who could not, in good conscience, accept alternative service of "national importance"—could legally be sent to the front lines and shot for insubordination. The day after Russell's letter was published, the government announced plans to send a contingent of C.O.s to France. A few days later Russell and other leaders of the NCF met with Prime Minister Asquith who issued an order that no C.O.s be shot.*

Sir, —In the present temper of the governing classes it is too much to hope that the conscientious objectors can escape serious persecution. Most of them are believed to be cowards, who can be forced to fight by making it clear that the alternative is even more unpleasant. Those who are acknowledged to be sincere are still more hated, since they are seen to be a danger to that condition of international suspicion and ill-will by which the tyranny of force is kept in being. Probably the most that can be actually accomplished is to mitigate in some degree the penalties inflicted for the crime of refusing to kill.

There are about 10,000 objectors who have failed or are failing to obtain such exemption as would satisfy their consciences. Some of these have been awarded what is called "non-combatant service," but more than half have obtained no relief at all. In either case they are arrested as absentees and handed over to the military authorities, whose orders they cannot conscientiously obey.

It is not, I think, generally realised that these men are legally liable to be taken to France, and there shot for continuing to disobey orders. The military authorities have already been hinting that this fate is not unlikely to befall them; and there is nothing in the Military Service Act to prevent it, in spite of a clause which some optimists imagined to have that effect. (This has been admitted by Mr. Tennant,[17] in a correspondence published in the *Labour Leader*, April 27, p. 4.) In France a court-martial can be held and an execution carried out without the knowledge of the public at home; the name of the victim can be simply published in casualty lists, and the truth need not leak out until the war is over.

It must be remembered that the majority of conscientious objectors, having failed altogether to receive recognition from the tribunals, are deemed by the military authorities to be simply ordinary soldiers, and have no acknowledged claim to special treatment. Unless something is done by the Government it is natural to suppose that commanding officers will proceed as they would in any other case of insubordination.

It was certainly not the intention of Parliament that conscientious objectors should suffer the death penalty. Yet this will happen automatically unless all those who claim to be conscientious objectors are placed in civil custody instead of being placed in the custody of the military authorities. It is a monstrous thing that men whose whole protest is against militarism should be taken to barracks, subjected to a discipline against which they must rebel, and imprisoned, with or without hard labour, in a military prison, from which, at any moment, they may be shipped off to France or Salonica or Mesopotamia, or whatever place is thought most opaque to friendly eyes.

Before any other steps are taken to solve the problem raised by the conscientious objectors, the system of subjecting them to military law ought to be stopped. This must apply not only to those whose consciences have had the good fortune to be visible to the tribunals, but to all who have claimed to be conscientious objectors, and who have proved by their subsequent contumacy that their claim was not frivolous.

This measure would have the support of the officers responsible for discipline in camps and barracks, if experience up to the present time is any guide. Men who will not obey, who win respect by their courage, and who are often persuasive missionaries of pacifism, are by no means con-

17. H.J. Tennant (1865–1935) was Under-Secretary of War at this time. Despite the Prime Minister's assurance in May that no C.O.s would be shot, 34 C.O.s in the Non-combatant Corps in France were sentenced to death in June. Their sentences were commuted to prison terms.

ducive to discipline. And most officers, though professional duty requires that they should inflict punishment, feel the task an odious one, and would be thankful to be relieved of it. Few officers and few privates share the persecuting ferocity of the elderly civilians to whom war does not bring danger or painful duties, but only an opportunity of indulging bad passions normally repressed. And yet the ruthlessness of military law makes the worst result almost inevitable if the conscientious objectors are allowed to remain subject to it. To place them under civil control, if necessary in civil prisons, would be a simple and easy measure. However the majority may disagree with them at the moment, it cannot be denied that they are the kind of men who will make useful citizens when the war is over, and who ought not to be treated with a severity which is normally reserved for murderers. Is it too much to hope that the Government will agree to this very slender measure of relief, as a preliminary to a more complete solution of the problem?

—Yours, &c., Bertrand Russell.

[25]

## "Adsum qui Feci"

*The Times* (17th May, 1916), p. 9 | C16.11

*Ernest Everett, a young school teacher from St. Helens, Lancashire, was granted exemption from combat service on grounds of conscience. He then ignored the military notice for non-combatant duties. He was arrested and sentenced to two years' hard labor. Russell wrote an unsigned leaflet for the NCF explaining the case, which began: "Two Years' Hard Labour for Refusing to Disobey the Dictates of Conscience." He said that Everett was "fighting the old fight for liberty, and against religious persecution . . ." And he asked "Will you join the persecutors? Or will you stand for conscience . . . ?" When Russell learned that several people had been arrested for distributing the leaflet, he wrote the following letter to* The Times.

*Russell was then accused under the Defence of the Realm Act of "impeding recruiting and discipline." He was found guilty and fined one hundred pounds. His conviction also led to his dismissal from Cambridge University and caused the Foreign Office to deny him a passport to America to lecture at Harvard.*

*The letter's Latin title (assigned by the editor) roughly translates: 'Here I am; I did it.'*

Sir, —A leaflet was lately issued by the No Conscription Fellowship dealing with the case of Mr. Everett, a conscientious objector who was sentenced to two years hard labour by court-martial for disobedience to the military authorities. Six men have been condemned to varying terms of imprisonment with hard labour for distributing this leaflet. I wish to make it known that I am the author of this leaflet, and that, if anyone is to be prosecuted, I am the person primarily responsible.

Yours faithfully, Bertrand Russell.

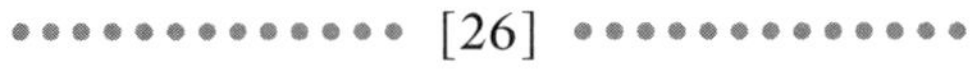

[26]

## "Liberty of Conscience"

*The Cambridge Magazine* (27th May, 1916), p. 505 | C16.12

*In this letter—refused by* The Nation*—Russell responds to a letter in the* Nation *signed "One of the Majority" and written in response to his letter ('A Clash of Consciences') to the* Nation *of April 15th. Here Russell emphasizes the role of fear in the cause of war, and defends conscientious objection against the charges of fallibility and anarchy. He also reaffirms his idea that non-resistance to aggression is generally a preferable alternative to belligerence.*

Sir, —A writer signing himself "One of the Majority", recently put various questions to me in *The Nation*. These I endeavoured to answer in the following letter, which *The Nation* has not inserted.

The writer states that if the majority had agreed with the conscientious objectors, England would now be in the same condition as Belgium. Now, to begin with, this would obviously be false if the views which he criticizes had also prevailed in Germany, such views have existed in Germany, and have been dealt with very severely by the German Government. But such an answer does not go to the root of the matter. I maintain that, if the majority among the Allies, or even in this country only, had agreed with the conscientious objectors, so far from England being as Belgium is, Belgium would be as England is—or rather as England was before the war. But for England, not only would the Belgiums not have resisted the passage of the German troops, and not have suffered any greater hardships than those that we are now inflicting upon the Greeks, but it is even in the highest degree probable that the war would not have occurred. Although national ambition inspires a certain proportion of the citizens of any great Power, the only motive that leads the bulk of the population to acquiesce in war is fear. The ordinary

German believes as firmly as the ordinary Englishman that his country was forced to fight in self-defence. If the Entente had been so obviously peace-loving as to make this view impossible, the militarist party in Germany would have had very little chance of securing popular support. How large a part fear played in German policy may be seen from the fact that Germany, after being pacific for thirty years, began to be war-like when we joined the Franco-Russian Alliance.

Your correspondent, in common with most critics, finds fault with the conscientious objectors for not undertaking some form of national service which would show a willingness for sacrifice as great as that of men who go to the front. I reply that, in making a stand for peace, in voluntarily suffering imprisonment (with or without hard labour), in incurring the risk of being shot for disobedience (which most of them believe, and I think rightly believe, to be very great), they are performing a national service, more useful, scarcely less painful, and demanding a higher order of courage, than that of men who fight for their country. Whatever may be urged in the name of liberty by those who sympathize with the conscientious objectors, they themselves do not ask to be spared the penalties attached to this form of service: if, by incurring the penalties, they can make their testimony against war more effective, they are glad to suffer. What many of them are not willing to do is to undertake a form of "national service" which would enable the authorities to conscribe other men whose labour is at present indispensable. If they did this, they would feel that they deserved the censure of sheltering behind those who do not share their scruples, which is now unjustly brought against them. Very many among them have always been willing and anxious to undertake any form of national service not open to this objection, but the tribunals, in the vast majority of cases, have refused to allow them to do so.

The other two points that are urged are that conscience is not infallible, and that liberty of conscience involves anarchy.

The claim to liberty of conscience does not depend upon any supposed infallibility: it depends upon the positive evil involved in coercing conscience. Your correspondent mentions the people who have a conscientious objection to the employment of doctors, and whose children die in consequence. I have as little sympathy with the views of these people as militarists have with the conscientious objectors; nevertheless, I should not wish to see them punished, and in fact they are usually not punished. Anti-vaccinators appear to be equally mistaken, but I am glad that their conscientious objection has been accorded legal recognition. To endeavour to force men to disregard their consciences must always involve great cruelty, and, if successful, it involves moral degradation and loss of self-respect, however mistaken these men may seem to be to others.

The plea that recognition of conscience involves anarchy is the old plea by which persecution has been justified in all ages, for the sake of which religious uniformity was enforced by the Inquisition and the stake. When at last religious toleration was tried, it was found that the State remained intact; and so it would be found now if freedom of conscience were permitted. In some men—especially in the small minority who make spiritual progress in each generation—there is an inner imperative, which religion has interpreted as the voice of God. Those in whom it exists dare not disregard it, on pain of moral death. For this reason, in every age, the men whom posterity has most honoured have found themselves in conflict with the State, which embodies always the maxims of the past, not the nascent wisdom of the present. Until lately, we might have hoped that civilized nations had learnt from history the danger that repression, however necessary it might seem, would be directed against the very things of most value to mankind. But under the stress of war, everything that had been learnt has been forgotten, and conscience must once more fight the old fight to free the human spirit from the tyranny of fear.

—Yours, etc., Bertrand Russell.
Trinity College, Cambridge, April 30, 1916.

[27]

## "The Conscientious Objector"

*The Daily News* (10th August, 1916), p. 4 | C16.20

*Public sentiment against conscientious objectors continued to grow throughout the war. The law allowed exemption for men claiming C.O. status, subject to determination by a citizens' tribunal. These tribunals rarely granted absolute exemption. Many were granted exemption from combat but required to perform alternative service of "national importance." This was the case with about 16,000 C.O.s. But some 1,300 "absolutists" also refused alternative service on grounds of conscience.*

*David Lloyd George (1863–1945) was a Liberal Member of Parliament for 54 years. He became the Secretary of State for War in June of 1916, and would become Prime Minister of a coalition government in December. His attack in the House of Commons on the absolutists distressed Russell and the NCF.*

Sir, —Mr. Lloyd George recently announced in the House of Commons that the milder treatment of conscientious objectors is not to extend to those who are unwilling to accept civil alternative service as the condition of their exemption for military service. Speaking of these men, he said: "I do not think they deserve the slightest consideration . . . I shall only consider the best means of making the path of that class a very hard one."

The public, while dissenting utterly from the views of all conscientious objectors, has nevertheless been shocked to learn of the persecution which they have had to undergo, and has become convinced of their sincerity through their willingness to suffer. Is it wise, at this date, to except one class of conscientious objectors from the proposed amnesty? Whatever may be thought as to the wisdom or unwisdom of these men's opinions, there can be no doubt whatever as to their earnestness. Those who stand out for absolute exemption, having been court-martialled and imprisoned, having been offered liberty on condition of engaging in what is called "work of national importance," are deliberately choosing to go back to prison, because they believe they have a work to perform which is not recognised as of national importance by the Tribunals or the Pelham Committee. For the sake of this work they are willing to remain in prison when their comrades have been released.

Such men (of whom many are known to me personally) may be called fanatics, may be thought utterly wrong-headed, but cannot possibly be regarded as cowards, shirkers, or hypocrites. By singling them out for special persecution the government is taking the best means of concentrating public sympathy upon them. The Military Service Acts allow of absolute exemption: the second Act made this clear because the first had been ambiguous. Is it not time to have done with persecution for conscience' sake, and to give to each kind of conscientious objector that form of exemption which meets his case? These men have shown by their previous record that they are anxious to serve the community. They cannot be turned into soldiers. What public purpose can be served by keeping them in gaol merely because they feel that their service can only be conscientiously given if it is not part of a bargain with what they regard as evil?

Bertrand Russell.
August 8.

[28]

## "Rex v. Russell"

*The Manchester Guardian* (14th August, 1916), p. 8 | C16.21

*The NCF put together a pamphlet ("Rex v. Russell") giving a verbatim report of Russell's trial in which he defended himself against charges stemming from his leaflet regarding the Everett case (see above, document [25]). 'Rex', Latin for 'king', indicates a government prosecution. Ironically, this pamphlet was seized by the authorities as illegal because it contained a transcript of Russell's trial which included the words of Russell's "mischievous" leaflet read into the record by the prosecuting attorney.*

Sir, —In the House of Commons on August 10 Mr. Forster[18] gave a reply to a question from Mr. Philip Snowden[19] regarding the seizure by the military authorities of a pamphlet consisting of the verbatim report of the case "Rex v. Russell" which shows a misconception of the facts on his part. He stated that "in addition to giving the official report of the trial" the pamphlet "contains a reprint of the mischievous pamphlet the publication of which led to Mr. Russell's conviction and punishment."

As a matter of fact, there is not a single word in the pamphlet beyond the verbatim report of the trial, and in order to ensure that the report should be unobjectionable the official shorthand notes of the Public Prosecutor were used. Even the title was made carefully neutral. It seems that what the military authorities dislike is that Mr. Bodkin, the prosecuting counsel, quoted the original leaflet paragraph by paragraph with his criticism.

Are we to understand that the report of the case is only rendered dangerous by the fact that it includes the speech for the prosecution?

—Yours, &c., Bertrand Russell
34, Russell Chambers, Bury Street, London, W.C., August 12.

18. H.W. Forster was Financial Secretary to the War Office.

19. Philip Snowden was a Member of Parliament in the Independent Labour Party. He was an ally in the anti-war effort and much admired by Russell.

[29]

## "Bertrand Russell's Advice"

*The Labour Leader* (7th September, 1916), p. 4 | C16.23

*Russell had learned a few days earlier that his London flat had been searched "top to bottom" by Scotland Yard who were looking for the NCF pamphlet "Rex v. Russell."*

Dear Sir, . . . There is nothing to do about the police. Domiciliary visits from the police are one of the customs of the country. If you desire less interference with personal liberty I should advise you to emigrate to Russia.

—Yours faithfully, Bertrand Russell.

[30]

## Mr. Bertrand Russell and His Lectures; Reply to Mr. Lloyd George

*The Glasgow Herald* (21st October, 1916), p. 8 | C16.27

*During the summer of 1916 Russell came under increased surveillance by the government who considered him a serious threat to the war effort. His anti-war lecture tour in Wales in July was seen as dangerous, and the government restricted his travel in certain 'prohibited' regions, especially those where labor unrest and anti-war sentiment were widespread.*

Sir, —As Mr. Lloyd George's statements concerning my lecture in the House of Commons yesterday show that he has been gravely misinformed as to my intentions, I hope you will allow me to correct the erroneous impression which he has unintentionally conveyed. According to "The Times" of to-day, Mr. Lloyd George stated: "We had information from very reliable sources that Mr. Bertrand Russell was about to engage in the delivery of a series of lectures which would interfere very seriously with the manning of the Army." There is not a word of truth in this. I do not know what the "very reliable sources" may have been, but I can only earnestly hope that the Secret Service is less inaccurate as regards the Germans than it has proved itself to be where I am concerned. The only series of lectures which I contemplate delivering is a series on "The World as it can be Made." As regards these lectures, I have published a statement (which has been read by the War Office authorities) explaining why I cannot give an undertaking and saying, inter alia, that the course "Is not intended to deal with the immediate issues raised by the war; there will be nothing about the diplomacy preceding the war, about conscientious objectors, about the kind of peace to be desired, or even about the general ethics of war." The syllabus of the course was sent to the War Office. The first lecture, on "Political Ideals," which is a perfectly fair sample, has been delivered by me in Manchester and by Mr. Robert Smillie in Glasgow, and is now on sale, having been published by the National Council for Civil Liberation. I hope, before the War Office view as to my lectures is accepted, this lecture will be read. Mr. Lloyd George stated that my lectures "undoubtedly interfere with the prosecution of the war, they lead to weakness and inefficiency." Even if I had the worse intentions I could not achieve this result by lectures, for which there is a fee, which are addressed to audiences of 200 or 300. But in fact they have no such aim and are quite incapable of having any such effect. And if they are so pernicious, why are they permitted in Manchester?

[31]

## "Mr. Bertrand Russell's Case"

*The Times* (27th October, 1916), p. 7 | C16.28

*Russell was prevented from traveling to Harvard University shortly after his June conviction for writing the Everett leaflet. In September he was restricted from travel in much of the U.K., and he published some of his correspondence with the War Office concerning the prohibition, including his explanation for his refusal to give "an honourable undertaking" not to use his public talks as a "vehicle for propaganda" in exchange for freedom to travel and lecture.*[20]

*In this letter Russell challenges the Home Secretary's assertion in the House of Commons that Russell's travel to the U.S. was contingent on his acceptance of the "understanding."*

Sir, —Will you allow me to correct a misapprehension, which is liable to arise out of Mr. Herbert Samuel's[21] answers in the House of

20. 'Bertrand Russell and the War Office'. *The Manchester Guardian* (27th September, 1916), p. 6.

21. Herbert L. Samuel (1870–1963) was Home Secretary in 1916.

Commons on October 19 and 25, as regards the Government's refusal to permit me to go to America? No correspondence of any kind, and no verbal communication, official or unofficial, ever passed between me and any Government office on this subject. The only communication of which I have any knowledge is a letter from our Ambassador in the United States to the President of Harvard stating that a passport could not be granted to me because of my conviction at the Mansion House under the Defence of the Realm Act. This letter was dated June 8, at a time when the Mansion House decision was still *sub judice*, as I had appealed to Quarter Sessions. I was never asked whether I would give such an undertaking as Mr. Samuel now says would be sufficient. Throughout my recent correspondence with the War Office I not only did not know, but did not in any way suspect, that the undertaking demanded would carry with it permission to go to America. It is now too late for me to fulfill my engagement at Harvard, as the Harvard authorities have been compelled to make other arrangements, as I have also. Mr. Samuel stated on October 25 "that Mr. Russell could at any time have obtained a permit to go to America on giving such an undertaking". Not the faintest hint of this was given to me, and I neither knew nor guessed that it was the case.

Yours faithfully, Bertrand Russell,
57, Gordon Square, W.C., October 26.

[32]

## "Mysterious Girl Brings Russell's Peace Plea Here. Famous English Philosopher and Mathematician Asks Wilson to Stop War ere Europe Perishes"

*The New York Times* (23rd December, 1916), pp. 1, 3 | C16.31

*Russell was heartened throughout 1916 by American neutrality and a growing sentiment for peace negotiations, and he had great hopes that Wilson could mediate an end to the war and thus save Europe from complete destruction. In early December he wrote an appeal to President Wilson which was smuggled out of the country, into the U.S. The letter was taken to the American Neutral Conference Committee in New York, and then onto to Washington where it was placed before President Wilson by Walter Lippmann, the American author and editor. The letter was published in many newspapers, including* The New York Times *and the* Los Angeles Times.

Sir, —You have an opportunity of performing a signal service to mankind, surpassing even the service of Abraham Lincoln, great as that was. It is in your power to bring the war to an end by a just peace, which shall do all that could possibly be done to allay the fear of new wars in the near future. It is not yet too late to save European civilisation from destruction; but it may be too late if the war is allowed to continue for the further two or three years with which our militarists threaten us.

The military situation has now developed to the point where the ultimate issue is clear, in its broad outlines, to all who are capable of thought. It must be obvious to the authorities in all the belligerent countries that no victory for either side is possible. In Europe, the Germans have the advantage; outside Europe, and at sea, the Allies have the advantage. Neither side is able to win such a crushing victory as to compel the other to sue for peace. The war inflicts untold injuries upon the nations, but not such injuries as to make a continuation of fighting impossible. It is evident that however the war may be prolonged, negotiations will ultimately have to take place on the basis of what will be substantially the present balance of gains and losses, and will result in terms not very different from those which might be obtained now. The German Government has recognized this fact, and has expressed its willingness for peace on terms which ought to be regarded at least as affording a basis for discussion, since they concede the points which involve the honour of the Allies. The Allied governments have not had the courage to acknowledge publicly what they cannot deny in private, that the hope of a sweeping victory is one which can now scarcely be entertained. For want of this courage, they are prepared to involve Europe in the horrors of a continuance of the war, possibly for another two or three years. This situation is intolerable to every humane man. You, Sir, can put an end to it. Your power constitutes an opportunity and a responsibility; and from your previous actions I feel confident that you will use your power with a degree of wisdom and humanity rarely to be found among statesmen.

The harm which has already been done in this war is immeasurable. Not only have millions of valuable lives been lost, not only have an even greater number of men been maimed or shattered in health, but the whole standard of civilization has been lowered. Fear has invaded men's inmost being, and with fear has come the ferocity that always attends it. Hatred has become the rule of life, and injury to others is more desired than benefits to ourselves. The hopes of peaceful progress in which our earlier years were passed are dead, and can never be revived. Terror and savagery have become the very air we breathe. The liberties which our ancestors won by centuries of struggle were sacrificed in a day, and all the nations are regimented to the one ghastly end of mutual destruction.

This drawing of Russell by J.F. Horrabin appeared in the Quaker socialist monthly, The *Ploughshare* (February 1917), the first British publication to reprint Russell's open letter to President Wilson in its entirety. See document [32].

But all this is nothing in comparison with what the future has in store for us if the war continues as long as the announcements of some of our leading men would make us expect. As the stress increases, and weariness of the war makes average men more restive, the severity of repression has to be continually augmented. In all the belligerent countries, soldiers who are wounded or home on leave express an utter loathing of the trenches, a despair of ever achieving a military decision, and a terrible longing for peace. Our militarists have successfully opposed the granting of votes to soldiers; yet in all the countries an attempt is made to persuade the civilian population that war-weariness is confined to the enemy soldiers. The daily toll of young lives destroyed becomes a horror almost too terrible to be borne; yet everywhere, advocacy of peace is rebuked as treachery to the soldiers, though the soldiers above all men desire peace. Everywhere, friends of peace are met with the diabolical argument that the brave men who have died must not have shed their blood in vain. And so every impulse of mercy towards the soldiers who are still living is dried up and withered by a false and barren loyalty to those who are past our help. Even the men hitherto retained for making munitions, for dock labour, and for other purposes essential to the prosecution of the war, are gradually being drafted into the armies and replaced by women, with the sinister threat of coloured labour in the background. There is a very real danger that, if nothing is done to check the fury of national passion, European civilization as we have known it will perish as completely as it perished when Rome fell before the Barbarians.

It may be thought strange that public opinion should appear to support all that is being done by the authorities for the prosecution of the war. But this appearance is very largely deceptive. The continuance of the war is actively advocated by influential persons and by the Press, which is everywhere under the control of the Governments. In other sections of society feeling is quite different from that expressed by the newspapers, but public opinion remains silent and uninformed, since those who might give guidance are subject to such severe penalties that few are willing to protest openly, and those few cannot obtain a wide publicity. From considerable personal experience, reinforced by all that I can learn from others, I believe that the desire for peace is almost universal, not only among the soldiers, but throughout the wage-earning classes, and especially in industrial districts, in spite of high wages and steady employment. If a plebiscite of the nation was taken on the question whether negotiations should be initiated I am confident that an overwhelming majority would be in favour of this course, and that the same is true of France, Germany, and Austria-Hungary.

. . . Above all, I see that none of the issues in the war are as important as peace; the harm done by a peace which does not concede all that we desire is nothing in comparison to the harm done by the continuance of the fighting. While all who have power in Europe speak for what they falsely believe to be the interests of their separate nations, I am compelled by a profound conviction to speak for all the nations in the name of Europe. In the name of Europe I appeal to you to bring us peace.

Bertrand Russell
Dec. 4, 1916.

[33]

## "The Pacifist at Large. Mr. Bertrand Russell Explains Himself."

*The Morning Post* (15th January, 1917), p. 9 | C17.04

*Russell's letter to Wilson was published in the* Morning Post *on 10th January, followed by a critical editorial the next day which, in part, impugned his patriotism.*

Sir, —Your leading article on the subject of my open letter to President Wilson in your issue of January 11 calls for a few words of reply.

You say: "Mr. Russell, if he is so much set on an immediate peace, might realise that the unlikeliest way to obtain it is to assure Germany that she is invincible." Do you seriously suggest that the German Government is going to be influenced in its view of the military prospects by anything I may say, or that it will regard me as the mouthpiece of the British Cabinet? You do me too much honour.

When I say that "the desire for peace is almost universal," you infer without any reason that I mean peace on any terms. I mean, of course, peace on terms which will restore Belgium and the North of France, and respect the principle of nationality in the Balkans—terms which there is every reason to believe are now obtainable.

You state that I "gave the Germans a certificate of good character." I do not know on what you base this assertion. As for the German people, every one who knows them is aware that they have many good qualities. As for the German Government, I have never concealed and often expressed my conviction that its guilt in regard to the present war is much greater than that of our Government.

Finally you say, "he has the satisfaction of knowing that, in spite of the Censor, he has rendered his country a very signal disservice." Do you, sir, really believe that I wish to render my country disservice? If so, I can only assure you, most solemnly, that you are absolutely mistaken. It is my conviction that the course upon which we have embarked is very dangerous, and possibly fatal. In attempting to bring the war to an end I am as much actuated by love of my country as you are in advocating the opposite policy. I believe that your policy is calculated to do untold damage to the British Empire, but I do not impugn your patriotism: I acknowledge a sincere difference of opinion. Cannot you do the same?

—Yours, &c., Bertrand Russell.
57, Gordon Square, W.C., Jan. 12.

[34]

## "Conscientious Objectors."

*The Manchester Guardian* (19th March, 1917), p. 8 | C17.16

*In this letter, Russell responds to "Artifax," the pen name of Canon Peter Green (1871–1961) of St. Philip's parish, one of the* Guardian's *regular correspondents who frequently criticize the Church for ignoring Christ's messages of pacifism and poverty. In his letter of 15th March, Green had criticized the conscientious objectors as being guilty of a kind of social irresponsibility.*

Sir, —In your issue of March 15 there is a discussion by "Artifex" of the position of the conscientious objector, which, while very temperate in tone, contains two sentences to which I wish to reply. "Artifex" says:—

> I think that to be a real conscientious objector a man must be, consciously or unconsciously, an extreme individualist with little sense of the solidarity of mankind and of our membership one of another.

There are no doubt many kinds of reasons which lead men to become conscientious objectors, but I am convinced that the chief reason, and the most valid, is precisely, that sense of "the solidarity of mankind," of "our membership one of another," which "Artifex" denies to us. It seems to me that when he wrote "mankind" he was thinking only of the Allies. But the Germans too, are included among "mankind." The conscientious objector does not believe that violence can cure violence, or that militarism can exorcise the spirit of militarism. He persists in feeling "solidarity" with those who are called "enemies," and he believes that if this feeling were more widespread among us it would do more than armies and navies can ever do to prevent the growth of aggressive Imperialism, not only among ourselves but also among potential enemies.

"Artifex" repeats the argument that the conscientious objector accepts the protection of those who are willing to fight, and that he "will accept protection from the police and from penal laws, and pay taxes which support not only the gaol but the scaffold." But the conscientious objector only "accepts" this "protection" because there is no way of avoiding it. He has not asked for it and does not believe it necessary. For my part, nothing would induce me to prosecute a thief, and if there are any burglars among your readers they are welcome to take note of this announcement; but I shall be very much surprised if I lose as much through them as I have lost through the operation of the law. And is it not rather ironic to speak of the protection of the law to men whom it has deprived of the means of livelihood and shut up in prison for the duration of the war with only occasional brief intervals for fresh courts-martial? Is there really such a vast gulf between Wormwood Scrubs and Ruhleben?[22]

Yours, &c., Bertrand Russell.
57, Gordon Square, London, W.C.

[35]

## "Conscientious Objectors: Lord Derby and the Absolutists"

*New Statesman* (9th June, 1917), p. 229 | C17.33

*Throughout 1917 Russell served as Acting Chairman of the NCF while Clifford Allen, its permanent Chairman, was in prison for conscientious objection. Much of his time and writing focused on the problem of conscientious objectors, especially the so called "absolutists."*

*This letter is signed "Margaret Hobhouse," but it has been identified as Russell's. At the time Margaret Hobhouse was co-authoring a book on conscription with Russell, and she had an "absolutist" son who was sentenced to two years' hard labor in prison. Here, Russell defends the unpopular position of the absolutists against Lord Derby, the Secretary of State for War.*

22. Wormwood Scrubs had the reputation of being one of London's harshest prisons. Ruhleben was a German internment camp outside Berlin where several thousand Britons were held.

Sir, —Lord Derby's[23] pronouncement on the subject of the Conscientious Objectors who have refused work of national importance under the Home Office came as a great disappointment to those—and they are many—who had hoped that the Government was going to adopt a more lenient policy towards these men. He announced bluntly that the men must either do work of national importance or stay in prison.

It is quite clear from his speech that he had failed altogether to understand the nature of their conscientious scruple. He said: "They were prepared to let other men fight to retain them their liberties, and would not themselves assist their country by undertaking any work for the nation at all at the time of its greatest crisis."

Apart from the irony of alluding to the "liberties" of men who are kept in prison, their position, however unreasonable we may think it, is, at any rate, different from this. They are willing and anxious to undertake work for the nation—provided that the work is not imposed by the Military Service Acts, and is not designed for the prosecution of the war. The great majority of them were engaged in useful occupations up to the time of their arrest, and would return to those occupations if they were set at liberty; but they will not return to those occupations, or to any others, as part of a bargain. They claim the right to the absolute exemption which is allowed by the Acts, and which, according to a Government statement, has actually been granted to some 400 men.

However strange it may appear to us, they do sincerely believe that they would be doing wrong in so far bowing to Conscription as to purchase their liberty by undertaking work which is imposed as a result of Conscription.

An account of their position—with their numbers and an analysis of their occupations, politics, and religions—has been published by the Friends' Service Committee under the title "The Absolutists' Objection to Conscription." Those who find it impossible to understand how sincere men can take up such a position would perhaps find this little book useful.

The principle of liberty of conscience ought not to be extended only in favour of consciences which we can easily understand. We all know that Mahommedans object to pork and Hindus to beef. If we were to hear of these scruples now for the first time, they would seem to us so strange that we should hardly be able to believe in their genuineness. Yet experience has shown that it is absolutely necessary to respect them; and it can

23. Lord Derby was Edward George Villiers Stanley (1865–1948), the seventeenth Earl of Derby. He was a conscriptionist with no sympathy for absolutist C.O.s

hardly be maintained that they are less fantastic or unreasonable than the refusal to participate in war.

The Government has now had the experience of some 800 men enduring repeated terms of imprisonment (some have reached their third and even fourth term) for refusal to accept work under the Home Office Scheme. There has been enough experience to prove conclusively that these men are sincere, and will not alter their view in order to escape punishment.

The alternative to prison for these men is not the Army, but civil work in Home Office camps. There can, therefore, be no question whatever of cowardice as a motive to their continued resistance. Moderate opinion, from the Archbishop of Canterbury downwards, has urged the Government to set these men at liberty.

Moreover, the inhumanity of our prison system is such that it is quite wrong that such brutality and harshness should be possible in treating human beings at all, and investigation and reform seem urgently needed.

Further, at present it would seem as if the cases of doubtful conscience were treated with leniency, while those of unquestionable convictions were treated with barbarity.

In spite of Lord Derby's pronouncement, it is to be hoped that wiser counsels will prevail, and that the absolute exemption which has been granted in some cases will be extended to those whose conscientious objection has proved incapable of being satisfied by anything else.

—Yours, etc., Margaret Hobhouse.

[36]

## "The German Peace Offer"

*The Tribunal* (3rd January, 1918), p. 1 | C18.01

*News of the Russian Revolution in March of 1917, and the Russian call for a negotiated peace without annexations or indemnities encouraged those like Russell who called for a swift end to hostilities and a rebuilding of post-war Europe on the basis of peace and social justice. But the entry of America into the war the next month served to dampen hopes for an impending armistice.*

*Although Russell's association with* The Tribunal, *the weekly publication of the NCF, had officially ended at the close of the year, he was asked to write a piece for this edition. Despite the article's up-beat tone, the Allies' declaration in February 1918 that they would push for victory and Russian capitulation to Germany's harsh demands in the Treaty of Brest-Litovsk caused Russell to doubt the effectiveness of continued peace work, and he resolved to return to professional philosophy. Ironically, it was at this time that the government pressed hard to prosecute Russell.*

*This article, not a letter to the editor, was the basis of the government's case under the Defence of the Realm Act that Russell had made a statement "likely to prejudice His Majesty's relations with a foreign power." Describing the likely effects of continuing the war, Russell wrote: "The American Garrison which will by that time be occupying England and France, whether or not they will prove efficient against the Germans, will no doubt be capable of intimidating strikers, an occupation to which the American army is accustomed when at home." For that Russell was sentenced to six months in prison.*

## The German Peace Offer

The more we hear about the Bolsheviks, the more the legend of our patriotic press becomes exploded. We were told that they were incompetent, visionary and corrupt, that they must fall shortly, that the mass of Russians were against them, and that they dared not permit the Constituent Assembly to meet. All these statements have turned out completely false, as anyone may see by reading the very interesting dispatch from Arthur Ransome in the *Daily News* of December 31st.

Lenin, whom we have been invited to regard as a German Jew, is really a Russian aristocrat who has suffered many years of persecution for his opinions. The social revolutionaries who were represented as enemies of the Bolsheviks have formed a connection with them. The Constituent Assembly is to meet as soon as half its members have reached Petrograd, and very nearly half have already arrived. All charges of German money remain entirely unsupported by one thread of evidence.

The most noteworthy and astonishing triumph of the Bolsheviks is in their negotiations with the Germans. In a military sense Russia is defenceless, and we all supposed it a proof that they were mere visionaries when they started negotiations by insisting upon not surrendering any Russian territory to the Germans. We were told that the Germans would infallibly insist upon annexing the Baltic Provinces and establishing a suzerainty over Poland. So far from this being the case, the German and Austrian Governments have officially announced that they are prepared to conclude a Peace on the Russian basis of no annexations and no indemnities, provided that it is a general Peace, and they have invited the Western Powers to agree to these terms.

This action has placed the Governments of the Western Powers in a most cruel dilemma. If they refuse the German offer, they are unmasked before the world and before their own Labour and Socialist Parties: they make it clear to all that they are continuing the war for purposes of territorial aggrandizement. If they accept the offer, they afford a triumph to the hated Bolsheviks and an object lesson to democratic revolutionaries everywhere as to the way to treat with capitalists, Imperialists and war-mongers. They know that from the patriotic point of view they cannot hope for a better peace by continuing the war, but from the point of view of preventing liberty and universal peace, there is something to be hoped from continuation. It is known that unless peace comes soon there will be starvation throughout Europe. Mothers will be maddened by the spectacle of their children dying. Men will fight each other for possession of the bare necessaries of life. Under such conditions the sane constructive effort required for a successful revolution will be impossible. The American Garrison which will by that time be occupying England and France, whether or not they will prove efficient against the Germans, will no doubt be capable of intimidating strikers, an occupation to which the American Army is accustomed when at home. I do not say that these thoughts are in the mind of the Government. All the evidence tends to show that there are no thoughts whatever in their mind, and that they live from hand to mouth consoling themselves with ignorance and sentimental twaddle. I say only that if they were capable of thought, it would be along such lines as I have suggested that they would have to attempt to justify a refusal to make Peace on the basis of the German offer, if indeed they do decide to refuse.

Some democrats and Socialists are perhaps not unwilling that the war should continue, since it is clear that if it does it must lead to universal revolution. I think it is true that this consequence must follow, but I do not think that we ought on that account to acquiesce in the refusal to negotiate should that be the decision at which our Governments arrive. The kind of revolution with which we shall in that case be threatened will be far too serious and terrible to be a source of good. It would be a revolution full of violence, hatred and bloodshed, driven by hunger, terror and suspicion—a revolution in which all that is best in Western civilization is bound to perish. It is this prospect that our rulers ought to be facing. It is this risk that they run for such paltry objects as the annexation of African Colonies and Mesopotamia. Labour's war aims accepted almost unanimously on December 28th are on the whole very sane, and might easily form the basis for the immediate initiation of negotiations. Labour at the moment has enormous power. Is it too much to hope that it will use this power to compel some glimmer of sanity on the part of the blinded and maddened rulers of the Western Powers? Labour holds the key. It can if it chooses secure a just and lasting peace within a month, but if this opportunity is allowed to pass by, all that we hold dear will be swallowed up in universal ruin.

••••••••••••• [37] •••••••••••••

## "Mr. Bertrand Russell and the War"

*Morning Post* (9th February, 1918), p. 4 | C18.03

*Russell's letter is a response to a review of a collection of Russell's essays (*Mysticism and Logic, *1918) printed in the* Morning Post. *Here Russell clarifies his "understanding" with the government and defends himself against the charge of being "pro-German." The letter was published on February 9th, the same day that Russell was officially charged, for the second time, with violating the Defence of the Realm Act.*

Sir, —Your review of me in your issue of February 1, which has only just come into my hands, contains a misstatement which, in the interests of justice, I feel sure you will wish to correct. You speak of my "sending a stop-the-war message to America when an express promise had been made not to indulge in such propaganda." There is no shadow of truth in this; I always refused to give any promise, although the government offered to withdraw its orders restricting my movements if I would enter into such an undertaking. My views on the sacredness of promises are as strict as your own.

One more point. You speak of me as "pro-German," which I am not. I have repeatedly stated in public, and I repeat, that I consider Germany more to blame than the Allies, and that I would rather see a victory of the Allies than a victory of Germany; but I consider war so grave an evil that I would rather see an inconclusive peace than an indefinite prolongation of the struggle. This has been my attitude from the first.

Yours, &c., Bertrand Russell
57, Gordon-square, Feb. 8.

••••••••••••• [38] •••••••••••••

## The Role of Truth in Art

*The Nation* (27th July, 1918), p. 446 | C18.06

*This letter in defense of the poet Siegfried Sassoon was written while Russell was in prison and was smuggled out with the help of Ottoline Morrell. Hence, the pseudonym "Philalethes," which means 'lover of truth', (from the Greek* phil- *for love and* aletheia *meaning truth).*

*Sassoon (1886–1967) was a Cambridge-educated poet and novelist. He was also a highly decorated soldier who came to protest against the war and defy military authority. His courage was much admired by Russell and the NCF. Here Russell defends Sassoon's anti-war poems* (Counter-Attack and Other Poems, *1918) against a critical review which had appeared in the* Nation *two weeks earlier.*

Sir, —Your review of Mr. Sassoon's poems in your issue of July 13th lays down certain dogmas which, ancient and respectable as they are, should not be regarded as unquestionable. In criticism of Mr. Sassoon's attempt to portray the war, your reviewer says: "We feel not as we do with true poetry, or true art, that something is, after all, right, but that something is intolerably and irremediably wrong." And again, "There is a value in the plain, unvarnished truth; but there is another truth more valuable still." Why are we to be asked to accept such statements? Being told that "God's in His Heaven" may in the end grow more wearisome to those who certainly are not there, and they may refuse to be put down by being reminded of the serenity of Sophocles, and having it pointed out that Shakespeare, after making a fortune and retiring to Stratford-on-Avon, took a more cheerful view of life than he did when he was writing "King Lear." For my part, I believe that art is important and that truth is important, and that the union of the two is very important, but that it is untrue that something is, after all, right. It is just as easy to turn the "after all" the other way round, to point out how all happiness, even when it seems most innocent, is obtained at the expense of intolerable misery to others and how even the emotions that seem noblest to those who feel them, are often mere disguises for vanity, despotism, or greed. I do not say that such a view of life would be wholly true; I say only that it is as true as the optimistic view. If art is to remain living, it must be combined with truthfulness. Those who cannot believe that something "is, after all, right," must make and seek an art which is free from this dogma. And among the young they are the vast majority, for it is not only their lives that they are losing in the war.

—Yours, &c., Philalethes.

PART III

# Between the Wars

(1919–1938)

Bertrand Russell

The two decades represented here take us up to the beginning of World War II. These were busy years for Russell in which, as his public letters reveal, he displays passionate concern over a wide variety of issues. This is, after all, a time when he visited Russia and China, stood for Parliament twice, divorced and married twice, became a parent thrice, founded a progressive school for children, and watched, in horror and frustration, the approach of yet another world war. It was also, as I noted in the Introduction, a period during which Russell wrote scores of articles and 19 books on subjects including mathematics, politics, education, history and science.

His concerns in these years included foreign policy, and we find a surprisingly large number of letters on China, Russia, and India. From the earliest years after the Russian Revolution he made clear his criticisms of the Bolsheviks, but he also made plain his disapproval of capitalism and its imperialistic excrescences in the non-Western world.

During this period he identified largely with the socialist politics of the Labour Party. But we glimpse some differences, such as his position on birth control, which he openly favored, and his criticisms of orthodox religion, especially Christianity.

Throughout these two decades he continued to espouse the brand of pacifism he had defended in the First World War, and several of the letters concern his response to critical reviews of his *Which Way to Peace?* But by the end of the period he felt that, with the growing menace of Naziism, his pacifist arguments were becoming more and more difficult to justify.

Certainly war and peace were a major focus in this period, but we also find letters covering human rights, sexual ethics, science, religion, and education. In short, Russell the polymath is very much in evidence.

The 54 letters below are representative of the 68 known published letters to the editor written in this period. For the reader's convenience, they are divided into five categories and presented chronologically within each category.

# War and Peace

•••••••••••••• [39] ••••••••••••

## "The Biology of War"

*The Athenaeum* (16th May, 1919), p. 344 | C19.16

*In this letter Russell defends his earlier (11th April) review of G.F. Nicolai's* The Biology of War *against the complaints of the English translators, Constance and Julian Grande. Russell had objected to some of the translators' ethnocentric comments.*

*The letter is signed "The Reviewer." Internal evidence and Russell's diaries have revealed it to be by Russell.*

Sir, —The translators of Dr. Nicolai's[1] "Biology of War" are aggrieved because I criticize their work. I had not the original German before me, and relied upon such facts as their admitted insertion of quotations from English poets, together with the remark in their Introduction (to be interpreted in the light of such admissions) that "the present English translation has been simplified as much as possible without doing violence to the author's ideas." The officially admitted fact which the translators deny is "the English use of the flags of neutral countries"—a recognized naval *ruse de guerre.* They say in their footnote to this: "Even Dr. Nicolai does not seem to be above repeating unproved and unprovable statements of the German Press during this war" (p. 172n.). As examples of other footnotes, we may cite the following. Dr. Nicolai remarks that the Englishman's love of country is not of a sort to make him unwilling to travel, and continues: "He has conquered the world, in short, just because for him 'Home, sweet home,' is no longer anything but a romantic idyll." On this they comment "Dr. Nicolai, like every one else, is entitled to his own opinion. His writing affords much more proof of knowledge of biology than of knowledge of English character, his notions of which seem to be purely theoretical" (p. 232n.). When, however, Dr. Nicolai happens to praise a compatriot of theirs, the translators are no better pleased. He remarks that "Tolstoy, Ibsen and Bernard Shaw have

1. Georg F. Nicolai was a member of the physiology faculty of the University of Berlin during World War I. At that time Nicolai drew up a pacifist document, *Manifesto to Europeans,* calling for peace and a united Europe. It was signed by Albert Einstein who was teaching at the University of Berlin.

their schools in every country." On this they comment as follows: "Like many foreigners, Professor Nicolai seems to take Mr. Bernard Shaw much more seriously than do most of that dramatist's own fellow-countrymen. Mr. Shaw will of course retort that a prophet has no honour in his own country" (p. 294n.1). It seems a pity thus to go out of their way to point out our national inability to appreciate our great men.

Yours, etc., The Reviewer.

## [40]

## "Why I Support the Labour Party"

*Labour Leader* (17th March, 1921), p. 1 | C21.07

*Russell wrote an open letter to a 'capitalist' [Henry C. Emery]*[2] *explaining his belief in the possibility of socialism without class war. Both his open letter and his covering letter were written in January while he and Dora Black were in China. The letters were published in mid-March, about the time that Russell fell ill in China and reports of his death were circulated throughout the world by the Japanese press. The rows of asterisks were in the letter to Emery, as published.*

Government University, Peking
January 18, 1921

To the Editor of the Labour Leader

Sir, —As I find that my views on Russia and on Communism are widely misunderstood, I should be grateful if you would publish the enclosed letter to a capitalist who considers the universal class-war inevitable, and accuses me of being a "knight of the impossible," and of "tilting at windmills" because I still believe that at any rate in Great Britain, it may be possible to introduce a better economic system without civil war. The letter was not intended for publication, but I think it may

2. Henry C. Emery (1872–1924) was a professor of economics at Bowdoin and Yale before the Russian Revolution. He toured Russia (1917–18) and worked in banking in China (1920–24). His doctoral dissertation (Columbia, 1896) on the economics of the stock exchange was considered authoritative.

help to remove the misapprehensions which appear in reviews of my book on Russia.

Yours etc., Bertrand Russell

Government University, Peking, January 14, 1921

Dear , —Your view is that "we only befog the issue by trying to evade the fact of class-war," and you believe it useful to "stimulate clear thinking."

I have considerable sympathy with this view; I merely find it impossible to understand how anybody who follows your advice on this point can come down on the side of the capitalists, except on grounds of simple egoism. It is this point, among others, that I should like to see you explain in a book.

Again, as to "clear thinking": if we are to embark upon it, we had better carry it through to the end. If the class-war becomes world-wide, the issue will be neither the establishment of Communism nor the re-establishment of capitalism, but the ruin of industry and education, and the downfall of our whole civilisation.

I therefore consider that, however small may be the chance of averting the universal class-war, we ought to try and avert it so long as the chance is not nil; and in view of the uncertainty of human affairs, the chance will not be nil until the disaster has actually occurred. I find that those who desire the class-war, and also those who prophesy it without desiring it, are helping to bring it on.

I disagree with your attitude for the same reason for which I disagree with that of the Third International, namely, that it tends to hasten the advent of a (catalyst) which may not be inevitable, but will probably produce utter and total collapse if it comes soon.

I am anxious that my own position in the matter should be clear, since I find that it is widely misunderstood. I believe the following propositions:

(1) If the class-war becomes world-wide, the quick victory of the proletariat would be a very great good.

(2) The quick victory of the capitalists would be a very great evil, but a far smaller evil than the prolongation of the struggle.

(3) The most probable result would be a warfare lasting for many years, taking the form of unprecedently bloody and brutal civil war in all civilised countries, involving universal starvation and ferocity, destroying the means of industrial production, reducing the population of the world

by about fifty percent, and leaving at the end an uncivilised peasant population terrorised by robber bands.

(4) The class-war is not yet by any means certain; there is still a considerable chance that it can be averted by making both sides conscious of the immensity of the danger, and by giving the Russians peace and trade, out of which will come prosperity with a consequent diminution of fanaticism.

(5) If the class-war comes and is as prolonged as I fear, the only men who will bring into the new world the seeds of progress and reconstruction will be those who take no part in the struggle, but retire to whatever refuge is available, as the monks retired to their monasteries at the time of the barbarian invasion of the Roman Empire.

My disapproval of Bolshevism, in so far as I do disapprove, is on the ground that I do not think it can achieve the end at which it aims. I regard the Bolsheviks as "knights of the impossible," and the whole development of Russia during the last three years confirms me in this view.[3]

It is as a practical man, not as an idealist, that I object to them: I think the capitalists sufficiently strong, sufficiently bestial, and sufficiently reckless to make the quick success of the Communists in a class-war impossible, and I therefore hold that, if the ends which I desire are to be achieved, a longer period of peaceful propaganda and industrial development is essential.

I do not think the capitalists, even now, sufficiently strong to preserve their own system by victory in a class-war, but only sufficiently strong to wreck civilisation. I therefore support the British Labour party as against both Moscow and Wall Street. And no one can accuse the British Labour Party of "tilting at windmills."

* * * * *

You object to my speaking of the capitalist system as "unjust," and the communist system as "just." I grant that the logical definition of these terms is difficult, but, as you yourself point out, politics is a matter of sentiment rather than of logic.

* * * * *

3. Russell here refers to Lenin's New Economic Policy, introduced in 1921 after the end of the Allied intervention. The Policy abandoned the requisitioning of grain and established liberal-market reforms.

I am, I confess, a little surprised by your allusions to "liberty."

What "liberty" is there now except for rich members of powerful nations?

What "liberty" have German mothers had since 1914? The "liberty" to see their children die of starvation or grow up stunted and diseased, because rival groups of rich men had decided that proletarians should kill each other.

What "liberty" has the Sinn Feiner at the present day? The "liberty" of having his house burnt down and his children shot before his eyes.

What "liberty" has a man of unpopular opinions in the United States? The "liberty" of being shot in his home, or trampled to death by a hired mob.

What "liberty" has a moderate Socialist in France? The "liberty" of being publicly assassinated, and having his assassin acquitted.

What "liberty" has the Hindoo, or the Korean, or the Japanese Trade Unionist?

What "liberty," in any country, has the intellectual who can only live by selling his brains to capitalists, whom he hates and despises, for whom he must do work that he knows to be evil, until cynical despair destroys whatever good his nature once contained?

And what of the restrictions on liberty in Russia?

True, there are political restrictions due to the state of war, and of the same kind as those imposed by your own Espionage law, or our Defence of the Realm Act. What of other restrictions?

In a climate much colder, in winter, than that of Peking, it is impossible to obtain warm clothing because of the blockade; it is impossible to obtain coal, because of the blockade and Denikin's reckless destruction of the Donetz basin; it was possible to obtain wood, and vast piles were brought to Moscow during last summer, but they were burnt by incendiaries—Polish, French, possibly English—but certainly agents of capitalism. The result is that, because capitalists dislike a threat to their income, the inhabitants of Moscow have to endure the winter insufficiently clad and in unwarmed houses.

It is impossible to obtain medicines, disinfectants, or soap (except of very bad quality and in very small quantities) because of the blockade; consequently millions of Russians have died of typhus and other diseases, because the comfortable plutocrats of other countries consider every inhabitant of a Communist country deserving of death by slow torture.

When operations have to be performed, it is impossible to obtain anesthetics because capitalists are of opinion that the anguish endured is deserved by those who threaten to make them less rich. Meanwhile education is starved, vitality lowered, and civilisation imperiled throughout European and Asiatic Russia—not by the fault of the Bolsheviks, but by the fault of the rich foreigners who cause Russia to be blockaded and exhausted by civil and external wars.

All the graver restrictions of liberty in Russia are due to this state of affairs, not to any inherent vice of Communism.

* * * * *

I note that you personally oppose the blockade. But it is an inevitable result of the capitalist system, and whoever supports that system is in effect a supporter of the blockade, however much he may regret that other capitalists are less far-sighted than himself.

Yours sincerely, Bertrand Russell

[41]

## "The Practice and Theory of Bolshevism"

*The New Statesman* (2nd April, 1921), p. 755 | C21.09

*Here Russell writes to give credit to his secretary, Dora Black, for her contribution to his 1920 book on Russia. Dora and Russell were both in Russia in 1920, although they traveled separately. They married in September 1921; their first child, John Conrad Russell, was born in November.*

Sir, —In your review of my *Practice and Theory of Bolshevism,* on December 18th, 1920, there is an error for which I feel some responsibility, and which I shall be grateful if you will correct, in spite of the lapse of time. You say "His descriptions of what he actually saw in Russia are often admirable, particularly his description of a Bolshevik pageant." This description, and the whole chapter in which it occurs, are (as stated in the preface) not by me, but by my secretary, D.W. Black. If you will kindly acknowledge this correction you will be doing an act of justice to a young and hitherto little-known writer.

—Yours, etc., Bertrand Russell.
Government University, Peking. February 16th.

[42]

# "Ireland and Japan"

*The Daily News and Leader* (10th September, 1921), p. 4 | C21.16

*The Home Rule movement for a political autonomy in Ireland led to the formation of a militant Irish nationalist society Sinn Fein ("We Ourselves") in 1902 and resulted in insurrection against the British from 1919 to 1922. A truce was established in the summer of 1921, and the British offered to negotiate a treaty creating an Irish Free State, which took effect in 1922. Among those influential Irishmen who supported the struggle for Irish independence was the playwright George Bernard Shaw.*

*In this letter Russell points up the importance of the Irish-Anglo accommodation for improving relations—and, he says, avoiding war—between the U.S. and Great Britain. Russell alludes to Anglo-American friction over Japan, a matter which he addresses in his December letter to the* Daily Herald.

Sir, —I observe that two correspondents in to-day's "Daily News" treat Mr. Bernard Shaw's views on England and America as either mischievous or mere fireworks. For my part, I thought Mr. Shaw's article the first I had seen in England which tackled the main problem connected with Sinn Fein, namely, Anglo-American relations. Partly for commercial reasons and partly owing to our alliance with Japan we have incurred the hostility of Americans interested in the Far East. Their Press has utilised our atrocities in Ireland as our Press utilised German atrocities in Belgium. I do not doubt that the Government's offer to Sinn Fein is chiefly actuated by a desire to improve our relations with America. A few more years of the policy we had been pursuing until that offer would have generated a spirit in America which would have made war sooner or later almost inevitable.

Bertrand Russell.
Strand Cottage, Winchelsea, Sept. 8.

•••••••••••• [43] ••••••••••••

## "How Washington Could Help China"

*The New Republic* (4th January, 1922), pp. 154–55 | C21.30

*This letter originally appeared in the* Daily Herald, *16th December, as an article. Here Russell notes Anglo-American and Chinese mutual interests in curbing Japanese ambitions. He warns of possible war between Japan and the U.S., and he denounces American economic and cultural imperialism in the Far East.*

Sir: In international dealings it is useless to expect any nation to pursue any end which it does not believe to be in its own interest. No good to China could be expected to come out of the Washington Conference[4] but for the fact that the interests of both England and America are, for the present, identical with those of China, except in a few points, such as our possession of Hong Kong. The immediate and pressing aims of any Chinese patriot must be two: to end the internal anarchy and to recover the independence and integrity of China. The aims of English and American statesmanship in China, from a purely selfish point of view, may be taken to be the extension of trade and the opportunity to exploit Chinese natural resources. Territorial ambitions have no place in America's programme, and ought to have none in ours; I believe that, in fact, our ambitions in that respect are limited (in China) to the retention of what we already possess, or rather of part of it, for our Government seems to have realised that our true national interest would be furthered by the restitution of Wei-Hai-Wei.[5] What both English and American interests most urgently require in China is stable government and the open door; that is, to say, the ending of anarchy and of Japanese territorial aggression. Our interests are, therefore, for the present almost completely identical with those of China.

The interests of Japan, at any rate as conceived by the militarists who control policy, are different from ours, and not compatible with the welfare of China. Japan wishes to be a Great Power, in territory, population, and industrial resources. Japan has not much of the raw materials of industry, whereas China has them in abundance. If Japan is to be able to conduct a long war successfully, control of mines in some portion of China is essential. Moreover, Japanese statesmen have not merely

4. The Washington Conference was a conference on armaments that met from November 1921 to February 1922. It agreed upon reductions in the navies of Britain, America, Japan, France and Italy, and concluded treaties for the territorial, integrity of China, including restoration to China of Japanese held territory in Shantung.

5. Returned to China in 1930.

economic aims, but also the desire for dynastic grandeur and a vast empire. Psychologically, one of the fundamental causes of the whole situation is the Japanese inferiority complex. At every moment they are afraid that they are being insulted or cold-shouldered on account of not being white, and this makes them aggressive and ill-mannered. This is by far the strongest part of the Japanese case. Europeans do not beat Japanese rickshaw drivers to make them hurry, nor do their chauffeurs dismount to cuff pedestrians who are slow in getting out of the way, as I have seen the chauffeur of an American do in Peking. The Japanese are not liked by either Europeans or Americans, but they are treated with a respect which few white men show to the Chinese. The reason is simply that Japan has a strong army and navy. White men, as a rule, only respect those who have power to kill them or deprive them of their means of livelihood; and as wealth depends upon success in war, skill in homicide is, in the last analysis, the only thing that secures tolerable courtesy from a white man. If the Japanese are defeated in war by the Americans or by an Anglo-American alliance there will be a setback for the colored races all over the world, and an intensification of the intolerable insolence displayed towards them by white men. There will be an immediate catastrophic destruction of the Japanese civilisation, which still has many merits that our civilisation lacks. And following upon this there will be a slow destruction of the civilisation of China, not by war, but by Americanisation. The big towns will become like Chicago, and the small towns like "Main Street." Americans would feel that they were conferring a boon in effecting this transformation, but no person with any receptivity or aesthetic sense would share their view.

We may, therefore, diagnose the situation as follows: Japan is in a bad mood, and is more immediately dangerous to China than any other nation; but England and America—especially the latter—are, by the very nature of their civilisation and outlook, destructive of all that is best in the Far East, and doomed, willy-nilly, to be oppressors if they have the power. Under these circumstances the worst thing that could happen would be a Japanese-American war, leading to the destruction of everything distinctive in the civilisation of the yellow races, the increase of white tyranny, and the launching of America upon a career of militarist Imperialism. On the other hand, the best thing that could happen would be a diplomatic humiliation of the Japanese military party, causing Japan itself to become less aggressive and less anxious to subjugate the adjoining mainland.

The difficulty is that Japan will not yield except to the threat of war. If England and America, at Washington, join in insisting on the evacuation of Shantung,[6] one may presume that Japan will give way sooner than

---

6. Shantung was a region in northeast China, part of which had been occupied by the Japanese since 1915. It was the birthplace of Confucius and the place of origin of the Boxer

face a war against both combined. If America alone threatens, Japan will probably choose war, and be destroyed.

What is, of course, to be expected is that America will give way, in substance though not in form, about Shantung, in return for Japanese acceptance of the naval ratio; that after a few years American spies will report (truly or falsely) that Japan is building secretly; that in the meantime America will have fortified naval bases in the neighbourhood of Japan; and that then America will proceed to destroy Japan with a good conscience. I do not see any issue from this cycle of disaster except a change of heart in Japan. Of course, a change of heart in America would be just as good, but nothing will convince Americans that they need a change of heart.

China, unfortunately, cannot escape being industrialised. It would be far better for China to develop her industries slowly with native capital; but they will, in fact, be developed quickly with foreign capital. So much, I fear, is independent of the issue at Washington. For the immediate interests of China it would be well if America and England combined to force Japan by diplomatic pressure, not by war, both to accept the naval ratio and to evacuate Shantung. This would also be good for Japan, since it would be a blow to the military party, and perhaps introduce a much more liberal regime. (Evacuation of Vladivostok[7] and friendly relations with the Far Eastern Republic should also be insisted upon.)

But in the long run it is not in the interests of Asia that the one genuinely independent Asiatic Power, should be crushed. England and America can, if they choose, exercise despotic sway over the world. There is much good that they might do in that case. They might curb the ambitions of France and Japan, make all nations except themselves disarm, undertake the economic rehabilitation of Germany and Russia for the sake of their own trade, and liberate China from the fear of Japan. But if they were able to accomplish all this they would also acquire the habit of bullying and become confirmed in the ruthless certainty of their own moral superiority. They would soon come to display an economic and cultural despotism such as the world has never known—always, of course, in a missionary spirit. From such a tyranny the world could only escape by a universal rebellion, possibly with Great Britain at the head of the rebels.

From the alternative of tyranny or war there is, so far as I can see, no escape while the industrial nations continue their system of capitalist

---

Rebellion against foreigners in 1900. At the Washington Conference (1921–22), Japan agreed to evacuate Shantung.

7. The Russian Pacific port in far eastern Siberia. Japan kept troops there until 1922 as part of a post-World War I Allied intervention in Russia to defeat the Bolsheviks.

exploitation. Nothing offers any real escape except Socialism—i.e., in this connection, production for use instead of production for commercial profit. America is still in the phase of Liberalism which more experienced nations have outgrown since the war. President Wilson attempted to save the world by Liberal ideas, and failed; President Harding is making a second attempt and will fail even if he seems to have succeeded. He will fail, I mean, as a humanitarian, not as the champion of American capital. The existing capitalist system is in its very nature predatory, and cannot be made the basis of just dealing between nations. So long as America draws nearly all the dividends derived from Capitalism, she will continue to think the present system heaven-sent, and will employ Liberal futilities which will delude fools into supporting knaves.

But in all this I am speaking of the future, not of the immediate situation. For the moment, Anglo-American cooperation at Washington can secure two important things: (1) the naval ratio; (2) a breathing space for China by a curbing of Japanese ambitions.[8] If these ends are achieved the Washington Conference will have been useful. If it leaves Japan's activities in China unchecked, it will have been futile; but if it leads to war with Japan it will have been immeasurably harmful.

Bertrand Russell
London

[44]

## "Our Promise to China"

*The Daily Herald* (21st April, 1924), p. 4 | C24.21

*Towards the end of the nineteenth century the Western powers and Japan were in the process of carving up China into "spheres of influence." In 1898 Britain extracted from China a 22-year lease for the port city of Wei Haiwei in northeast Shantung where a British naval base was constructed. In 1900 a Chinese society (the Boxers) staged a rebellion to drive foreigners out of China. In response, Great Britain, France, Germany, Russia, the U.S., and Japan sent troops against China, and imposed an indemnity of $320 million as a punishment. Only the U.S. gave up its share of the indemnity.*

I am writing concerning two non-controversial questions which appear to have been overlooked by the present Government owing to matters which have seemed to it more pressing.

8. Both of these goals were essentially achieved by the Washington Conference.

The first is Wei-Hai-Wei. At the Washington Conference in 1921, Lord Balfour publicly promised to restore this port to China; neither the late Government nor the present one has kept this promise, thereby causing great indignation in China, with consequent damage to our trade.

The second is the Boxer Indemnity. America long ago devoted the surplus of this money, after paying claims for actual damage, to the promotion of Chinese education. The late Government announced that, in principle, it was in favour of similar action by Great Britain.

The matter is of great importance in Chinese opinion, and it is to be hoped that the present Government will immediately announce its willingness to consider definite schemes for devoting what remains of the Boxer Indemnity to Chinese educational purposes.

The Chinese are a quarter of the human race, and their friendship may before long be very important to us. Apart from this consideration, both the above measures are demanded by elementary justice, and one of them cannot be longer delayed without exposing the British Government to the charge of bad faith.

Bertrand Russell.
Sidney Street

[45]

## "Under Which Flag?"

*The New Leader* (21st November, 1924), p. 6 | C24.49

*In this letter Russell expresses his international sentiments, and he reminds some elements of the Labour Party of the close connection between nationalism, imperialism, and war.*

Sir, —I read with a feeling akin to despair the letter headed "Under Which Flag?" which appeared in your issue of November 14, since I fear that it represents the views of a considerable section of the Labour Party. With what it says about non-co-operation with Communists I am in agreement; what I dissent from is the advice to "leave the Red Flag to the Communist" and "use the union Jack—we are the only patriotic party."

If "patriotism" means desiring the welfare of our own country, I agree; but as symbolised by the Union Jack, it bears a more sinister meaning. The Union Jack is the symbol of imperial pomp, and helps to generate the emotions which lead us to cause misery to countless millions in Asia and

Africa. Nationalism and imperialism are the most cruel and destructive features of modern civilisation. In effect—though not, of course, in intention—your correspondent's proposal would mean that the Labour Party would cease to protest against these evils. If this happened, it would no longer deserve the support of those who seriously believe in the possibility of a world freed from the menace of great wars.

Yours, etc., Bertrand Russell.

••••••••••••• [46] •••••••••••••

## "Why He Distrusts 'Gentlemen'"

*The Daily Herald* (3rd December, 1924), p. 9 | C24.54

*In this letter, Russell responds to a correspondent who took issue with his statement in an earlier article ('What Really Is Happening in China; Will the Meek Inherit the Earth?'* Daily Herald, *19th November, 1924) that "gentlemen" were less than decent human beings. In his answer Russell itemizes several ungentlemanly activities—foreign and domestic—of recent Conservative governments, "including Lloyd George's Coalition Government."*

*The editor of the* Daily Herald *introduces the controversy and Russell's response follows.*

Mr. Geoffrey Williams writes from Crickett Court, Crickett Malherbie, Ilminster, Somerset, to complain of a remark in the Hon. Bertrand Russell's recent article on China. The remark was:

"Perhaps 100 years ago the 'gentleman' was not such a finished product as he is now. Now, on the average, he is a man who hires others to commit forgery, libel, and murder for the purpose of maintaining or increasing his income. It is decent human beings, not 'gentlemen,' that ought to be sent to China."

"Though I venture," says Mr. Williams, "to differ from the methods by which the HERALD proposes to improve the condition of the wage-earner, and disagree with its views, I read Mr. Russell's virulent paragraph with considerable surprise. I should be genuinely sorry to have to state publicly that the Labour Press uses such weapons."

In reply, Mr. Bertrand Russell writes:

The statement which your correspondent complains of is one which is susceptible of exact proof. The definition of a "gentleman" is a matter about which disputes are possible, but whatever definition (consistent with usage) may be adopted, gentlemen, on the average, are Conservatives, and on the average approve of the acts of Conservative Governments, including Lloyd George's Coalition Government.

In 1920, Scotland Yard had pretended copies of "Pravda" forged, and these copies were distributed by the help of the Foreign Office and the Admiralty; their purpose was to cause Englishmen to kill Russians, and Russians to kill each other, with a view to making good the losses of "gentlemen" who had invested in Russia. The DAILY HERALD protested, but the "gentlemen" of the Conservative Party were silent.

At the present moment, the death of the Sirdar at the hands of a misguided fanatic is made the excuse for a demand for unlimited irrigation in the Sudan, which will put money into the pockets of rich "gentlemen" in England but leave Egyptian peasantry without enough water to support life.[9] In the late General Election, as everyone knows, the Conservative Party indulged in a campaign of slander unexampled in our political annals.

I shall give personal instances, because they are what I know most about. My wife, who stood in Chelsea,[10] was said to be not legally married; this fact had no doubt not been previously known to her opponent, Lieut. Colonel the Right Honourable Sir Samuel Hoare, Minister for Air, but when it was brought to his notice he refused to say publicly that such statements, if made, were untrue and not sanctioned by him.

When I stood on a former occasion the wives of gentlemen put it about that I was in the habit of distributing indecent literature to children.[11] Most Labour candidates had far worse libels and slanders to endure. At the last minute a headquarters Conservative leaflet was distributed accusing the Labour Party of being in favour of free love. The "nationalisation of women" lie about Russia was deliberately repeated in leaflets issued by Conservative headquarters, which, I understand, is run by gentlemen.

When gentlemen cease to support the Party which obtains power by such means, and uses it for such ends, I will withdraw my charge. Until then, I shall maintain it.

Bertrand Russell.

---

9. In 1922 Britain recognized the independence of Egypt but not the Sudan. Bad feeling led to the assassination of Sir Lee Stack, the Sirdar (governor-general) of the Sudan, in Cairo in 1924. Egypt was made to pay reparation in the form of irrigation rights.

10. In the General Election of 1924, Dora stood unsuccessfully for Parliament as a Socialist candidate.

11. Russell had stood unsuccessfully as a Socialist candidate in Chelsea in 1922 and 1923. Concerning his electoral efforts, he told friends: "I never wanted to get in but only to do propaganda" (Clark, p. 414).

[47]

## "Force in China"

*The Nation and Athenaeum* (5th February, 1927), p. 619 | C27.06

*In this letter Russell speaks forcefully against British military intervention in China.*

Sir, —It becomes increasingly difficult to read with patience your commentaries and warnings on the present situation in China. Is it not time that all people of humane ideals and aims were frankly told that the dispatch of the large forces that have gone to China is not only likely, but probably intended, to provoke a war between us and the Chinese, in which there would not be a shadow of right or justification on our side, nor any possible final issue but shameful and deserved defeat, involving the almost complete loss of our already fast diminishing trade with the Chinese.[12] In these circumstances all those who do not demand the immediate recall of all British forces from China, and the recognition of Cantonese rights in all provinces where the Cantonese Government has jurisdiction, are doing a grave disservice, not only to the English people, but also even to the misguided British merchants out in China, who still hope to extend their trade at the bayonet point as they did at the time of the opium wars.[13]

Not long since you were urging the Government to explain the Wanhsien incident.[14] No English explanation has been given; and now you speak of the necessity of large forces in order to avoid a "repetition of the Wanhsien fiasco." In what did the fiasco consist—in the fact that not more than one thousand Chinese were killed, and not more than one thousand Chinese houses destroyed? Surely Mr. Chen's[15] "rodomontade" on Imperialism has a considerable "bearing on the existing situation," when he is faced by the dispatch of more troops by a Power which has not hesitated to bombard without compensation or apology an open unfortified town. This act is against the laws of warfare, even were we at war with the Chinese.

---

12. There was a Chinese nationalist movement, supported by the Communist Party, to resist foreign domination and unite the country under Chiang Kai-shek's Kuomintang Party. The Party's headquarters were in Canton.

13. The Opium War, concluded by the Treaty of Nanking in 1842, put Canton under foreign control.

14. This could be the 'May 30th Incident' (1925), in which British police killed many people in an uprising in Shanghai initiated by Chinese Communists.

15. Chen Yi (1901–1972) was a Chinese general who participated in the Northern Expedition (1926) against the war lords in northern China.

The lives and persons of British nationals are in no danger. Persons of other nationality are walking about and doing business freely. It must be admitted, of course, that they have not seen fit to take part in the recent shooting of Chinese as we have done. But it is time that the six thousand odd British in Shanghai faced the situation like the British gentlemen they claim to be. They are free to return to England, or to move northward if they do not like the Cantonese regime.[16]

The Cantonese are the accepted and functioning Government now of nine provinces, practically all the South and West of China. The treaty rights, about which we generously offer to "negotiate," were forced on China by war. No self-respecting Chinese Government could continue to accept them, and our trade and prestige in China stand to gain by their immediate abandonment. There is nothing outrageous or "impossible" in the whole of the Cantonese demands. They are modern people, ready for peace and trade. They have not taken, nor will they take, unless bitterly provoked, the life of any foreigner not engaged in war with them. In fact they are a model of sweet reasonableness, in comparison with what the English would be like, had Chinese gunboats sailed up the Thames for a lark and bombarded Reading and Oxford.

Unless this Government is severely handled, telegraph agencies will soon be busy manufacturing "riots in Shanghai," and the British troops privily engaged in the Chinese civil war, on the side of the North against Canton.

Yours, &c., Bertrand Russell. Dora Russell.
31, Sydney Street, S.W.3. January 29th, 1927.

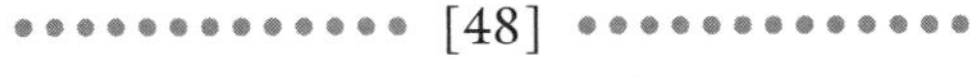

[48]

## British Anti-War Council

*The New Statesman and Nation* (19th November, 1932),
pp. 622–23 | C32.64

*This letter is an early warning of the coming of war and of Russell's efforts to organize resistance against it. The letter is co-signed with Havelock Ellis (1859–1939), a British psychologist and physician best known for his* Studies in the Psychology of Sex.

---

16. An apparent reference to the Chinese nationalist Northern Expedition with which, no doubt, Russell sympathized.

Sir, —The increasing intensity of the international situation is now very generally admitted. The continued crisis in the Far East, the rapid degeneration of the European situation typified by the imminent rearming of Germany, and lastly the denunciation of the Anglo-Russia Trade Treaty as a first result of the attempt to align the British Empire against the rest of the world at Ottawa must surely have convinced even the most sceptical that the danger of war is real and growing.

As a result of an important International Conference, attended by over 2,000 delegates, held at Amsterdam on August 26th last, National Anti-War Councils have been set up in all the major countries of the world. These bodies do not attempt to recruit individual members, but rather to unite the activities of all organisations which are determined to resist war. Some forty local Anti-War Councils are already in existence in different parts of this country, and a very large number of Trade Union branches of political parties, and similar bodies are linked together with these local councils. Thus a formidable organisation for the resistance to war and to war preparations, not by the method of individual protest but by organised action on the part of the relevant categories of workers, is coming into being. (Anyone wishing to acquaint himself further with the principles of the Anti-War Council may obtain a pamphlet, entitled *The United Front Against War*, from the Hon. Sec. the National Anti-War Council, 53 Gray's Inn Road, London, W.C.1, price 1d.)

The British National Anti-War Council is faced with rapidly growing responsibilities. It is in urgent need of money. As British members of the International Committee, we appeal to those who wish to take part in a truly practical and effective effort at war resistance to send us a donation. Cheques should be made payable to the Treasurer, the National Anti-War Council, 53 Gray's Inn Road, London, W.C.1.

Bertrand Russell, Havelock Ellis

## [49]

# Internationalising the Air

*The New Statesman and Nation* (24th December, 1932), p. 830 | C32.70

*After World War I, Russell was constant in his view that world government was a required for the solution to the problem of war. Here he underscores one of the central themes of that idea: the internationalization of military force.*

Sir, —It was with a painful emotion that I read the letter in your issue of December 17th, from Mr. C.G. Grey,[17] against internationalising aviation. Mr. Baldwin[18] has told us that this measure is necessary if civilisation is to survive; Mr. Grey tells us it is an impossible measure, because British aeronauts would not be willing to risk their lives in French machines. I cannot believe them to be such poltroons, and I am convinced that Mr. Grey has cast a wholly undeserved aspersion upon a very gallant body of men.

Bertrand Russell
47 Emperor's Gate, S.W.7.

[50]

## The British Labor Party and Hitler

*The New Republic* (3rd July, 1935), p. 224 | C35.27

*In this letter to the* New Republic *Russell explains the British Labour Party's position regarding Hitler.*

Sir,—In your issue of June 5, there is a letter from Mr. Werner Hegemann[19] about Karl von Ossietsky,[20] a man whom all pacifists must reverence. With the wish that he should be awarded the Nobel Peace Prize I am strongly in agreement: I cannot imagine any man more deserving of this honor.

What prompts me to write to you, however, is a different matter.

Mr. Hegemann speaks of "Hitler's most perverse bodyguard: the English Labor Party." These words are either very ignorant or very

17. C.G. Grey was an aviation historian. He wrote many books on the history of aircraft and edited several editions of *Jane's All the World's Aircraft.*

18. Stanley Baldwin (1867–1947) was a British statesman and Conservative Party leader. He was three times Prime Minister, including (his last term) 1935–37.

19. Werner Hegemann was a German author and expert on European art and architecture.

20. Karl von Ossietsky (1898–1938) was a German pacifist who led the German peace movement after World War I. He was imprisoned, 1931–32, and held in a concentration camp, 1933–36. The Nazi government protested when Ossietsky was awarded the Nobel Peace Prize in 1935.

thoughtless, and are surprising in a pacifist context. The English Labor Party abominates Hitler and all his ways, but is anxious not to be hurried by indignation into the support of war, or into abandonment of its previous demands for justice to Germany. It is all very well for American radicals, at a safe distance, to urge Europeans to go crusading while their own country remains neutral. But for sane Europeans other considerations must be dominant. We know that war, if it comes, will destroy everything that we value, however the Powers may be grouped and whoever may enjoy "victory." We feel little doubt that, in the course of the war, what remains of democracy in Europe would disappear. We expect disaster to civilization through the maddened terror of urban populations. In these circumstances, we resent being scolded for attempting to preserve all that we care for (both publicly and privately) rather than ruin our Continent to gratify the resentments of men who will remain spectators of our possibly heroic folly. A writer who praises pacifism should understand this point of view.

Bertrand Russell
Petersfield, Eng.

[51]

## Air Raid Precautions

*The New Statesman and Nation* (10th August, 1935), p. 191 |

*Here Russell forcefully states his objections to the Air Raid Precautions issued by the National Government (headed by the Conservative Party's Stanley Baldwin), and warns of the folly and false sense of security in defending against air warfare.*

Sir, —The recent Home Office Circular on Air Raid Precautions has aroused wide-spread indignation, on two grounds: (1) that the precautions suggested are, in the main, only available for the well-to-do; (2) that the precautions which are possible are known to be far less effective than the circular would lead people to believe. Lord Marley[21] in the House of Lords argued these two points in a speech to which the Government were totally unable to find any adequate reply. The proposed gas-drill should

21. Lord Marley (1884–1952) was a member of the House of Lords and the Labour Party. He was Under Secretary for War in 1930.

be resisted, first, because it is calculated to give an entirely fallacious sense of security, and, secondly, because resistance will make the Government far less willing to go to war.

In these circumstances, it is profoundly regrettable that the Labour Party has been officially advised to co-operate with the Home Office by the National Executive Committee, in a document of which the decisive words are: "the risks must be faced and provision made for coping with the direst possibilities." By such advice, the sound impulses of members of the Labour Party throughout the country are discouraged. The Home Office circular does not make "provision for coping with the direst possibilities" of war. At the present stage in the development of the art of war, there is only one way of coping with them, and that is to keep out of war. In all the densely populated countries of Western Europe, it seems almost certain that, within a few days of the outbreak of war, panic will seize the surviving inhabitants of the capitals and the industrial areas, leading to anarchy, starvation, and paralysis of all warlike effort. The only sensible course, therefore, is to prevent war if possible, and to remain neutral if war occurs. The neutrals will be the only victors, and the only Powers whose policy will have a chance of prevailing. It is the duty of all who care for their country or for civilisation to point out that we cannot further any of our ideals by participation in the next war, and that we ought therefore to resist all measures based upon the assumption that we shall take part in it.

In the late war it was arguable that victory, being possible, might do some good. With the modern technique of gas attack, no belligerent can hope for victory. Absolute pacifism, therefore, in every country, in which it is politically possible, is the only sane policy both for Governments and individuals.

Bertrand Russell
Telegraph House, Harting, Petersfield.

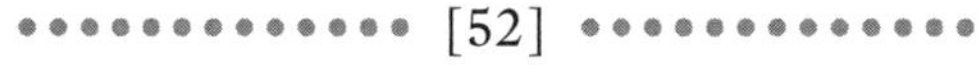

[52]

## British Foreign Policy

*The New Statesman and Nation*, n.s. 12 (18th July, 1936), p. 82 | C36.19

*In this remarkable letter, Russell sardonically suggests that British foreign policy is preparing to fight a war "on the side of Hitler." Of course he's not quite serious. But he does mean to point out what later came to be recognized as a Baldwin-Chamberlain policy of accommodation and appeasement towards Germany. And he implies that greater British co-operation with France and Russia is the proper way to stem the threats to democracy from fascist Germany and Japan.*

*In early 1935, Hitler had won a plebiscite in the Saar basin to return the area to Germany from French control, contrary to the provisions of the Treaty of Versailles. He also reintroduced military conscription and announced the creation of the Luftwaffe, both in violation of the Treaty. And in the spring of 1936, while the League of Nations was deciding what to do about Italian aggression against Ethiopia, Hitler sent troops into the Rhineland to claim German territory, again undermining the Treaty and the security of Europe.*

*In his book* Which Way to Peace?, *written at this time, Russell urges repudiation of, and non-cooperation with, Hitler. But he insists on a pacifist foreign policy on the grounds, as stated in this letter, that a general war in Europe would be even "worse than subjugation by Hitler." Russell was to publicly change his mind about this, shortly after the onset of World War II.*

Sir, —Various clear indications prove that our Government considers a European war in the near future by no means unlikely. Other indications, rather less clear, suggest that, when the war comes, we are to fight on the side of Hitler. The clearest of these indications is the line we have taken on the Dardanelles question, and the leading article, "Enter Russia," in the *Times* of July 9. As yet, however, we are not definitely committed. I wish to suggest reasons why all possible efforts should be made to prevent the irrevocable adoption of such a policy.

First: the Nazi Government is undoubtedly the one most disposed to risk a general war. Support by us makes it much more likely that they will make the venture.

Second: France, after a period of reaction, has lately acquired a vigorous democratic socialistic government, which is attempting to carry out a policy—e.g., in regard to the munitions industry and the Bank of France—that all Socialists must view with sympathy. Shall we join in ruining France and substituting a Fascist government?

Third: Russia has been engaged in a great experiment, and seems now on the point of success; moreover, with success, there is to be some measure of democracy. The desire to prevent Soviet success is, apparently, the principal motive of our reactionaries in wishing to help the Nazis to establish a White Terror in Russia.

Fourth: Japan, which is allied to Germany, is engaged in enslaving China, and will almost certainly succeed if we help in making Japan invincible.

Fifth: from the point of view of British Imperialism, the support of Germany and Japan is madness. We shall lose, first, what remains of our position in the Far East; then, after the destruction of France and Russia, we shall be unable to prevent the Japanese from taking India or the Germans from taking our Crown Colonies. But this argument may be left to Mr. Winston Churchill.

Sixth: a German victory means the extension to all Europe (including Great Britain) of the Fascist method of keeping wage-earners in subjection; it may well mean the establishment, for centuries, of a new kind of serfdom.

We have, I admit, grievances against France, but they are not of the same order of importance as the above considerations. For neutrality in the next war there are strong arguments, the strongest of which is that the effects of a great war would be worse than subjugation by Hitler; but for siding with Germany the only reasons are so sinister that they cannot be avowed. I agree with Miss Rathbone that this is no time for the Labour Party to attack those Ministers who remain friendly to France, and therefore to Russia also. What matters at this moment is to see that our weight is not thrown against peace, freedom, democracy, and the rights of wage-earners, in favour of war, dictatorship, suppression of all intelligent thought, and a system of permanent social and political inequality.

Bertrand Russell
Telegraph House, Harting, Petersfield.

[53]

## A Struggle for Liberty Against Tyranny

*Manchester Guardian* (12th August, 1936), p. 18 | C36.23

*In July 1936, revolution against the Republican government of Spain broke out, led by the fascist forces of General Francisco Franco with support from Germany and Italy. In this letter, which includes a letter from an "English friend" in Spain at the time, Russell conveys a sense of the calamity of fascist repression.*

Sir, —I have received from an English friend[22] who has lived many years in Spain, who is now living near Malaga, and who is well qualified to form a judicial estimate of the present situation a letter which I think likely to be of interest to your readers. He says:

22. Probably Gerald Brenan.

This is not a struggle between Fascism and Communism, but a struggle for liberty against tyranny. The Fascist generals are of the true brand: I hear them talking on the wireless from Seville and Africa; patriotism, death for Mother Spain, resistance to the "international Jewish bankers of Amsterdam." That gives their quality; then threats of summary execution to loyal soldiers caught by them, workers who remain on strike, &c. Without any necessity they have brought on the most terrible civil war known in Europe since the religious wars in Germany. They proposed to win it by bringing over from Africa the *Terejos* or Foreign Legion, a collection of 15,000 ruffians of every nation mixed with Moorish tribesmen who loot and rape and murder whenever they can. They did so in the November, 1934, rebellion of the miners at Oviedo. The few hundreds they have been able to get across have taken Carmona (a town near Seville) by storm and "exacted reprisals, which were necessary but most regrettable."

They brought on these calamities without any reason, for as you know from my letters the danger of Communism had disappeared and moderate opinions were winning everywhere; a government such as there is now in France was to be expected in October. And now? I do not even now think that Communism will follow on a victory of the Government.

It is the police and the soldiers who are fighting these battles, not the armed work men, who are mostly useless. Azana is as much opposed to Communism as you are and he is organising the defense, and he will hold the laurels if the people win.

I beg you to point out the extraordinary wickedness of this thing that the Fascists have done. In every town, in every village almost in Spain troops or police or plain clothes Fascists rose and began killing their fellow citizens, without warning, at moment's notice. In Malaga, for instance the soldiers began to fire on the *guardias de asalto* and Fascists sniped from roofs. All that the English here notice is the next morning workers with red handkerchiefs burned those houses from which they had sniped and others belonging to the instigators of this outrageous assault. Even Hitler refused to bring a civil war upon his country. A coup in some garrison town a "Putsch" in Madrid could have been forgiven to a losing party perhaps—but this. . .

Yours, &c. Bertrand Russell
August 10.

[54]

# Logic of the Pacifist Case— Relying on World's Better Mood

*The Daily Telegraph* (23rd November, 1936), p. 12 | C36.31

*Here Russell defends his pacifism as expressed in his most recent book,* Which Way to Peace?, *against the charge of bad logic. Russell maintains that his pacifist program requires a transition period when the nations are "in a pacific mood."*

Sir, —Mr. Harold Nicolson's[23] letter in your issue of Nov. 18, accusing me of lack of logic, calls for a reply.

I will begin by observing that logic—a subject to which I have paid some attention—shows that arguments which seem valid are often not so. When non-logicians accuse me of lack of logic, they usually mean that I accept A, but not B, which seems to them to follow from A. In this they are probably mistaken, as it is rare, outside mathematics, for one proposition to follow from another.

For example, if it is urged that a large-scale European war with modern weapons would be disastrous, it does not follow that all use of armed force is always to be condemned.

Mr. Nicolson urges that it is not pride, but "profound human indignation," that would urge us to resist Goering by force.[24] I wish I could agree with him, but I have found indignation, as a mass phenomenon, only powerful when associated with pride.

Which of us have failed to see the pacifist argument against forcible resistance to the British Government on account of its crimes in India? Which of us fought on the side of the Irish during the Black and Tan horrors?[25] So long as pride does not mislead, the grounds for pacifism are easily apprehended.

---

23. Sir Harold G. Nicolson (1886–1968) was a statesman and writer. A Labour Party member, he served as a minister in Churchill's wartime coalition government (1940–45).

24. Hermann Goering (1898–1946) was a Nazi Party leader who established the Gestapo and the concentration camps before becoming head of the *Luftwaffe*. He was sentenced to death at Nuremberg but committed suicide before sentence could be carried out.

25. The Black and Tans were temporary English recruits—mostly jobless former soldiers—used as an auxiliary force to keep order among the Irish republicans from July 1920 to July 1921. They took brutal revenge on Irish citizens after the Irish Republican Army's anti-English violence on 'Bloody Sunday' (21st November, 1920).

## Transition Period Needed

I seem to imagine, says Mr. Nicolson, "that there is some alternative between resistance and complete surrender." He ignores the necessity for a transition period, if we are to aim at a new policy.

The pacifist policy is incompatible with Empire, and the problem of surrendering our Empire is a difficult one, which will require time. Of course, Italy, Germany and Japan will want their share of the booty; but I doubt whether Russia covets any part of our territory. The pacifist, aware that his full policy is not practicable immediately, will seek, in the meantime, to secure the adoption of policies likely to postpone war, and in any case prevent British participation in it.

My long-term peace policy, as I thought I had made clear, is one which, in my opinion, has no application in the world as it is at present. It will only become applicable at a moment when all the Great Powers are in a pacific mood. I only mentioned it to show its remoteness from practical politics, and the impossibility of basing our day-to-day policy on the principle of collective security.

If it is said that the way to turn Goering into a pacifist is to defeat him in war, I reply that we have already done this once, without its having the desired effect.

## Treatment of the Brigands

As to the final parody of my argument, it is easy to parody Mr. Nicolson's parody; "You are about to traverse a country infested with brigands. You may, by calling up all your forces, succeed in killing the brigands, but you cannot prevent them from destroying your property, and your followers, being reduced to destitution, will have to become brigands themselves. Certain cowardly persons suggest that in those circumstances, you had better postpone your journey, but your profound human indignation with brigandage will not allow you to listen to their poor-spirited advice. The only right course is to fight them, and to dismiss from your mind the fact that, by so doing, you put off the end of the brigandage."

We are all descended from brigands, Hengist and Horsa[26] were brigands; William the Conqueror was a brigand. I do not suggest that it is "wicked" to defend yourself against brigands; I say it is foolish when, as

26. Hengist and Horsa were the legendary leaders of the first Anglo-Saxon settlers in Britain in the fifth century. They were supposedly invited by the British king to help him fight against the Picts.

now, resistance is certain to bring upon both them and you greater misfortunes than would result from non-resistance, and is certain also to postpone the day when nations cease to practice brigandage.

Yours &c., Bertrand Russell
Petersfield, Nov. 20

[55]

## Which Way To Peace?

*The New Statesman and Nation* (28th November, 1936), pp. 847–48 | C36.32

*Russell responds to a correspondent's criticisms of his recent book. He points out that there is no defense against air bombardment, and that defenses can even work against the interests of peace in some cases.*

Sir, —The letter from Mr. Jonathan Griffin[27] in your issue of November 14th raises an important question which deserves to be considered in no controversial spirit. He advocates what he calls "defence without menace." If this were feasible, I should not, on pacifist grounds, have anything to say against it. On the subject of food supply, in particular, "Which Way to Peace?" contains suggestions which go even farther than those of Mr. Griffin. But I am afraid what can be done in this way is very limited. "Bomb-proof architecture," for instance, involves—so the Government asserts—a quite prohibitive expenditure, which even total disarmament would not enable us to support. Nor does it seem probable that anti-aircraft batteries can protect a large area such as that of London. They can make it impossible to aim accurately at a small objective, such as, say, Downing Street; but even from a height of 20,000 feet it is easy to hit London, and exact aim becomes unimportant when gas and thermite bombs are used. It is impossible to say what defences against air attack may hereafter be discovered, but at present, as Mr. Baldwin has said, no adequate defence is possible. There is, moreover, an important psychological argument: what is making this country peaceable is fear of attack, and if that were removed Mr. Griffin would find less support than at present for his purely defensive policy. And there is always a danger—a

27. Jonathan (Robert John Shurlow) Griffin (1906– ), an English poet, author, and translator of French works, including Charles de Gaulle's *War Memoirs*.

very real one, as the Home Office circulars[28] have shown—that the authorities may lull the civilian population into a false sense of security as to defensive possibilities.

Mr. Griffin accuses me of sophistry is [sic] saying that "whatever weakens one side diminishes its will to war as much as it increases that on the other side; on the balance, therefore, it has no more tendency towards war than towards peace." Yet there is a recent and important example of the truth of this: when the Germans marched into the Rhineland[29] there can be little doubt that the French would have wished to fight if they could have counted on our support.

As for Denmark, I spoke, when in that country last year, with people of all shades of political opinion, and met none who regarded forcible resistance to Germany as possible. This is only to say that the Danes recognise obvious facts.

The statement that my book may "drive people in despair towards Fascism" is curious and unintelligible. Why should the realisation of the evils of war make people adopt the most warlike creed now in existence? Why should the view that there are better ways than war for fighting Fascism make people Fascists? Only if we suppose that, at all costs, they are determined to have a war, and will have it for a bad object if they cannot deceive themselves into thinking that they can have it for a good one. Is this Mr. Griffin's view?

Bertrand Russell
Telegraph House, Harting, Petersfield.

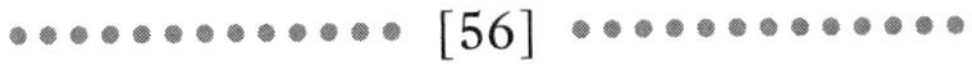

[56]

## Which Way to Peace?

*The United Services Review* (14th January, 1937), p. 15 | C37.02

*Russell controverts the editor's claim, in a recent review of his* Which Way to Peace?, *that Germany's annexation of Denmark would be used as a casus belli by Britain. He points out (a) the absence of treaty obligation and (b) the failure to respond in 1864 even when commitment to the defense of Denmark was strongest.*

---

28. See above, Russell's letter 'Air Raid Precautions', document [51].

29. On 7th March, 1936, Hitler sent troops to the Rhineland in violation of the Versailles treaty.

*In* Which Way to Peace? *Russell urged British neutrality and passive resistance even if subject to German aggression on the grounds that a general war would bring an even greater evil to all of Europe. This position he would finally repudiate publicly in 1940 when he reassessed the nature of the German threat.*

Sir, —In your courteous review of my book "Which Way to Peace?" in your issue of December 24 there is one point on which I should wish to controvert what you say, namely, the position of Denmark. You say the great nations would make the annexation of Denmark a *casus belli* with Germany. I have met no one in Denmark who believes that this would happen. Mr. Eden.[30] recently enumerated the issues which Great Britain would regard as necessitating war and said not a word about Denmark. No Great Power, so far as I know, has any treaty obligation to that country. As regards Belgium, we had, and have, treaty obligations, yet they did not prevent invasion in 1914.

"In 1864," you say, "when such conditions did not obtain Germany had no scruples about helping herself to a portion of Danish territory." The Schleswig-Holstein question is so complex that no short statement can fail of inaccuracy; but the truth, so far as it can be shortly stated, is that the Powers were far more committed to the defence of Denmark in 1864 than any of them are now. The diplomatic position was governed by the Treaty of 1852, concluded when my grandfather[31] was Prime Minister, which declared the integrity of the whole Danish Monarchy; to this treaty all the Great Powers were parties. Throughout the diplomatic crisis in 1863 the Danes believed that they could count on our armed support and were encouraged in this belief by the "Times" and the "Morning Post," as well as by the recent marriage of the Prince of Wales to a Danish Princess.

In December, 1863, Palmerston, as Prime Minister, wrote to my grandfather as Foreign Secretary: "Schleswig is no part of Germany and its invasion by German troops would be an act of war against Denmark, which would in my clear opinion entitle Denmark to our active military and naval support." Our Government finally remained neutral because it could not secure the support of France except by helping France to insist on the liberation of Poland, and French ambitions were feared.

30. Anthony Eden (1897–1977) was a British statesman who resigned as foreign minister in 1938 because of the appeasement policies of Prime Minister Neville Chamberlain. He was Foreign Minister under Churchill, 1942–45, and Prime Minister, 1955–57.

31. John Russell, the First Earl Russell (1792–1878) was Foreign Secretary (1860–65) and twice Prime Minister (1846–52, 1865–66).

At the end of it all my grandfather wrote to Lord Cowley: "I am very glad we have not given in to the temptation of a war between France and Germany. The French, if they get an inch, would certainly take and ell." The Government's policy of inaction was, however, so unpopular that a hostile motion was carried in the Lords and defeated by only 18 in the Commons.

Thus the only occasion, since the time of Napoleon, when Denmark has been invaded has been the only occasion when a diplomatic guarantee gave that country good hope of foreign support.

Bertrand Russell.
Telegraph House, Harting, Petersfield

[57]

## Methodism and Armament Firms

*The Methodist Recorder* (London), 78 (21st January, 1937), p. 22 | C37.03

*Russell had written* Freedom and Oranization *1814–1914 in 1934 in collaboration with Peter Spence whom he married in 1936. Here Russell corrects a passage that had charged the Methodist Church with armaments investments.*

*Mr. Bertrand Russell writes:—*

In my book *Freedom and Organisation,* there is on page 248 a statement quoted from "The Secret International" (Union of Democratic Control), which I hear with regret is inaccurate and which I wish hereby to correct. The statement is to the effect that on June 5, 1931, the trustees for Wesleyan Chapel Purposes (Ltd.), Manchester, were shareholders in Handley Page, Ltd. The fact is that they were asked to hold an investment in Handley Page Ltd., as custodian trustees, but after considerable correspondence with the body which made the request they refused to continue to hold the investment. I am informed, and I fully believe, that no department of the Methodist Church holds any investment in an armament firm.

# Science, Philosophy, and Religion

•••••••••••• [58] ••••••••••••

## Taking Dr. Rabagliati to Task

*The Ploughshare* (July 1919), *p. 158 | C19.21*

The Ploughshare *was a monthly publication of the Socialist Quaker Society. It was the first British publication to publish, in full, Russell's war-time appeal to President Wilson. Here Russell objects to the "righteous persecution" implied in A. Rabagliati's*[32] *article of the previous week on national health and venereal disease.*

To the Editors of "The Ploughshare":

I was surprised to find in "The Ploughshare" for June, in the course of an article on the national health, an argument in favour of the punishment of sinners, which seems to me directly contradictory of your position on the war, and of pacifism as I understand it. The article says: "The proposals for the treatment of venereal disease are an outrage on the self-respecting portion of society." Apropos of free treatment, it says: "Is no question of morals involved in this? That is, we not only condone what ought not to occur, but we do what we can to reduce the effects by free treatment of sufferers. Is this not also encouraging sufferers to continue in their evil courses?" I cannot think that the writer realised what is implied in these sentences. To begin with, his objection seems to be to the fact, which is administratively vital, that the treatment is free; this means, in effect, that he objects when those who are not well-to-do escape the punishment of sin, more than when the rich do. If he took his own argument seriously, without class bias, he ought to wish all treatment of venereal disease forbidden, so that all who contract the disease, together with their wives and children, may slowly perish. But this is not his view: he objects only when the treatment is gratuitous. What he protests against is "free treatment for those who have wilfully broken the laws of life and health."

---

32. Dr. A. Rabagliati was the author of several books on medicine, nutrition, and exercise, indluding an 1895 pamphlet, *On Some Symptoms Which Simulate Disease of the Pelvic Organs in Women; And Their Treatment By Allo-Piesto-Myo-Kinetics (Massage) and By Auto-Piesto-Myo-Kinetics (Self-Movements of Muscles Under Pressure)* (New York: William Wood and Company).

Let us take some analogies. A man who attempts to cut his throat has "willfully broken the laws of life and health." If Dr. Rabagliati found such a man bleeding to death, would he delay staunching his wound until he had ascertained whether the man could afford to pay? You Sirs, as pacifists, would presumably admit that those who are wounded in battle have "wilfully broken the laws of life and health"; but I do not think you would maintain that the Red Cross should only attend to those who have a bank account.

Next, we are told that these proposals are "an outrage on the self-respecting portion of society." Why? I claim to belong to that portion of society, but am apparently mistaken, since I fail to see how I am outraged. Is it necessary to the happiness of the self-respecting to feel that nothing is done for others? The argument is exactly the same as that used against feeding the Germans. In "John Bull" or any other equally "self-respecting" contemporary, you may read almost verbally similar arguments against mitigating the punishment of German sinners. True, the penalty of the blockade falls most heavily upon innocent women and children, and so does the penalty of venereal disease. But our "self-respecting" citizens harden their hearts with muttered words about "the third and fourth generation." No humane solution of the problem of sexual conduct will ever be found until we abandon the conception of sin, which is one of the root causes of present evils in this respect.

It is time we had done with all this righteous persecution. Is there not enough inevitable misery in the world without our adding to it by what we are pleased to call the punishment of sinners? If we are to believe in sin, are we not all sinners? And is not the man who indulges in condemnation perhaps a greater sinner than the man he condemns? Rightly or wrongly, this view is taken in the Gospels. The religion of love is a different thing from the religion of righteousness, and we look to those who refused to believe in a "righteous" war to refuse also to believe in a "righteous" callousness to the sufferings of venereal disease.

Bertrand Russell.

[59]

## The Mystic Vision

*The Athenaeum* (11 July, 1919), p. 599 | C19.23

*In his review of A. Clutton-Brock's* What Is the Kingdom of Heaven? *("The Mystic Vision,"* The Athenaeum, *June 20th), Russell criticized Clutton-Brock's mysticism as a dubious path to knowledge, and defended scientific rationality against charges of scepticism.*

*In this letter, Russell points up a contradiction between Clutton-Brock's acceptance of Christ's teaching and his support for the war; and he explains to J.W. Harvey the sense in which emotions can retard the quest for knowledge.*

Sir, —The two letters on "The Mystic Vision" in your issue of July 4 call for a few words of reply. I am sorry if Mr. Clutton-Brock thinks I misrepresented him in saying that "loving a man affords no argument against killing him"; I tried in these words to summarize his attitude on the war, which he supports (p. 110). The war could not be fought without killing Germans, yet, if I understand Mr. Clutton-Brock rightly, he holds that we ought to love all human beings, even Germans. Mr. Clutton-Brock says that "Christ, in telling us to love our enemies, meant that, if we loved them, we should not wish to kill them." Does he maintain that a soldier could fight well without wishing to kill? And if not, what becomes of his reconciliation of fighting with Christ's teaching? I certainly hold that all emotion is misleading, love as much as hate, if regarded as a source of knowledge of its object; but that is too large a question to be argued here.

With regard to Mr. J.W. Harvey's letter, I would point out, to begin with, that "the free man's worship" was republished with express reservations, stated in the preface to "Mysticism and Logic." And as for the "despair" spoken of in that essay, it is not an emotion with which we begin our study of the world, but one which comes (as I held) as an outcome of unemotional study: it is not a cause, but an effect, of philosophical opinions. Of course emotions arise in the course of study; it is not the feeling of emotions that I regard as misleading, but the belief that they afford data as to the nature of the objects towards which we feel them. I do not aim at "an agony of neutral detachment," but only at avoiding the fallacy of regarding my emotions, which are in me, as evidence concerning something outside me. This is a commonplace of scientific method; but I suppose it is too much to ask that men should approach ultimate questions in a scientific spirit.

—Yours, etc., Bertrand Russell.

[60]

# Bolshevism—Some Light on the Theory

*The Peking Leader* (28th December, 1920), p. 8 | C20.24

*Shortly after Russell returned from his travels in Russia in the summer of 1920, he set off for a year's lectureship at Government University in Beijing, China.*

*This letter was written while Russell was in China, about a month after the publication of his book on the new Soviet state,* The Practice and Theory of Bolshevism. *In his letter to the* Peking Leader, *Russell responds to an article dealing with his critique of Bolshevism and draws similarities between it and Christianity.*

Christmas Day, 1920

Sir, —The article in your issue of Dec. 19, dealing with my views on Bolshevism, has only just come to my notice. You argue that "the antithesis of Bolshevism—the doctrine of the whole for the part—is not, as we see it, science, but the philanthropic doctrine of love—the part for the whole—of the Christian religion."

For my part I can see little difference between Christianity and Bolshevism either as regards their theory or as regards their practice. The principles of the Sermon on the Mount are admirable, but their effect upon average human nature was very different from what was intended. Those who followed Christ did not learn to love their enemies or to turn the other cheek. They learnt instead to use the Inquisition and the stake, to subject the human intellect to the yoke of an ignorant and intolerant priesthood, to degrade art and extinguish science for a thousand years. These were the inevitable results, not of the teaching, but of fanatical belief in the teaching. Even admitting all the charges ever made against the Bolsheviks by their most embittered opponents, their record of bloodshed is infinitesimal compared with that of the Christian Church, yet I have never refused to meet a bishop on the ground that I would not "shake hands with murder."

Christianity has had every opportunity of regenerating the world during the last one thousand nine hundred and twenty years, yet I fail to observe that the world is very regenerate. Bolshevism has only been in the world three years, but if it is to have rivalled Christianity's record of effectiveness in crime and ineffectiveness in virtue by the year three thousand eight hundred and forty, it will have to mend its pace.

People by this time have nearly forgotten that Christianity was once in earnest and that the early Christians made a serious effort to practise communism. The Wise Men of the East once had the same opinion of Christianity as they now have of Bolshevism. As pilgrims once traversed the desert to Bethlehem, so now to Baku, enquiring as eagerly for Lenin as then for Christ. Possibly when Bolshevism has been in the world for one thousand nine hundred and twenty years, there will remain only a few antiquaries to remind ordinary believers that it also once believed in communism.

Yours etc., Bertrand Russell

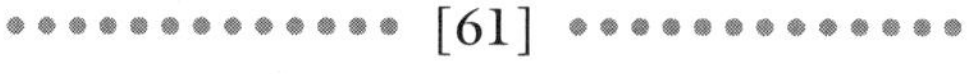

[61]

## Capitalism in South China

*The Japan Weekly Chronicle* (26th July, 1921), p. 5 | C21.12

*While on a brief stay-over in Japan on his way back to England from China, Russell wrote this letter in defense of John Dewey (1859–1952). Russell had met Dewey, the famous American philosopher, during his visit to Harvard in 1914. Dewey was in China at the same time as Russell, and was present when Russell was near death in March. Russell liked Dewey personally, but philosophically they disagreed. Russell once described him to Ottoline Morrell as "a good man but not a very clever one."*

Sir, —In your issue of July 24th there is a leaderette with whose general scope I am in agreement, but ending in a suggestion which seems to me misleading and not wholly just, to the effect that "Professor Dewey . . . is not a good authority or an unprejudiced witness." I do not know that any one of us could claim to be an unprejudiced witness where national bias enters in. I have myself struggled against the distorting influence of nationalism on my own thoughts for many years, yet I am still conscious of being by no means unprejudiced in an issue between Britain and a foreign country. Doubtless Professor Dewey also may be described—along with the rest of the human race—as a prejudiced witness in this sense, but in this sense only. He favours the Consortium. I do not. He sees in the extension of America's influence on China the best hope of China's regeneration. I do not. But these are very difficult questions in regard to which either opinion may be held rationally.

As to the statement that Professor Dewey "is not a good authority," he has been in Canton and seen the leading men, and is, no doubt, repeating what they told him. Nor is he the only authority for the statement in question, which is repeated with more detail by Mr. Philip

Haddon in the *Review of the Far East* for July 16th. And certainly some explanation has to be sought for the extreme hostility of Hongkong to the Government of Dr. Sun Yat-sen. The favour shown to that government by the Americans also needs explanation, which, I hope, will be provided by some American as "unpatriotic" as myself.

—Yours, &c., Bertrand Russell.
Tokyo: July 24, 1921.

[62]

## Mr. Bertrand Russell's 'Analysis of Mind.'

*The Japan Weekly Chronicle* (20th April 1922), p. 575 | C22.11

*Russell's* Analysis of Mind *(1921) was one of his most important works in metaphysics and theory of knowledge. It developed his new doctrine of neutral monism, which differed in important ways from the dualism and representative realism of his* Problems of Philosophy *(1912). Here he offers a non-technical explanation of that doctrine especially its difference from Berkeleyan idealism, according to which all reality is mental.*

Sir, —In the course of a very kind review of my "Analysis of Mind" in your weekly edition of January 26th,[33] there is a rather important misunderstanding which, with your permission, I should like to remove. Your reviewer believes that I regard matter as a "collocation of sensations" and naturally finds difficulty in understanding what I mean by a "purely physical world." I had tried to guard against this misconception by the illustration of a photographic plate. I believe the world to consist of floating particulars, some of which enter into those mnemic contexts which I regard as constituting minds. It is by means of mnemic phenomena that "experience" is defined. Thus we may say (omitting niceties) that "sensations" are to be defined as "those particulars which happen to be experienced." It follows tautologically that I cannot give an instance of a particular which is not a sensation. This, however, is not an important metaphysical truth, any more than the fact that I cannot give an instance of a man I have never heard of, although, in common with the rest of mankind, I believe there are such men.

33. Russell refers to the review by Dr. N.G. Munro (1863–1942), a Scottish physician who lived in Japan, and wrote a classic study of the aboriginal people of Japan, *Ainu Creed and Cult* (1963).

The philosophy which your reviewer imputes to me is a Berkeleian idealism,[34] whereas the philosophy I hold is neither idealism nor materialism, and allows the possibility of a world containing nothing mental.

—Yours, etc., Bertrand Russell.
London: March 8, 1922.

[63]

## Einstein

*The Japan Weekly Chronicle* (1st February, 1923), p. 5 | C23.06

*In addition to his popular* The ABC of Relativity *(1925), Russell wrote several articles explaining Einstein's theories. Perhaps the article most accessible to the general reader appeared in* The Kaizo *(October, 1922). In this letter Russell clarifies a point in that article about the speed of light.*

Sir, —In your weekly issue of November 9th a correspondent writes on the sense in which Einstein assumes (as a result of the Michelson-Morley and other experiments) the constancy of the velocity of light. You appeal to my article in the Kaizo as giving a different sense. But your correspondent is right and says exactly what I meant to convey. In the article in question I say: "However a body may be moving, the velocity of light, as measured relatively to an observer on that body is the same." You will find in my article an illustration of a fly causing ripples on a pool which I think makes the point clear. If the ripples behaved as light does, the fly would remain at the centre of the ripples (from its own point of view), and so would the spot on the pond where the fly touched the water (from the water's point of view), no matter how the fly might move. It is this paradox that has to be explained. The part of my article which explains this point is later than the part about the train, which is concerned with the definition of simultaneity.

—Yours, etc., Bertrand Russell.
London: Dec. 21, 1922.

34. Berkeleian (or Berkeleyan) idealism, the view that only perceptions are real and there are no material objects represented by perceptions, is the metaphysical philosophy of George Berkeley (1685–1753), Bishop of Cloyne, an important British empiricist, after whom Berkeley in California was named.

••••••••••••• [64] •••••••••••••

# Missionary Influence in China

*The Manchester Guardian* (13th April, 1923), p. 7 | C23.13

*On April 4th Russell had published an article in the* Manchester Guardian, *'The Boxer Indemnity and Chinese Education'. Here he responds to a correspondent's objections to that article. Russell had published his book on China,* The Problem of China, *the previous year. He expressed great admiration for the serenity and beauty of Chinese civilization, and he saw Christian influence as linked with certain undesirable features of Western civilization, especially militarism.*

Sir, —The objections of your correspondent Mr. Sylvester Lee in your issue of April 7, to my remarks on missionary influence in Chinese education sufficiently illustrate the points I wished to make. As to the number of converts, "hundreds or thousands" in a population of 400 millions may justly be described as few. As to denationalisation, that is a matter of opinion; I can only say that I came across a great many foreign-educated Chinese and that while something of this tendency seemed to me to exist in almost all of them, it was especially marked (at least so I thought) among those who had become Christians, who had in most cases a somewhat abject reverence for foreign culture which no one conscious of European short comings could admire.

We have heard a great deal about the Chinese Christian general. If efficient militarism of the Western type is to be claimed as one of the blessings brought by missionary activity, my case is conceded. The Chinese point of view is illustrated by Lao-Tze's saying: "The best soldiers are those who do not fight." Are we to congratulate ourselves on altering this attitude? No one denies that the missionaries have done valuable educational work in China, especially before the Chinese had efficient educational institutions of their own. But unfortunately their influence is indissolubly bound up with that of Western civilisation, which values "strong" government, militarism, and preferential trade, so that the "heathenism" of the Chinese comes to consist in their preferring enjoyment to predatory activity, learning to "useful" knowledge (such as poison gases), and the peace of the sceptic to the military prowess of the fanatic.

—Yours, &c., Bertrand Russell.
Carn Voel, Treen, Penzance. April 9

[65]

## An Agricultural Religion?

*The New Leader* (12th March, 1926), p. 7 | C26.08

*In the London* New Leader *of 26th February ('Trotsky on Our Sins'), Russell had referred to Christianity as an "agricultural religion." Here he responds to letters of 5th March which took issue with his earlier characterization of Christianity.*

I am sorry that two of your correspondents should have been annoyed by my referring to Christianity as an agricultural religion; I had thought this was now generally admitted. The evidence is collected in Frazer's *Golden Bough,* which is too long a book to be summarised. With regard to the ethics of Christ (as opposed to Christian ethics) I have two things to say. First, they are in no way peculiar; they are to be found in Buddhism and Confucianism. Secondly, they are historically unimportant, since they have never influenced the conduct of Christian communities or prominent Christian individuals. Take, e.g., "a warm place in one's heart for little children." Does not Mr. Watcyn Williams know that what is being done for them at the present moment is being done in the teeth of bitter opposition from organized Christianity? Does he not know that priests refuse to allow anything to be done, e.g., to prevent the birth of syphilitic children except among the well-to-do? Ever since the thirteenth century, every diminution of cruelty has been opposed by the recognised leaders of Christianity; and this is still the case now.

Bertrand Russell.

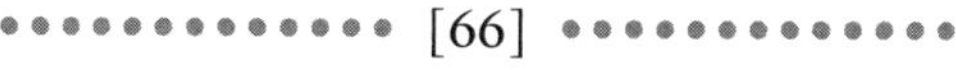

[66]

## Philosophy and Common Sense

*The New Statesman and Nation* (5th March, 1938), p. 365 | C38.05

*Hyman Levy (1889–1975) was an English mathematician, political activist and philosopher. After joining the Communist Party in 1931, he became one of the British Communist Party's leading spokesmen. Russell's letter is in response to an earlier letter from Levy, which in turn was a reply to Russell's review of Levy's book,* A Philosophy for Modern Man, *in the same magazine. In the late 1950s, after protesting persecution of Jews in the U.S.S.R., Levy was expelled from the Communist Party.*

Sir,— Professor Levy's letter in your issue of February 26th calls for some words of reply from me. I will take his points seriatim.

His first point is that Left Book Club discussion groups are not interested in "the old philosophical issues." If this is taken as evidence that such issues no longer deserve to excite interest, one wonders why Professor Levy is so much concerned about the reality of matter, which is one of the oldest of them.

His second point is that, if physical processes can be most conveniently described without using the category of substance, then "Spain, Italy, China, Abyssinia, Depressed Areas, Armaments are so much metaphysical lumber." He qualifies this by saying, "if this means what you and I understand by it." I do not know, sir, what you understand by it, but it certainly does not mean what Professor Levy understands by it. I hold, in common with most modern logicians, that numbers are linguistic conveniences, not Platonic realities, but this view has no bearing on their utility in accounts or in measurement. I hold, in common with Einstein, that position in space is relative, and that "Spain, Italy, China, Abyssinia" are relative terms; but I do not see how this view bears on my interest in the fate of Spaniards, Italians, Chinese, and Abyssinians. I hold in common with all (not some) who have attempted to formulate modern quantum theory, that the atom is most conveniently treated as a series of events, not as a persistent entity; but no person with even a slight sense of relevance can suppose that this view has any bearing whatever on politics.

Professor Levy continues: "I refuse at a time like this to be a party to increasing the confusion that already prevails. Matter is simply what we pick up and handle." What "a time like this" can have to do with the nature of matter I fail to see. The Pope, frightened by the Thirty Years War, thought that, "at a time like this," the earth could not be allowed to go round the sun. The argument that "matter is what we pick up and handle" is reminiscent of Dr. Johnson's refutation of Berkeley. I gather that Professor Levy, like the early Ionians, does not consider gases to be matter.

The next point maintained is that, unless one accepts the Marxist theory of social dynamics, "human group action becomes irrational." Why? We can organize the food supply, for instance, without any particular theory of social dynamics. He exaggerates rhetorically the degree of unpredictability which I had asserted to exist, but he advances no refutation of my arguments except that without faith life is insupportable—a contention which is urged even more eloquently by the Buchmanites.

He accuses me of a "non-possumus attitude to the making of history." Apparently he means "to the making of a theory of history," for otherwise his words are meaningless. I do not dogmatically assert that a theory of history is impossible; I say only that the Marxist theory is

This caricature of Russell appeared in *John Bull* (1st October, 1932), accompanied by Hannen Swaffer's open letter to Earl Russell, entitled 'Your Lash Is Good for Us'. Swaffer writes: "Mankind, today, needs the chastening lash with which you point out how religion is often used to encourage war, how patriotism . . . has been turned to worship of the flag . . . not to guide man on to victory over evil, but to wholesale murder."

not supported by such arguments as would be found convincing in a science that made less appeal to the passions.

Professor Levy speaks of me as arguing for "the immateriality of the world about us." The suggestions of this phrase are quite misleading. He thinks, or affects to think, that, if we do not use the category of substance in the scientific treatment of physical phenomena, we must hold that reality is spiritual, or some such doctrine. Apparently he does not know that, in physics and psychology alike, the belief in substance is obsolete, and matter and the soul have vanished together.

Finally he maintains that he and I cannot possibly have similar ideals because I contend for "the immateriality of the world about us" "in a world trembling on the brink of social transformation." I am happy to have found at last a point on which I can agree with him. I hold that one should advocate a doctrine because one sees some reason to think it true, and I fail altogether to see how the fact that the world is trembling on the brink of social transformation bears on quantum theory. Professor Levy apparently holds that one should advocate a metaphysical doctrine (a) because it interests Left Book Club discussion groups, (b) because it is supposed by some, owing to their incapacity for logical thought, to be useful to one's political party. This does prove, I agree, that he does not have "ideals much the same as mine."

Bertrand Russell
Amberley House, Kidlington, Oxfordshire.

# Human Rights and Civil Liberties

••••••••••••• [67] •••••••••••••

## "To Save an Innocent Man"

*The Manchester Guardian* (22nd March, 1920), p. 8 | C20.09

*The end of the war brought political chaos to Hungary which, as part of the Dual Monarchy of Austria-Hungary, had been on the losing side. In 1919 a Communist government came to power in Hungary on the model of the Bolsheviks in Russia. In 1920 a 'White' (or anti-Bolshevik) government was established with the intervention of the Allies, and many supporters of the Communist regime were persecuted.*

*In his letter Russell shows, as he did on countless occasions throughout his life, his genuine concern for civil liberties and human rights, and his willingness to speak out for the downtrodden and the voiceless.*

Sir, —The victims of the White Terror in Hungary have been so numerous that it may seem invidious to write on behalf of any one of them, but it so happens that among the Communists now awaiting trial is a philosopher whose work on fundamental logical ideas is of more interest to me than to most people, and rouses in me a specially strong desire that he should escape, if possible, from the death penalty with which he is threatened. His name is Alexander Varjas. He was a teacher of philosophy in the University of Budapest. He was not in favour of terrorism, but, on the contrary, a pacifist. I do not know whether we have the same horror of pacifism among our late enemies as among ourselves, but it is not on the ground of his opinions that I am appealing on his behalf. It is on the ground of the contributions which he is likely to make to learning. He has a width of erudition which is rare among philosophers and very considerable original powers. In the midst of war and revolution he found time for exceedingly interesting speculations on the relations of logic, mathematics, and the theory of aggregates. He has now been seven months in gaol awaiting trial. I cannot think that after all the destruction and waste of the war the world is so rich in civilisation that it can afford to squander the best lives that remain to it, merely because their political opinions happen to be, at the moment, out of favour in the country in which they live. It is clear that the Entente Governments are in a position to suggest leniency to the Hungarian regime, and I could wish that they would inaugurate such a course by intervening on behalf of a man of really distinguished intellectual attainments.

—Yours, &c., Bertrand Russell.
70, Overstrand Mansions, Prince of Wales Road, Battersea, S.W., March 18.

[68]

## The Relief of the Russian Famine

*The Nation and The Athenaeum* (17th December, 1921), p. 468 | C21.31

*In this letter Russell says that although he has been "a severe critic of the Bolsheviks," the main cause of the famine is drought and not bad government from the Bolsheviks.*

Sir, —It has been urged constantly, and was repeated in the recent debate in parliament, that the Russian famine is due to Bolshevik misrule. Although I have been a severe critic of the Bolsheviks, particularly as regards their agrarian policy, I am convinced that they have had only a small share in causing the famine, and that even that small share is due to past mistakes now rectified. The main cause is the drought. Tsarist Russia was equally liable to famine; so is China. When I arrived in China last autumn, many millions of peasants were starving, but no one attributed the calamity to the Government. When, in the summer of last year, I traveled down the Volga, the peasants in the regions now suffering were obviously well fed in spite of Bolshevik rule. Famines occur periodically wherever there is peasant agriculture with inadequate transport facilities. It is true that the Bolshevik policy of requisitions formerly discouraged grain production, but this policy was reversed last spring, very wisely as I think.

Even were the Bolsheviks far more to blame than they are, there is no logic in starving anti-Bolshevik peasants because we dislike a Government to which they are opposed. If, some day, we were to have an advanced Labor Government and foreign Governments were to stop the export of grain to Great Britain, I am sure the opponents of Labor in this country would consider themselves very ill-used. Moreover, our policy inflicts upon the Russian peasants a penalty far worse than that which our law inflicts upon murderers, since death by starvation is far more painful than hanging; yet surely their guilt cannot be judged greater than that of a murderer even by the most vehement anti-Bolshevik.

From the point of view of policy, the argument for relieving the Russian famine immediately and effectively is at least equally strong, as Mr. Hoover[35] has perceived.

—Yours, &c., Bertrand Russell.
31, Sydney Street, S.W. 3.

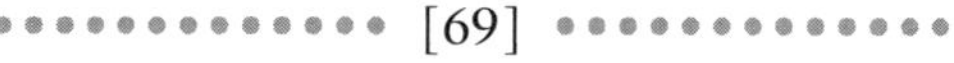

[69]

## The Case of Margaret Sanger.

*The Nation and The Athenaeum* (27th January, 1923), p. 645 | C23.04

*Russell defends two Britons accused of obscenity for publishing a Margaret Sanger pamphlet on birth control. Freedom of the press and a rational sexual ethic are issues in evidence here, and both were themes that Russell defended throughout his life.*

Sir, —The prosecution of Margaret Sanger's's[36] pamphlet, "Family Limitation," by the Public Prosecutor, on the ground of obscenity, demands more publicity than it has obtained. Margaret Sanger is well known, not only in America, but throughout the world, for her fearless attempt to spread knowledge on this important matter. Her pamphlet (which I have read carefully) is as free from obscenity as any medical textbook, plain language being necessary if information is to be given. If it is condemned, all treatment of birth control in print will be rendered impossible.

In the West London Police Court Guy and Rose Aldred (who printed and published the pamphlet in this country) were ordered to destroy all copies of it. No evidence of obscenity was given. The only evidence for the prosecution was that of a policeman who, acting under instructions,

35. Herbert Hoover (1874–1964) was President of the United States, 1929–33. When he was Secretary of Commerce in 1921-22, his Food Relief Administration provided food for ten million Russians.

36. Margaret Sanger (1883–1966) was an American pioneer in the movement to disseminate knowledge of birth control. She organized the first American conference on birth control in 1921 and the first international conference in 1925.

had written various letters, one saying his wife wanted the pamphlet, others saying that he was a woman who had been at a birth control meeting, and that he and two friends desired copies of the pamphlet. On the first page of the pamphlet is a declaration in the following terms: "This booklet is supplied at the special request of . . . who has declared that he or she is over twenty-one years of age, and considers the Artificial Limitation of the Family justifiable on both individual and national grounds, and wishes to know the various Hygienic Methods of Family Limitation, and undertakes to keep it out of the hands of unmarried persons under the age of twenty-one years." Believing in the bona fides of the supposed married man, &c., the defendants sent the pamphlet to the policeman without first exacting the signature of this declaration. This was the whole case for the prosecution.

Mr. Maynard Keynes[37] and my wife are sureties for the expenses of the appeal. If an adequate defence is to be made on appeal, funds will be needed, which may be sent either to Mr. Keynes (King's College, Cambridge) or to my wife. It is to be hoped that those who realize the importance of the population question will be willing to come forward.

—Yours, &c., Bertrand Russell.
31, Sydney Street, S.W. 3.

[70]

## The Case of Margaret Sanger

*The Nation and The Athenaeum* (10th February, 1923), p. 719 | C23.08

*Here Russell responds to Dr. Marie Stopes's letter* (Nation and Athenaeum) *critical of Russell's letter of 27th January.*

Sir, —If Dr. Stopes[38] was surprised by my letter, I was amazed by hers in your issue of February 3rd. She was, of course, aware, when she wrote, that I cannot reply to her statements while the case is *sub judice*. Anyone who will take the trouble to follow the case when it comes up for appeal will have no difficulty in judging between her and me. Although I feel the

---

37. John Maynard Keynes, later Lord Keynes (1883–1946), was a famous British economist and a friend of Russell at Cambridge.

38. Marie C. Stopes (1880–1858) was a British eugenist and founder of Britain's first birth control clinic.

rashness of differing on a point of logic with so great an authority on that subject, I adhere to the opinion I expressed before, which I shall be glad to argue fully as soon as the case is disposed of. At this moment the Aldreds are in trouble through taking part, with somewhat less circumspection, in the movement which Dr. Stopes adorns. Her many friends will be sorry that she should have chosen this moment to make things harder for workers in the same cause.

—Yours, &c., Bertrand Russell.

[71]

## "Birth Control"

*The New Leader* (11th July, 1924), p. 6 | C24.27

*In the following letter both Russell and his wife Dora protest the government's repressive policy on birth control.*

Sir, —At the Baby Week Conference great emphasis has been laid by Mr. Wheatley[39] and others on maternity care (particularly ante-natal) as the best means of saving the lives of infants as well as mothers.

These pronouncements savour of hypocrisy to those who reflect that the Ministry of Health is causing the deaths of a large number of women and babies every year, and ensuring the birth of blind, syphilitic, and tuberculous children by its obstinate prejudice against giving birth control information at its centres.

Every year a large number of women die in childbirth whose lives could only have been saved by the prevention of conception, because they are medically unfit to produce another child. Public Health officers are not allowed to help them. What is more, the reports of the Ministry of Health itself confess that the large number of maternal deaths from puerperal sepsis result from the prevalence and even from the increase of abortion.

The present Minister of Health seems to assume that the provision of adequate houses and lying-in hospitals is all that is needed to produce a healthy population. He talks glibly of not relieving the mother of her

39. John Wheatley (1869–1930) was Minister of Health in Ramsay MacDonald's Labour government from January to November, 1924.

duties and responsibilities. She seeks relief only to perform them better. A woman is a human being, and every mother has a right to two years' rest between babies. No amount of sentimental blindness will prove that this is possible on the average without the use of contraceptives.

The Ministry professes itself ready to consider schemes from local authorities likely to minister to the health of babies and mothers. We suggest that local authorities less blinded by the prejudice than the central body should put forward permission to give birth control advice when medically advisable as an essential part of such schemes. We do not suggest that this is more than a part of what should be done, or that it be done in a propagandist fashion. But prejudice and that class attitude which allows the information to the rich and not to the poor make continual protest necessary.

—Yours, etc., Bertrand Russell, Dora Russell

[72]

## Birth Control and the Labour Party

*The Daily Herald* (9th October, 1926), p. 4 | C26.31

*Here Russell explains to a correspondent the Labour Party's position on birth control.*

Mr. Middleton states that he cannot understand why lovers of liberty (among whom he mentions me) desire liberty for medical authorities at health centres to give information on birth control, and wish the Labour Party to favour this extension of liberty.

Apparently he would abolish the whole programme of the Labour Party, as an interference with the freedom of its members. Would he have left members free on the Miners' Eight Hours Bill? It was the Executive's actions at Liverpool that compelled Mr. Thurtle to present birth control as a non-party issue.

But a political party exists to achieve certain objects, and I had supposed that among the objects of the Labour Party was an increase in the well-being of wage-earners and their wives and children. Some of us hold that when a woman is nearly certain to die of her next confinement, or to give birth to a syphilitic child, common humanity demands that a medical man employed at a health centre should have a right to tell her how to avoid those misfortunes.

We think also that women have a right to a voice in the matter which is of most importance to them. Those who think otherwise have a right to their opinion, but should not pose as friends of freedom.

Bertrand Russell.
Sydney-street, S.W.3.

[73]

## "Birth Control and Housing. Views of the Hon. Mr. and Mrs. Russell."

*The Daily Express* (2nd May, 1927), p. 2 | C27.18a

*This letter, signed by both Russell and Dora, is their reply to an article of the previous week concerning the issues of birth control and housing. The Russells' letter was printed with the editor's introduction.*

The following letter has been received from the Hon. Bertrand and Mrs. Russell, dealing with the subjects of birth control and housing. Mr. Russell is the son of the late Viscount Amberley, and heir-presumptive to Earl Russell, and is the noted writer on economics:—

To the Editor of the "Daily Express."

Sir, —Straightforward opposition to birth control is one thing, but it is difficult to regard the misrepresentation contained in your issue of April 25 as honest.

It is common knowledge, both in the Labour movement and outside, that the demand for birth control advice has come from married women and mothers, and has been opposed—what trifling opposition there has been—by the unmarried women. There are only two unmarried women concerned with the Labour birth control group. Both are women invited to give their support because of their eminent position in the party.

### The Remedy

The remedy for the promiscuous spread of pamphlets and propaganda, to which you object, lies in granting the women's demand for clinical advice at welfare centres.

As to housing, we are not aware that the "Daily Express" or its political supporters have contributed anything towards the solution of that problem. They demand more citizens, and compel them to live in conditions not fit for pigs or cattle.

Thousands of women are rendered "haggard and unhealthy," but by excessive child-bearing under such conditions, not by contraception.

If the "Daily Express" cannot provide us with a better world for the children, by what right does it demand that they be born?

Bertrand Russell. Dora Russell.
Carn Voel, Porthcurno, Penzance.

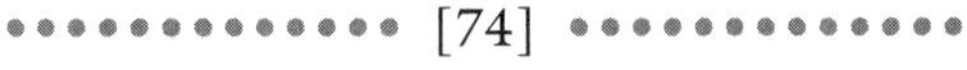

[74]

## "An Advertisement"

*The Daily Herald* (20th January, 1928), p. 4 | C28.01

*Russell and Dora opened their new, alternative school for children, Beacon Hill, in the autumn of 1927. One of the features of the school was the non-religious content of the curriculum. Russell here calls attention to the fact that an advertisement for the school was refused by one of the major London newspapers* (The Times). The Daily Herald *was a pro-Labour newspaper.*

Being recently in want of a matron for our school at Beacon Hill, we sent an advertisement to the *Times* for a MATRON for small Nursery Boarding school, run on free, modern lines. No religion taught. Sympathy with school's attitude is essential. Also good technical training.

This advertisement the *Times* refused to print: apparently, in its opinion, Free Thinkers, alone among human beings, should be deprived of the right to impart their theological opinions to their own children.

Bertrand Russell.
Beacon Hill School, Harting, Petersfield.

[75]

## "Pour Encourager les Autres"

*The Nation and Athenaeum* (23rd August, 1930), p. 642 | C30.17

*In the following letter Russell relates a disturbing story of British police excesses against an American journalist friend of the Russells. The friend, Griffin Barry, had lived with the Russells intermittently at their Beacon Hill school. A month earlier Dora gave birth to Barry's child. Russell had apparently been unable to give her a third child. And when, while on tour, he learned of Dora's pregnancy by Barry, he wrote: "Since I cannot do my part, it is better someone else should, as you ought to have more children."*[40]

*Nevertheless, the arrival of Barry's child created difficulties for Russell's marriage; they separated in 1932 and divorced in 1935.*

Sir, —Probably not many of your readers know of the activity of the British police in encouraging tourist traffic. The following incident will show what a debt of gratitude in this respect we owe to the defenders of law and order.

An American friend of mine, Mr. Griffin Barry, was intending to proceed from Plymouth to Cherbourg on August 4th. When he attempted to take his ticket, a Scotland Yard agent asked to see his passport, and discovered that, in common with the great majority of Americans, he had forgotten to register as an alien. For this purely technical offence, he was then and there cast into prison, his papers and luggage were seized and searched, bail was fixed at the preposterous figure of £1,000, offers of bail made to the police were not communicated to him, and the newspapers were informed that bail was not forthcoming.

The police endeavoured to prevent his friends from coming to his defence by assuring them that the matter was trivial, although when it came into Court they endeavoured to secure the maximum penalty (£100 fine and/or six months' imprisonment) by false accusations of Communist activities, for which they offered no evidence, because none exists. The four days during which he was kept in prison were spent by Scotland Yard in interviewing every person in London whose name they had been able to ascertain from his papers.

It is charitable to suppose that when they arrested him they really believed that they had caught a Communist "agent," but they must have discovered their mistake before the case came on. Nevertheless they persisted in the accusation, and caused it to have prominence in the Press

40. Cited in Clark, p. 443.

reports of the case, in spite of the failure of Scotland Yard working at high pressure for four days to secure one iota of evidence in support of this wholly unfounded accusation.

Is it not time the police were instructed to show courtesy and fair play in their dealings with unoffending Americans? Better still, the Aliens Order of 1920, which was made during the panic about Bolshevism, should be rescinded.

—Yours, &c., Bertrand Russell
Carn Voel, Porthcurno. August 16th, 1930

[76]

## The Untouchables in India

*The Manchester Guardian* (13th January, 1933), p. 16 | C33.04

*In this, the first of five letters to the editor of the* Manchester Guardian *concerning freedom in India—four of which are reprinted here—Russell appeals to the British people not to allow their government to obstruct social reform there. At this time India was part of the British empire, and was in the throes of a long struggle for emancipation, which finally came in 1947.*

*In August 1932, Prime Minister Ramsay MacDonald announced his Communal Award—a unilateral attempt to resolve electoral disputes among India's religious groups. Gandhi and his Congress Party objected to electoral provisions which they said discriminated against the untouchables, India's lowest caste. Gandhi and his followers were imprisoned for civil disobedience. While in prison Gandhi undertook a "fast unto death" until MacDonald's plan was withdrawn.*

Sir, —I have received a cable from Mr. C. Rajagopalachari, a leader of the Congress and an intimate colleague of Mr. Gandhi.[41] It denies the assumption so readily held in this country that our Government's proposals at the Round-table Conference[42] are such as to satisfy Indian

41. Mohandas K. Gandhi (1869–1948) was a religious and political leader in India who led his country to freedom from British rule. Gandhi's form of non-violent resistance, known as Satyagraha, served as a model for the American civil rights reformer, Martin Luther King, Jr.

42. The Round Table Conference (1930–32) consisted of three meetings in London between representatives of India and the British government to consider a constitution for future India. The first and the third meetings were not attended by representatives of Gandhi's Indian National Congress Party.

opinion and lead to peace. The Congress rejects the safeguards and limitations upon which his Majesty's government insist. Recent experience has shown that in the absence of Congress co-operation government in India has to be carried on by coercive laws and mass repression. Unless our government changes its policy and is prepared to transfer real power to Indian hands, a state of conflict as at present or worse is inevitable.

Meanwhile a fresh crisis is imminent in connection with the social rights of the untouchables. Some time ago Mr. Gandhi stated that he would be obliged to resume his fast if the temple at Guruvayur were not opened to the untouchables. This public demand for the extension of social rights to the untouchables, however, cannot be made effective in existing circumstances without certain changes in the law.

Mr. Rajagopalachari's cable states that the Government is unwilling to permit the necessary bills to be introduced in the Legislature. British authority is thus actually impeding the progress of social reform which Indian opinion demands.

The following is the text of the cable:

The nature, reservations, safeguards, adumbrated Round Table, and unchanged attitude Government India toward Gandhiji render all hopes peace impossible. Emancipation untouchables impossible without removal social bar. Therefore entry public temples all important. Trustees bound by British Court decisions as well as positive enactments maintain established usage, including untouchability, even where local opinion clearly expressed in favour of abolition—example Guruvayur. Government seems unwilling sanction necessary legislation. Withholding sanction most unusual procedure. Many measures affecting long-established socio-religious customs sanctioned and passed before. Dr. Subbarayan's bill simply provides scheme local option for authorising trustees temple allowing untouchables, and does not itself throw open temple. Madras Council has passed resolution without dissentient favouring legislation temple entry. Withholding sanction despite great awakening readiness for reform prevents due fulfillment; solemn pledges given September last depressed classes. His Majesty's Government must intervene and at risk enhancing prestige Gandhiji instruct sanction legislation. Gandhiji consider resumption fast obligatory. If public fail secure Viceroy's sanction for necessary legislation and thereby Guruvayar Temple remains unopened situation critical in my opinion. Have explained everything Madras Governor personally, No valid grounds for withholding sanction. —Rajagopalachari

It is our responsibility as British people to see that our Government here and our agents in India do not obstruct the cause of social reform or block the way to political peace.

Bertrand Russell,
Chairman, the India League
148, Strand, London, W.C. 2, January 11

[77]

## Meerut Sentences: What is Meant by "Rigorous Imprisonment"?

*The Manchester Guardian* (27th January, 1933), p. 18 | C33.07

*Russell raises some important questions about the nature of the punishment—"rigorous imprisonment"—of the convicted Meerut prisoners, so named after the Indian town in which they were tried. Thirty-two trade unionists, including three Englishmen, were arrested and charged in 1929 with conspiracy to deprive the King-Emperor (George VI) of the sovereignty of India. The prisoners were held in jail under appalling conditions until and throughout their three-year trial (1930-33), which resulted in harsh sentences for 27 men. Six months later the sentences were greatly reduced on appeal after public protest in Britain.*

Sir, —A good many people have been startled by the severity of the sentences on the "Meerut prisoners,"[43] British and Indian trade union officials who have already been in prison for two years awaiting trial and being tried. One man has been transported for life, another—an Englishman—for twelve years, another Englishman for ten years, others have been transported for seven and five years, while sentences of three and four years "rigorous imprisonment" have been passed on others.

I know that you have yourself criticised the method of trial and the nature of the evidence admitted, and I have no doubt that you had exceedingly good ground for the objections you made. But even supposing the trial had been entirely satisfactory, some of us would like to know a little more about the punishment which has been inflicted. For example, where is the "penal colony" to which these men are being sent? Their friends allege that conditions there are so bad that they suggest that most of the men will not live to complete their sentences. What is the official reply to this?

Then what does the term "rigorous imprisonment" mean? Their friends say that it means being shut up alone in a cell in which it is impossible to read after nightfall.

Many of us go to see films about Devil's Island or chain gangs in the belief that "nothing of that sort could go on under British rule." But is our smugness justified? Can any of your readers give any information as to conditions to which these men are being sent? I see that several trade union and I.L.P. branches have passed resolutions of protest.

—Yours, &c., Bertrand Russell
47 Emperor's Gate, London, S.W.7, January 25.

[78]

## The Viceroy's Attitude

*The Manchester Guardian* (31st January, 1933), p. 18 | C33.08

*Russell defends his earlier assertion that British authority is "impeding the progress of social reform."*

Sir, —Mr. Ritchie, writing in your issue of January 26, demands an explanation of my assertion that British authority in India is impeding social reform. He appears to think that the decision made by the Government of India last week disproves my statement. It does nothing of the kind.

The Government of India is still the ally of social reaction. The Viceroy has sought safety in procrastination and avoided an immediate conflict with Mr. Gandhi. It is the insistence of Mr. Gandhi and his followers that has compelled Lord Willingdon[43] to retreat one step. The Government's antipathy to the cause of social reform, however, is evident in the Viceroy's statement which permits the Indian Legislature to discuss a measure to remove the disabilities of the untouchables and at the same time insists on proclaiming that the Government will not be bound by the decisions of the Legislature.

Meanwhile the bill for enabling the untouchables to enter temples in Madras is disallowed on the ground that the question is an all-India one. I understand that in Madras the legal power for preventing untouchables entering temples is derived from the Hindu Religious Endowment Act of

43. Freeman Freeman-Thomas Willingdon (1866–1941) became Viceroy of India in 1931 and resisted Gandhi's demands.

that province. This Act is not an all-India measure; yet it was sanctioned by a former Viceroy not long ago.

The Indian Government's present attitude only confirms the view that I have expressed that it is impeding social reform. It is meeting the demand for reform with delaying tactics and spurious argument.

—Yours, &c., Bertrand Russell,
Chairman, the India League
140, Strand, London, W.C.

[79]

## The Meerut Case

*Week-End Review* (11th February, 1933), p. 144 | C33.12

*Russell calls attention to one of the Meerut prisoners and the harshness of his sentence. He notes the charge of Communism which he claims obscures the real issue, trade unionism.*

Sir, —The Meerut Conspiracy Case has attracted widespread attention, though even now few are aware of the full harshness of the Government's conduct of the trial. In the case of at least one of the men condemned—namely, Hugh Leicester Hutchinson[44]—there is considerable reason to hope that an appeal might be successful in reversing the verdict. He was unanimously acquitted by the five assessors, whose decision was completely ignored by the judge. I am informed, on the best authority, that he is not a Communist. Indeed, the principal point relied upon by the prosecution in his case was the fact that in his library there was a book by Stalin. The animus of the British Government is shown in the fact that, while the former Secretary of the State for India gave an explicit promise that his two years in prison before the trial should be counted in as sentence that might be imposed, this promise is now ignored, and he is to serve his full four years from the date of the sentence. If sufficient funds can be raised an appeal will be lodged in his case, and, if possible, in other cases also. For this purpose it will be necessary to raise about £1,000 within the next sixty days.

---

44. Hutchinson was an Englishman from Manchester. He was arrested in 1929, three months after the other 31 Meerut prisoners. He spent four years in jail awaiting trial and sentence. On appeal he was found not guilty. He was active in the anti-colonial movement and wrote several books about India's struggle for independence, including *Conspiracy at Meerut* (Ayer, 1972). He was elected to Parliment in 1945.

The accusation of Communism by the prosecution has obscured the issue, as it was intended to do. The real issue is trade unionism. Wages in the jute mills are in general under six shillings a week, while profits have frequently amounted to between 20 percent and 40 percent, and sometimes even 100 percent. The real crime of the Meerut prisoners was that they resisted reduction of these very low wages.

This year the British trade unions are to celebrate the centenary of the famous case of the Dorchester labourers who, for an almost identical crime, were sentenced to almost identical penalties. The Government has already celebrated the centenary by repeating the crime of the Government of that day.

Contributions towards the expenses of an appeal should be sent to Mrs. Annabel Williams Ellis, Romney House, Hollybush Hill, Hampstead N.W. 3.

Bertrand Russell
47 Emperor's Gate, S.W.7

[80]

## Indian Prisoners

*The Manchester Guardian* (20th April, 1933), p. 18 | C33.33

*As Chairman of the India League, Russell makes a plea for support for civil rights in India and calls attention to the repressive nature of "British imperialism" in that country.*

Sir, —There is little hope that the policy which is being pursued by our Government will lead to a peaceful settlement with India. Meanwhile, repression, imprisonments, ill-treatment of prisoners, and unrest continue.

It is necessary that public opinion should be awakened to the facts of the situation in India and to the character of British Imperialism.

There should be emphatic protests against political persecution and imprisonments and an insistent demand for freedom for the Indians.

The India League would be glad to receive the support of all those, in different parts of the country, who are in agreement with these aims, and I hope that many of your readers will write and offer us their help.

—Yours &c., Bertrand Russell,
Chairman, the India League.
145, Strand. London, W.C. 2, April 18.

# Education

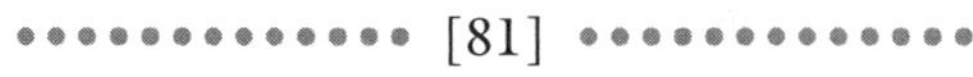

[81]

## "Freudianism"

*The Literary Guide and Rationalist Review* (February, 1929), p. 44 | C29.04

*Russell offers a qualified defense of Freud. When he says that the truth of some of Freud's "fantastic" doctrines is confirmed by his own "experiences with young children", Russell is no doubt referring to his experiences at Beacon Hill School, which he and Dora had been operating for a little over a year. J. M. Robertson (1856–1933) was a widely published Victorian scholar. Barbara Low was an early popularizer of Freud and author of* Psychoanalysis in Education *(Harcourt, Brace, 1928). See below, document [85].*

As a constant reader of the *Literary Guide*, I am writing to you to suggest that its tone is somewhat unduly hostile to Freud. I am moved to this the more by the article at the beginning of the January number by Mr. J.M. Robertson; but I have been on the point of writing earlier—for example, in connection with the review of Barbara Low which appeared a few months ago. Some of the hostile expressions of opinion which I have seen have struck me as ill-informed and prejudiced; indeed, I suspected that they were inspired by the belief that Freudianism leads to immorality, and that it is important to prove that Atheists are as virtuous as other men. Such motives are unscientific in judging the truth of a doctrine. I am myself by no means an out-and-out Freudian, and I have in the past criticized Freud somewhat severely; but experience with young children has led me to think that much of what appears fantastic in his psychology is nevertheless largely true. I quite agree that Freud does not, in his published works, prove the truth of his doctrines; but that is often very difficult for him owing to the fact that he has arrived at them through relations with his patients, which it is the duty of a medical man to treat as confidential. Consequently there is often more truth in what he says than one would suppose from reading his arguments. In any case, he is not a man whom it is rational to treat as some Rationalists treat him in the *Literary Guide*.

Bertrand Russell.
Harting, Petersfield, December 19, 1928

[82]

## "Mr. Russell Replies"

*The Nation* (11th December, 1929), p. 720 | C29.31

*Shortly after he arrived in New York on his fourth visit to the United States (25th September, 1929), Russell was quoted by* The New York Times *as saying that the scarcity of men teachers in the educational system was lamentable because "the scientific attitude toward life can scarcely be learned from women." This alleged quotation was vigorously protested by Mary Dudderidge of New York whose letter appeared above Russell's.*

Sir: The quotation given in Miss Dudderidge's letter is substantially correct. I would explain, however, that I say nothing as to women's congenital capacities—it is only women as hitherto educated that I regard as unscientific in outlook. So are most men, but not all. America seems to me to have less respect for the fact than any other civilized country, and I attribute this partly to feminine influence. I hold that children, from six on, should have at least one man among their teachers.

I'm afraid this explanation makes matters worse, but I shall probably be out of the country before there is time for maenads to tar and feather me.

New Orleans, November 11
Bertrand Russell

[83]

## "The Bertrand Russell School"

*Time and Tide* (3rd January, 1930), p. 12 | C30.01

*In this letter, and in the next three, Russell responds to various correspondents about the nature of discipline and freedom at the Russells' Beacon Hill School.*

Sir, —In the course of Mr. St. John Ervine's Notes about Tolstoy and his wife in your issue of December 20th, I notice a remark about my wife and myself which seems to call for some comment. He appears to think that the principles upon which we run our school can be described as —"Back-to-Nature—Don't discipline-the-Child theories." It may possibly interest you to know that self-discipline, and more particularly intellectual discipline, is one of the main things taught in our school. It seems that at the school at which Mr. St. John Ervine was educated, "wammering" intellectuals (whatever that may mean) were not taught to ascertain the facts before expressing an opinion.

—Yours, etc., Bertrand Russell
Harting, Petersfield

[84]

## Free Speech in Childhood

*The New Statesman and Nation* (27th June, 1931), p. 575 | C31.08

*Russell responds to two correspondents regarding freedom and creativity at Beacon Hill. W. E. Williams was a scholar of English literature and author of a book on the poet William Wordsworth.*

Sir, —Two letters concerning Beacon Hill School in your issue of June 6th call for a few words of reply.

First, as regards Mr. Schofield's, the limitations of freedom which exist at Beacon Hill School are such as we have found necessary in the interests of health. We see to it that the children are clean twice a day, and that they get a sufficient length of time in bed. Neither of these things would happen if the children were left completely free, but neither entails any curtailment of free speech, and we find both easy to carry out without resort to punishment. During the first term of the school there was a certain difficulty in establishing the routine; but once established it continues through the force of habit and example.

As regards the letter of Mr. W.E. Williams, I should like to say that I have been surprised myself at the success of co-operative poetry. Some of the poems are individual, some are produced by two or three together, some by as many as four or five. The children all know each other so well that a kind of instinctive co-operation among them has become possible, such as I have seen described in anthropological accounts of the Melanesians and such people.

Take the case of the poem, "In the Graveyard," which was printed in your issue of May 30th. Having just seen a graveyard, the five concerned spontaneously decided they would like to write a poem on the subject. One of them contributed the idea of an old crone; another the idea of the love-bird. Even the tone of the poem is, I think, generally co-operative; certainly the detail was so. For the end of the third verse, for example, one child suggested: "One was her love-bird wild"; a second said, "That is too short"; a third said, "Yes, we must have another word with a 'w,'"; and the fourth suggested, "One was her love-bird weird and wild," which was adopted. I do not think this suggests the existence of a poetic Mussolini in the group.

May I suggest that Homer and the Authorised Version were not products of individual genius, and that the individualism of the artist is perhaps over-emphasised in modern times?

—Yours, etc., Bertrand Russell
Harting, Petersfield. June 8th, 1931.

[85]

## "Free Speech in Childhood"

*The New Statesman and Nation* (27th June, 1931), p. 643 | C31.09

*In this letter to the* New Statesman and Nation *Russell responds to two correspondents and defends Beacon Hill's approach to education against that of "conventional education" which all too often is dogmatic, unscientific, and "inspired by national, imperialist or commercial propaganda." See document [81].*

To the Editor of the New Statesman and Nation.

Sir, —I am interested by Miss Barbara Low's letter in your issue of June 20th, as it illustrates the tendency to dogmatism without experience from which even psycho-analysis is unable to free the victims of conventional education. Psycho-analysts, in the main, derive their ideas of childhood from the reminiscences of neurotics; those whose impressions are derived from direct contact with children, combined with careful observation, are regarded by the psycho-analysts as unscientific outsiders.

It really amazes me that any person professing a scientific outlook should at this date quote Samuel Butler[45] as an authority. He was an admirable writer, and a man of incomparable wit, but if Miss Low counts among her

45. Samuel Butler (1835–1902) was an English author best known for his utopian satire *Erewhon* (1872) and *The Way of All Flesh* (1903), a novel attacking Victorian family life. Butler also wrote some biological works challenging Darwin's theory of evolution, which he regarded as too mechanistic.

acquaintances any person with a competent education in biology, let her ask this person what is thought about Butler's views on heredity.

I suggest to Miss Low that before she dogmatises as to the emotions that are innate in children, she should try to observe children brought up in unusual environments. If the matter concerned sweet peas or green flies, or salamanders, this method would be adopted as a matter of course; but since it concerns children Miss Low feels free to dogmatise on data derived almost wholly from adults or from children in one kind of environment.

As for "cheap catchwords," let Miss Low read how Pavlov turned dogs into neurasthenics by applying to them the methods commonly applied to children, and let her study also the methods which he adopted for curing these victims of higher education.

In so far as M.R. Le Fleming attempts not to teach the customary national and class prejudices, my remarks on that subject clearly do not apply to him (or her?). But most of the current geography and history books for schools (which we find we cannot use) suggest to me that, if there are teachers of wider views, they are not very successful in making themselves felt in the educational world.

A recent attempt under this present Government to introduce better history and science books in State schools utterly failed.

Looking to a new teaching method—the cinema—we have found that the majority of films made available in libraries for small projectors are inspired by national, imperialist or commercial propaganda. If the children happen to be interested in something other than the American view of industry, or Empire marketing, it is not easy to provide for them.

The efforts of the few teachers who resemble M.R. Le Fleming will surely be helped rather than hindered by public denunciation of the manufacture of prejudiced matter for children. It is inescapable unless they are forbidden to read, or even to see.

—Yours, etc., Bertrand Russell
Beacon Hill School, Harting, Petersfield

## Free Speech in Childhood

*The New Statesman and Nation* (4th July, 1931), p. 11 | C31.11

Sir, —I am reluctant to trespass still further upon your space, but the letter of Richard Sellier Jefferies in your issue of June 27th calls for a few words of reply. He says: "The whole idea of Mr. Bertrand Russell's group creation seems to be quite unhealthy." The fact is that no grown-up person suggested group creation to the children, and we were as surprised as your readers appear to have been at the discovery that the children like to write poetry in this way.

Does Mr. Jefferies suggest that I should punish them whenever they write a collective poem, on the ground that what they have been doing is unhealthy?

—Yours, etc., Bertrand Russell
Beacon Hill School, Harting, Petersfield. June 27th

[87]

## Changes on the School Front

*Time and Tide* (19th May, 1934), p. 641 | C34.22

*In June of 1932 Russell and Dora separated. Dora continued to run the school until the outbreak of World War II, although not at Telegraph House. At the time of this letter Russell and Dora were going through a bitter divorce which was finally concluded in 1935. Russell and Patricia ('Peter') Spence were married in 1936, and she gave birth to Russell's third child, Conrad Sebastian Robert, in 1937.*

Sir, —With regard to your paragraph about Beacon Hill School in the current issue, I have two observations to make:

(1) I have had no connection with the school since June 1932, and nothing that I may write now is to be taken as expressing the present policy of the school.

(2) While I was connected with the school, it was run in accordance with the principles which I lately expressed in the *New Statesman*,[46] and which you regard as a new departure. This would be known to anyone who had either (a) visited the school (at any rate before June 1932) or (b) read my earlier writing on education. The only people to whom it would seem that there was a change in my views are those whose information is derived from sensational and intentionally misleading newspapers.

I am, etc., Bertrand Russell
The Hotel Portmeirion, Penryndeudraeth, N. Wales

46. Russell's article, 'Education and Civilisation', appeared in the *New Statesman and Nation* (5th May, 1934). It is reprinted in his *In Praise of Idleness* (Unwin, 1935).

# Miscellaneous

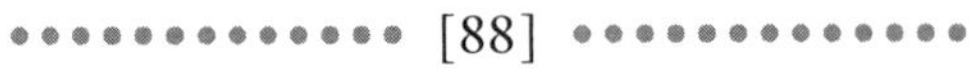

## "Mr. Bertrand Russell and the Japanese Press"

*Japan Weekly Chronicle* (8th September, 1921), p. 356 | C21.14

*Russell and Dora visited Japan for twelve days on their way home from China. Russell's annoyance with some elements of the Japanese press is evident. What he doesn't mention is that it was the Japanese press that circulated reports of his death in March. In Tokyo Russell, not yet fully recovered from his illness, was hard pressed by reporters for an interview. Dora finally drove them off by pointing out that since he was, by their own reports, deceased, he could not give an interview.*

Sir, —I learn both from your columns and from other sources that my brief visit to Japan gave rise to a number of statements in the Press, some of them merely inaccurate, others pure fabrications. As an example of the latter, I may mention that a newspaper called the *Chuo*, on July 29th, printed what purported to be a message from me to the Japanese nation. I had given no such message, nor made any statement remotely resembling the sentiments attributed to me. You mention also an assertion that I showed no desire to get in touch with the labour movement in Kobe. So far is this from being the truth that I returned from Osaka on purpose, had a long conversation with Mr. Kagawa,[47] saw something of the poorer quarters of Kobe, and addressed a meeting of strikers. None of this would have been possible if I had not escaped momentarily from the persecutions of reporters by a sudden change of plans.

The Press of Japan were informed that both Miss Black and I were in bad health, but they took no account of this fact, and never mentioned it in their complaints. The Doctor in Peking who was attending us both was convinced that we ought to return to England, but doubtful whether we could stand the journey. He was only led to sanction it when it appeared that Miss Power,[48] with very great kindness, was willing to cancel her passage by another route and accompany us as far as Vancouver, in order to

47. Toyohiko Kagawa (1888–1960) was a Japanese Christian social worker. He was imprisoned for his pro-labor activities in 1921 and arrested for pacifism in World War II.

48. Eileen Edna Le Poer Power (1889–1940) was a friend of Dora's from Girton College, Cambridge, where she was a medieval historian.

minimise the fatigues of travelling. It is very unfortunate that her kindness has exposed her also to annoyance.

I stated repeatedly that I was willing to give interviews to Labour or Socialist newspapers, but I saw no reason to sacrifice health in order to make money for capitalist journals. However, I devoted two hours to a collective interview with all journalists who cared to come at the appointed time. Apart from this occasion and the brief speech in Kobe mentioned above, I made only two statements for publication, namely a lecture in Tokyo and a short written message to a Yuai-kai meeting. No other pretended statement is genuine.

It is clear that the Press of Japan imagines it is imitating Western methods, and does not know what damage it does to its country. I found much to admire in Japan, particularly its energy, the remarkably thorough erudition of its professors, and the spirit of many of the young men. But I was entirely prevented from having any conversation with some of the most interesting men whom I met, owing to the interruptions of flashlight photographers. These boys caused serious injury to Miss Black's health, which is doubtless considered a small matter in Japan, where women are of no account. But no other civilised country will share this opinion.

—Yours, etc., Bertrand Russell.
SS. Empress of Asia: August 3, 1921.

••••••••••••• [89] •••••••••••••

## ["Tuchuns", Not "Teachers"].

*The Atlantic Monthly* (March 1922), p. 431 | C22.06

*Russell had a great sense of humor, as the following brief letter to the* Atlantic Monthly *shows.*

Dear Atlantic, —Would you kindly correct a misprint on p. 774 of your December number? You make me say: 'The Government had just spent nine million dollars in corrupt payments to three teachers who had descended upon the capital to extort blackmail.' Instead of 'teachers,' it should be 'Tuchuns,' i.e. Military Governors. I am afraid that, if you do not correct the misprint, China will be flooded with impecunious members of the scholastic profession, under the impression that it is an Eldorado.

Yours, etc., Bertrand Russell.

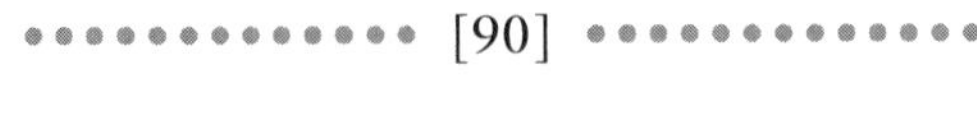

[90]

## Snobbery

*The New Statesman and Nation* (25th June, 1932), p. 824 | C32.39

*Russell became Lord Russell (the third Earl Russell) when his older brother Frank, the second Earl Russell, died in 1931. In this letter Russell eschews public use of the title.*

Sir, —By an inadvertence for which I am not responsible, my signature appears in your issue of June 18th as "Russell." Ever since, through no fault of my own, I became a peer, I have been trying to persuade my snobbish countrymen not to use my title, but it is up-hill work. I shall therefore be grateful if you will publish this letter.

Bertrand Russell
Carn Voel, Porthcurno, Penzance.

[91]

## Art and Sex-Appeal

*Time and Tide* (17th October, 1936), pp. 1, 44 | C36.27

*Russell writes in defense of John Yerbury Dent's* Reactions of the Human Machine *against an "illiberal" review by Geoffrey Gorer.*[49]

Sir, —I was distressed to read in your usually liberal Review such illiberal sentiments as those expressed by Mr. Geoffrey Gorer in his notice of Dr. Dent's "Reactions of the Human Machine." Mr. Gorer apparently holds that any person whose views differ from his own must be a fool, and should be prevented from publishing. "It would appear," he says, "that Dr. Dent is a general practitioner;" the tone implies that Mr. Gorer is a Harley Street specialist. Is this the case?

Though I do not subscribe to all Dr. Dent's opinions, I consider his book excellent; and, unlike Mr. Gorer, I do not think that nothing with which I disagree should be published. What right has Mr. Gorer to his lofty tone of superior wisdom? "It is such books as this," he says,

49. Geoffrey Gorer was an anthropologist and author whose published works included *The Life and Ideas of the Marquis de Sade.*

"which make one wonder whether a state censorship which would stop the publication of misleading and inaccurate statements as though they were facts would be altogether an unmitigated evil." Mr. Gorer's objection to the publication of statements which he finds startling or considers inaccurate would be more defensible if he himself never ventured upon rash and disputable assertions as, for example, his contention (in your issue of July 25th) that "sex-appeal is a respectable and even desirable component of most works of art." This may or may not be true; but Mr. Gorer should remember when expressing such opinions that they would be more liable to the censorship he advocates than any of those of Dr. Dent, some of whose remarks he seems to have been unable to understand.

For my part, while I admit that artistic merit and sex-appeal are not infrequently conjoined, I consider that they have no inherent connection, and that each often exists without the other. No one ever pretends that "sex-appeal" is usually accompanied by artistic merit: why, therefore, assume the converse? The examples that Mr. Gorer chooses to support his thesis lack force because they are obviously exceptional; they prove nothing about "most works of art." Other examples chosen at random could be used to support an equally sweeping and less untrue assertion on the other side. How about the Parthenon? How about Chinese painting; the poems of Po Chui, Milton, Dante, Leopardi, and a thousand others? How about Bach and Rembrandt, Titian's portrait of Charles V and Bellini's portrait of the Doge Loredano? If these arouse sexual emotion in Mr. Gorer he must be in a bad way; if he says they do not, is he, to use his own phrase, "decadent, unhealthy and suspect"? In either case few people would think it worth while to prevent him from "airing his views."

I am, etc., Bertrand Russell
Telegraph House, Harting, Petersfield.

## [92]

# The Amberley Papers

*The Times Literary Supplement* (20th March, 1937), p. 222 | C37.09

The Amberley Papers *(a mammoth work of two volumes each over 500 pages) concerns the lives of Russell's parents, Lord and Lady Amberley, who died when he was an infant. Russell is anxious to see that his new wife, Patricia 'Peter' Spence, with whom he wrote the book, gets due recognition.*

Sir —The kind review of "The Amberley Papers" in *The Times Literary Supplement* of March 13 is such as to give great pleasure to the editors, not only by its praise, but by its sympathetic understanding of their purpose and subject. There is, however, one point which ought, perhaps to have been made clear in the preface, as to which I feel that some explanation is called for. Your reviewer treats the work as more mine and less my wife's than is in fact the case. She did more than half, not only of the very considerable drudgery, but of the selecting, arranging and annotating. For example, the last chapter, which your reviewer singles out for praise, was entirely my wife's work; and, indeed, the whole book is so unlike my usual work that I should never have attempted it alone.

Bertrand Russell

PART IV

# World War II and the Early Cold War

(1939–1953)

Bertrand Russell

Towards the end of 1938, Russell, his third wife Patricia ('Peter') Spence and their 17-month-old son Conrad, came to the United States where Russell taught philosophy briefly at the University of Chicago and at UCLA before becoming embroiled in the controversy over his appointment at City College of New York in 1940. This controversy was bitter and exposed Russell to much personal abuse by certain sectors of the conservative community. For a while he found himself unable to get a job—he was too controversial for most academic institutions to hire—and cut off from England which was in the throes of World War II.

Shortly after the City College case, Russell, by this time unable to accept the pacifist arguments he had set forth in his 1936 *Which Way To Peace?*, publicly repudiated his opposition to the war in Europe in a long letter to *The New York Times*. He and his family remained in the U.S. until they returned to England in 1944, and Russell was soon reinstated as a Fellow at Cambridge University.

Russell's concern for civil and human rights is very much in evidence during this period. Several of his letters concern the plight and suffering of German civilians in the immediate post-war situation. He also addresses the subject of Indian independence in three letters. But his most intense focus regarding civil liberties is his worry over the rise of McCarthyism in the United States, despite his personal dislike in the early post-war years of Communism and Soviet Russia. Russell defends Albert Einstein's public opposition to the investigation by the "new Holy Office into the lives and opinions of American citizens," and he strongly criticizes what he sees as a growing attack on freedom in America.

But this period is also the one which saw the advent of the atomic bomb and the danger of nuclear war—matters which formed the focus of much of his life's work after World War II. Russell, along with Einstein, was one of the first to see clearly the threat to human civilization in the nuclear age if war were not abolished. During the first few years after the Second World War, we see Russell weighing the evils of nuclear war and Soviet Communism. And though he briefly thought the U.S. ought to use its temporary monopoly on the Bomb to force the Soviets to accede to world government, by the early 1950s he was emphasizing peaceful coexistence and the paramount importance of avoiding nuclear holocaust. His changing ideas on the role of nuclear weapons during these years were set forth in many articles. But Russell also made important use of the letter to the editor to explain his evolving ideas regarding nuclear weapons and to defend himself against the charges by some of his critics that he favored war with Russia.

# Human Rights and Civil Liberties

[93]

## Bertrand Russell Explains

*The New York Times* (26th April, 1940), p. 20 | C40.06

*This letter was written at the end of the two-month controversy surrounding Russell's appointment (by the city's Board of Higher Education) to the College of the City of New York—an appointment which was ultimately revoked on grounds that Russell was morally unfit to teach. According to Justice McGeehan's verdict of 30th March, Russell's books were filled with "immoral and salacious doctrines," and his appointment would establish "a chair of indecency" at City College. The Board's and Russell's plans for appeal (supported by the Committee for Cultural Freedom, the American Civil Liberties Union, the City College Department of Philosophy and the Student Council) were thwarted by Mayor La Guardia and Judge McGeehan who refused to allow Russell to intervene.*[1]

*Russell writes from the University of California at Los Angeles where he was completing a one-year position teaching philosophy. Russell justifies his efforts to sustain his City College appointment on civil libertarian grounds. In the Bertrand Russell Archives, one copy of this clipping is labeled "P", suggesting that Peter Spence, Russell's third wife, may have written it.*

To the Editor of *The New York Times:*

I hope you will allow me to comment on your references to the controversy originating in my appointment to the College of the City of New York, and particularly on your judgment that I "should have had the wisdom to retire from the appointment as soon as its harmful effects became evident."

In one sense this would have been the wisest course; it would certainly have been more prudent as far as my personal interests are concerned, and a great deal pleasanter. If I had considered only my own interests and inclinations I should have retired at once.

1. An excellent acount of the Russell City College case may be found in Thom Weidlich's *Appointment Denied: The Inquisition of Bertrand Russell* (Prometheus, 2000).

But however wise such action might have been from a personal point of view, it would also, in my judgment, have been cowardly and selfish. A great many people who realized that their own interests and the principles of toleration and free speech were at stake were anxious from the first to continue the controversy. If I had retired I should have robbed them of their *casus belli* and tacitly assented to the proposition that substantial groups shall be allowed to drive out of public office individuals whose opinion, race or nationality they find repugnant. This to me would appear immoral.

It was my grandfather who brought about the repeal of the English Test and Corporation Acts, which barred from public office any one not a member of the Church of England, of which he himself was a member, and one of my earliest and most important memories is of a deputation of Methodists and Wesleyans coming to cheer outside his window on the fiftieth anniversary of this repeal, although the largest single group affected was Catholic.

I do not believe that the controversy is harmful on general grounds. It is not controversy and open difference of opinion that endanger democracy. On the contrary, these are its greatest safeguards. It is an essential part of democracy that substantial groups, even majorities, should extend toleration to dissentient groups, however small and however much their sentiments may be outraged.

In a democracy it is necessary that people should learn to endure having their sentiments outraged. Minority groups already endure this, although according to the principles of the founders of the American Constitution they are equally entitled to consideration. If there is 10 per cent of the population of New York that holds opinions similar to mine, then 10 per cent of the teachers in New York should be allowed to hold those opinions. And this should apply to all unusual opinions. If it is once admitted that there are opinions toward which such tolerance need not extend, then the whole basis of toleration is destroyed.

Jews have been driven from Germany and Catholics most cruelly persecuted because they were repugnant to the substantial part of the community which happened to be in power.

Bertrand Russell
Los Angeles

[94]

## Mass Deportations

*The Times* (23rd October, 1945),
p. 5 | C45.20

*In this, and in the following two letters, amidst the assessment of German war crimes, Russell calls attention to the crimes being carried out against the civilian refugee population of eastern Europe by "our allies."*

Sir, —In your leading article of October 19 you refer to the third count of the indictment of German war criminals which deals with an "immense array of charges of murder and rapine, including mass deportations and the murder of hostages" and the fourth count which includes crimes against humanity such as " the attempt to exterminate the Jews". In eastern Europe now mass deportations are being carried out by our allies on an unprecedented scale and an apparently deliberate attempt is being made to exterminate many millions of Germans not by gas but by depriving them of their homes and of food, leaving them to die by slow and agonized starvation. This is not done in an act of war but as part of a deliberate policy of "peace".

Is it possible for the British nation, with its tradition of humanity, to watch these trails without shame while in the words of a British officer now in Berlin "we acquiesce in the perpetration by our allies of these very injustices against which we have so recently fought." Are mass deportations crimes when committed by our enemies during war and justifiable measures of social adjustment when carried out by our allies in time of peace? Is it more humane to turn out old women and children to die at a distance than to asphyxiate Jews in gas chambers? Can those responsible for the deaths of those who die after expulsion be regarded as less guilty because they do not see or hear the agonies of their victims? Are the future laws of war to justify the killing of enemy nationals after any resistance has ceased?

These are questions discussed far more in England now than the past sins of the Nazis. It was decreed by the Potsdam agreement that expulsions of Germans should be carried out "in a humane and orderly manner." And it is well known both through published accounts and through letters received in the numerous British families which have relatives or friends in the armies of occupation that this proviso has not been observed by our Russian and Polish allies. It is right that expression should be given to the immense public indignation that has resulted and that our allies should know that British friendship may well be completely alienated by the continuation of this policy.

I am, Sir, yours faithfully, Russell
Trinity College, Cambridge, Oct. 19

[95]

## Mass Deportations

The Times (31st October, 1945), p. 5 | C45.21

Sir, — Mr. J. H. Flexman accuses me of exaggeration in suggesting that an apparently deliberate attempt is being made by our Russian and Polish allies to exterminate many millions of Germans. He also remarks that I produce no evidence.[2]

Evidence of the scale of these deportations has for some months been freely available to Mr. Flexman as to myself. That a large proportion of those deported must die this winter unless the western allies rescue them is obvious, since the food available in Germany is officially admitted to be only enough for bare sustenance for the population already there. Indeed there is no reason to doubt that the Russians know how bare the German bone is picked. Mr. Flexman thinks it is better for these people to be deported to or within Germany than to slave labour abroad. This is a matter of opinion. I gather from Mr. Bevin's speech in last Friday's debate that an unknown number of men have in fact been deported "to work in Russia"; it is only the women and children who are turned loose in Germany. It is, I fear, unlikely that many families so separated will in future be reunited and enabled to compare notes that would provide evidence for Mr. Flexman.

As to our acquiescence: our Government has made representations it is true. It has not made a public protest, although a flagrant breach of the Potsdam agreement[3] has been committed. Moreover, governmental representations have not been adequately supported by public opinion. It is

2. Flexman's letter had appeared in *The Times* on 26th October.

3. The Potsdam agreement resulted from a meeting (17th July–2nd August, 1945) of the principal allies in World War II. It provided for the occupation and demilitarization of Germany.

frequently said that the entire German nation is responsible for the horrors of Belsen and Buchenwald[4] which were committed in its name. This contention is unjust, since the facts were never fully made public, and the penalties for criticism were more than the bravest man could be expected to face. The facts in this case are accessible to anyone who cares to know them, and there are no penalties for criticism. Every thoughtful man and woman, therefore, who knows these facts and makes no protest acquiesces no only in cruelty but in a breach of faith, and in the hypocrisy of condoning in our allies the deeds that fill us with such horror when committed by our enemies.

I have no doubt that courageous action in Great Britain and America could halt these expulsions until provision can be made for them to be carried out in a "humane and orderly manner." Fear of friction prevents courageous action. But friction now would be not only less distasteful but ultimately less harmful than a deliberate choice of cowardice and hypocrisy.

I am Sir, yours faithfully, Russell
Trinity College, Cambridge, Oct.27

[96]

## Food Parcels Still Needed

*The New York Times* (3rd November, 1945), p. 14 | C45.23

To the Editor of *The New York Times:*

Together with the Master of Balliol, Prof. Gilbert Murray,[5] and others, we recently addressed an appeal to the British public, calling attention to the desperate plight of the Germans, mainly old men, women and children, who have been expelled from their homes in eastern Germany and the Sudetenland. Many are dying; many millions, it has been stated in responsible papers, will die this winter if nothing is done. Burgomasters have been instructed to have graves dug now, since the people will be too weak to dig them in a few months' time.

---

4. Belsen and Buchenwald were sites of notorious concentration camps under the Hitler regime.

5. Gilbert Murray (1866–1957) was an Oxford classical scholar and a life-long friend of Russell.

In response to this appeal many people have signified their willingness to have their rations cut, "if, thereby alone men, women and children of whatever nationality may be saved from intolerable suffering." Many others ask for abolition of the present ban on voluntary gifts of food to Europe, which might be sent as and when they could be spared.

Meanwhile some of us still receive food parcels from the United States, which we are not allowed to pass on to those whose need is so much greater. These gifts from our American friends have been a most welcome addition to our austere but adequate diet; but there are, we feel sure, few people in England who can comfortably accept little luxuries which are not strictly necessary while they know that not far away children cry for bread. We therefore suggest that those who acquired the habit of sending food parcels to England while other countries were inaccessible should send them now, through a relief organization, to be distributed wherever they are most needed.

Bertrand Russell,
George Cicestr (Bishop of Chichester),
Victor Gollancz[6]
Cambridge, England, Oct. 11, 1945

••••••••••••• [97] •••••••••••••

## Science and Democracy

*The Listener* (6th February, 1947), p. 245 | C47.03

*Upon his return from the United States, Russell enjoyed a brief period of respectability in England which included invitations to participate in BBC broadcasts. Russell gave a talk on the BBC Third Programme entitled 'Science and Democracy' on January 5th, printed in* The Listener *(16th January) as 'A Scientist's Plea for Democracy'. The following is a response to three letters in the* Listener *of January 30th concerning Russell's BBC talk.*

Sir, —Three letters in *The Listener* of January 30 call for some reply from me.

6. Victor Gollancz, a renowned publisher, was a leader in the effort to bring relief to post-war European refugees. He later played an important role in the British anti-nuclear movement.

First, Mr. H. Perry's and Mr. Blatchley's remarks on genetics in Soviet Russia express a view widely held in this country, but not borne out by the facts. For English readers, the facts are set forth, objectively and impartially, in *The New Genetics in the Soviet Union,* by Hudson and Rickens (Cambridge School of Agriculture). I do not think that any candid reader of this report can doubt the accuracy of what I said on the subject. The work of Lysenko, whom the Soviet Government has supported, has a very slender experimental basis, and relies to a very large extent upon its metaphysical Marxist orthodoxy. To criticise Lysenko in Russia is dangerous; his scientific opponents are apt to disappear mysteriously.

As regards 'inculcating stupidity', I will not be lured into saying anything favourable to the Tsarist government, but I should like to point out, in connection with the increase of literacy, that modern methods of causing populations to accept unquestioningly dogmas for which there is no evidence are only effective where most people can read. There are people in this country who regard as gospel truth whatever their favourite newspaper says, with the result, not infrequently, that their opinions are even more stupid that if they were illiterate. If there were no diversity among newspapers, this result would be much more marked that it is.

On the other hand I agree with Mr. Perry that the Soviet Government has been admirable in dealing with Asiatic race problems. As for ossification, which I predict, that is a process that takes time.

Miss Marion Towndrow considers that I am unjust to Mary Wollstonecraft[7] in saying that the earliest advocates of the equality of women were 'mostly male'. I think my statement is numerically correct, and I certainly had no intention of belittling Mary Wollstonecraft. But she stood alone. Bentham,[8] though timidly, was a convert, and J.S. Mill,[9] at an early age, acquired his opinions from Bentham. It was through J.S. Mill that the movement first acquired political strength.

Yours, etc., Bertrand Russell
Cambridge

---

7. Mary Wollstonecraft (1759–97) was an English writer and feminist. Her *Vindication of the Rights of Woman* (1792) was one of the earliest great feminist documents.

8. Jeremy Bentham (1748–1832) was an English philosopher and founder of utilitarianism, according to which the goal of social ethics is to achieve the greatest good (or pleasure) of the greatest number of people.

9. John Stuart Mill (1806–73) was an English philosopher in the empirical tradition. His writings include *On Liberty* (1859), *The Subjection of Women* (1869), and *Utilitarianism* (1863). He was also Bertrand Russell's secular godfather.

[98]

## A Philosopher Gone Astray

*The Gates of Zion* (July, 1948), p. 32 | C48.17

*Russell's lectures at the Barnes Foundation shortly after his denial of appointment at City College, led to his book,* A History of Western Philosophy *(1945), one of the most popular works in philosophy and a welcome source of income for Russell. Russell responds to J. Litvin's review of his book which appeared in the July issue of* The Gates of Zion.

Dear Sir, Thank you for your letter and for the two numbers of *The Gates of Zion.*

I do not wonder that the intolerable sufferings of the Jews ever since 1933 have produced a mood of hysteria, but it is a pity when this takes the form of hostility to their warmest friends. I was a pacifist in the first world war, but not in the second; my horror of the Nazi anti-Semitism was one of the chief causes of my different opinion. Your reviewer never so much as mentions that, in my book, I call Spinoza the most lovable of the great philosophers. He is annoyed because I speak of Jews in modern times as having contributed individually. But no one can say that e.g. Spinoza or Einstein wrote as Jews.

As for Maimonides, what I say is taken from generally accepted authorities. If there is evidence that it is false, I will gladly correct it. But Jews, like other people, are not always at first receptive of new prophets, and no person who had a Christian upbringing can be expected to believe that they are. This is no peculiar demerit on their part. Even Aquinas, now the standard of orthodoxy, was at first banned both at Paris and at Oxford.

It may be true that I have given too little space to Jewish philosophers. If so, this is due entirely to my ignorance of Hebrew, which I regret.

Please believe me that you are wholly and completely in error in supposing that I have any hostile feeling towards the Jews.

Yours truly, Bertrand Russell
27 Dorset House, Gloucester Place, N.W.1.

•••••••••••• [99] ••••••••••••

## Professor Bernal

*The Manchester Guardian* (20th October, 1949), p. 4 | C49.26

*J.D. Bernal was an eminent British scientist and a prominent and active Communist. He was a founder and former president of the World Federation of Scientific Workers, and he played an important role in the world peace movement in the 1950s and 1960s. In 1955 he helped Russell bring together eminent scientists from Communist and non-Communist countries in support of the Russell-Einstein Manifesto denouncing nuclear weapons and war as instruments of national policy.*

*After his 1920 visit to Russia, Russell became a consistent critic of Soviet Communism. His anti-Soviet views were especially marked in the late 1940s and early 1950s. Then the Soviet possession of nuclear weapons and the advent of the H-bomb convinced him that nuclear war posed a greater danger to humankind than Communism.*

*In this letter, and in the next two, Russell criticizes Bernal and Soviet repression.*

Sir, —In your issue of October 17, Professor Bernal, speaking of the freedom of scientists in Russia, is reported as saying: "Those who were uncompromisingly opposed to Lysenko's theories had been given work in other fields." This is a charming and novel euphemism. I hope that, if the American Communists now on trial are condemned to penal servitude, Professor Bernal will be content to say that "they have been given work in other fields."

Yours, &c., Bertrand Russell
Festiniog, North Wales. October 17

•••••••••••• [100] ••••••••••••

## Professor Bernal

*Manchester Guardian* (26th October, 1949), p. 4 | C49.27

Sir, —Professor Bernal's evasive letter in your issue of October 24 calls for a few words of reply. Those who are not in the confidence of the Soviet Government cannot quickly ascertain facts which it wishes to conceal. I will therefore confine myself to a case old enough to be incontrovertible—the case of N.I. Vavilov.[10]

Which of the following facts does Professor Bernal deny?

1. Vavilov fell from favour because he disagreed with the Russian Government on a purely scientific question.

2. When in 1942, he was elected a foreign member of the Royal Society, Sir Henry Dale, as its president, vainly endeavoured to ascertain his whereabouts, and received no reply to official inquiries addressed to the Soviet Government.

3. He was arrested in 1941, and was seen in a concentration camp at Saratov.

4. He was sent to forced labour in the Arctic, where he died in 1942 or 1943.

I like Professor Bernal's argument that "it will be far more comfortable for all of us if we try to get on with them" (the Soviet Government). What a pity that Vavilov overlooked this obvious truth! It would have been "far more comfortable" for Christian martyrs if they had "tried to get on" with Roman emperors, and for Karl Marx if he had "tried to get on" with the Prussian authorities. But Marx is a back number among Marxists.

Yours &c., Bertrand Russell
Festiniog, October 24

[101]

## Professor Bernal

*The Manchester Guardian* (25th November, 1949), p. 6 | C49.28

Sir, —Professor Bernal's letter in your issue of November 22 calls for a few words of reply. The facts concerning Vavilov are set forth in Langdon-Davies's "Russia Puts Back the Clock," p. 116ff. Professor Bernal says the evidence is inconclusive because it comes from anti-Soviet sources. Of course it does. Professor Bernal would have us disbelieve everything about Russia except what the Soviet Government itself announces. He offers us two alternative hypotheses as to Vavilov's death,

10. Nikolai Ivanovich Vavilov (1887–1943) was a Russian botanist who opposed Lysenko's theory of heredity. He died in a Soviet concentration camp, but was rehabilitated by the Soviet government in 1956, after which his works were republished.

but does not explain why the Soviet authorities have never suggested either.

I am comforted to learn that "it is neither the policy nor in the interests of the Soviet Government to impose" its rule upon us. I hope he will let us know how he has ascertained this. We should all breathe more freely if he could persuade us of it.

Yours, &c., Bertrand Russell
November 22

••••••••••••• [102] •••••••••••••

## Bertrand Russell and the U.S.

*The Manchester Guardian* (12th January, 1952), p. 4 | C52.01

*In November 1950 Russell was on lecture tour in the United States where he learned, while at Princeton, that he was to be the 1950 recipient of the Nobel prize in literature. On October 20, 1951 Russell was back in the U.S. for another (three-week) lecture tour. He stirred up considerable controversy defending the British version of socialism while criticizing Soviet repression and lamenting what he saw as America's slide toward anti-Communist fanaticism which he perceived as a threat to civil liberty. He wrote a critical piece on the state of Indiana's school system which was reprinted in* The Manchester Guardian Weekly *(1st November, 1951) as 'Democracy and the Teachers in the United States'. This article drew fire from several readers. The following two letters are Russell's replies to two critical American academics.*

Sir, —Mr. William Henry Chamberlin,[11] in your issue of January 8, takes me to task for some remarks of mine about America. I should like to suggest, to begin with, that, living in the safe haven of Harvard, he probably knows little of average America, and would feel as alien as I do if planted down in the Middle West.

I will concede at once that the reign of terror in America is far less severe than in Russia, but I will not concede that it is non-existent. Apart from legal penalties there are economic penalties which cause acute apprehension. And it is now the law that prospective federal employees

11. William Henry Chamberlin (1897–1969) was an American journalist and author of many books on Soviet Russia and Japan.

must prove innocence; it is not necessary for the authorities to prove "guilt." Even legal penalties are to be feared: the Attorney-General has prepared vast lists of persons to be interned whenever, in his opinion, such a course shall seem wise.

Mr. Chamberlin's remarks about Jefferson surprise me. He mentions, as if it were relevant, that Jefferson "never stood higher in general American esteem." Christ stands almost equally high, but everyone knows that it is dangerous to quote the Sermon on the Mount in wartime. As for Jefferson, I commend the following quotations:

"A little rebellion, now and then, is a good thing, and as necessary in the political world as storms in the physical. . . It is a medicine necessary for the sound health of government," (Letter to James Madison, January 30, 1787. The rebellion concerned was in America, not in Europe.)

"What country can preserve its liberties, if its rulers are not warned from time to time, that this people preserve the spirit of resistance? Let them take arms . . . The tree of liberty must be refreshed from time to time with the blood of patriots and tyrants." (Letter to Colonel Smith, son-in-law of the second President, November 13, 1787.)

But for considerations of space I could multiply such quotations indefinitely.

Every alien wishing to visit America has to declare on oath his disagreement with such sentiments. And I think that if Mr. Chamberlin were to state (without mentioning that he is quoting Jefferson) that the United States ought to have rebellions oftener than once every 150 years he would secure the attention of the F.B.I. even in Cambridge, Mass.

I am amazed by what he says about Pitt and Burke in 1793 and 1794, particularly coming, as it does, after praise of Jefferson, who vigorously disapproved of their attitude. Does Mr. Chamberlin regret that Pitt failed to catch and hang Tom Paine? I quite agree that Pitt, that sinister Tory, said things that sound topical now, if one places them in the mouth of an American Republican. For my part, I was brought up in childhood to execrate Pitt, and see no reason to change.

In conclusion, I cannot agree that the first step in war for liberty should be the surrender of what you say you are fighting for.

—Yours &c., Bertrand Russell
Richmond, Surrey, January 9

[103]

## Russell and the U.S.

The Manchester Guardian (1st March, 1952), p. 4 | C52.04

*In this long letter Russell responds to Professor Eugene Bird's response to his* Manchester Guardian *piece referred to in the previous letter. Russell elaborates on his fears about the rise of illiberality in the U.S. including "Senator McCarthy's irresponsible accusations."*

Sir, —The interesting letter which you published in your issue of February 26 from Professor Eugene H. Bird of the University of Oregon demands some reply.

He has three accusations against me of (1) cultural snobbery, (2) over-simplification, (3) publishing criticism of America in English rather that American newspapers. His letter contains not one single fact concerning America except that he lives on the Pacific coast, and even that one fact does not seem to have registered since he has apparently never heard of the University of California.

I have noticed in all those Americans who take the same line as Professor Bird a considerable shyness about facts. Those who champion the victims of oppression are quickly inundated with facts, and one is led to the conclusion that the orthodox succeed in not knowing the facts. I must repeat what I have said before, that I do not for a moment suggest that the reign of terror in present-day America is anything like as bad as the reign of terror in Nazi Germany or in Soviet Russia. But where I do perceive a very disquieting parallel is in the ignorance of the general public as to what is occurring. Most Americans professed indignant incredulity when the Germans said that they had not known what went on in Nazi concentration camps. Their own ignorance of what goes on in America should show that such Germans may have been quite sincere. Most of the cases of oppression that occur in America cannot be publicised since any victim who did so would be even more severely victimised.

It is only those who have private incomes who can let the world know what they have suffered. Take, for example, a letter which appeared in the "Saturday Review of Literature" on February 23 from Dr. Burnham P. Beckwith, an economist who, after giving up a Federal position bringing him in £10,000 a year in order to write a book on price theory, was unable after writing the book to obtain re-employment because in the opinion of the authorities there is a reasonable doubt as to whether there is a reasonable doubt of his loyalty. Although he had never been a Communist or a fellow-traveller he is henceforth barred not only from government employment but from an academic post in the great majority of universities. He has not been informed of the ground on which he is suspect of being suspect and he has no method of redress. He is one of many thousands who are in this position, but most of them dare not mention their predicament.

Illiberality in America has reached proportions which are dangerous not only to mankind but even to the United States. Practically every American who has any knowledge of China has become disqualified from giving any assistance to the Government by Senator McCarthy's irresponsible accusations. Professors of economics who are told that it is their duty to indoctrinate the young against communism are considered subversive if they know what the doctrines of communism are: only those who have not read Marx are considered competent to combat his doctrines by the policemen who have professors at their mercy. To object to this, I am told is cultural snobbery. I suppose that, if I were not a culture snob, I should recognise at once that wisdom and virtue are only to be expected from ignorant hypocrites. Professor Bird takes me to task because I do not mention all the cases in which crimes have not been committed. There was a time when people made a fuss about the number of murders in Chicago, but it was not considered necessary to add that "of course there are many people in Chicago who are not murderers." When Dreyfus was sent to Devil's Island the world was shocked, and it was not considered that a Frenchman was giving an adequate defence if he said "Oh, but you ought to mention all the French Jews who are not in Devil's Island."

Professor Bird seems to think that when I protest against evils in America I do so because I am anti-American. This is not the case. There are in America a great many men and women for whom I have profound respect, and when I protest against what is being done I do so for their sake. Those who inflict the terror and those who pretend that it does not exist are attempting to destroy what is best in America and what every friend of America must wish to preserve. I have in my day protested with equal vigour against evils in my own country, but not because I hated my own country. At the present time whatever hopes there may be for humanity have to be centered upon America since America alone has enough power to resist the Soviet Government. But for that very reason not only America but the whole free world is vitally concerned in preserving freedom on America.

Professor Bird takes me to task for writing about American evils in English rather than in American newspapers. The first and most obvious answer is that it is extremely difficult to get letters accepted by most American newspapers except such as I should consider intolerably pro-Russian. And when I do succeed in getting published in America, I am exposed to editorial distortions without my knowledge or consent. I wrote an article for "Look" which I called "What is wrong with Anglo-American Relations". It was a balanced article attributing faults to both sides. To my amazement it appeared under the title "What is wrong with Americans," and owing to this change of title produced an effect totally different from what I had intended.[12] I have no wish whatever to damage Anglo-American relations. On the contrary, I think good relations between America and Britain quite enormously important. But there cannot be good relations if America does things which shock British opinion and refuses to know that British opinion has been shocked. The shocking things that are done in America are known in every country of the Eastern Hemisphere although most Americans remain unaware of them. It is no service to America to conceal the way that other countries feel about these things. I cannot remember any occasion since 1776 when Americans have concealed criticism of Britain. I do not blame them for this, but they should admit that liberty of criticism should be mutual.

Yours &c., Bertrand Russell
41 Queens Road, Richmond, Surrey, February 27

[104]

## Obeying Law in Testifying

*The New York Times* (26th June, 1953), p.18 | C53.13

*Russell expressed concern throughout the 1950s for what he perceived as a growing American receptivity to illiberal ideas and institutions, especially McCarthyism and the investigations of the House Committee on Un-American Activities. In this letter, and the next, Russell supports Einstein's refusal to testify before the Committee. This letter caused Einstein to reply two days later: "With your fine letter to* The New York Times *you have performed a great service for the good cause" (Einstein to Russell, 28th June, 1953).*

To the Editor of *The New York Times:*

In your issue of June 13 you have a leading article disagreeing with Einstein's view that teachers questioned by Senator McCarthy's emissaries should refuse to testify. You seem to maintain that one should always obey the law, however bad. I cannot think you have realized the implications of this position.

12. 'What's Wrong With Americans?', *Look* (24th April, 1951), pp. 34–35.

Do you condemn the Christian martyrs who refused to sacrifice to the emperor? Do you condemn John Brown? Nay, more, I am compelled to suppose that you condemn George Washington, and hold that your country ought to return to allegiance to Her Gracious Majesty Queen Elizabeth II. As a loyal Briton I of course applaud this view, but I fear it may not win much support in your country.

Bertrand Russell
London, June 15, 1953.

[105]

## Voice of Freedom

*The Nation* (15th August, 1953), inside front cover | C53.16

Dear Sirs: I am astonished that there is not more objection in America to the inquisition by your new Holy Office into the lives and opinions of American citizens and eminent aliens. The law which permits this inquisition is a bad one, and in my opinion everyone, whatever his opinion, ought to refuse to obey this law in order to promote its repeal. It is somewhat ironic that in America, which was once regarded as the land of liberty, the most resounding voice in favor of freedom should come from a German.

I sincerely hope that Einstein's splendid lead will be widely followed.

Bertrand Russell
Richmond, England

[106]

## British Guiana

*The Manchester Guardian* (13th October, 1953), p. 6 | C53.25

*In 1953, British Guiana was a British colony with limited self-government. Britain temporarily suspended the 1953 elections and the new Constitution because of alleged Communist subversion. British Guiana became Guyana following its independence in 1966.*

Sir —The action of our Government in British Guiana and still more its pronouncements are calculated to cause uneasiness and confusion unless and until they are clarified. We profess to favour democracy, and at the same time we say that we cannot tolerate a recently elected Parliament which has a Communist majority, because we are apprehensive of future illegalities. On the face of it this is an inconsistency, but the problem is not a new one.

What is an upholdher of democracy to do when a majority votes against democracy? I think the answer is that democracy involves legal opportunities for changes of opinion, and that it is anti-democratic to allow a momentarily popular clique to secure itself in power indefinitely no matter how unpopular it may subsequently become.

I hope that when a new Constitution is established in British Guiana it will be one which, with whatever safeguards, gives adequate scope to the opinion of the majority. We have, I think, a right to say that we will not have a Communist Government, for that is one which cannot be changed by subsequent changes of opinion; but I do not think that we have a right to say that we will not tolerate a Government containing Communists but not altering the Constitution. I wish I could feel confident that this distinction will be borne in mind.

—Yours &c., Bertrand Russell
41 Queen's Road, Richmond, Surrey, October 10.

[107]

## British Guiana

*The Manchester Guardian* (23rd October, 1953), p. 6 | C53.27

Sir, —The letter from Lady Huggins in your issue of October 21 calls for a few words of reply. She omits, in quoting me, my proviso that a new Constitution, when granted, must contain proper safeguards. Such safeguards are a normal part of all democratic constitutions except our own. The Constitution of the United States can only be amended by a very elaborate procedure involving an overwhelming majority. There is hardly any country with a written Constitution which allows it to be altered by a bare majority such as the 51 percent of voters in British Guiana. In the case of British Guiana, which has some special features, I think the British Government should reserve the right to intervene in the event of any serious threat to democracy.

—Yours &c., Russell.
41 Queen's Road, Richmond, Surrey, October 21.

# War and Peace

[108]

## Long-Time Advocate of Peace Approves Present War

*The New York Times* (16th February, 1941), section 4, p. 8 | C41.02

*Russell recorded his change of mind on the war as early as May 1940, in a private letter to Kingsley Martin of the* New Statesman *(see* Autobiography, *Volume 2, p. 357). In the following carefully reasoned letter, Russell details his arguments for giving up his earlier pacifism and supporting th war against Hitler.*

To The Editor of *The New York Times:*

In the years that preceded the outbreak of the present war I expected that I should be opposed to it, as I was to the war of 1914–18. Various circumstances, however, have led me to alter my view. This alternation is not as to any fundamental principle.

I have never been one of those who condemn all war. I have worked so much with people who were complete pacifists, opposed to all war, that it was natural that I should have been assumed to be one of them. Though I belonged to the Peace Pledge Union in the years immediately preceding the present war, I joined it on the explicit understanding that my objections to the war that was coming were not of principle but of expediency.

In 1915 I wrote an article on "The Ethics of War," in which I specified four justifiable kinds of wars, among which I included as examples the American War of Independence and (on the part of the North), the Civil War. My view was, in general, that modern wars are seldom justified, both because the propaganda and interference with freedom that are necessary for victory produce an atmosphere in which a good peace is unlikely.

In particular, I thought the arguments used by the Allies in the Great War were largely unsound: Germany was not as bad as was said, a war fought in alliance with Czarist Russia could not be genuinely a war for democracy, and imperialist motives (as the peace showed) were by no means confined to the German side. Moreover, at any time after the Battle of the Marne a reasonable negotiated peace would have been possible. On these grounds I opposed that war both in advance and during its progress. As to this, my opinion is unchanged.

## Munich Turning Point

Down to and including the time of Munich,[13] I supported the policy of conciliation. In this I was in agreement with the majority of my countrymen. I went further than the majority in believing that war should, at this moment in history, be avoided, however great the provocation.

I changed later through the influence of the same events that changed Chamberlain, Lord Lothian, Lord Halifax and most of the previous advocates of peace.[14] In view of what has happened since, it would seem that it might have been better for the world if Germany had been opposed at an earlier stage but I still think that the arguments for the policy of conciliation were very strong. These arguments, as I saw them, were three.

First: Germany had been treated with abominable injustice at Versailles and after war; what the Nazis demanded was no more than Germany had a right to claim—equality with other nations, and union under the German flag of all populations that so desired.

Whatever fears might be felt for the future, it would have been a dreadful thing to plunge Europe into war in order to perpetuate a wrong. The British (contrary to a belief which is common in America) had no treaty obligation to Czecho-Slovakia. France has such a treaty, but Britain was only bound to go to war to defend France if she were attacked.

## Czech Move a Factor

I leave out of account the fact, since made evident, that Britain and France were not prepared at the time of Munich, since this was not true at certain earlier times when we had a legal *casus belli,* for instance, when Hitler marched into the Rhineland.

This first argument collapsed with Hitler's occupation of the non-German parts of Czecho-Slovakia. Until then, the German Government had done nothing that could rightly be called foreign conquest. The world had been told, in the most emphatic terms possible, that Hitler's aspirations would be satisfied as soon as all Germans were in the Reich.

---

13. The Munich Pact was signed in September 1938 by Germany, France, Italy, and Britain. The Pact ceded the German-speaking Sudetenland to Germany. The pact was nullified in March 1939, when Germany seized the non-German part of Czechoslovakia and made it a German protectorate.

14. Chamberlain, Lothian, and Halifax were prominent members of the British government who were instrumental in negotiating the Munich Pact as part of Britain's policy of appeasement of Hitler.

One might be skeptical of these assurances, but in the absence of evidence to the contrary they had to be tentatively accepted. When Bohemia was occupied a new situation arose.

Second: it was expected by all the experts that a new great war, if it occurred, would be far more horrible than the last. The British Government distributed gas masks to everyone and prepared for casualties on a very large scale from air attack. So far, in spite of the German occupation of the Channel ports, the war, dreadful as it is, has not been as bad as was feared. This may cease to be true at any moment if a large-scale attempt at invasion is made; perhaps the horror has been only postponed to the moment that best suited Hitler's plans.

But in the case of aerial attacks on Great Britain, it seems clear that he has done his utmost; and this has been enormously less destructive than had been predicted in the most authoritative prognostications, the reason being, apparently, that defense against aerial attacks has made very great progress during the last few years.

On the other hand, the fate of subject populations, more particularly in Poland, has been a good deal worse than had seemed probable. There is reason to think that, if the conquered nations are not liberated by force of arms, they will be compelled for a long time to come to endure appalling suffering and unbearable tyranny.

On both these grounds the arguments for armed resistance to German ambitions have been shown to be stronger than they appeared to be before the war began.

Third: I feared that, if once there was war, the issue, whoever was nominally victorious, would be military dictatorship. It was obvious that, for the duration of the war, every belligerent government would need dictatorial powers, and it was far from certain that, if the previously democratic nations won, they would reestablish democracy when peace had been concluded.

### Discretion Shown

As to this, though the British Government has now very wide powers, it is using them, except in India, with admirable discretion. Free speech is still tolerated, except the most flagrant expression of pro-Nazi sentiment, and as the civil population has shown no tendency to panic, the strict military dictatorship that I expect has proved quite unnecessary. Malcolm MacDonald's[15] recent order that children should

15. Malcolm MacDonald (1901–1981) was Minister of Health in the British National Coalition government, 1940–45.

be compulsorily evacuated if medical evidence proves that their health is suffering is an example of the mild degree of government interference insisted upon. There is now obviously a good chance of preserving democracy if the democratic powers win, and none if Germany wins.

There came a moment—some will say one moment, some another—when it became evident that Germany would destroy the independence of the democracies one by one if they did not combine in armed defense. From that moment the only hope for democracy was war.

In this argument a vital factor is the military strength of Germany. A nation which is secure may reasonably pursue a conciliatory policy; but it is another matter if the price of conciliation is likely to be ultimate subjugation. The defeat of France showed what is possible, and must have increased Hitler's ambitions as much as it increased his enemies' fears.

Before the war began, it might have seemed preposterous to suppose that Hitler could aim at world domination. Now it seems probable that he does so and his success is sufficiently possible to call for the utmost vigor in resistance.

## Our Stand Discussed

Many people in America, though a rapidly diminishing number, take still, in regard to the United States, an attitude similar to that which I formerly took in regard to Great Britain. President Hutchins,[16] in a speech with which I feel some sympathy, is reported—I quote *The New York Times* of Jan. 24—as saying that "the United States can better serve suffering humanity everywhere by staying out."

If his opinion were based merely on the belief that England can win without American help, it would be one on which only the military experts would have a right to pronounce. But it appears from other parts of his address that is not what he means.

"We must show the world," he is reported to have said, "a nation clear in purpose, united in action and sacrificial in spirit. The influence of that example upon suffering humanity everywhere will be more powerful than the combined armies of the Axis."

I cannot understand the logic of this statement. In the first place, assuming that America rejects President Roosevelt's policy—which is what President Hutchins is advising—what reason is there to expect the country to be any more "clear in purpose, united in action and sacrificial in spirit" than at other times in its history?

---

16. Robert Maynard Hutchins (1899–1977) was a fiercely controversial American educator, dean of Yale Law School (1927–29), and president (1929–45) and chancellor (1945–50) of the University of Chicago.

Is it not certain, on the contrary, that it will be unclear in purpose owing to divided counsels, disunited in action owing to the existence of powerful factions pulling opposite directions, and so far from sacrificial in spirit that many men's opinions on the question of war or peace will be decided by considerations of self-interest?

But even if the United States, unlike every other nation known to history, were suddenly transformed into a community of saints, how would that help "suffering humanity"?

President Hutchins speaks of welcoming refugees; this is admirable as a mitigation of the sufferings of those who have escaped; but how would it help Polish industrial workers, of whom vast numbers have been sent by the Russians to forced labor in Siberia or by the German to forced labor in the Rhineland?

If Hitler wins, this will be the fate of all Europe, while Asia will suffer equally under Japanese taskmasters. What meanwhile may be happening in America, however "sacrificial," will be unknown to these hopeless serfs, and, if they did know of it, I fail to see how it could console them.

As for the Nazis, they would view the edifying spectacle with contempt, so long as it did not constitute a military menace. They have not in the past shown themselves susceptible to moral example.

## Hutchins View Disputed

If America goes to war, President Hutchins says, "for a generation, perhaps for a hundred years, we shall not be able to struggle back to where were were. ***Education will cease.*** We shall think no more of justice, the moral order and the supremacy of human rights."

If this were a plea for avoidance of war under all circumstances, it would at least be logical. But it is combined with the statement that America must arm for defense and must help England, China and Greece as much as is compatible with avoiding risk of involvement in the war.

This brings us down to questions of fact. If such limited help will suffice to enable the present belligerents to win, well and good; though there seems nothing particularly "sacrificial" in such a policy. But if not, then, given Hitler's ambitions, it seems likely that America will in the end be involved in a longer and more difficult war than would otherwise be necessary.

All the evils feared by President Hutchins will then exist in even greater measure, since the war will be more severe and more dangerous. The question, on his own premises, reduces to one of fact: what degree of help from America will suffice for the defeat of Hitler? On this question I cannot express any opinion.

It may be said, and truly: all these considerations should have been present, mutatis mutandis, to the minds of British statesmen during the era of "appeasement"; they should have been present to the governments of Norway, Holland, Belgium and Rumania during the period when they were struggling to preserve neutrality. But each fresh victim affords a fresh argument, and the later such views as those of President Hutchins are advanced the more overwhelming are the reasons afforded by the march of events for rejecting them.

**Evidence Counted**

The whole argument, either way, is necessarily based on hypotheses and probabilities, as to which no certainty is possible; but as immediate decisions are forced upon us, we have to act upon such data as can be obtained, knowing that even the most careful consideration may lead us astray. I have changed my own opinion as the evidence has changed.

I know that the war, even if it ends in victory, involves very grave dangers to democracy and freedom. I fear also that British war aims—which Mr. Churchill still refuses to state—will probably be found, if we win, to have contained an element of imperialism.

I deplore the short-sighted illiberality of British policy in India, particularly the harsh imprisonment of such a man as Nehru. I scarcely dare to hope that the world after the war will be a good world, if we win, but if we lose, it will be hell, probably for a long time to come.

It is a tragic alternative, but it must be met with such hope as the times permit and with a determination that in winning the war we shall not lose what we are fighting for.

There is one hope that is important and, I think, not utopian; that at the end of the war some step, less ineffective than the League of Nations, may be taken toward the Federation of the World.

Bertrand Russell
Cambridge, Mass, February 11, 1941

••••••••••••• [109] •••••••••••••

## Gandhi's Stand Disapproved

*The New York Times* (5th August, 1942), p. 18 | C42.04

*In this letter, and in the next three, Russell explains his position on the international status of India, his disagreement with Gandhi and his hopes that India will co-operate in the Allied effort against Japan.*

*At the time of Russell's* New York Times *letter, the Cripps Mission had failed to secure Indian co-operation in the defense of India against Japanese invasion, and Gandhi demanded immediate withdrawal of the British from India. Shortly after Russell's* New York Times *letter appeared, the Indian crisis came to a head with Gandhi's arrest and the imprisonment of the leadership of the National Congress Party.*

To the Editor of *The New York Times:*

As a past president of the India League in England and a supporter for many years of the movement for Indian self-government, I feel that I should make clear my strong opposition to the present policy of Mr. Gandhi.

I ardently desire freedom for India and I consider that Mr. Gandhi's policy is likely to assist India's enslavement. I hope that the British Government will grant India complete independence and not merely dominion status when the war ends, and I should favor the immediate granting of such civil independence as is compatible with the military necessities of India and all the other threatened nations.

Complete independence is not possible among nations involved in modern war. England and Australia have welcomed the presence of American troops. India, for their own safety, should do likewise, should continue to endure while war lasts the existing military status of the British in India, and also should invite the military collaboration of the Chinese.

I fully understand how galling to Indian feelings British military control must be, but the utility now of a trained and experienced military command should be obvious.

Mr. Gandhi's movement is calculated to hinder the victory of the United Nations and to assist Japanese conquest not only of India but also of China. Whoever supports this movement is no friend of either India or China.

Bertrand Russell
Malvern. Pa, July 31, 1942

[110]

## Bertrand Russell on India

*The Nation* (5th September, 1942), p. 200 | C42.07

Dear Sirs: The Indian situation is dangerous, and if it is to be wisely dealt with, clear thinking is very necessary. I find in some quarters a lack of clear thinking which may increase the dangers that we all wish to diminish.

There are some points about which we are all agreed. First, the Indian difficulty must be handled in the way most likely to help in winning the war. Second, as soon as the war is over, India is to have independence—as complete, at any rate, as Great Britain or any other country will have. The only practical question at issue is: what is to be done during the continuance of the war? I feel that neither the British government nor the Congress Party is treating this question in the way most likely to lead to victory. Many people in America seem to feel that Gandhi must be in the right since he stands for national independence; others feel that loyalty to an ally makes criticism of the British government impolitic. Both seem to me mistaken. On the one hand, insistence on immediate independence, with all the confusion resulting from a transfer of government in the middle of a war, would probably end in the enslavement of both India and China to Japan. On the other hand, the problem of India, since it is part of the problem of victory, is a problem on which all the United Nations have a right to a voice.

The question of India is much more complex than it appears to many American liberals. They do not know that one of the points on which the Cripps mission broke down was the unwillingness of the Hindus to admit that Moslems have the same right to independence from Hindus as Hindus from British. They do not face the difficulties of a complete change of government when a Japanese invasion is imminent. They profess to think that Sir Stafford Cripps's promises are not to be trusted. They imagine that if the demands of the Congress Party were granted, India would become enthusiastic for the war, although the example of Ireland should suggest the contrary. They attribute the poverty of Indians to the British, in spite of the fact that the poverty of China has always been at least as great. Mr Louis Fischer, in *The Nation* of August 22, mentions that the infant death rate is 274 in Bombay as against 66 in London and remarks that "such figures burn deep resentment, hatred, and disloyalty into the soul of India." The implication that the higher death rate of Bombay as compared with London is entirely the result of British misgovernment is most unfair. Bombay has a hot climate and a high birth rate; London a low birth rate and a temperate climate. I have

# On the Ball

"PROFESSOR AYER, the Hoad of philosophical discussion." (Sunday Times.)

Pancho Gonzales
Said, flexing his muscle,
"If Ayer is Hoad,
Then I'm Bertrand Russell."

Lew Hoad was an Australian tennis player who, in the mid-1950s, was arguably the best in the world, winning the British, Australian, French, and Italian men's singles championships in 1956. Gonzales was a player who had recently beaten Hoad. A.J. Ayer was an Oxford analytic philosopher whose style and doctrines were heavily influenced by Russell. See document [191] where Russell refers approvingly to Ayer's views on ethics and the irrelevance of ethics to the question of the existence of God. The cartoon and verse are from Peter Simple's column in the *Daily Telegraph* (11th February, 1959).

no doubt that the British government could have done more than it has done to reduce the high infant death rate, just as the government of the United States could have done a great deal more than it has done to reduce the death rate among the children of Southern Negroes; but there is no reason to suppose that fewer children would die in Bombay if British rule were to be succeeded by a government headed by Mr. Gandhi. Some years ago Mr. Gandhi stated that the earthquakes then troubling India were sent as a punishment for sin. This attitude has never been very effective against a high infant death rate. And Mr. Fischer should remember that there is every reason to think that the death rate in China, before the beginning of the war with Japan, was at least as high as in India.

Above all, American liberals refuse to face the difficulty of establishing Indian independence overnight when every scheme hitherto suggested, whether by Indians or by the British, is vehemently rejected by a large section of Indian opinion.

The British government has been gravely at fault in the past, and Mr. Churchill has been even more reactionary than the government, as appeared in his opposition to the Government of India Act. In these circumstances it is not surprising that Sir Stafford Cripps's promises were not received at their face value. This difficulty, had it stood alone, could have been easily overcome: his promises could have been guaranteed by the United Nations. But this difficulty did not stand alone. The demand that India should be given full independence here and now is incompatible with victory, and would not be made by the Congress Party if it thought the defeat of Japan more important than immediate emancipation from England. It is this demand that creates the apparently insoluble difficulty. I believe, however, that a solution is still possible, though at some cost to British *amour propre.*

India, as an imperial possession, is lost to England; everyone in England, including Mr. Churchill and Mr. Amery, knows this. The problem is to make the transition to self-government without handing India over to Japan. This problem concerns China and Russia just as much as it concerns England. It should be dealt with, not by England alone, but by the United Nations jointly. There should be appointed, with the consent of the British government, a commission of four men, chosen respectively by the British, American, Soviet, and Chinese governments, with full power to negotiate with all sections of Indian opinion and to make recommendations keeping in mind two objectives: first, that the war must be won; second, that Indian independence must be granted as soon as it can be granted without hindering the first objective. If, as I believe, complete independence cannot be granted now without retarding the conduct of the war, the commission would probably find that some of the functions of government could be transferred without delay. There should be, at the earliest possible moment, interim measures to produce an armistice in the present Indian conflict and, later, considered proposals for a permanent settlement. The British government should undertake to accept the findings of the commission, provided the other three governments did so. If any section of Indian opinion rejected them it would be in effect siding with the Japanese and would have to be treated as a hostile force.

The measure should be regarded as a first step toward the establishment of an inter-Allied authority for deciding questions of common concern; and such an authority, in turn, should be viewed as the nucleus of a future international authority for the preservation of peace. *Complete* national independence, even for the strongest nations, has become an anachronism, since it can only lead to successive enslavement by predatory powers. For the same reasons a private imperialism, such as that of England in India, is equally an anachronism. But those American liberals who think that insurgent nationalism is right while imperialist nationalism is wrong are still living in the nineteenth century.

Bertrand Russell
Malvern, Pa., August 27

[111]

## Americans and the Indian Problem

*The Manchester Guardian* (29th October, 1942), p. 4 | C42.11

To the Editor of *The Manchester Guardian:*

Sir, We doubt whether English people sufficiently realise the excitement that exists in the United States over the Indian deadlock. Many good-hearted Liberals of the type who automatically take up the cry of "Freedom" whenever they hear it have begun a passionate propaganda for Indian independence, which most of them, without adequate knowledge of the facts, interpret as unconditional surrender of the British Government to Mr. Gandhi and the Congress party. This propaganda has been jubilantly taken up by those Americans—and there are more of them than the English realise—whose deep distrust of "Britain" was imbibed with their mother's mild and fostered by textbooks which still treated England as the hereditary enemy.

Unfortunately, many Americans believe that England has not changed since George III and there is much in Mr. Churchill's speeches to confirm this view. On one of them even the "New Yorker" was moved to comment as follows:—

You hear it is said that this is a "people's war." And so it is. Then you read a speech of Winston Churchill's before the House of Commons and he calls Malta "as bright a diamond as shines in the King's crown" and you wonder whether it is a people's war or just another war. We're very fond of Mr. Churchill and of England and are working hard to make his and our side prevail, and for that very reason we wish he would not flash these old Imperial jewels. Malta is just a lot of guys.

It is natural that to emancipated colonies Empire should remain for ever a bugbear. To the majority of Americans the words "Empire" and "Imperialism " have been from childhood bad words rousing distaste and condemnation. It is useless to point out that exploitation and oppression within one nation are just as harmful. They learnt as infants that the United States were once a part of the British Empire and they celebrate their escape yearly on the glorious Fourth. The world "Empire", therefore produces in them a more immediate and hostile response than any other word signifying social injustice. And of course, we are all more liable to indignation over the injustices that are not to our own advantage.

Many people here are convinced that England is fighting this war to retain her Empire. This conviction was expressed in the recent pious and pontifical "Letter to the People of England" published in "Life" magazine. We and our English friends in this country keep up a constant struggle against this point of view. We protest that England is fighting for her own survival and for the right of nations to survive. We point out, waving our hands towards some city less than one hundred miles away, that one does not worry about Empire when the enemy is as near as that.

But the average audience cannot take it in. Vast oceans separate them from both enemies and they attribute the sanguine spirit that they derive from their geographical isolation and economic wealth to us, and magnify it, believing still that the British Empire is a mighty Power which even the the United States must fear. We have even seen a propaganda leaflet put out by an ultra-patriotic organisation protesting against the threatened "reannexation to the Empire."

We wish that our efforts to disabuse them of their suspicions were given more support from home. It is four years since we left England, and we do not know how many people there are—besides Mr. Churchill—who do not realise that the days of our Empire are drawing to a close. We wish that those who do realise it would be more vocal.

With regard to India in particular, something should be done to reassure not only India but the United States and our other allies.

It is, we think, obvious that India cannot be granted a Provisional National Government now. Even if Mr. Jinnah and Mr. Ambedkar and other minority leaders were willing and able to co-operate in such a Government—and Mr. Gandhi himself has repeatedly declared that he considers a period of anarchy and chaos more likely—it could not possibly organise efficient resistance soon enough to keep out the Japanese, the Indian Army, as Mr. Gandhi reminds us, having been disbanded with the withdrawal of British power.

But does it therefore follow that nothing can be done? In the utterances of Mr. Churchill and Mr. Amery Americans read a certain satisfaction with the status quo, almost a tone of relief that Gandhi, by being naughty, has relieved them of the bother of coping with the Indian problem at all. The Indian correspondent of the New York newspaper "P.M." remarks "What the Indians long for almost as much as freedom itself is a touch of humility from London. It is an attitude of spirit that seems to matter to Indians. There seems to be a note of righteousness in the London attitude that is injurious to the sensibilities of the people here."

Obviously the Government cannot be expected to negotiate while the civil disobedience movement still goes on. But is there any reason why the Government should not sacrifice its pride sufficiently to issue in India an appeal for the abandonment of the movement and a declaration that when once it is abandoned negotiations will be resumed? Such negotiation might fail, like the Cripps proposals: but there is evidence that Indian leaders are getting worried, and the attempt should at least be made, if only to prove our good intentions, which many in the United States, as well as in India doubt.

Such negotiations, we believe, should be carried on by a commission consisting of representatives of all the United Nations. Indian leaders might believe in our sincerity if we invoked the aid of our allies, and if they were once convinced of our sincerity they would surely consent to support the war effort while negotiations were going on.

If such negotiation succeeded they would be an auspicious inauguration of the practice of international arbitration. If they failed they would at least have the effect of allaying the doubts of Americans as to our sincerity and convincing them that the whole problem is a great deal more difficult that they, led by the naive criers of "Freedom," have hitherto believed.

Yours &c., Bertrand Russell, Patricia Russell
Malvern, Pa., October 14

•••••••••••••• [112] ••••••••••••••

# Future of India

*The Times* (3rd March, 1945) | C45.03

*Russell and his family returned to England in May 1944 where he was to begin a five-year lectureship at Cambridge University. In the previous year, Russell had lectured on the foundations of knowledge at Bryn Mawr College, at Wellesley College, and at Princeton University, where he took up residence and had frequent meetings with Einstein and Kurt Gödel, the mathematical logician.*

*In this letter, Russell reminds his countrymen that with the Japanese threat in decline, independence for India must be faithfully pursued.*

Sir, —I should like to endorse the suggestion made recently by Sir Muhammad Zafrulla Kahn and supported by Sir Frederick Whyte and Mr. R.A. Wilson in a letter in *The Times* to-day, that an immediate effort should be made to solve the deadlock in India which resulted from the failure of the Cripps offer. The resignation with which his Majesty's Government have accepted this failure has given rise to a widespread suspicion, especially in the United States, that the Cripps offer was made only because of the apparent urgency of the military situation at that time, and that our good intentions towards India have diminished with the threat of Japanese invasions.

Both in justice to India and for the sake of our honour and prestige among the United Nations a definite announcement should be made now of a fixed date—say one year after the cessation of hostilities with Japan—upon which we are prepared to hand over India to a representative provisional Government. I agree with Sir Muhammad that such declaration might be expected to accelerate agreement among the different parties in India. The present situation cannot continue indefinitely. Our seeming reluctance to initiate any further action brings us neither credit nor advantage, and may embitter our relations with India for many years to come.

Yours, &c., Bertrand Russell
Trinity College, Cambridge, March 1

# The Bomb

*Russell's early awareness of the danger to humankind posed by the atomic bombing of Japan resulted in an early article, 'The Bomb and Civilization', which appeared in* Forward *(18th August, 1945). In that article Russell advanced the argument that only an international authority with a monopoly on the means of producing weapons of mass destruction could render war practically impossible and thereby avert the catastrophe of nuclear holocaust. The ideal of world government had been one of Russell's since the First World War. And his preferred means of its coming about was by voluntary association. But he also thought that as a practical matter, and as a less desirable but acceptable alternative, American hegemony might bring about such an organization by coercion.*

[113]

## Resisting Russia

*The Observer* (28th November, 1948), p. 3 | C48.25

*Russell gave a talk at Westminster School in late November in which he was reported as advocating preventive war against Russia before she got the Bomb. Russell's position, from 1946 to 1948, was that the West should threaten Russia with war unless she agreed to international controls on armaments and joined a World Federation to ensure world peace. Russell believed that by such a threat Russian compliance could be obtained without war. Misunderstanding of Russell's position during this period continued until the end of his life and sometimes threatened to undermine the credibility of his anti-nuclear campaign in the 1950s and 1960s.*[17]

Sir, —An address which I gave recently at a New Commonwealth Schools Conference at Westminster School has been widely misrepresented. I did not, as has been reported, urge immediate war with Russia. I did urge that the democracies should be prepared to use force if necessary, and that their readiness to do so should be made perfectly clear to Russia.

It has become obvious that the Communists, like the Nazis, can be halted in their attempts to dominate Europe and Asia only by determined

17. See my 'Russell and Preventive War', *Russell*, n.s. 14 (Winter, 1994).

and combined resistance by every means in the democracies power—not excluding military means, if Russia continues to refuse all compromise.

Yours, etc., Bertrand Russell

••••••••••••• [114] •••••••••••••

## Lord Russell and the Atom Bomb

*The New Statesman and Nation* (21st April, 1951), pp. 448, 450 | C51.13

*The following letter represents one of Russell's many attempts to put the record straight regarding his alleged advocacy of preventive war against Russia. In this case, Russell and his lawyers secured a "correction" from the editor, Kingsley Martin, of* The New Statesman and Nation.

*This letter was published with the following note from the editor: "We are glad to publish Lord Russell's statement, which will remove misapprehension about his views on the use of the atomic bomb, and we regret having published a comment which may have increased and perpetuated the misunderstandings to which he refers."*

Sir, Through a series of accidents I have only quite lately learned of a statement about me which was made by Critic in *The New Statesman and Nation* of November 19, 1950. In this issue Critic says of me: "After the last war, even more deeply troubled by the spread of Communism than he was by the power of Rome, which he had often denounced, he decided that it would be both good morals and good politics to start dropping bombs on Moscow." At the time when you published this statement I was in the United States of America having fierce encounters with Republican journalists for advocating a policy diametrically opposite to that which you attribute to me.[18] I had previously conducted a campaign of public lectures, not only in the United States, but also in Australia and various Continental countries, to advocate policies which, I hoped, might prevent the need of a clash with Russia. These lectures were published at the time in the various countries in which they were delivered. Lest you should impugn my veracity I must ask you to allow me to quote various passages from them.

If a war is at all likely to have the sort of outcome that I have been suggesting, it is evidently the duty of every sane man to do what lies in

18. In November 1950 Russell was in the U.S. lecturing at Princeton and Columbia. At Princeton he learned that he was to be the recipient of the 1950 Nobel prize in literature.

his power to prevent war. To this, however, there are limits. Dreadful as a war would be, and disastrous as its consequences would prove, I, for my part, think that it would be even more dreadful and more disastrous if the Soviet system, with all its cruelty and all its obscurantism, were to extend over the whole world. I believe that a large majority of English-speaking people agree with me in so thinking. Our problem, therefore, is to avoid war without submitting. And if that should prove impossible, we must seek to be strong in defence, so as to avoid some of the worst misfortunes that war would otherwise bring. But victory should be a secondary aim: the primary aim should be the preservation of peace.

Again:—

Fanaticism on the issue of Communism is very common and very dangerous. A Communist is a fanatic if he thinks it worth while to make war in order to destroy capitalism. An anti-communist is a fanatic if he thinks it worth while to make war in order to destroy Communism.

Again:—

What , then, can we do in the meantime? The first step—and this is one which is eminently practicable—is a clear delimitation of spheres. The Russians should not give support to French or Italian Communists; we would make no official protest when Polish patriots or Hungarian Cardinals suffer, whatever we may privately feel. Africa would have to be allotted to the West; Asia would have to be divided. It should then be solemnly agreed that any interference of either in the other's domain, whether by arms or by propaganda, should be a legitimate *casus belli.*

Again:—

Matters will not improve until there is more sense of security, at least for a few years ahead. To create such a sense, on both sides of the Iron Curtain, is the main duty of statesmen in our time. But how is this to be done? There must be a change of emphasis: we must devote ourselves to showing not how to secure victory for our side, nor how desirable our victory would be, but how disastrous to everybody on all sides a war must be. In the West, where free discussion is possible, important men, especially scientists, of all shades of political opinion, should meet together. It should be agreed that never, in their discussions, must anyone raise the question as to which system is best, the Russian or the American. What should be made clear is: First, that if there is a war, then even if one side is completely victorious (which is unlikely) the victors will still be worse off than if there had been no war; second, that there is no reason, except mutual suspicion, why the two kinds of regime would not exist peaceably side by side; third, that it is possible to divide the world into spheres, leaving each side free in its own sphere, but agreeing not to interfere in the other. If, in the West, men of sufficient importance and sufficient political diversity, including Communists, had agreed on such a solution, it is not irrational to hope that governments, on both sides of the Iron

Curtain, would examine the proposals carefully, and would perhaps reach a basis of agreement. The alternative is disaster, not to this or that group, but to mankind.

Prosperity is generally admitted, in the West, to be the best preventive of Communist fanaticism, but no one seems to draw the conclusion that it would be a good thing if Russia were prosperous. Trade across the Iron Curtain ought to be encouraged. Everything possible should be done to turn the attention of Russians to the internal development of their own country. I admit that the Russians make these things difficult, but it is bound to take time and patience to dispel their suspicions.

During the last three years or more I have been giving almost all my time and energy to advocating these views in various parts of the world. It is, therefore, somewhat bitter to find my work impeded by statements such as yours.

I will admit that at one time I had hopes of a shorter road to general peace. At the time of the Baruch proposal for internationalising atomic energy, I thought it possible that the Russians might be induced by threats to agree to this proposal and thereby to save the world from the atomic armaments race upon which it is now embarked. But this hope proved vain. After the Berlin blockade and the rape of Czechoslovakia I stated emphatically, what I still hold, that the Russians ought to be informed that the West would not tolerate further aggressions of this sort. My statements were mis-reported and misunderstood, and men with whom I might have co-operated chose, instead, to regard me as an enemy. As you have contributed to this result, which does both public and private harm, I must ask you to correct publicly your misrepresentation of my views.

Bertrand Russell
41 Queen's Road, Richmond, Surrey.

[115]

## Preventative War

*The Nation* (17th October, 1953), p. 320 | C53.26

*The next letter appeared in* The Nation *with the explanation: "The following letter from Bertrand Russell was received by a reader of* The Nation *and is printed with the permission of Earl Russell and the recipient."*

Dear Sirs: The story that I supported a preventive atom war against Russia is a Communist invention. I once spoke at a meeting at which only one reporter was present and he was a Communist, though reporting for orthodox news papers. He seized his opportunity and in spite of my utmost efforts, I have never been able to undo the harm. Krishna Menon[19] with whom I had collaborated for years on Indian affairs, turned against me. *The New Statesman* in London wrote assuming the truth of the report and it was only by visiting the editor in company with my lawyer that I induced *The New Statesman* to publish a long letter of refutation from me. You are at liberty to make any use you like of this letter, and I shall be glad if you can make its contents known to anybody who still believes the slanderous report.

Bertrand Russell
Richmond, England

[116]

## Spot Letter From Earl Russell

*The Daily Herald* (27th October, 1953), p. 3 | C53.28

*Russell reports a provocative statement by Syngman Rhee (1875–1965), the president of South Korea (1948–1965).*

Dr. Syngman Rhee has announced to the world that if Korea is not unified within three months he will attack North Korea.

May we assume that, if this happens the United Nations, under the leadership of America, will rush to the defence of North Korea against unprovoked aggression? Or must we assume that the United States will support Syngman Rhee even though this act should lead to a world war?

I wish there could be a public opinion poll of Great Britain on the question: Are you willing to die for Syngman Rhee?

Bertrand Russell
Richmond, Surrey.

---

19. Krishna Menon (1897–1974) was a British-educated lawyer and Indian diplomat. He served as secretary of the Indian League (1929–47), as High Commissioner for India in Great Britain, as Indian delegate to the United Nations (1952–62), and as India's Minister of Defence (1957–62).

# Miscellaneous

•••••••••••••• [117] ••••••••••••••

## Mountaineering Courses

*The Times* (30th March, 1951), p. 7 | C51.10

*Russell was an avid hiker and mountaineer most of his life. In the early 1950s, as president of the Mountaineering Association, he wrote several letters to the editor on behalf of his beloved pastime. The following is typical.*

Sir, Your article on the growth of mountaineering clubs prompts me to call your attention to the work of the Mountaineering Association, which provides training for beginners. Mountaineering has its dangers, particularly for novices, but these dangers are minimized when the mountaineer possesses the necessary knowledge and technical skill for difficult expeditions. In the past beginners have found it difficult to obtain this knowledge and it was to meet this need that the Mountaineering Association was formed. Its courses give basic training in map reading, route finding, mountain rescue work, rock climbing, snow and ice climbing and ski-mountaineering.

The ultimate aim of the association is the establishment of permanent training schools and for this purpose a trust fund is being accumulated. The amount needed is £25,000 and subscriptions are invited from educational, industrial, commercial, welfare, and youth organizations as well as from individuals. The constitution of the association provides for such bodies to affiliate with us and take part in the administration and management. Until the permanent schools are established the association will continue to give training at interim courses in the British Isles and abroad. Four hundred pupils have been trained i the three years since we began to provide these facilities which are non-profit making; the 1951 training programme provides training for 300 pupils. The courses are open to all, and the secretary, 1, Kildare Gardens, W.2., will gladly give further information.

Yours, &c. Russell,
President, Mountaineering Association
41 Queens Road, Richmond, Surrey

••••••••••••• [118] •••••••••••••

## B.B.C.

*The Times* (29th March, 1952), p. 7 | C52.07

*After World War II, Russell frequently defended British socialism and the expansion of certain state functions. The suggestion that the B.B.C. should allow private advertising was met with much criticism. Here Russell adds his voice to the opposition.*

Sir, —I am utterly dismayed by the suggestion that the B.B.C. should admit sponsored programmes. I wish to endorse whole-heartedly every word of Miss Margery Fry's letter in your issue of March 26. It was my misfortune to be dependent on American radio in 1940 at the time of the fall of France. The most devastating news would be interrupted just at the point where one's anxieties had reached their highest pitch, to assure one that So-&-So's pills would cure worry, or that more men smoked So-&-So's cigars than anybody else's. I used to find it difficult not to smash the machine in fury. The B.B.C. is one of the most admirable of modern British institutions, and it will be a disaster if from commercial motives it is vulgarized and degraded.

Yours, &c., Russell
41 Queen's Road, Richmond, Surrey.

••••••••••••• [119] •••••••••••••

## Portraits From Memory

*The Listener* (14th August, 1952), p. 267 | C52.22

*During World War I Russell and D.H. Lawrence became friends and exchanged ideas on politics and the war. But there was a falling out owing in part to a difference in personalities, as Russell explained in his* Portraits From Memory *(Simon and Schuster, 1951). Russell clarifies the nature of their disagreement in response to a letter from Lawrence's biographer, Dallas Kenmare.*[20]

---

20. Kenmare's book, *Fire-Bird: A Study of D.H. Lawrence* (London: James Barrie, 1951), appeared about the same times as Russell's *Portraits from Memory.*

Sir, —Mr. Kenmare's letter on D.H. Lawrence in THE LISTENER of August 7 misses the point. The disagreement between Lawrence and me was not as to head and heart. On the contrary, one of his main objections to me was that I had a heart. I minded the suffering involved in the war; he did not, and regarded my minding as a pretence. That Lawrence had not much head, I will admit. But he had even less heart. As for Mr. Kenmare's idea that there are people who take reason as a guide in ultimate problems, I can only say that I have never come across such people either in life or in literature. They are, in fact, a figment in the brains of people who do not take the trouble to think things out.

Your, etc., Bertrand Russell
Richmond

PART V

# The Cold War and the Nuclear Peril

(1954–1962)

# Bertrand Russell

Russell's public letters in this period reflect his dual concerns for civil liberties in the United States and his fears regarding nuclear war. They also reveal some changes in his attitudes towards both Russian Communism and the United States which he explains in his *Autobiography*:

> Later [after his strong anti-Communist attitude of the early post-war years] I was brought around to being more favourable to Communism by the death of Stalin in 1953 and by the Bikini [U.S. H-bomb] test in 1954; and I came gradually to attribute, more and more, the danger of nuclear war to the West, to the United States of America, and less to Russia. This change was supported by developments inside the United States, such as McCarthyism and the restriction of civil liberties.

By the mid-1950s, Russell's anti-nuclear campaign came into conflict with official Western establishment policy regarding the Bomb and national defense. The Russell-Einstein Manifesto in 1955, penned by Russell and signed by prominent scientists of international repute, attested to the dangers of nuclear weapons and urged the world to abolish war; it concluded with a simple but poignant appeal: "Remember your humanity, and forget the rest."

At this time Russell criticized both superpowers for their confrontational rhetoric and posturing, and, by the end of the decade, he urged the British government to give up its nuclear weapons unilaterally, withdraw from NATO and assume a neutralist role to help defuse East-West hostilities. These themes concerning the dangers of nuclear war and of Britain's role as neutralist recur in many of Russell's letters throughout this period.

In the Cold War climate of the day, Russell's anti-nuclear appeal was often criticized as pro-Communist, and the idea that avoidance of nuclear holocaust transcended political ideology met with considerable resistance. Fear of Communism continued to feed McCarthyism and to threaten civil liberties in the U.S., a fact illustrated by Russell's concern in the famous Rosenberg-Sobell spy case.

For several years, starting in 1959, Russell served as President of the Campaign for Nuclear Disarmament, an organization that had wide public support in England and considerable influence abroad. But by the early 1960s, he thought the CND was losing its effectiveness and that only a movement featuring mass civil disobedience could stem the drift to nuclear catastrophe. Thus, the Committee of 100 was brought into being. In 1961, at the age of 89, Russell was sentenced to two months in prison for civil disobedience.

During the Cuban Missile Crisis of October 1962, the 90-year-old philosopher assumed global center stage as the world tottered on the brink of nuclear war. In his telegram exchanges with Khrushchev and Kennedy he pled for the triumph of reason over ideological fanaticism. Russell down-played his own efficacy. But he insisted that it was Khrushchev, not Kennedy, who had practiced proper restraint and to whom the world owed a debt of gratitude—an opinion which provoked much antipathy among pro-American Cold Warriors. In this period (and the next) we have several letters in which Russell explains his position and defends his actions during the Crisis.

There are 92 known published letters in this period of which 82 are reproduced here.

# War and Peace

## *The Bomb*

••••••••••••• [120] •••••••••••••

### Atomic Weapons

*The Manchester Guardian* (22nd April, 1954), p. 6 | C54.10

*Russell reminds the editor that the U.S. is committed to a nuclear policy which allowed for first-use of atomic weapons as a response to conventional (non-nuclear) attack.*

Sir, —In a leading article in your issue of April 20 you say, "The United States is not so foolish or wicked as to fire the first shot in a war with atomic weapons." This statement as it stands is ambiguous. If you mean that the United States would not fire the first shot, the statement may be correct. But if you mean that the United States would not be the first to use atomic weapons, you are almost certainly mistaken. The United States authorities have declared that any aggression anywhere by Russia or China will be met by all-out retaliation, which certainly means the bomb.[1]

It is apparently the opinion of experts that in a world war the Western Powers will be defeated if they do not use the bomb, but victorious if they use it. If this is the view of the Russian authorities, they will abstain at the beginning of a war from using the bomb and leave to our side the odium of its first employment. Can anybody seriously suggest that the Western Powers will prefer defeat? There is only one way to prevent the necessity for this choice and that is to prevent a world war.

—Yours &c., Bertrand Russell
41 Queen's Road, Richmond, Surrey, April 20.

---

1. Russell no doubt has in mind the policy of the 'massive retaliation' articulated by U.S. Secretary of State John Foster Dulles. The nuclear response was not to be as automatic as Russell suggests. Rather, it was to be a live option—"by means and places of our own choosing." But Russell is right in so far as first use and pre-emption have been part of U.S. national security doctrine since 1950.

[121]

# 1948 Russell vs.1954 Russell

*The Saturday Review* (16th October, 1954) | C54.30

*In 1946–47, before Russia had the bomb (which it was to acquire in 1949), Russell advocated threatening the Soviets with war unless they agreed to international controls on armaments. For a while he thought the threat would secure Russian agreement without war. But in mid-1948, with the Czech coup and the Berlin crisis, he became temporarily doubtful that effective international controls could be achieved without war with the Soviets which he saw as preferable to other alternatives—a view which he expressed in a private letter at the time. Later, after the Soviets got the bomb, Russell ruled out war, or the threat of war, as a rational possibility, and headed a world-wide campaign against nuclear war and nuclear weapons as posing the greatest danger to humankind. Some of Russell's critics noted the apparent inconsistency in Russell's thinking and tried to use it to discredit his anti-nuclear campaign in the 1950s.*

The Saturday Review *published Russell's private 1948 letter along with his current (1954) views with the following editor's note.*

Editor's Note: The two letters which follow constitute the record of an important change in opinion of one of the world's most influential thinkers. In May 1948, commenting on a paper of Dr. Walter Marseille of Berkeley California, Bertrand Russell noted his agreement that an aggressive anti-Soviet policy, even considering a possible World War III, as the proper one for the United States to pursue. Six years later, in "A Prescription for the World" [SR Aug. 28, 1954], Lord Russell appeared to reject this view; he ruled out any consideration of World War III. Dr. Marseille remarked the discrepancy and sent SR the 1948 letter. SR then requested Lord Russell to submit his own reasons for this revision in thinking, which he generously consented to do.

1948: I have read your paper [Dr. Marseille's] with great interest. I agree entirely with all the underlying assumptions. As soon as Russia rejected the Baruch proposals I urged that all nations favoring international control of atomic energy should form an Alliance, and threaten Russia with war unless Russia agreed to come in and permit inspection. Your proposal is, in effect, the same, for compulsory inspection would be, legally, an act of war, and would be so viewed by the Soviet Government.

During the past year conversations with professional strategists have slightly modified my views. They say that in a few years we shall be in a better position, and that Russia will not yet have atomic bombs; that the economic recovery and military integration of Western Europe should be carried further before war begins; that at present neither air power nor atomic bombs could prevent Russia from overrunning all West Europe up to the Straits of Dover; and that the most dangerous period for us is the next two years. These views may or may not be correct, but at any rate they are those of the best experts.

There are some things of which Europeans are more vividly conscious than Americans. If Russia overruns West Europe, the destruction will be such as no subsequent reconquest can undo. Practically the whole educated population will be sent to labor camps in Siberia or on the shores of the White Sea, where most will die of hardships and the survivors will be turned into animals. (See what happened to the Polish intellectuals.) Atomic bombs, if used, will at first have to be dropped on West Europe, since Russia will be out of reach. The Russians, even without atomic bombs, will be able to destroy all big towns in England, as the Germans would have done if the war had lasted a few months longer. I have no doubt that America would win in the end, but unless West Europe can be preserved from invasion, it will be lost to civilization for centuries.

Even at such a price I think war would be worthwhile. Communism must be wiped out, and world government must be established. But if, by waiting, we could defend our present line in Germany and Italy, it would be an immeasurable boon. I do not think the Russians will yield without war. I think all (including Stalin) are fatuous and ignorant. But I hope I am wrong about this.

Bertrand Russell
Trinity College, Cambridge.

1954: I am much obliged to the Editor of *The Saturday Review* for giving me this opportunity of explaining why my views on policy towards Russia have changed since the writing of the above letter to Dr. Marseille in 1948.

The main cause in my change of opinion is the shift which has occurred in the balance of forces. In the letter above I say that it would be desirable to postpone war for a time, because in the opinion of such experts as I had been able to consult our military position was likely to improve. In fact, however, the exact opposite has happened. Russia acquired atom and hydrogen bombs much sooner than we expected. China became Communist. Western Europe failed to unite, and Western Germany is not yet rearmed. For all these reasons, of which the Russian possession of the bombs is the most important, it seems to me that a policy which was feasible in the first years after 1945 can now no longer achieve its objects.

Immediately after Hiroshima it seemed obvious that a nuclear war in which both sides were armed with bombs must be avoided if the human race was not to suffer shipwreck. This was the view of the American Government and led to the Baruch Plan. Considering that America at that time had a monopoly of the bomb, the offer of the Baruch Plan was an act of the highest generosity as well as the most statesmanlike wisdom. I thought at that time that perhaps the Russians could be compelled to accept the offer by the threat of war in the event of their continued refusal. Whether such a threat would have been wise became a purely academic question as soon as Russia also had the bombs. The situation now is that we cannot defeat Russia except by defeating ourselves.

Those who still advocate war seem to me to be living in a fool's paradise. I must add, however, that I do not now, any more than at an earlier time, advocate either appeasement or a slackening in rearmament, since either might encourage the Communist powers in aggressive designs and would therefore make war more likely. The problem for statesmanship in the present situation, as I see it, is to avoid war without surrender on our side or the expectation of surrender on the other.

I should not be wholly sincere if I did not admit that my opinions have undergone a change somewhat deeper than that warranted by strategic considerations. The awful prospect of the extermination of the human race, if not in the next war, then in the next but one or the next but two, is so sobering to any imagination which has seriously contemplated it as to demand very fundamental fresh thought on the whole subject, not only of international relations, but of human life and its capabilities. If you were quarreling with a man about some issue that both you and he had thought important just at the moment when a sudden hurricane threatened to destroy you both and the whole neighborhood you would probably forget the quarrel. I think what is important at present is to make mankind aware of the hurricane and forgetful of the issues which had been producing strife. I know it is difficult after spending many years and much eloquence on the evils of Communism or capitalism, as the case may be, to see this issue as one of relative unimportance. But, although this is difficult, it is what both the Soviet rulers and the men who shape the policy of the United States will have to achieve if mankind is to survive. To make such a realization possible is the purpose of the policy which I now advocate.

Bertrand Russell
Richmond, Surrey.

[122]

# Communism and War

*The Manchester Guardian* (22nd November, 1954), p. 6 | C54.33

*Russell reaffirms his belief that war is not a rational option for either the U.S. or the U.S.S.R.*

Sir, —A letter from Mr. Colin Clark[2] in your issue of November 18 gives a misleading statement of what is at stake in the relations between East and West. The question he is discussing is whether it would be better to have a world war than to submit to the Communists. He says that the question is whether, for the sake of prolonging our own lives for a few more years, it is worthwhile to sell our children and descendants into perpetual enslavement. This is not the question at issue. If there is a third world war it is likely that neither in the West nor in Communist countries will there be any children or descendants either to enjoy freedom or to suffer slavery. It is this issue that both East and West have to face.

—Yours &c., Russell
41 Queen's Road, Richmond, Surrey.

[123]

# Earl Russell Praises Acland

*The Bolton Evening News* (18th May, 1955), p. 7 | C55.24

*Although Russell did not always agree with Sir Richard Acland (see below, document [183]), he applauds Sir Richard's "courage" in resigning from the Labour Party over its nuclear policy. Russell's letter was included in the text of the* Evening News *article.*

Earl Russell (Bertrand Russell, the philosopher) who today celebrates his 83rd birthday, has written a letter of support to Sir Richard Acland, the former Labour M.P. for Gravesend, who resigned his seat in protest at Britain's decision to manufacture the hydrogen bomb.

2. Colin Grant Clark (1905–1989), an English statistician and economist. He served as Under Secretary for Labour from 1946 to 1952.

Sir Richard is fighting the Gravesend seat in the general election as an Independent.

In his letter to the electors of Gravesend, Lord Russell says: "I am not sure that I agree at all points with Sir Richard Acland's policy, but I am sure that his return to Parliament is of very great national and even international importance.

"Political courage and independence have become rare and Sir Richard has displayed them in a high degree. The menace of the H-bomb is the most serious that has ever threatened mankind, and Sir Richard is doing all that is in the power of an individual to make the nation aware of the catastrophe that must be avoided."

[124]

## Prime Minister's Reply to Lord Russell

*The Times* (16th July, 1955), p. 5 | C55.31

*The editor of* The Times *printed the exchange of letters between Russell and the British Prime Minister (Anthony Eden) just before the latter's departure to Geneva for a summit conference with the U.S and Russia.*[3] The Times *editor included the following introduction:*

On the eve of the Prime Minister's departure for Geneva there was an exchange of letters between him and Lord Russell (Bertrand Russell) on the subject of nuclear warfare. The text of the letters was issued from 10, Downing Street yesterday. It was as follows:

Dear Mr. Prime Minister, —I enclose a statement,[4] signed by some of the most eminent scientific authorities on nuclear warfare, pointing out the danger of utter and irretrievable disaster which would be involved in

3. Two months earlier, in London, the Soviet Union had shocked the West by accepting a Western arms control proposal on conventional forces and offering to eliminate weapons of mass destruction under a plan replete with an intrusive system of inspection. The West withdrew its previous offers and put forward an alternative plan in July at Geneva—Eisenhower's 'Open Skies' plan, whereby the U.S. and the Soviet Union would exchange "complete blue prints" of each other's military establishments, a plan which prompted I.F. Stone to quip that "we had long accused the Russians of proposing disarmament without inspection; now we were proposing inspection without disarmament." See Stone's *Polemics and Prophecies* (Random House, 1970), p. 270.

4. The "statement" to which Russell refers was the Russell-Einstein Manifesto, decrying the danger of nuclear weapons and affirming the need to abolish war, drafted by Russell with Einstein's approval and the endorsement of ten eminent scientists.

such warfare, and the consequent necessity of finding some way other than war by which international disputes can be settled. It is my earnest hope that you will give public expression to your opinion as to the problem dealt with in this statement, which is the most serious that has ever confronted the human race.

Yours faithfully, Bertrand Russell.

[125]

## Britain's Bomb

*The Manchester Guardian* (21st March, 1957), p. 6 | C57.08

*Britain became a nuclear power in 1952 with its first nuclear test, followed by another in 1953. Nuclear testing by the U.S., U.S.S.R., and Britain increased dramatically in 1957, creating much concern and initiating a world-wide campaign for a test ban led by Linus Pauling, Albert Schweitzer, and others. Russell played an important role in the British efforts for a test ban.*

Sir, —I wish to join in the already influential protests against the British Government's decision to carry out a nuclear test at Christmas Island. The hazards are unknown, and the arguments in favour appear to be only those of a rather foolish national vanity.

In addition to the arguments against the tests in general, there is in this case the entirely justifiable anger of the Japanese at the wanton and undeserved injury which we propose to inflict upon them. The political disadvantages of carrying out the test far outweigh, on any sane computation, the technical advantages of the knowledge to be gained.

Apart, however, from such arguments, there are the much weightier moral considerations. A general agreement to discontinue tests is probably attainable, and it is this that our Government should be seeking to realise.

Bertrand Russell
Plas Penrhyn, Penrhyndeudraeth, Merioneth.

[126]

## Britain's Bomb—Can we defend ourselves?

*The Manchester Guardian* (26th March, 1957), p. 6 | C57.10

*The question of the wisdom of a British nuclear deterrent independent of America's would vex the British political scene for the next few years with Russell playing a prominent part advancing the case against a British Bomb.*

Sir, —Mr. R.R. Stokes[5] is pursuing a delusive vision in hoping to make us "independent of anyone else in defence of our own shores." If we were engaged in a nuclear war with Russia while the United States remained neutral, we should be obliterated within a day or two. The possession of nuclear weapons increases the likelihood of this fate and therefore augments our insecurity. I am shocked to learn from a report in your issue of March 23 that Mr. Aubrey Jones, the Minister of Supply, contemplates our entry into a nuclear war without the support of America and imagines that we can be in a position to defend ourselves against Russia in such a war. I had supposed that only a few aged Colonel Blimps still lived in this land of happy dreams, and I am amazed to find that the British Government is so completely ignorant of things known to all well-informed persons.

—Yours &c., Bertrand Russell
Plas Penrhyn, Penrhyndeudraeth, Merioneth.

[127]

## Britain and the H-Bomb

*The New Statesman* (9th November, 1957), p. 617 | C57.28

*Russell agrees with J.B. Priestly's article (2nd November) which criticized Aneurin Bevan, the shadow Foreign Secretary, for abandoning the idea of unilateral British nuclear disarmament.*

Sir, —I have read with great pleasure and almost complete agreement

5. R.R. Stokes (1897–1957) was a Member of Parliament and a minister in the Labour Government, 1950–51.

the article by Mr. Priestley[6] on Britain's share in nuclear warfare. It has seemed until recently that Britain might make nuclear weapons but eschew tests; this, however, I understand is technically impossible. I deeply regret Mr. Bevan's[7] capitulation to the Foreign Office, which follows the precedent of Ernest Bevin and Ramsay MacDonald. If the Labour Party is to offer a substantial alternative to the present government, it will have to find in its ranks some statesman bold enough to ignore the so-called experts, who are blinded by tradition to the apprehension of present facts.

There are three issues which British foreign policy has to consider: first, shall there continue to be human beings on this planet; second, shall Soviet Communism dominate the world, or may others systems survive here and there; third, can Britain continue to be regarded as in the same rank as Russia and America among great powers? The government and Mr. Bevan agree that the third of these issues is the one which should decide our policy. They do not face the inevitable development that nuclear weapons will, within a very short time, be manufactured by a great many states, and that, when this stage has been reached, if any one of such states is governed by a lunatic (as will probably be the case) the rest of the world will have to submit to him or perish. For this development Britain will have a grave responsibility unless the present British policy is reversed.

Bertrand Russell
Penrhyndeudraeth

6. J.B. Priestly (1894–1984) was a popular English novelist and a vigorous critic of nuclear weapons. Priestly's November 2nd article rallied the anti-nuclear forces and sparked the founding of the Campaign for Nuclear Disarmament.

7. Aneurin Bevan (1897–1960) was an outspoken leader of the left wing of the Labour Party. As Minister of Health in the Labour Government (1945–51) he introduced the socialized National Health Service. In coming out as a supporter of a British bomb, Bevan made the much-quoted remark that Britain "should not go naked into the conference chambers."

••••••••••••• [128] •••••••••••••

# Bertrand Russell on Negotiations

*The New Republic* (27th January, 1958), p. 9 | C58.05

*Russell wrote an 'Open Letter to Eisenhower and Khrushchev' (*New Statesman and Nation, *23rd November, 1957), urging a summit meeting to consider "the conditions of co-existence." That letter prompted Khrushchev to respond that peace could indeed be served by such a meeting. Russell elaborated his views in* The Observer *(5th January) and proposed a cessation of nuclear weapons production—unilaterally by Britain if necessary—and a Germany "freed from all alien armed forces and pledged to neutrality in any conflict between East and West." Eventually John Foster Dulles, the U.S. Secretary of State, replied for Eisenhower. The exchange of letters was published as* The Vital Letters of Russell, Khrushchev, and Dulles *(MacGibben and Kee, 1958).*

*In this letter Russell responds to a request from* The New Republic *to detail his views on world peace still further.*

Dear Sirs: I suggest the following terms as a basis for negotiations:

Nuclear weapons tests to cease immediately by agreement. Negotiations to be inaugurated for abolition of H-bombs under guarantee of neutral inspection (say by India and Sweden, jointly). There will also be need for inspection of the industrial use of atomic energy to insure its not being diverted to war uses. Conventional weapons to be cut down in such a way as not to alter the balance of power.

A Neutralized Zone to be established in Central Europe comprising, as a minimum, Germany—East and West—Poland, Czechoslovakia and Hungary. No alien armed forces, whether Russian or Western, to be allowed in the Zone. Each country in the Zone to be free to choose its own political and economic system and, in particular, East and West Germany to be allowed to unite with whatever form of constitution they prefer. No State in the Neutralized Zone to conclude an alliance with any State outside the Zone. Germany to accept the Oder-Neisse frontier.

In the Middle East, the West must avoid opposing Arab Nationalism or supporting reactionary Governments. Arab nations should be left free to develop as they may prefer, but Israel must be protected from aggression, and prevented from committing it, by a United Nations force on its frontiers. Friendly relations with Arab nationalism offer the best chance for Western oil interests.

Communist China should be recognized and admitted to the United Nations with a permanent seat on the Security Council.

As regards procedure, I should wish to see, first negotiations between the US and the USSR along with a view, not to reaching binding decisions, but to discovering whether a compromise agreement is possible. If it is found to be possible, it should then be proposed to the other Powers of NATO and the Warsaw Pact as something that the US and the USSR could both accept.

I think it may be assumed that neither the US nor the USSR desire a nuclear war, but there are risks of its occurring unintentionally. The first and most urgent steps should be those which diminish this risk. These have to do with H-bomb tests and with the constant flight of planes armed with nuclear weapons. Agreements to stop these should therefore have priority. Almost equally urgent is the prevention of the acquisition of H-bombs by Powers which do not have them at present. I should wish to see the US and the USSR jointly agree to prevent the acquisition of H-bombs by new Powers, and, if it would facilitate such agreement, I should wish to see Britain renounce H-bombs as part of the agreement.

Bertrand Russell
Plas Penrhyn, Penrhyndeudraeth, Merioneth. 10 January, 1958

[129]

## The Right Grade of Deterrence

*The Times* (4th March, 1958), p. 9 | C58.15

*In a House of Commons speech on 27th February, 1958, Emmanuel Shinwell (1884–1986) an M.P. and a leading member of the Labour Party for more than three decades, referred to Russell as a "superannuated philosopher." Shinwell, already in his mid-70s, gets as good as he gave.*

Sir, —May a "superannuated philosopher" permit himself a few words in reply to that juvenile politician Mr. Shinwell? In common with the rest of the politicians of east and west, Mr. Shinwell has not grasped the fact that the problems raised by nuclear energy are not such as a politician's training enables him to understand. I should advise Mr. Shinwell to retire from politics and study theoretical physics. When he has understood the subject, his opinions will perhaps become worth listening to—though I fear that by that time he will be "superannuated."

Yours, &c., Bertrand Russell
Plas Penrhyn, Penrhyndeudraeth, Merioneth.

[130]

## The Nuclear Dilemma

*The Times* (6th March, 1958), p. 11 | C58.16

*In this and the next letter in response to Emmanuel Shinwell, Russell emphasizes his contention that the supposed security of nuclear deterrence is "an illusion."*

Sir, —Mr. Shinwell's letter in your columns today illustrates the difficulty that politicians experience in grasping the nature of the nuclear dilemma.

He begins by remarking very truly that he knows a nuclear war would be disastrous. In his next sentence he points out that in a major conflict between the United States and Russia we should be involved whether we have nuclear weapons or not. It is not only we who should be involved but all the nations of the world whose quarrels would be ended in one vast graveyard.

Those who oppose the British possession of H-bombs are not concerned with guesses as to possible Russian benevolence. They are concerned with the fact that possession of nuclear weapons does not increase security. The supposed great deterrent is an illusion not only because neither side can use it without disaster to itself but also because of the appalling risk of an unintended war brought on by some misunderstood "incident."

I see no reason to believe in the "benevolence" of the Russian Government or of any other, but the hope that we can defend the west by means of the H-bomb is illusory because to use this weapon would be suicide. The human race can only survive if governments realize the dangerous futility of H-bombs, and I should like the British Government to lead the way towards sanity in this respect.

Yours &c., Bertrand Russell
Plas Penrhyn, Penrhyndeudraeth, Merioneth

••••••••••••• [131] •••••••••••••

# The Choices Before Us

*The Times* (8th March, 1958), pp. 4, 7 | C58.17

*Russell sharpens the logical alternatives for Mr. Shinwell, and points out the danger of unintended war due to nuclear proliferation.*

Sir, —Mr. Shinwell still misses the point. Which of the following propositions does he deny?

(1) If there is a nuclear war, Britain is finished, whatever policy our Government may have pursued.

(2) Unless we renounce the H-bomb and seek its restriction to America and Russia, it will soon be possessed by France, Germany, China, Egypt, Israel, and the Principality of Monaco.

(3) When this has happened, a nuclear war not intended by either Russia or America will be far more probable than it is at present.

Yours &c., Bertrand Russell
Plas Penrhyn, Penrhyndeudraeth, Merioneth, March 7.

••••••••••••• [132] •••••••••••••

# Nuclear Dilemma

*The Times* (18th March, 1958), p. 11 | C58.19

*Russell gives a* Times *correspondent two reasons for British unilateral renunciation of the H-bomb.*

Sir, —Allow me to say a few words to correct misunderstandings in the letter of Mr. Carl H. Stern[8] published in your issue of March 13. Mr. Stern seems to think that the argument for unilateral renunciation of the H-bomb by Britain is that this action would win the admiration of the world. This is not the argument that influences me. Experience has taught me that sensible actions are seldom admired by fools. The arguments which influence me are two.

First: As things stand, H-bombs will soon be possessed by all and sundry, Communist, anti-Communist, Middle Eastern Powers, and the

8. Carl H. Stern (1937– ), an American journalist. He served as host of *Program P.M.* from 1959 to 1961 and as a legal journalist for the *Cleveland Reporter*, 1961–67.

rest. The greater number of Governments possessing this weapon, the greater is the likelihood that at least one will prefer the extermination of the human race to the victory of its enemies—a point of view already expressed by many Americans and some western Europeans. For this reason, it is important that H-bombs should be possessed by as few Powers as possible. America and Russia already provide a deterrent which sane men should find adequate, and what Britain can add is negligible. British renunciation of the bomb would make it more possible for America and Russia to agree, as they easily could, that no other Power should possess the bomb. This, in itself, would be a useful step and would make more possible the ultimate renunciation of the bomb throughout the world.

Second: I do not care to owe a few years of precarious liberty to ability to participate as an accomplice in a crime which has no parallel in human history.

Yours, &c., Bertrand Russell
Plas Penrhyn, Penrhyndeudraeth, Merioneth.

[133]

## Central Question

*The Observer* (20th April, 1958), p. 8 | C58.27

*Russell writes in support of* The Observer'*s editorials on preserving world peace. Here he draws attention to the psychological obstacles to peace and the need for "subordination of national pride."*

Sir, —Your three editorials on the "Central Question" give genuinely constructive suggestions for the preservation of world peace. There are innumerable schemes designed for this end; my post brings me a new one about every other day. The difficulty is not to think of schemes which would be good if adopted, but to think of a scheme which has some chance of being adopted. This is the merit of your suggestion that the United States and the U.S.S.R. should co-operate for the one purpose of safeguarding peace by preventing the spread of nuclear arms.

The obstacles to the adoption of such a plan are psychological. Many people, especially in the United States, think that the extermination of the human race would be preferable to the victory of Communism. I do not know whether the correlative opinion exists in Russia, but its influential existence in the United States would, for the moment, make any co-operation between the United States and the U.S.S.R. very difficult.

If the plan that you put forward is to have any chance of success, it is necessary that fanaticism on both sides should diminish. Both sides must make contributions which will have to be more important than any of them seem willing to make at present. One could wish that a summit conference would be a means to this end, but, as yet, such an outcome seems very doubtful.

There is one point in your programme that deserves whole-hearted support, but is likely to meet with vehement opposition. You suggest that all Powers other than the United States and the U.S.S.R. should acquiesce in a more or less subordinate role. Britain has hitherto refused to do so, and France and Germany and perhaps China seem likely to follow Britain in this dangerous course. In urging the subordination of national pride to the supreme end of preserving peace, you deserve the praise of all who realise that the continuation of the human species is in jeopardy.

Although all the above difficulties are serious, it is nevertheless not irrational to hope that the Governments of the United States and the U.S.S.R. may gradually become more and more aware that their common interest in the preservation of peace outweighs the rival interests of power politics and must prevail if anything of what either side desires is to be achieved.

Bertrand Russell
Merioneth.

[134]

## Progress

*The Observer* (20th July, 1958), p. 21 | C58.42

*In this letter and the next, Russell criticizes the British scientist and novelist, C.P. Snow, for what Russell regards as an unduly benign view of nuclear war.*

Sir, —Your issue of July 13 contains an article by Sir Charles Snow which will give comfort to all escapists. He assures your readers that, in his opinion, a great many people would survive a nuclear war. He does not mention how he came to know this. I assume that it was a revelation from On High. He appears to have never heard of fall-out.

Russell
Merioneth.

[135]

## Progress and The Bomb

*The Observer* (27th July, 1958), p. 2 | C58.43

*Snow's response to Russell's first letter appeared on the same page. He accused Russell of being overly emotional, and he stated that no one knows the consequences of nuclear war, but that most experts sided with him as against Russell's "apocalyptic inflation."*

*Russell cites Einstein on the probability of survival and defends his emotional posture.*[9]

Sir, —Sir Charles Snow's reply to my letter in your issue of July 20 calls for a few words of rejoinder from me. He and I are agreed that no one knows how many people would survive a nuclear war. His guess is two-thirds of the total population of the world. I, following a great mass of expert opinion, to which Einstein was the first or one of the first to give expressions, think it quite likely that no one would survive. Neither of us professes to know, but his guess is quite peculiarly optimistic. The opinions of experts differ according to their temperament, their politics and the source of their income. I do not think a man is serving a public object by minimising the risks.

As for Sir Charles Snow's objection that my letter is "emotionally charged," I have no apology to offer. I think the prospects of the destruction caused by a nuclear war *should* cause emotion, because, unless there is emotion, nuclear war will not be prevented.

Russell.
Merioneth.

9. On the same page, Joseph Rotblat (who helped Russell organize the Pugwash Conference and received the Nobel Peace Prize in 1995) comes to Russell's defense by pointing out that even if destruction of the human race is not possible now, the trend in the growth of nuclear stockpiles makes it not unlikely in the near future.

In the 1970s and 1980s many scientists stated that a war using ten thousand megatons of TNT equivalent would likely wipe out the human race. See Jonathan Schell, *The Abolition* (Knopf, 1984), pp. 15–16. In 1958 the U.S. had sixteen thousand megatons; the Soviets had only 100, but would attain omnicidal levels by 1968. See *Bulletin of the Atomic Scientists* (December 1989), p. 52.

••••••••••••• [136] •••••••••••••

## Nuclear Disarmament

*The Manchester Guardian* (6th November, 1958), p. 6 | C58.53

*The Campaign for Nuclear Disarmament was brought into existence in 1958 by Russell (who served as its first president) and other anti-nuclear advocates, including J.B. Priestly, Kingsley Martin, Denis Healey, and Canon John Collins of St. Paul's.*

*Russell and Collins (Chairman of the Campaign for Nuclear Disarmament), denounce nuclear testing and call for donations to help continue the work of CND.*

Sir, —Many thousands of your readers must have been appalled during this past week at the spectacle of the three nuclear Powers competing desperately to keep abreast of each other in nuclear explosions,[10] ignoring the fact that every ten megatons of fission kills or maims 15,000 of our unborn children.

May we suggest a practical way in which sympathetic people may show their feelings: £2,000 is urgently needed for the winter programme of the Campaign for Nuclear Disarmament, which will include, among other things, a European Congress in London on January 17 and 18. Donations should be sent to the Secretary, 146 Fleet Street, London E.C. 4.

—Yours &c., Russell, President
L. John Collins, Chairman
October 30.

••••••••••••• [137] •••••••••••••

## The Unborn Victims of Nuclear Tests

*The Manchester Guardian* (12th November, 1958), p. 6 | C58.54

Sir, —A letter from Mr. P.R.J. Burch[11] in your issue today takes me to task for making a statement concerning the evils due to nuclear

---

10. At the end of October the three nuclear powers (U.S., U.K., U.S.S.R.) agreed to observe a moratorium on atmospheric testing. But all three nations dramatically increased testing in the weeks leading up to the moratorium which collapsed in 1960 when France tested a nuclear device.

11. P.R.J. Burch, a British biologist and medical researcher. He is the author of *The Biology of Cancer: A New Approach* (Baltimore: University Park Press, 1976).

explosions in terms which are too positive. I will agree that instead of saying "The fact that . . . [every ten megatons of fission kills or maims 15,000 of our unborn children]" and so on, I ought to have said, "The fact that according to the most careful estimates available." I think that with that addition my statement is unimpeachable. The evidence upon which it is based is set forth quite fully in Dr. Linus Pauling's[12] book "No More War," chapters four and five.

—Yours &c., Bertrand Russell
Penrhyndeudraeth, November 11.

[138]

## "Summit Agreement"

*The Guardian* (23rd May, 1960), p. 6 | C60.14

*Russell's concerns about nuclear war, and his conviction that both the Americans and the Soviets were embarking on disastrous policies, leads him to remark, with a kind of Swiftian sarcasm, about their "identical purposes."*

Sir, —Can we assume that the Pentagon and the Praesidium have enough intelligence to perceive the consequences of their respective policies? If so, we must conclude that they have an identical aim—namely, the extinction of the human species. Since their purposes are identical, is it not time that they ceased their pretended mutual hostility and formed a firm alliance against all sane men?

—Yours & c., Bertrand Russell.
Plas Penrhyn

12. Already a Nobel Laureate in chemistry, Linus Pauling received the Nobel Peace Prize in 1962, for publicizing the health risks of nuclear fallout and for rallying the global scientific community in support of an atomic test ban.

[139]

# "Case for A Neutral Britain"

*The Guardian* (15th June, 1960), p. 8 | C60.17

*Russell was a founder and first president of the Campaign for Nuclear Disarmament (CND). He had been an early opponent—along with Canon Collins, J.B. Priestly, and other prominent Britons—of British nuclear armament. Despite some critics' claims, he never advocated unilateral nuclear disarmament by the West. But throughout the 1960s he did advocate British unilateralism: that Britain should both unilaterally give up its nuclear weapons and leave the NATO alliance, on the general grounds that (1) Britain would reduce its chances of nuclear attack by the U.S.S.R., and (2) Britain would be in a better position to foster an East-West rapprochement.*

*In this letter, one of many on the subject of British unilateralism, Russell argues his case.*

To the Editor of the "Guardian"

Sir, —In your issue of June 13 there is a carefully dispassionate discussion by Mr. Anthony Howard[13] entitled "Labour Party and Pacifism." This article implies, perhaps justly, that the strongest support for unilateralism comes from believers in complete pacifism. There is, however, a case for breaking with N.A.T.O. and abandoning the "protection" of nuclear weapons which has nothing to do with theoretical pacifism or with any principle not generally accepted in international relations.

Anyone who takes the trouble to examine present-day facts must soon become aware that Britain derives no degree of safety whatever from the American alliance or from nuclear weapons, whether British or American. On the contrary, reliance upon America and nuclear weapons increases the likelihood of the total destruction of the population of Britain.

The Soviet Government has given notice that any satellite of America which permits its territory to be a starting point for U-2 flights over Russia will be exterminated.[14] We have been assured by our Government that British territory will, henceforth, not be used for this purpose, but it is exceedingly probable that, if the American occupation of Britain

---

13. Anthony Howard (1934– ), an English journalist. He served on the editorial staff of the *Guardian* from 1959 to 1961.

14. In May 1960, American U-2 pilot, Gary Powers, had been shot down over the U.S.S.R., creating an international crisis which wrecked the Paris summit conference.

continues, British territory will be used for some purpose equally obnoxious to Russia. Will the American alliance, in that case, protect us from obliteration? Only if the Russians believe that after Britain had been wiped out, the United States would honour its obligations to our no longer existing country.

America can only do this by inaugurating a general nuclear war which would involve wiping out not only the population of Russia, but also that of the United States and perhaps the whole of the rest of the world. If the Russians do not believe that the American Government will adopt this suicidal course, they may think it worth while to devote the necessary few hours to destroying us.

If, on the other hand, we are not allied with America and do not possess H-bombs, the Russians will have no motive for attacking us, and strong propaganda motive for letting us alone. Moreover, if we become neutral, we can be far more useful than we are at present in devising measures for the prevention of a nuclear war, which should be the supreme aim of statesmanship in our time. Neutrals can do more than can be done by States belonging to either camp in the way of devising and urging upon each side equally possibly acceptable compromises and other means of lessening tension. It is on such work that I, for one, should wish to see Britain engaged.

—Yours & c., Bertrand Russell.
Plas Penrhyn

•••••••••••••• [140] ••••••••••••••

## A Question of Survival

*The Guardian* (30th June, 1960), p. 30 | C60.18

*Russell presents a similar, if more succinct, argument for British unilateralism and supports his case by reference to the American nuclear strategist, Herman Kahn.*

To the Editor of the "Guardian"

Sir, —From your article "Labour Quarrel over Defense," it appears that Conservatives and the orthodox section of the Labour party are agreed that the security of the nation is the first duty of any Government. I profoundly agree, and, if I thought that either party had a programme likely to secure this end, I should support it. I observe, however, on this occasion as on many previous ones, that practical politicians are too busy to know the facts on which their decisions ought to be based.

These facts are: a) the Soviet Government has announced that any satellite of the United States which permits U-2 flights from its territory will be exterminated; b) Although the British Government has announced that it will not permit such flights, it is almost certain that the United States authorities will soon find, too suddenly for us to object effectively, that it is necessary to use our territory in some way which will be equally obnoxious to the U.S.S.R.; c) A Soviet attack upon Britain alone could obliterate our population in a few hours; d) It is unlikely that, after we were all dead, the United States would think it worth while to come to our defense by causing the rest of the human race to be obliterated; and it is still more unlikely that the Soviet Government would think that the United States would do so; e) It follows that, if we wish any part of the population of Britain to survive, we must leave N.A.T.O. and not allow American armed forces on our territory.

Most of this argument is set out in detail in an article called "The Feasibility of War and Deterrence" by Mr. Herman Kahn (an American) in "Survival." vol. ii. number 2.

—Yours & c., Bertrand Russell
Plas Penrhyn, Penrhyndeudraeth, Merioneth

[141]

## Great Britain as a Neutral

*The Guardian* (14th July, 1960), p. 8 | C60.24

*Russell presents his ideas for a neutral Britain and responds to letters from three prominent Britons. The idea of World Government is very much a part of Russell's conception of a secure and peaceful world. On July 15th, the Labour Party came out against Britain's role as an independent nuclear power, and at the annual Party Conference in October, the Party voted to support a policy of British unilateral nuclear disarmament—a vote overturned the following year (1961).*

To the Editor of the "Guardian"

Sir, —Three letters in your issue of July 11 call for a reply. I will begin by restating my own position: 1) No policy will secure safety either for our own country or for the human species until there is a World Government with a monopoly of the major weapons of war. 2) A general nuclear war would be an absolute disaster to the whole world. 3) Britain in common with other satellites of the United States is exposed to the danger of extinction without a general war. I am persuaded that America intends to honour her obligations under NATO, but if all the inhabitants of Britain were already dead I think the American Government might reasonably doubt whether any purpose would be served by extending the same fate to the rest of mankind. 4) NATO and American bases in Britain might be held by the USSR to afford a motive for obliterating Britain. This motive would not exist if Britain were neutral.

I come now to the arguments of my critics. Mr. Sorensen,[15] so it seems to me, envisages quite a different sort of general war from that which is probable. The war which seems probable is one in which each side launched its bombs and by the end of the first few days the population remaining in either country is moribund. I cannot think it likely that during the few hours of war either country would concern itself with Britain or any other territory outside the United States and the USSR. Mr. Sorensen imagines "economic strangulation with its resultant misery and chaos." This is altogether a slower process than any that is probable since we should all be dying or dead anyhow. He also mentions as possible a "strategically limited" war between the United States and the USSR. I cannot think that there is the faintest likelihood of any strategic limitation and in this I agree with all the military authorities that I have been able to consult.

Mr. Sorensen argues that if Britain were neutral both America and Russia would have a motive for occupying Britain. As to this, one might argue that there are many neutral countries, none of which has been occupied by either. But I think the more cogent argument is that Russia's ICBM's are good enough or bad enough to make the occupation of Britain unimportant to Russia. As for America, I find it impossible to believe that she would set to work to occupy territory of any neutral Power. Moreover, if America were to attempt to occupy a neutral Britain, Russia would undoubtedly consider this a hostile act. America would recognize that and would, therefore, abstain from occupying Britain. In fact, as a result of becoming neutral, we should ensure the protection of both Russia and America, and not only of one of them.

---

15. R.W. Sorensen (1891–1971) became a Life Peer in 1964 and served as a minister in the Labour government from 1964 until 1968.

Mr. Green's[16] letter is one with which, in part, I have considerable sympathy, but I cannot agree that either NATO or the Warsaw Pact is in any degree a step towards World Government. It would only become such a step if one or other bloc had a chance of achieving victory and of imposing imperialist control on vanquished enemies. But there is practically no chance that either side could achieve such a victory. Nor would the resultant World Government, if it could be established, be such as any liberal-minded person could welcome.The road to World Government, if it is to become possible, must be through the United Nations, enlarged and strengthened, and not through rival military alliances.

Mr. Graham[17] ignores the argument, which I have accepted from influential American sources, that the American forces in Britain would not be considered by America sufficiently important to justify a war against Russia if the Russians made it clear that their attack was only against Britain. As for the possibility which Mr. Graham suggests that the British Government might involve itself in another Suez, this surely becomes a quite fantastic hypothesis if Britain were no longer a member of either bloc, since we should then be defenseless against universal hostility.

Yours & c., Bertrand Russell
Penrhyndeudraeth [Wales], July 11

[142]

## Disarmament Policy

*The Guardian* (1st August, 1960), p. 4 | C60.27

*Russell's letters to the editor frequently involved exchanges with notable personalities, including Members of Parliament. In this letter, and in the next three, Russell defends, sometimes with humor, the nuclear disarmament campaign against the criticisms of Desmond Donnelly, M.P.*

16. A. Green (1911–1991) served as a minister in the Conservative government from 1961 until 1964.

17. T.E. Graham (1925– ) became a Life Peer in 1983 and served as a minister in the Labour government from 1976 until 1979.

To the Editor of the "Guardian":

Sir, —In your issue of July 27 there is an article by Mr. Desmond Donnelly, M.P.,[18] in the course of which he says, "There has never been in modern political history a more pathetically muddled or foolish policy than the nuclear disarmament campaign." I agree with this statement down to the word "than," but after this I should substitute the words "the policy pursued jointly by the United States and USSR with the support of the British Government."

This policy is to discuss disarmament endlessly with the tacit understanding that no agreement is to be reached, while the daily probability of unintended war mounts steadily towards certainty. For Britain, there is the additional risk that our whole population might be exterminated in an hour or two without causing a general war, and that, therefore NATO fails to protect this country against attack by the USSR. Nor would our own armed forces offer us safety even if we spent so much upon them as to reduce our whole population to subsistence level.

I do not know whether Mr. Donnelly is ignorant of the facts or indifferent to the survival of his compatriots. If he is not ignorant of the facts, his letter implies that only "pacifists and fellow travellers" desire our national survival. Undoubtedly there are pacifists and fellow travellers in the CND, but there are, also, those who are neither, but have taken the trouble to understand the present international situation. Among these are not to be included the governments of NATO or the Warsaw Pact, or the majority of the Labour Front Bench.

Yours & c., Bertrand Russell.
Plas Penrhyn, Penrhyndeudraeth, Merioneth.

18. Desmond L. Donnelly (1920– ), a Labour Member of Parliament, 1950–68. He authored several books on Cold War history, including *The March Wind: Explorations behind the Iron Curtain* (London: Collins, 1959). He joined the Conservative party in 1971.

[143]

# Greatest Threat

*The New York Times Magazine* (14th August, 1960),
Section 6, pp. 90–91 | C60.28

*In* The New York Times Magazine *of July 24th, Russell and British Labour party leader, Hugh Gaitskell, had taken opposing sides in dueling articles on the question of British unilateralism. In this letter Russell writes in rebuttal of Gaitskell's views.*

To the Editor: Mr. Gaitskell's reply to my arguments in favor of British neutralism calls for a rejoinder on certain points. First, as to the likelihood of a nuclear war by accident: Oskar Morgenstern, a politically orthodox American defense expert, in an article reprinted in Survival, says, "The probability of thermonuclear war's occurring appears to be significantly larger than the probability of its not occurring."

Ohio State University inaugurated a study of the possible causes of unintended war, which are numerous and have already on several occasions very nearly resulted in disaster. Adlai Stevenson has said: "There can be no deterrent to war by accident." I suppose it is proneness to such remarks which caused him to be thought unfit to be President.

The next question is what would occur in a nuclear war. Mr. Gaitskell brushes this aside with an acknowledgement that it would be horrible—which is oddly combined with a refusal to adopt policies making it less probable. The United States Secretary of Defense in 1958, summarizing a Pentagon report, maintained that in a nuclear war there would be 160 million deaths in the United States, 200 million in the U.S.S.R. and, in the United Kingdom, everybody.

Some authorities are more optimistic. A.G. Field, our civil defense expert, has stated: "It cannot be said categorically that in these countries [NATO allies of the U.S.] there would be no survivors after a nuclear attack."

I should certainly agree that this cannot be categorically asserted. Until the experiment is made, doubt is permissible, but it seems somewhat remarkable that the British Government, with the connivance of a majority of the Labor Front Bench, should support a policy of which the best that can be said is that it may leave a few Britons alive.

We were impressed by the seriousness of Hitler's threat to Britain in 1940, but it was not nearly as serious as the U.S. threat to Britain at the present moment. This threat arises not only from a possibility of a general war, but also from an entirely different source—namely, the risk that we might be dragged by the U.S. into acquiescence in measures regarded by the U.S.S.R. as provocative, and that we might, in consequence, be subjected to a completely destructive attack directed against Britain alone, and not also, against the U.S.

Mr. Gaitskell is surprised that I should consider this not unlikely. I cannot understand his surprise. At the time of the U-2 crisis, Khrushchev and Malinovsky loudly proclaimed that this would be their policy if incidents such as the U-2 flight continued. Malinovsky said of any NATO nations other than the U.S. which tolerated such incidents, "We shall deal them such a blow that nothing will be left of them."

He uttered on this occasion no similar threat against the United States. All the British newspapers, especially on May 10 and 11, were full of these threats, which were headlined. But apparently Mr. Gaitskell failed to see them.

Mr. Gaitskell asks, as if it were an argument against me, "Need brinkmanship continue?" Of course, it need not; but it will continue if the governments of the West persist in present policies which Mr. Gaitskell, in the main, supports.

A third point for which Mr. Gaitskell finds fault with me is as to the expense of the arms race. At present (to quote Sir R. Adams' "Assault at Arms") we in Britain spend only £30 per head per annum for every man, woman and child, but already we are being told that the estimates will have to be increased, and in America the Democrats have adopted a program rejecting any attempt at a ceiling for expenditure on armaments. I think Mr. Gaitskell seriously underrates the ingenuity of armament experts of both East and West in inventing new weapons.

The manned bomber is obsolescent; the guided missile is to have its little day; but clearly the future lies with manned satellites containing H-bombs. My arithmetic does not run to computing what they would cost.

Mr. Gaitskell rejects my view that ideological differences play a very small part in the hostility between East and West. I do not believe that, even if Russia became as liberal as our ally Franco's Spain, we should become friendly to the Soviet regime. We have been sometimes friendly with Russia, sometimes hostile, without any change in the Soviet governmental system.

Mr. Gaitskell says (1) that a nuclear war will almost certainly not happen, (2) that "the present peace is highly precarious." Which does he mean?

I do not wish to think that the whole world will become Communist, but I wish even less to see mankind obliterated. Neither disaster need occur. Mr. Gaitskell speaks favorably of disarmament, but fails to note that the most serious approaches to disarmament have been made by the U.S.S.R. and have been foiled by niggling opposition from the West.

Western policy, through blindness, has done everything to pose the alternative, "Red or dead." Those who advocate a policy which would evade this alternative are regarded as fellow travelers. As to this, however, public opinion in Britain is changing, and there seems now some hope that, in spite of our "patriots," there may be Britons alive at the end of the present century.

Bertrand Russell
London

[144]

## Britain's Two Perils

*The Guardian* (16th August, 1960), p. 5 | C60.29

*In this second letter in response to Donnelly, Russell distinguishes between the threat of general nuclear war and the threat of attack by the U.S.S.R. on Britain alone. He also quotes himself on the need to abolish war and not merely ban nuclear weapons.*

To the Editor of the "Guardian":

Sir, —I am grateful to Mr. Donnelly for his attempt to cure me of emotional muddleheadedness. I hope he will establish a seminar to instruct us in the art of logical thinking. If he permits it, I shall attend this seminar with all due humility. Perhaps he may begin his therapeutic activities on my behalf by replying to the following considerations, for, as yet, I still retain an emotional and muddleheaded feeling that it would be rather a pity if no Britons remained alive at the end of the present century. The chain of argument which Mr. Donnelly considers muddleheaded proceeds as follows:

The population of Britain is exposed to two quite distinct perils: the first, as to general nuclear war; the second, that of attack by Russia on Britain alone. The former peril is one of which, by this time, most politically conscious people are aware. But the second is a new peril, brought into prominence by the reaction of the Soviet Government to the U-2 incident. Khrushchev and Malinovsky have stated with great emphasis that any satellite of the United States which permits the US to use its territory in ways to which the Soviet Government objects will be obliterated. This could be done in an hour or two, and nothing that an individual satellite could do in the way of creating its own nuclear weapon would afford any serious protection.

It seems highly probable that, after an individual satellite (say Britain) had been obliterated, the US, in spite of NATO, might see no point in obliterating the rest of the population of the world as an act of futile vengeance. At present, therefore, the USSR has a motive for obliterating the satellites of the US one by one. Any satellite which became a neutral would no longer offer this temptation to the USSR.

I am interested to learn from Mr. Donnelly that the crisis in which we are living has nothing to do with nuclear weapons. The sort of situation which Mr. Donnelly describes in which poorer nations and classes attack richer ones has occurred frequently in history and does not distinguish our age from many others. What distinguishes the present situation from the former ones is the danger of obliteration by nuclear weapons. I infer that, when one has acquired Mr. Donnelly's capacity for thinking clearly and unemotionally, one regards the extermination of the human race as a triviality which serious politicians can ignore. Of course, Mr. Donnelly is entirely in the right in saying that the international problems presented by nuclear weapons cannot be solved by any unilateral action on the part of Britain. What unilateral action on the part of Britain can do is, first to diminish the risk of unilateral action by Russia against Britain, and second, to set an example of wise statesmanship.

Mr. Donnelly advances as an argument against me that even if an agreement were reached to abolish nuclear weapons, such weapons would be created afresh in time of war, and therefore only the prevention of war will save mankind. What he says on this point is almost verbally identical with what I have said myself with all the emphasis of which I am capable. In my original manifesto entitled "Man's Peril," I said: "Whatever agreements not to use hydrogen bombs had been reached in time of peace, they would no longer be considered binding in time of war, and both sides would set to work to manufacture hydrogen bombs as soon as war broke out, for if one side manufactured the bombs and the other did not, the side that manufactured them would inevitably be victorious." I summed up the situation in the words: "Here, then is the problem which I present to you, stark and dreadful and inescapable: Shall we put an end to the human race; or shall mankind renounce war?"[19]

One final point: Mr. Donnelly thinks that the sort of men who support the CND are the sort of men who supported Munich. This is a curi-

19. 'Man's Peril' was originally a talk given by Russell on the BBC on 23rd December, 1954. Some of its language was borrowed for the Russell-Einstein Manifesto the next year, especially its moving conclusion: "I appeal as a human being to human beings: remember your humanity, and forget the rest. If you can do so, the way lies open to a new Paradise; if you cannot, nothing lies before you but universal death."

ous illusion. It was the high Tories who supported Munich. They did so because they thought Russia a greater danger than Germany. They and most of the Labour Front Bench are at present repeating this same mistake.

In the world in which we are living no policy is free from risk. The best that can be done is to weigh the risks of various policies and to choose the policy in which the risk is least. I should add, as an admonition to the East and West equally, that the risk of the extermination of mankind should outweigh the risk of advantage to the bloc to which we do not belong.

Yours &c. Bertrand Russell
Plas Penrhyn, Penrhyndeudraeth, Merioneth

[145]

## Britain's Hope of Survival

*The Guardian* (29th August, 1960), p. 6 | C60.30

*In his third letter in response to Donnelly, Russell insists that his central point has not been touched: that Britain would be safer to abandon NATO.*

To the Editor of the "Guardian":

Sir, —Mr. Donnelly's letter in your issue of August 24 calls for a reply which, following his example, I will make as brief as possible. I will begin by acknowledging that he makes a good point by his quotation from my book "Which Way to Peace?" I publicly abandoned the opinion which he quotes soon after it was printed.

Mr. Donnelly's incursions into history have been rendered largely irrelevant by the H-bomb. As for dictators being impelled to fight Britain, he seems to have overlooked the fact that in 1793, 1914, and 1939 it was Britain that declared war.

As to the substance of our debate, I should of course infinitely prefer a general renunciation of nuclear weapons by agreement to a unilateral renunciation by Britain. But experience of disarmament conferences has caused me to despair of such agreement in the near future.

Mr. Donnelly does not grapple with my central argument, which is as follows: While we allow America to use our territory for purposes to which Russia objects, the Russian Government has threatened to obliterate the population of Britain without attacking the United States. This could be achieved in an hour or two. There is reason to think, and even to hope, that, in spite of NATO, the US would not retaliate by obliterating the rest of mankind. If Britain abandons NATO, Russia will no longer have this motive for exterminating us.

It is to this argument that I should like to know Mr. Donnelly's reply. The argument does not depend upon pacifism or any other ism, but merely upon a wish (surely not unpatriotic) that some Britons may survive.

Yours &c., Bertrand Russell
Plas Penrhyn, Penrhyndeudraeth, Merioneth

[146]

## The Wrong Address?

*The Guardian* (8th September, 1960), p. 8 | C60.31

*In his final letter in response to Donnelly, Russell answers the charges that he changed his views on war and peace in 1939, and he admits that the nuclear policy he attributes to the Soviet Union is "foolish and wicked," but he insists that that is no criticism of his position.*

To the Editor of the "Guardian".

Sir, —Mr Donnelly's letter in your issue of September 5 is interesting. He takes me to task for having changed my opinion in 1939.[20] He, I gather, has never held any opinion which he now believes to have been mistaken. In other words, he has never learnt anything from experience. I do not ask people to agree with me on account of any personal weight my individual opinion may have. I ask them to examine the argument and use their own judgment, in accepting or rejecting it.

The major part of Mr. Donnelly's letter should have been addressed not to me but to Khrushchev. It consists in saying that the policy which I attribute to the Soviet Government is a foolish one. I agree; it is both foolish and wicked. What he has failed to notice is that Khrushchev and Malinovsky have announced this policy as that of their Government. Mr. Donnelly says, "Lord Russell's proposition is nonsense." He should

20. Russell's change of opinion was first made public when a private letter of his was printed in the *New Statesman* (8th June, 1940).

have said, "The Soviet Government's proposition is nonsense." I hope he will succeed in persuading the Soviet Government that this is the case.

Mr. Edward Talbot, in your issue of September 2, has an argument identical with Mr. Donnelly's and the answer to it is the same.

Yours &c. Bertrand Russell
Plas Penrhyn, Merioneth

[147]

## Neutrality

*The Observer* (16th October, 1960), p. 18 | C60.40

*Russell the logician was ever sensitive to the charge of inconsistency. He replies to C.W.K. Mundle, an American analytic philosopher, regarding alleged logical lapses.*

Sir, —A letter from Mr. C.W.K. Mundle in your issue of October 9 accuses me of lack of logic and therefore calls for a reply. The apparent inconsistency which he points out arose from a desire for brevity.

I maintained: a) that Britain adds little to America's deterrent power; b) that for American military purposes German territory is more convenient than that of Britain. In the latter contention, I was speaking from the point of view of American military authorities which for my part, I consider to be based upon fallacies.

I hold that any country in Western Europe increases the risk of its own nuclear obliteration by membership in NATO. I have already published the reasons for this opinion, but I will here repeat them briefly. In the opinion of eminent and orthodox Americans, Russia could exterminate the population of any European member of NATO without bringing on a general nuclear war. The Soviet Government might consider this advantageous, but would be very unlikely to see any advantage in such an attack upon a neutral Power.

As for a nuclear war between the United States and the U.S.S.R., I do not think that either side is likely to bring this on deliberately; but I do think, in common with almost all who have studied the matter, that the risk of an unintended war is very great. This risk does not depend upon any supposed equality of power between East and West, but upon the risk of accident in the technical measures taken by both sides in the hope of preventing a surprise attack.

For these reasons, I think that American bases in Britain or Western Europe increase, rather than diminish, the danger to the countries in whose territories they are situated and do nothing to diminish the risk of general war. Neutrals are in a position to suggest and to press, as no other Powers are, possibly acceptable measures designed to lessen East-West tension, and Britain, as a neutral, would be in a greatly improved situation in promoting such measures.

Merioneth. Bertrand Russell

[148]

## High Treason

*The Scotsman* (7th November, 1960), p. 6 | C60.43

*In this letter Russell's vexation is evident, and he resorts to the sort of emotive rhetoric that would bring him criticism from more "responsible" commentators.*

Sir, —The British and American Governments have agreed to the establishment of a Polaris base on Clydeside. The Prime Minister[21] told the House that missiles would not be fired from submarines depending on the base without the consent of the British Government. The U.S. State Department has denied this, and has informed us that missiles will be fired whenever the U.S. Government sees fit. It follows that the British Government has handed over to the U.S. authorities the lives of all the inhabitants of Clydeside and the rest of Great Britain to be expendable whenever U.S. militarists think it in the interests of the U.S. that they should die.

Since the Queen is one of the inhabitants of Great Britain, this decision amounts to high treason. I call upon all who deplore this savage policy to protest in whatever way they may think most effective.

I am &c. Bertrand Russell

21. Harold Macmillan (1894–1986) was Prime Minister and leader of the Conservative Party, 1957–63.

[149]

## Russell Writes for Forum

*The Los Gatos Times—Saratoga Observer* (16th November, 1960), pp. 1–2 | C60.44

*A remarkable forum on nuclear weapons and nuclear war in the* Los Gatos Times—Saratoga Observer *featured guest columns and letters from experts in the field. Russell responds to a "dogmatic" letter from Edward Teller, the American physicist and father of the H-bomb. Earlier in the year Russell had had a TV debate with Teller on CBS's* Small World, *hosted by Ed Murrow.*

Sir, —In your issue of October 11 there is a letter from Dr. Edward Teller written in his usual pontifical style and making dogmatic assertions which do not accord with the opinions of such experts as have no reason for bias. He says that it is "nonsense" to maintain that an all-out nuclear war might put an end to the human race. He also says that it is "incorrect" to suppose such a war would "wipe out our technical civilization". He thinks it unnecessary to support these statements by anything except his personal authorization as the inventor of the H-bomb—a weapon which he apparently considers much less formidable than it is generally thought to be. In fact no one knows what percentage of the human race, if any, would survive such a war as Dr. Teller portends. I do not think there is a single disinterested expert who will deny this.

Yours faithfully, Bertrand Russell

[150]

## British Neutralism

*The Guardian* (25th November, 1960) | C60.46

*Russell defends British neutralism against Prime Minister Harold Macmillan's charges of defeatism, and he emphasizes the potential for peace that a neutral Britain could effect.*

Sir, —In your issue of November 19 you report some words of the Prime Minister condemning the advocates of British neutralism. According to your report he said "No one can believe that we have suddenly become a neutralist, a defeatist country." I must not presume to speak for other neutralists, but I must protest that so far from British neutralism being a defeatist policy it is the only policy at present being advocated in Britain that is not defeatist. The case for neutralism, briefly is this:

The greatest danger before the world at present is the danger of all-out nuclear war. This can only be averted by some agreement between the US and the USSR. Experience since 1945 has shown that, so long as the parties are left to negotiate directly with each other, no agreement will be reached, although, meanwhile, the daily and hourly risks of all-out war will mount up. The best hope of a detente between the two giants lies in friendly mediation by the neutrals, who should draw up suggested impartial agreements giving, in their opinion, no net advantage to either side and such as both sides could accept without loss of face. I wish to see Britain neutral in order that we may be able to take part in the work of peace. So far from being defeatist, such a policy affords the only hope of relief from imminent disaster. I agree with the Prime Minister when he says that "if this small country is to have greatness it must stem from the character of its people." Greatness for Britain, in present circumstances, demands an assertion of independence.

It is thought that our risk from Russia will be greater if we leave NATO than it is at present. This is a sheer mistake. At present, Russia can obliterate our whole population in half an hour without (in all likelihood) bringing on war with America. Russia could still do this if we were neutral; but would have far less motive for doing so than at present. It is, however, not only for the sake of the safety of my own country that I advocate neutralism for Britain, but for the sake of the continued existence of the human race, which is threatened by the present policies of Russia and America.

Yours &c. Bertrand Russell
Plas Penrhyn, Penrhyndeudraeth, Merioneth

[151]

## Mistaken Identity at Thule

*The Manchester Guardian* (30th December, 1960), p. 6 | C60.49

*The danger of accidental nuclear war is one which Russell took seriously. Here he mentions a notable false alarm in October 1960 involving the Ballistic Missile Early Warning System in Thule, Greenland, which falsely reported that the United States was under missile attack.*

Sir, —I am sorry to see from your leading article "Too Tense," which was part of your Christmas Eve good wishes to the world, that you have joined the "Die-quietly Brigade." In connection with the incident when observers in Thule mistook the moon for Russian missiles, you find fault with the American Air Force authorities and with certain new agencies for what you allege to have been an exaggeration of the danger.

You say: "The tone of the report suggested that if this exceptional man had not been on the job the decision might have been different. This sort of thing is a depressing example of lively modern journalism out of its element." So far as I have been able to discover, it was "lively modern journalism" that told the truth, while more expensive newspapers tried to calm their readers with soothing syrup.

The attempt to conceal from the public that at every moment of every day the human race is in danger of annihilation because some official observer is sleepy or drunk or mad is one of the most dastardly characteristics of certain present day Governments—including our own, since the Prime Minister has had the temerity to assure us that there will be no war by accident. It is sad that you are supporting this attempt to lure us to destruction by official deception.

—Yours, &c. Bertrand Russell
Plas Penrhyn, Merioneth

[152]

## "Marchers"

*The Observer* (9th April, 1961), p. 22 | C61.16

*Russell responds to the leading article of 2nd April and defends his version of British unilateralism which he distinguishes from American unilateral disarmament, a position which he did not advocate but which was often attributed to him.*

Sir, —Your leading article, "Marchers" (April 2), shows a serious misapprehension of the position of those who are called "unilateralists." As they have not yet agreed on a creed, I cannot be certain that my own opinions would receive unanimous consent among unilateralists, but when I set forth my opinions at a conference on March 11, they seemed to meet with general approval.

I do not advocate American unilateral disarmament; I advocate unilateral disarmament for Britain, and I think that the same arguments are valid for other allies of America in the eastern hemisphere. I advocate this as a step towards general disarmament.

The arguments are twofold: British and international. From the British point of view, the main argument is that Russia could obliterate the population of Britain completely in half an hour without bringing on a general nuclear war. While nuclear weapons exist, there is nothing that Britain or the United States can do to prevent this possibility, but if Britain were neutral, Russia would have not motive for such an act.

Internationally, Britain adds nothing to the power of America, but only a very burdensome liability. Disarmament conferences, so far, have always failed since 1945. The best hope for success would be a proposal drawn up by neutrals making no change in the balance of power, but possible for each side to accept since it would not be suggested by the other side. Britain as a neutral could do important work in this direction.

For the sake of brevity, I have made the above assertions dogmatically. Unfortunately, opponents of British unilateralism refuse to know what we stand for or what Americans think about our policy.

Bertrand Russell
Wales

[153]

## Bertrand Russell Replies

*Encounter* (June, 1961), p. 94 | C61.20

*Russell responds to an earlier letter from Christopher Mayhew,*[22] *attempts to dispel some misunderstandings concerning the label 'unilateralism', and he teaches a logic lesson concerning an alleged inconsistency.*

Mr. Christopher Mayhew's letter, in your issue of March 1961, calls for some reply from me. He says:

> The reason why the great majority of us oppose his views is not because we have not heard them or do not understand them, but because we disagree with them.

22. Christopher P. Mayhew (1915– ) served as a minister in the Labour government, 1945–51, and again (as Minister of the Navy) in 1964–70.

There are, however, many things in his letter which show that he does not understand my views. He supposes that those of us who are called "Unilateralists" are only anxious for British nuclear disarmament. This is an entire delusion on his part, though a not uncommon one among those whom he calls "us". A day or two before reading his letter I said in a speech at Birmingham:

> The policy that we advocate is called "unilateralism," but, unless accompanied by some explanations, this name for our policy is somewhat misleading. We want multilateral disarmament, but we think that British unilateral disarmament is the most effective step that Britain can take towards that end. This conclusion has been forced upon us by the utter failure of all disarmament conferences since the end of the last war.

All of us hope for general nuclear disarmament, but we have been forced by the repeated failure of direct negotiation between East and West to find some other means of bringing it about. We have come to think that the best hope of obtaining agreed disarmament by Russia and America is to be sought in the friendly intervention of neutrals. These neutrals could draw up impartial suggestions which each side could accept without loss of face, and we think that Britain would be more usefully employed as a member, and perhaps a leader of such a band of neutrals than as an impotent satellite of the U.S.

Mr. Mayhew, like many of our British opponents, says that the crucial question is, "If the Russians keep nuclear weapons, should the British renounce them?" This question would not be asked by anyone who had studied the strategy of nuclear war. If Mr. Mayhew is prepared to make such a study I advise him to look up Herman Kahn's article in *Survival*, Vol. II, No. 2; or, if he is prepared for a more serious study, to read the same author's book *On Thermonuclear War.* What he and the rest of "us" do not realise is something very damaging to British pride—namely, that nothing that Britain, or even NATO, can do will prevent Russia from destroying our whole population in half an hour if so disposed. Britain cannot have enough nuclear armament to inflict appreciable damage upon Russia, whereas Russia would require, at most, two per cent of her nuclear armament to destroy us completely. American orthodox authorities are agreed that, if we British were all corpses, America would see no point in turning all the rest of the world into corpses for the sake of a revenge which could not benefit us. And, again from national pride, most of "us" refuse to realise that we add practically nothing to the strength of America, but impose a difficult treaty obligation which probably cannot be fulfilled. America would be, if anything, stronger without us than with us, and we should be in less danger if we were not allied with America than we are at present.

Mr. Mayhew considers it illogical to be both a Unilateralist and a Multilateralist. This arises only from his willfully or ignorantly distorting the aims of those who are called "unilateralists." Where is the lack of logic in saying: "We wish everybody to disarm; but, meanwhile, let us disarm ourselves." I am, of course, willing, in all humility, to derive lessons in logic from Mr. Mayhew, but so far, my logical capacities are not equal to following his argument on this point.

Mr. Mayhew finds fault with the C.N.D. for getting "excited." To my mind, it is those who do not get excited who are to blame. Suppose Mr. Mayhew had been a Member of Parliament in the time of Guy Fawkes. Would he not have got excited? And yet the crime that Guy Fawkes attempted was infinitesimal compared with the crime that present-day Governments contemplate. It is the magnitude of the crime that prevents "us" from feeling the appropriate emotion. If I proposed to massacre a hundred children chosen at random and had some prospect of being able to do it, I believe that even Mr. Mayhew would get excited. But when people propose to practise this same crime against everybody, we are expected to keep calm and to regard the intending perpetrators as great statesmen. I suppose we are to be inspired by the example of Nero fiddling. But then it was only Rome that was burning.

Bertrand Russell
Penrhyndeudraeth

[154]

## From Lord Russell

*Columbia University Forum* (Winter, 1961), p. 3 | C61.42

*Russell appraises Amitai Etzioni's review of Herman Kahn's* On Thermonuclear War. *Russell thinks Kahn too "rationalistic" and blind to "human passion and human suffering."*

I have read with great interest and almost complete agreement Amitai Etzioni's devastating criticism of Herman Kahn's big book *On Thermonuclear War*. ["Our First Manual of Thermonuclear War": Fall 1961]. I read Mr. Kahn's book with appreciation of his candor. He has been found morally horrifying by many critics, but, for my part, I think him open to less moral criticism than is deserved by those who support

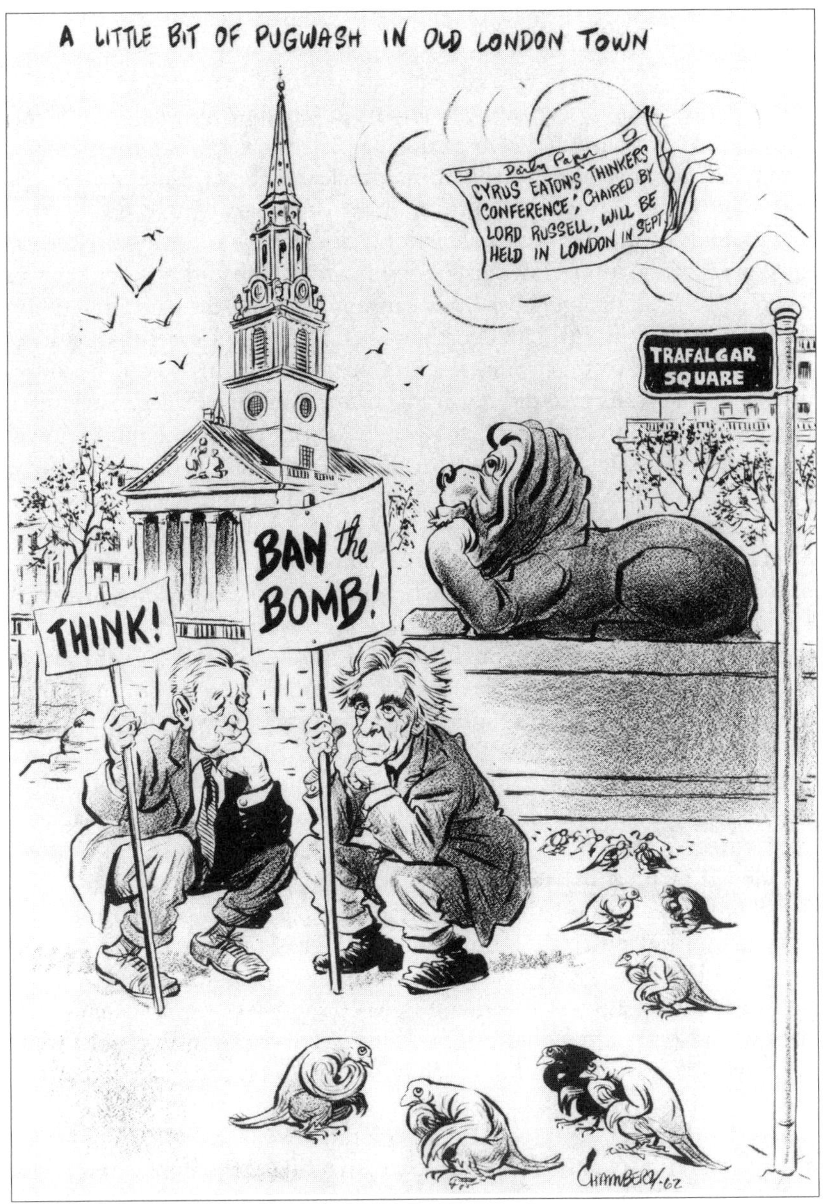


Cyrus Eaton was a Canadian industrialist and philanthropist who offered a forum, in Pugwash, Nova Scotia, for scientists from East and West to consider the dangers and prevention of nuclear war. Established in 1957 with Russell as president, the forum became known as the Pugwash Conference of Scientists. It was largely responsible for the 1963 Partial Test Ban Treaty, and in 1995 it (and its president Joseph Rotblat) received the Nobel Peace Prize. In 1962 a worldwide Pugwash Conference took place in London. See document [159]. This 1962 cartoon by Chambers was a gift to the Russell Archives from Eaton himself.

NATO policy but hypocritically shrink from recognizing what it involves. One of the few points at which I think Mr. Etzioni is too lenient with Mr. Kahn is as to what would happen in a nuclear war. Mr. Kahn's attempts to minimize the casualties omit a number of factors. There would be a complete disruption of communications, destruction of hospitals, and an enormous proportion of deaths among medical men and hospital nurses. There would be prolonged fallout causing renewed casualties for years. And if one may judge by advertisements about civil defense and pronouncements of Jesuit divines, a great many Americans would be killed by other Americans who did not want their shelters over-filled. Such matters, being not purely military, tend to be ignored by Mr. Kahn.

I agree with Mr. Etzioni that Mr. Kahn's suggestions of arms-control pacts between Russia and America, to be conscientiously observed by both sides during actual war, are utterly and totally fantastic. Mr. Kahn forgets everything that he and his friends have ever said about the untrustworthiness of the Soviets when it is a question of disarmament. He is also blandly unconscious of the passions which govern men during war. He assumes that, in the middle of the most terrible war ever to have occurred in human history, the Russian and American Governments and populations will remain as calmly rational as Mr. Kahn while he is making his calculations. I am myself accustomed to the accusation of being unduly rational and believing that reason can play a part in shaping policy, but I have never in my most wildly rationalistic moments imagined such a degree of general rationality as Mr. Kahn expects of populations maddened by utter disaster.

There is one superlatively important matter which is mentioned by Mr. Etzioni but deserves, I think, more emphasis than it has in his discussion. Mr. Kahn argues that neither Russia nor America would be mortally damaged in a nuclear war, and he even suggests that, after ten years, they would be ready to fight again. He never raises the question: what good will come of the war for which he asks us to prepare? Assuming that both sides recover as quickly as he expects, what will either side have gained by the war? If, to take the other alternative, Mr. Kahn thinks that, after a war, the two sides will agree to negotiate a secure peace, why should they not do so before the war and so avoid fighting it?

Mr. Kahn at no point offers any reason whatever for the hostility between Russia and America. We must be grateful to him for avoiding the cant about a war for freedom, and for admitting that, after a war, there would be as little freedom in America as in Russia. But one cannot help being surprised that this admission never makes him ask himself whether the projected war is worth-while. He imputes to the Russians, in his schemes for arms-control, a degree of rationality which, if it really exists, must make them conscious of an obvious fact which seems never to have entered his mind—namely, that in the nuclear age the hostility between East and West is simply silly since it cannot conceivably further the interests of either.

Mr. Kahn's whole book smells of the lamp. At no point does he show any awareness of human passions, good or bad, of the unimaginable sufferings that a nuclear war must entail, or of the good things that it must render for centuries, perhaps forever, unattainable. As Mr. Etzioni very justly observes, Mr. Kahn imagines the state of mind of those directing a nuclear war to be like that of two men engaged in a game of chess. I fear that there are all too many among militarists on both sides who share this total unimaginative blindness to human passion and human suffering.

Bertrand Russell
Merionethshire, Wales

[155]

## Long-term Remedies

*Tribune* (15th December, 1961), p. 8 | C61.45

*Russell's book* Has Man a Future? *(Simon and Schuster, 1961) was a continuation of the main themes of his* Common Sense and Nuclear Warfare *(Simon and Schuster, 1959).*

I am grateful to Mr. Arblaster for his very kind review of my *Has Man a Future?* (*Tribune*, December 8). There are, however, some things that I should like to say in reply to his gentle criticism.

I used to deal with wide sociological questions—for example, in *Principles of Social Reconstruction, Roads to Freedom* and *Power*—but the Bikini test of March 1, 1954, persuaded me that there was no time for long-term solutions and that some more immediate and specific movement was necessary for the preservation of mankind.

In the above books, I believe that I have dealt with social questions in a manner of which Mr. Arblaster would approve. I still hold what I formerly advocated, provided the immediate danger is overcome.

But, if you saw a man dropping lighted matches on heaps of TNT, you would feel it necessary to stop him without waiting for vast schemes of social reform. And that is the present situation as I see it.

Bertrand Russell
Penrhyndeudraeth

[156]

# [Nuclear Testing]

*Tribune* (18th May, 1962), p. 9 | C62.20

*The issue of atomic testing took on great significance in the early 1960s as it became clear that testing (a) made possible the acceleration of the nuclear arms race, and (b) posed great risk to human health due to radioactive fall-out. Russell denounces the hypocrisy of Labour Party leaders who condemn Russian nuclear tests while they support American tests.*

The statements of Gaitskell, Brown and Williams[23] are disgraceful. They lay themselves open to a charge of hypocrisy. They are on record at their own Conference to oppose the resumption of atmospheric tests.

The Right-wing of the Labour Party has no respect for opinion within its own party or without it. While the so-called Opposition presses the Government to withdraw the freedom to advertise smoking because of cancer they take upon themselves the freedom to advocate genocide up and down the country.

Those who are or have been members of their party feel revolted at the betrayal. How dare Gaitskell, Brown and company condemn Russian tests and support American tests? We who have been to prison for demonstrations against Russian tests have the right to oppose them. The suggestion that we are Communists is sufficient testimony of the bankruptcy of the leadership of the Labour Party.

Let me make this point clear: there are without doubt Communists who support our movement. Mr. Gaitskell should not complain of the few Communists who support a movement which opposes Soviet nuclear policy. We do not hold it against him that the majority of his supporters are Conservatives.

Both major parties advocate a course which will lead to the extermination of the whole population of Britain and a majority of the people of the world. This issue is greater than the petty ambitions of mediocre politicians.

On Gaitskell's reasoning, the British Government is surely Communist-inspired, for they imprisoned us when we protested against the resumption of Communist tests. Gaitskell cannot inspire such dedication from anybody; everyone knows of the total absence of any opposition on his part. That is the root of the matter and he knows it.

Bertrand Russell
London, SW 1

23. The three mentioned were Labour Party leaders.

[157]

## Crimes Against Humanity

*The Guardian* (13th June, 1962), p. 6 | C62.25

*Col. P.A.J. Graham had written a letter to the editor (June 9th) angrily protesting a letter from Jon Tinker, an environmentalist with the Committee of 100 who also served at this time as one of Russell's personal secretaries. Tinker had compared Air-Commodore Magill's willingness to participate in a nuclear war to Eichmann's crimes against the Jews. Graham dismissed the comparison as "tinkers and peanuts."*[24] *Russell replies to Graham with the help of Lewis Carroll.*

Sir, —With apologies to Lewis Carroll, I should like to reply to Colonel Graham, whose letter appeared in your issue of June 9:

The Peanuts answered with a grin
Why what a temper you are in.

Yours faithfully, Russell
Penrhyndeudraeth

[158]

## A Protest Ship

*The Guardian* (2nd August, 1962), p. 8 | C62.34

*Russell asks for financial support for a protest project against threatened Soviet resumption of nuclear testing.*

Sir, —A project is being organised by the World Peace Brigade[25] to send a ship from London to Leningrad to protest against the threatened

24. Apparently, the controversy can be traced back to Hugh Gaitskell's denunciation of the CND and the Committee of 100 at a Labor rally on 1st May 1: "When it comes to the ballot and to voting in elections, these people are not worth a tinker's curse. They are peanuts." Cited in Monk, *The Ghost of Madness*, p. 436.

25. The World Peace Brigade was launched in early 1962 under the leadership of A.J. Muste and Michael Scott. It was one of several international peace organizations active in the 1960s—including the Committee for Nonviolent Action and War Resisters International—against nuclear weapons.

resumption of tests by the Soviet Government. This ship will be called Everyman III,[26] since it is a sequel to Everyman I and Everyman II which were protests against Western tests. It is intended that eight large meetings should be organised in various Western countries to welcome the crew and encourage their effort. It is also intended to do everything possible to establish contact with inhabitants of the USSR. I am writing as a sponsor of this project, which has my wholehearted support. The difficulty is as to funds, and it is hoped that, among those who approve the project, enough funds can be raised to make it possible to carry it out. Contributions should be sent to the organiser of this project, Barnaby Martin, at 6 Endsleigh Street, London, WC 1.

Yours faithfully, Bertrand Russell
Penrhyndeudraeth

[159]

## To Detect Atom Testing

*The New York Times* (25th November, 1962), Section 4, p. 8 | C62.53

*Russell accuses both the United States and the Soviet Union of being less than sincere in negotiating an atomic test ban. He proposes a "technological innovation" as a hedge against cheating, an innovation that grew out of a Pugwash meeting of scientists from East and West—a series of conferences founded and sponsored by Cyrus Eaton, a Canadian millionaire, and chaired by Russell. The Pugwash Conference grew out of the 1955 Russell-Einstein Manifesto. The Conference, and its head, British physicist Joseph Rotblat, received the Nobel Peace Prize in 1995.*

*Curiously, Russell's letter elicited a response in* The New York Times *from Henry Kissinger (10th January) which in turn elicited one from Joseph Rotblat (25th January)—both Nobel Peace laureates.*

To The Editor of *The New York Times:*

The current inability of the Great Powers to agree on an end to nuclear tests is without any justification that can be noted by men of sin-

26. Everyman III was a 48-foot ketch which sailed out of London in September 1962 and arrived in Leningrad in October. The Soviets prohibited anti-nuclear leafletting, and the ship was towed away.

cerity and goodwill. The United States insistence upon on-site inspection is unjustifiable, since even underground tests do not demand such inspection, and those tests which might conceivably escape detection would be of such small magnitude as to be of marginal interest. The Soviet Union is not justified in being unwilling to agree to a ban on testing in the atmosphere independent of any agreement to be reached on underground tests.

Neither side, it would appear, is sincere in the negotiations. The British Government is perhaps the most culpable at the moment, because it insists upon endangering whatever prospect of settlement may exist with an absurd insistence upon holding tests of its own, the purpose of which is as ludicrous as it is damaging.

It is important to point out that even if the unreasonable request for inspection of underground tests is to be insisted upon by the Government of the United States, and even if the Soviets are to insist upon the inclusion of agreement about underground tests before being willing to accept a moratorium on tests in the atmosphere, there exists a scheme which answers both objections and which is known to both powers.

At the last Pugwash meeting, the technical innovation of a "black box" was agreed upon by scientists of East and West. This "black box" serves to detect and can be so arranged that tampering cannot go without recognition. It will be able to report on any devices which ordinary seismographic equipment would fail to notice.

It is important for Americans to realize that their scientists and Russian scientists have already agreed upon the viability of this arrangement. It is important to recognize that the seismographic station of Harvard University has vigorously declared its confidence in the Pugwash proposal.

I am anxious to have Americans appreciate that nothing stands in the way of an end to nuclear tests in the atmosphere or underground but the stubbornness of governments whose concern for the welfare of the population of our planet is clouded by the mad dictates of power.

No on-site inspection could give greater security, no on-site inspection is safe against paranoia. Without the urgent desire to end this threat to future generations, nothing can be done. It is essential that we understand that the pretext for failure to agree has been removed.

The "black box" will show beyond doubt any potential violation of a very small kind. Those larger can be detected without it.

Bertrand Russell
Penrhyndeudraeth, Wales, Nov. 16, 1962

## *The Middle East and the Far East*

[160]

### Peril in the East

*The Manchester Guardian* (29th January, 1955), p. 4 | C55.07

*Tensions between the U.S. and China had mounted since the Communist victory in the Chinese civil war (1945–49) and the Nationalist Chinese retreat to the island of Taiwan. In 1954, China vowed to liberate Taiwan and began artillery shelling of the Nationalist-held islands of Quemoy and Matsu. The U.S. government supported the Nationalists and issued a pledge of defense in 1955.*

*In this letter Russell suggests that the perilous U.S.-Chinese hostilities might be prevented with the help of two prominent statesmen (Churchill and Nehru) who, in Russell's view, had attained genuine realization of the danger of war in the nuclear age.*

Sir —Two powerful men, President Eisenhower and Mr. Chou En-lai,[27] are at the moment placing the continued existence of the human race in imminent peril. It is clear that neither of them is adequately aware of the danger. I say nothing as to the rights and wrongs of the dispute: when a house is one fire it is the duty of the fire brigade to save the inmates without first deciding who is to blame for the conflagration. Two wise men, Sir Winston Churchill and Mr. Nehru,[28] are meeting at the Commonwealth Conference. Both have shown their sense of the disaster to be expected in a third world war. Cannot they join hands in suggesting a method of postponing actual hostilities? Sir Winston has a long-standing friendly association with the President: Mr. Nehru has had recent friendly contacts with the Government of Communist China. What is needed, and what these men might secure, is a suspension of hostilities while a search is made for some method of arbitration. If no such method can be found it is not unlikely that the human race will cease to exist before the end of the present year.

—Yours &c., Bertrand Russell
41 Queen's Road, Richmond, Surrey.

---

27. Chou En-lai (1898–1976) was the first premier of the People's Republic of China (1949–76) and leader of the Chinese communist movement.

28. Jawaharlal Nehru (1889–1964) was India's first prime minister (1947–64).

············· [161] ·············

## The Suez Canal

*The Manchester Guardian* (11th August, 1956), p. 4 | C56.11

*When the U.S. and Britain withdrew pledges of financial aid to build the Aswan Dam, Egypt nationalized the Suez Canal on July 26th and expelled British oil interests and embassy officials.*

Sir, —I wish to express complete agreement with the statement by a number of Labour members in your issue of August 9 against the use of force in the Suez Canal dispute, except on one point. They suggest that the use of force should require the sanction of the Security Council. But the Security Council is subject to the veto, which either side may use obstructively. I suggest that the proposed conference should appoint, or ask the United Nations to appoint, an ad hoc authority in which the Communist and anti-Communist States should have equal voting power, and representatives of uncommitted nations should hold the balance. Such a body could act by a majority. The existence of the veto makes unanimity essential and where unanimity exists no organisation is necessary. Constructive internationalism demands the creation of an authority which can take enforceable decisions by a majority when unanimity is unattainable.

—Yours &c., Bertrand Russell
Plas Penrhyn, Penrhyndeudraeth, Merioneth

············· [162] ·············

## Britain's Act of War

*The Manchester Guardian* (2nd November, 1956), p. 4 | C56.19

*Israel, barred from the Canal and frustrated by terrorist raids, invaded the Gaza Strip and the Sinai Peninsula. Britain and France, after demanding Egyptian evacuation of the Canal Zone, attacked Egypt on October 31st. World opinion, including that of the U.S., condemned the actions of Israel, France, and Britain. The U.N. effected a cease-fire on November 7th.*

Sir, —The criminal lunacy of the British and French Governments' action against Egypt fills me with deep shame for my country. I endorse every word of Mr Gaitskell's indictment and of your leading article of

November 1. Only one hope remains, that the United States will use its power to stop the fighting and so save us from the worst consequences of our Government's insanity.

—Yours &c., Bertrand Russell
Penrhyndeudraeth

[163]

## The Atlantic Alliance

*The Manchester Guardian* (4th December, 1956), p. 6 | C56.22

*In the wake of the U.S. condemnation of Britain's "mad folly" against Egypt, Russell defends America against a growing anti-American campaign among some Conservatives.*

Sir, —My purpose in this letter is to make an appeal to those Conservatives, of whom I am sure there must be many, who put the welfare of their country above the temporary interests of their party. I do not propose to say anything about the interests of other parts of the world, except that I believe our national interests, rightly understood, to be wholly in harmony with those of mankind.

It seems that a large section of Conservative opinion, not content with the mad folly of the attack on Egypt, is now prepared to follow it up with an anti-American campaign. I have been at times critical of some things American, more particularly as regards Communist China and police action against American alleged Communists, but in the recent crisis I have thought America wholly in the right and our Government wholly in the wrong.

Apart from rights and wrongs, however, it should be obvious to everybody not blinded by reckless resentment that our alliance with America is vital to our national survival. But for N.A.T.O. we could not prevent the Russians from overrunning Western Europe including Britain. Having by our own action caused the Suez Canal to be closed we have made ourselves dependent upon American oil and without American aid our industry must suffer catastrophically. It is a shocking fact that we have been nearly indifferent when America has been in the wrong but are filled with indignation when America is in the right.

There is nothing new in Tory preference of party interests to national welfare. From the Treaty of Utrecht in 1713, which the Tories forced through the Lords by the creation of peers, and the ending of the Seven

Years War by a treaty which sacrificed British interest to the discrediting of Chatham, and on through the Ministry of Lord North, which succeeded in losing the American Colonies by a ruthless use of a parliamentary majority, we find ourselves brought to the present day, in which a Government is imitating Lord North to the utmost limit of what the changed circumstances make possible.

I realise that it is difficult for a Conservative to vote against his party, but when his party embarks upon a headlong rush towards utter destruction, as it is in danger of doing, it is time for sane men to think of a duty higher than party loyalty. We cannot recover the good opinion of the world until the present Government falls, and it will not fall until some Conservative M.P.s place patriotism before party.

—Yours &c., Bertrand Russell
Plas Penrhyn, Penrhyndeudraeth, Merioneth.

[164]

## Intervention and Its Risks

*The Manchester Guardian* (18th July, 1958), p. 6 | C58.41

*Muslim rebellion in Lebanon against the pro-Western regime broke out in May. In an effort to forestall an alleged Soviet and United Arab Republic attempt to overthrow the Lebanon regime, the United States, with British support, sent 10,000 Marines on 15th July.*

*Russell underscores the danger of the situation and pleads for a negotiated settlement.*

Sir, —In the Middle East, the American and British Governments have taken steps involving a risk of world war. The Soviet Government has made a pronouncement which seems to mean that it also, is prepared for world war.

I have no wish to express a view as to the rights and wrongs of controversies in the Middle East. What I do wish to say is that this dispute and any others that may arise should be settled by negotiation, and that the attempt by either side to settle them by the use or threat of armed force is madness, in view of the danger of the extermination of the human race.

At the moment, it is the Western Powers which appear to neutrals to be the aggressors. Mr. Khrushchev has taken advantage of this situation by a solemn declaration that the U.S.S.R. "is invariably guided by principles of self-determination of the peoples." I suppose he hopes that the world has already forgotten Hungary and Eastern Germany, where alien armed forces suppressed insurrections supported by great majorities of the populations.

If mankind is to survive, it will be necessary for the Great Powers to abandon their pretences to exclusive righteousness. I doubt whether the inhabitants of India, Africa, or South America, as they die in agony, will be much impressed by the nobility of either side. But if universal death is not to be the fate of mankind, the only hope lies, I repeat, in negotiations aimed at a just settlement giving no net advantage to either side.

—Yours &c., Bertrand Russell
Penrhyndeudraeth, July 17.

[165]

## Quemoy: The Price of Prestige

*The Manchester Guardian* (9th September, 1958), p. 6 | C58.48

*Increased shelling of Quemoy by mainland Chinese forces prompted the United States to reaffirm its defense commitment, and the U.S. 7th Fleet escorted Nationalist supply convoys to Quemoy during the bombardment.*

*Russell reminds us of the awesome power concentrated in the hands of a few individuals and which could be unleased over an issue of "schoolboy prestige."*

Sir, —The crisis over Quemoy is tragic and ridiculous, both in the highest possible degree. It matters nothing to the world whom Quemoy belongs to, and the only thing at issue is schoolboy prestige.

But over this entirely unimportant question the whole world is running an appalling risk. If, tomorrow morning, Mr. Dulles's breakfast disagrees with him, or Mao Tse-tung gets up in a bad temper, many hundreds of millions of human beings will die, not only in China, Russia, and America but also in Europe, Africa, and the uncommitted nations of Asia.

This risk illustrates the folly of our present institutions. The risk will continue to exist until nuclear weapons are abolished or internationalised.

—Yours &c., Bertrand Russell
Plas Penrhyn, Penrhyndeudraeth, Merioneth.

## *The Berlin Crisis*

[166]

# "After Paris: Obligations to West Berlin"

*The Times* (21st May, 1960), p. 9 | C60.13

*The problem of West Berlin plagued the West from the beginning of the Cold War and threatened on several occasions to explode into hot war. Berlin, like Germany itself, had been divided at the Potsdam Conference into four occupation zones under joint Allied command with the intention of eventual German unification and neutralization. Increase friction between the Soviet and Western Allies resulted in two separate cities—West Berlin, the combined French, British and American sectors, and East Berlin, the Soviet sector. Berlin itself was deep within the Soviet controlled zone of Germany (East Germany). In 1948, Stalin tried to drive the West out of Berlin by cutting off all traffic between Berlin and the Western zones. The U.S. answered by mounting a huge air lift that lasted 324 days.*

*In 1958 Khrushchev demanded that the Western allies withdraw their 10,000 troops from West Berlin, make it a "free" city and negotiate with the East German government (which none of the western allies recognized) for access into Berlin. If agreement was not reached within six months, Khrushchev threatened to turn the access routes over to East German control. U.S. Secretary of State, John Foster Dulles, rejected Khrushchev's demands and promised the use of NATO military force if access were denied to Western vehicles. Khrushchev replied that that would mean World War III.*

*In this letter, Russell proposes that the East and the West back away from the brink of war by bringing neutral powers into the negotiations over Berlin.*

To the Editor of the *Times:*

Sir —What should the west do if Khrushchev hands over west Berlin to the east German Government? This Government, which communists facetiously call "the German Democratic Republic", is, in fact, a brutal military tyranny imposed upon a reluctant population by alien armed force.

Western nations have obligations to the population of west Berlin. They cannot fulfil these obligations except by a threat of general war. If there is general war it is nearly certain that almost all the inhabitants of west Berlin will perish.

Protection by the western Powers is, therefore, only effective if Russia shrinks from a general war. If Russia does not shrink, we bring upon west Berlin by our intended protection a much worse fate than submission to the east German Government—and not only upon west Berlin but upon the whole world. Should the west play the game of brinkmanship in defense of west Berlin? It is likely that the Russians will think we are bluffing and will call our bluff. If we show that it was only bluff, Russia will proceed to a series of rash demands. Ultimately we must either resist or submit completely.

From this impasse, there seems no escape so long as only the Powers of Nato and the Warsaw Pact are involved in the negotiations. The matter is of vital interest to neutral Powers since they would all suffer catastrophically if there were a nuclear war.

It is open to neutral Powers to propose a way out of this impasse. The neutral Powers, great and small, having jointly examined the situation, should propose a compromise solution. Before doing so, they should attempt to induce east and west alike to make no decisive moves in the meantime. It is possible that neither east nor west would wish to offend neutral opinion by refusing such a proposal. It is, in any case, highly desirable that neutrals should emphatically assert their legitimate interest in preventing an east-west nuclear war.

Yours faithfully, Russell.
Plas Penrhyn, Penrhyndeudraeth, Merioneth, May 19

[167]

## The Berlin Crisis

*The New Statesman and Nation* (18th August, 1961), p. 212 | C61.25

*The Berlin Crisis grew critical in the summer of 1961. Khrushchev threatened to turn over access routes to East Germany; Kennedy put National Reserve troops on active duty and announced a 25 percent increase in American forces world wide. On 13th August the Soviets built the Berlin Wall, separating East and West Berlin, to staunch the flow of East German talent to the West. According to some experts, the United States came perilously close at this time to launching a pre-emptive first strike against the Soviet Union.*[29]

---

29. See Fred Kaplan, *The Wizards of Armageddon* (Simon and Schuster, 1983), pp. 298–301.

Sir, —In your issue of 4 August, A.S. Neill[30] says that I "should declare to the nation what it must do to save itself". I have been doing everything within my power to fulfill this suggestion. The Committee of 100, which in my opinion is doing the most effective work, has held demonstrations in which I have participated and is planning very much larger demonstrations in the near future. Some of your readers may wonder why I do not avail myself of television. It is only because I cannot. One television company offered me two minutes, but when I said I should wish to speak on Berlin the offer was withdrawn. It is the difficulty of making the peril widely known which has driven those with whom I work to methods of nonviolent civil disobedience. I think it is only by such methods that we can prevent the government from marching us, for the most part in ignorance of our fate, to the universal death which the government apparently hopes that we shall suffer while still sleep-walking to the sound of their Siren song. I hope that Mr. Neill and those who agree with him will hasten to join the Committee of 100 (13 Goodwin Street, N.4).

Bertrand Russell
43 Hasker Street, London, SW3

[168]

## The Berlin Crisis

*The New Statesman and Nation* (8th September, 1961), p. 304 | C61.28

Sir, —It should be accepted by all parties that war over Berlin or Germany is to be avoided. Two kinds of questions are involved: one of these is an ideal solution to the German problem; the other is a search for a possible compromise in the present dispute concerning West Berlin.

It is difficult to see any ultimate solution of the German problem without general disarmament. German reunification would involve Russian surrender of East Germany, which Russia could not be expected to accept if Germany were an armed force on the side of the West. Nor could the Germans be expected to accept German disarmament except as part of general disarmament. Khrushchev has repeatedly suggested general disarmament, and it is regrettable that the West has made no response.

30. A.S. Neill was a radical and progressive British educator, founder of Summerhill school.

As regards the immediate problem of Berlin: the USSR threatens to make a peace treaty with East Germany and to insist that the future status of West Berlin must be negotiated afresh with East Germany; the West fears that this would end the guarantee of free communications between West Berlin and West Germany. This fear could be obviated if the peace treaty between the USSR and East Germany contained a clause guaranteeing the preservation of the freedom of West Berlin and of its communications with West Germany. In return, the West should recognize East Germany—it would no longer have any good ground for refusing to do so—provided the guarantee concerning West Berlin were repeated in the treaty of recognition.

There can be no doubt that Russia is alarmed by the prospect of West German rearmament and, in view of what happened in Hitler's time, it can hardly be maintained that this fear is unreasonable. On this as well as on other grounds, it should be agreed that Germany should not possess nuclear weapons. The Oder-Neisse frontier[31] should be acknowledged to be final, as in any case it is *de facto*.

The above concessions to the USSR are only acknowledgements of facts which could not be changed at present without a world war. In return for such concessions, the rights of West Berlin, for which the western powers have a responsibility, would be more firmly secured than they are now, with the consequence that there would be a gain to West Berlin and a fulfillment of western obligations to it. Provided these conditions are fulfilled, a stubborn refusal to recognise the East German government is not defensible.

Bertrand Russell

## *Cuba and the Missile Crisis*

*Russell played a highly visible role in the Cuban Missile Crisis of October 1962 when the United States learned of Soviet emplacement of medium range missiles on the island. On 22nd October Kennedy announced a blockade of Cuba and warned of war if the missiles were not removed. Earlier in the year in the wake of the CIA's abortive Bay of Pigs invasion Russell had*

---

31. A boundary established in 1945 formed by the Oder and Neisse rivers separating East Germany from Poland. Its recognition was resisted by West Germany until 1970.

*made an appeal to the U.S. to desist from interference with Cuban sovereignty, saying with some prescience, "United States action against Cuba could lead to a nuclear war."*[32]

*During the Crisis, between 22nd and 28th October, Russell sent cables to both Kennedy and Khrushchev, insisting that the American actions were a "threat to human survival" and urging the U.S.S.R. away from precipitous action and to seek condemnation of the U.S. through the United Nations. On 24th October Khrushchev sent Russell a long reply thanking him for his concern and proposing a "top level meeting" to avoid nuclear war. The next day, the front page of the* New York Herald Tribune *read: "Khrushchev calls for Summit Meeting with Kennedy—He Replies to Lord Russell." We now know that Khrushchev's telegram to Russell came up in President Kennedy's White House deliberations no fewer than three times on 24th October, although he and his advisors dismissed the idea of a summit meeting as "useless."*[33]

*The crisis was averted at the last minute when the Russians chose not to challenge the blockade and agreed to remove the missiles in exchange for a pledge not to invade Cuba plus withdrawal of U.S. missiles from Turkey near the Soviet border—which is precisely what Russell had urged in a cable to Kennedy on 25th October, responding to Kennedy's cable to Russell of the same day. The events of that hair-raising week are recounted by Russell in his book* Unarmed Victory *(1963). See also documents [223–231] below.*

[169]

## Lord Russell on Cuba

*The Washington Post* (29th November, 1962), p. A14 | C62.54

I am profoundly concerned at the recent American statements on Cuba and on outstanding issues with the Soviet Union. Under public threat, Mr. Khrushchev withdrew missiles from Cuba and his so doing prevented conflict the consequence of which could only have been World War III. It is questionable whether Mr. Kennedy would have responded in similar manner had the blockade been of Formosa and by China. Nonetheless, in withdrawing all missiles Mr. Khrushchev received the

---

32. 'Atacar a Cuba Ilevaria a Una Guerra Nuclear'. *Revolucion*, Havana (15th February, 1962).

33. Ernest R. May and Philip D. Zelikow, *The Kennedy Tapes: Inside the White House During the Cuban Missile Crisis* (Harvard University Press, 1997).

unequivocal assurance that the sovereignty of Cuba would be respected by the United States.

Since this solemn assurance, American officials have declared that they intend to continue application of trade embargoes, of economic boycott, and to reserve the right of military intervention. It is declared that Dr. Castro's form of government can not be tolerated in the Western Hemisphere. This is the grossest imperialism. It is without a shred of justification in international law and it is a principle which, if adopted, means that the strong may forever destroy the sovereignty of those weaker than themselves if they decide to disapprove of the policies of the latter.

The attempt to wriggle from a public promise is a danger to peace and a display of bad faith. I wish to call to the attention of the American public that those not partisan to the Cold War are appalled by the bellicosity of the Government of the United States. Honesty requires that every conscientious person insist upon American adherence to her pledge and upon American willingness to cease the attempt to destroy the government of Dr. Castro.

The resolution of the Cuban crisis affords an opportunity such as has not been available before to a suffering world. The Russians have taken a painful decision which they honor in deed. It is for the United States to respond with magnanimity and to enable agreement on Berlin, nuclear tests, missiles around the world and all issues which, should failure to agree take place, will lead inexorably to the final crisis.

We all know that Mr. Khrushchev has based his leadership upon the possibility of agreement with the United States Government on outstanding issues. I consider it a matter of personal integrity for men and women around the world to insist that such an agreement take place and that every effort be made by the United States to be reasonable and just.

Bertrand Russell
Penrhyndeudraeth, Wales.

•••••••••••••• [170] ••••••••••••••

## [Cuba and Mass Murder]

*The Idaho State Journal* (5th December, 1962), p. 4 | C62.56

*Russell replies to an editorial of 6th November criticizing his conduct in the Cuban missile crisis.*

Dear Sir: Your editorial of November 6th has been brought to my attention. I cannot in any way agree with what you say. The fanaticism which made the Thirty Years' War possible and the mentality which allowed the War of the Roses to carry on for a half-century are present with us in the conflict between the Soviet Union and the United States.

Your objections to Communism are fanatical, and because they are fanatical they are evil. The consequences of what you say is mass murder, and I suggest that you cease attempting to cover it up. In order to carry out your objections to a political system, you are prepared to incinerate hundreds of millions of human beings. I am not.

Yours faithfully, Bertrand Russell
The Earl Russell, OM, F.R.S.
Plas Penrhyn, Penrhyndeudraeth, Merioneth, Wales

# Human Rights, Civil Liberties, and Disobedience

[171]

## Correspondence [Homosexuality as a Crime]

*The Twentieth Century* (June 1954), p. 574 | C54.12

*Russell writes in support of the decriminalization of homosexuality.*

Sir, —I wish to express my very complete agreement with the letter from Mr. Bernard Wall[34] published by you in May 1954. I do not think that making homosexuality a crime serves any purpose except to relieve the vindictive feelings of people who have failed to understand the right principles of the criminal law. Homosexuality of adults with mutual consent is a private matter in which society has no legitimate interest. There is no better reason for punishing it than for punishing extra-marital hetero-sexual intercourse. Most Continental countries recognize this, and I earnestly hope that the English law may before long become equally humane.

Yours faithfully, Bertrand Russell
41 Queen's Road, Richmond, Surrey. May 15, 1954.

[172]

## The Sobell Case

*The Manchester Guardian* (26th March, 1956), p.6 | C56.04

*In this letter and the next, Russell pleads the case of Morton Sobell, a co-defendant in the famous and controversial Rosenberg spy case. The Rosenbergs, Julius and his wife Ethel, were charged with espionage and brought to trial in 1951. They were found guilty and sentenced to death. Despite many court appeals and pleas for executive clemency, the Rosenbergs*

34. Bernard Wall (1908–1974) was a British writer and editor associated with the Catholic intellectual movement. His books include *These Changing Years* (1947) and his autobiography *Headlong Into Change* (1969).

*were executed on 19th June, 1953. Sobell received a 30-year prison sentence for his role in the Rosenberg conspiracy and was released in 1969. In his autobiography,* On Doing Time *(1974), he details his experience in the Rosenberg case and maintains his innocence.*

*The following letter, a summary of which appeared in* The New York Times *(27th March), prompted a letter to Russell from James T. Farrell, Chairman of the American Committee for Cultural Freedom. Farrell chastised Russell, charging him with "false and irresponsible statements" about American justice. Farrell's letter was published in* The Manchester Guardian *and in* The New York Times. *Russell, an honorary chairman of the International Congress for Cultural Freedom of which the American Committee was an affiliate, was outraged and resigned from that organization. In 1967 it was revealed that this worldwide cultural organization, unbeknownst to most of its sponsors, was CIA created and funded.*[35]

Sir, —I am writing to enlist your support in the case of Morton Sobell, an innocent man condemned as a result of political hysteria to thirty years in gaol and at present incarcerated in Alcatraz, the worst prison in the United States. He was sentenced as an accomplice of the Rosenbergs in espionage. I am ashamed to say that at the time of the Rosenbergs' trial I did not look into the evidence. I have now done so. I am almost certain that the Rosenbergs were innocent and quite certain that the evidence against them would not have been considered adequate if prejudice had not been involved. But the Rosenbergs are dead and nothing can be done for them now except to hold up their official murderers to obloquy. Sobell, however, is alive and it is not too late for the United States Government to make some reparation to him.

The facts in his case are briefly as follows:— He had a friend named Elitcher, who had been his best man. Elitcher had stated on oath that he had never been a Communist. The F.B.I. discovered that in making this statement he had committed perjury. They let him know that he could escape punishment if he would denounce other people as accomplices in treasonable activities. He decided to save his own skin by denouncing his best friend, Sobell. While negotiations in this sense were going on between him and the F.B.I. Sobell and his wife and their two small children went to Mexico. Sobell toyed with the idea of not returning to the United States, but rejected it. His decision to return became known to the F.B.I., which had determined to present him as a fugitive from justice. In order to be still able to present him in this light, they hired thugs,

---

35. See F.S. Saunders, *The Cultural Cold War: The CIA and the World of Arts and Letters* (New York Press, 2000).

who beat him into unconsciousness, hustled him and his wife and their two children into fast cars, and drove them without stopping from Mexico City to the United States frontier. There they were handed over to an immigration officer, who falsely stamped their card of entry with the words "Deported from Mexico" although the Mexican Government had not been privy to the kidnapping and had expressed no intention of deporting them.

When Sobell was brought to trial these facts were not mentioned as his counsel considered that any criticism of the F.B.I., however justified, would only increase the severity of his sentence, his condemnation being regarded by his counsel as certain in spite of lack of evidence. The judge instructed the jury that they could not find Sobell guilty unless they believed Elitcher. Elitcher, because he was useful in this trial, has never been indicatd for his acknowledge perjury and, in spite of his being known to be a perjuror, every word that he said against Sobell was believed.

People express scepticism when it is said that most Germans did not know of Nazi atrocities, but I am sure that the immense majority of Americans are quite ignorant of the atrocities committed by the F.B.I. They do not know of the standard technique of these defenders of what with cynical effrontery, they still call "The Free World." The technique is one with which we have been made familiar in other police States such as Nazi Germany and Stalin's Russia. The police find a man whom they can prove to be guilty of some offence and they promise him immunity if he will manufacture evidence against people who could not otherwise be indicted. Perjury is especially useful as a lever because many people who have been Communist in their student days rashly hope that this can be concealed and swear that they were never Communists. After a sufficient number of secret interviews the F.B.I. descends upon innocent people with a posse of terrified perjurors and in the general hysteria every word uttered by the perjurors is accepted as gospel truth.

I do not suppose for a moment that President Eisenhower is aware of this well-established technique. If he knew of it, he would not only feel the revulsion which all decent people must feel, but would realise that every such case which becomes known outside the United States turns hundreds of thousands of people, if not into Communists, at least towards neutralism and away from the policy of N.A.T.O. For this large reason of public policy, as well as from motives of humanity and justice, it is to be hoped that something will be done to curb the F.B.I. A beginning might be made by the release of Morton Sobell or, at least, by ordering a new trial of his case.

—Yours &c., Bertrand Russell
41 Queen's Road, Richmond, Surrey.

[173]

# The Case of Morton Sobell

*The Manchester Guardian* (5th April, 1956), p. 6 | C56.06

*Russell responds to the letters of Professor Bradford Perkins and others written in reaction to Russell's earlier letter (26th March) on Sobell.*

Sir, —The letter from Professor Perkins[36] which appeared in your issue of March 31 demands an answer. It is possible to read through the whole of the official report of the judicial proceedings in the Sobell case without learning many of the most important facts. Some, however, can be learnt from the official report. Professor Perkins objects to my saying that Sobell was condemned on the evidence of Elitcher[37] alone. As to this, Judge Irving Kaufman in his charge to the jury said: "If you do not believe the testimony of Max Elitcher as it pertains to Sobell, then you must acquit the defendant Sobell." Elitcher's motives for giving false testimony do not, of course, appear in the official report. But the interesting fact does appear there that the chief agent in the prosecution was McCarthy's now discredited henchman Cohn.[38]

I should be glad to know how Professor Perkins would defend the kidnapping of Sobell and the illegal stamping of his card by the United States immigration officer as "Deported from Mexico." As for the "blanket indictment" of the F.B.I., everybody knows at least the use that the F.B.I. has make of repentant Communists. It is generally recognised in modern times that confessions extorted by torture in past ages are unreliable, but it is thought that testimony extorted from confessed perjurors by the threat of prosecution should be accepted without question.

Professor Perkins doubts whether my letter can have any useful effect. I had hoped that it might induce a re-examination of Sobell's case in America, though Professor Perkins's letter makes me fear that I was too optimistic in this respect. To pass to more general considerations, I most earnestly desire good relations between the United States and my country, and I think it important that Americans should realise what an obstacle to such relations is created by authorised injustice. The cases of

36. Bradford Perkins was a professor of history at the University of California at Los Angeles.

37. Max Elitcher was Sobell's good friend who worked with Sobell at the Navy Bureau of Ordnance in Washington and who testified that Sobell attempted to recruit him to do espionage work.

38. Roy M. Cohn (1927–86) was a U.S. anti-Communist lawyer and assistant to Senator Joseph McCarthy in 1953–54.

Oppenheimer and Lattimore[39] did much harm in this respect, and even more has been done by the Rosenberg-Sobell case. It is not only for the sake of justice, but also for the preservation of Anglo-American friendship that I think a revision of Sobell's trial important. Such cases supply ammunition for Communist propaganda in Britain and Western Europe, and do far more than most Americans realise to help the Communist cause.

Mr. Wade N. Mack points out the limitations to the legal powers of the F.B.I. Has he never heard the ancient quip "Quis custodiet custodes?"?[40] He goes on to say that he has never known a "thug" to work for the F.B.I. beating up anybody. This I do not deny: but I think he might remember Dr. Johnson's remark, "Sir, what you don't know would fill a very large book." Mr. Mack is mistaken in saying that I implicate the Mexican Government. On the contrary, it was not a party to the action against Sobell.

Mr. Corliss Lamont[41] of the well known American banking family, writes to me:

"I was much interested in the 'New York Times' story of March 27, giving a summary of your views on the Federal Bureau of Investigation. From my own personal experience I can assure you that you have not exaggerated the situation. . . . Liberals and Radicals throughout the U.S.A. are fearful that the F.B.I. is tapping their phone, has installed a secret microphone in their living-room or car, opens their mail, or goes over the contents of their wastepaper basket. Because I have an independent income, I am not bothered by such possibilities as much as many other people."

Mr. Robert H. Rose seems to object to my quoting facts which have never reached the public and to accuse me of some secret source of knowledge. My sources of knowledge were all in published material. There is a very full account both of the Rosenberg case and of the Sobell case in a large book called "The Judgment of Julius and Ethel Rosenberg" by John Wexley, published by Cameron and Kahn, New York. Mr. Elmer Davis, the radio commentator, said after reading this: "Assuming that the record is here correctly cited (and I have no reason

39. J. Robert Oppenheimer (1904–1967) was director of Los Alamos laboratory for the Manhattan Project (1943–45). Accusations of disloyalty in 1953 caused him to lose his security clearance. Owen Lattimore (1900–1989) was a China scholar at Johns Hopkins. In 1950 he was accused by McCarthy of being a Soviet spy. He was exonerated by the Justice Department in 1955.

40. 'Who will guard the guards?'

41. Corliss Lamont (1902–1995) was a U.S. civil liberties activist and socialist.

to suppose that it is not) I cannot believe the testimony of Elitcher and the Greenglasses, or much if any of that of Harry Gold." There is a brief summary in a leaflet called "The Facts in the Case of Morton Sobell," published by "The National Committee to Secure Justice for Morton Sobell," 1050 Sixth Avenue, New York 18. There is also a pamphlet called "U.S. Senator William Langer Asks Justice for Morton Sobell." and an informative pamphlet published by the same committee called "Atomic Scientist Harold Urey Asks Justice for Morton Sobell."

Dr. Harold Urey,[42] who is a Nobel Prize man of by no means Left-wing opinion, said: "The integrity of justice as it is administered in the United States is at stake . . Mr. Sobell was not properly tried and the verdict and sentence were not justified." Judge Patrick H. O'Brien, Detroit, Michigan, said: "In accordance with our inheritance as a liberty-loving nation I urge the immediate release of Morton Sobell." Perhaps when Mr. Rose has studied these documents he will admit that my letter was not full of unsupported claims.

In conclusion, I cannot do better than offer him the advice which he so kindly offers to me, "that he re-examine his facts, review his paucity of knowledge of the case, re-evaluate his emotional fervour, restrain his crusading zeal, and rewrite his letter."

—Yours &c., Bertrand Russell
41 Queen's Road, Richmond, Surrey.

[174]

## The State of U.S. Civil Liberties

*The New Leader* (18th February, 1957), pp. 16–18 | C57.04

*On 7th January,* The New Leader *had published an open letter to Russell from Norman Thomas, the former head of the American Socialist Party, attacking Russell for his critical assessment of the state of American civil liberties in his preface to Corliss Lamont's* Freedom Is As Freedom Does.

My Dear Mr. Thomas: I am sorry that you have thought it necessary to publish your open letter to me. You and I are on the same side in most

42. Harold Urey (1893–1981) received the Nobel Prize in Chemistry in 1934. He was invited to sign the Russell-Einstein Declaration in 1955, but he declined owing to his anti-Communist sentiments.

matters, and I have every wish to avoid magnifying our differences. I shall, therefore, in replying to you, be as unprovocative as possible.

I am as much opposed to Soviet Russia as you are. Indeed, I think perhaps more so, since I object more than you do to the pale imitation of Russian methods which has been taking place in the United States. My attitude to Soviet Russia has been hostile ever since 1920. It is still that which I expressed in 1951 in a preface to *A World Apart* by Gustave Herling, a Norwegian, originally a Communist, whom the Russians imprisoned without cause while he was still on their side:

"Communists and Nazis alike have tragically demonstrated that in a large proportion of mankind the impulse to inflict torture exists, and requires only opportunity to display itself in all its naked horror. But I do not think that these evils can be cured by blind hatred of their perpetrators. This will only lead us to become like them. Although the effort is not easy, one should attempt, in reading such a book as this one, to understand the circumstances that turn men into fiends, and to realize that it is not by blind rage that such evils will be prevented. I do not say that to understand is to pardon; there are things which for my part I find I cannot pardon. But I do say that to understand is absolutely necessary if the spread of similar evils over the whole world is to be prevented."

I should like to mention that my appeal against hatred in the above quotation won the emphatic approval of Gustav Herling, in spite of all that he had suffered. You will doubtless agree that fellow-travelers share the guilt of Communist crimes by refusing to admit them; but presumably you will not agree that anti-Communists, equally, share the guilt of admittedly lesser crimes committed by the police and the law courts in the United States.

I am willing to believe that you do not know many of the facts about such crimes, but I do not think that ignorance in the face of available evidence is a valid excuse for those who make public pronouncements. I hope that, before you make any more such pronouncements, you will read Max Lowenthal's book *The Federal Bureau of Investigation*. You will doubtless say that things have grown better since the fall of McCarthy, just as Communists say that things have grown better since the death of Stalin; but I am afraid the improvement is as temporary in the one case as in the other.

For a little while after the death of Stalin, I, like others, had hopes that the Soviet regime was improving. These hopes have been shattered by events in Hungary—so far, I am in agreement with you.

You object to my writing a preface for a book by Mr. Corliss Lamont because of his record as a fellow-traveler. Before undertaking to do the preface, I had some correspondence with him, and explained that in the preface I would feel bound to state that I consider the infringements of liberty in Russia very much worse that those in the United States. (This I did.) You may, nevertheless, think that I ought not to have given seeming support to the point of view of a fellow-traveler. I was led to do so by the extreme paucity of strong protests by non-Communists against American malpractices. There have been a few such protests, highly honorable to those who have made them. I should mention, especially, what has been said by Dr. Harold Urey, the eminent atomic scientist, and Professor Malcolm Sharp, professor of law at the University of Chicago, on the Rosenberg-Sobell case. When I have agreed with Corliss Lamont, it is because what he says is confirmed by independent evidence and would be easily refuted if false.

Whoever pursues even-handed justice must expect to incur the hostility of both sides. In Russia, I am regarded as a rabid advocate of American imperialism. For example, *Bolshevik*, in an article devoted to the enumeration of my crimes, says:

"Russell now serves the American dollar and tirelessly trumpets the glories and unrivaled virtues of 'the American way of life,' of American 'democracy.' It costs him nothing to announce that the U.S.A. is the promised land for all nations and to summon nations to submit meekly to the undisputed military and civil power of Wall Street."

You, on the other hand, accuse me of evincing a desire lately, and "perhaps unconsciously, to use the blackest possible paint in depicting the American scene." I have no such desire. On the contrary, when recently there was a wave of anti-American feeling among Conservatives in this country, I wrote to the *Manchester Guardian* (December 4, 1956) to point out that, in the matter of Suez, America was in the right and we were in the wrong:

"It seems that a large section of Conservative opinion, not content with the mad folly of the attack on Egypt, is now prepared to follow it up with an anti-American campaign. I have been at times critical of some things American, more particularly as regards Communist China and police action against American alleged Communists, but in the recent crisis I have thought American wholly in the right and our Government wholly in the wrong."

What has given you the impression that my attitude to America has become more hostile recently is the action which I have been led to take by the realization that the Rosenbergs and Sobell, especially the latter, were condemned on evidence which no unbiased person could think conclusive. The argument from a purely legal point of view is set forth in Professor Sharp's *Was Justice Done?*, with an introduction by Dr. Urey from the point of view of a nuclear physicist. Neither of these men is a Communist or a fellow-traveler; each is actuated solely by a love of justice. The question whether a given person committed a specified crime is logically quite independent of the merits or demerits of Communism. If a murder has been committed and Mr. A is accused, if I think that there is not sufficient evidence against Mr. A I shall not on that account be thought to favor murder. But if a man is accused of the sort of crime that Communists are expected to commit, anybody who thinks that he did not commit it is supposed to be a Communist. This is only possible in an atmosphere of hysteria, and it is only in such an atmosphere that Sobell could have been found guilty.

It is through my interest in this case that I have been led to study the methods of the FBI. This body, ever since the 1914–18 war, has been steadily increasing its power, except in the early days of the New Deal. It has behaved for the past forty years with a disregard for law, truth and common humanity which should have aroused overwhelming public protest. I say this deliberately and with a full sense of responsibility. The evidence exists in published sources.

You say that I go beyond Mr. Lamont's book "in statements which his book does not properly support." You seem particularly surprised at the suggestion that people are exposed to suspicion if they support equal rights for colored people. I should have thought you would have known that is in fact notorious, that, in the South especially, any championship of the rights of colored people is regarded as evidence of Communism, and renders the champion liable to the hardships to which suspected Communists are exposed. I am convinced that what I said on this subject is not exaggerated.[43] Mr. Lamont quotes the chairman of a Government loyalty board as saying: "Of course, the fact that a person believes in racial equality doesn't prove that he's a Communist, but it certainly makes you look twice, doesn't it? You can't get away from the fact that racial equality is part of the Communist line." (See also the chapter "Mississippi Comes North" in Cedric Belfrage's *The Frightened Giant.*)

I have perhaps said more than Lamont said about the way in which a general state of terror has been produced. I will cite in illustration a case mentioned in the London *Observer* of July 18, 1954. This is the case of a man who was an American University professor, not a Communist or a fellow-traveler, but a friend of another professor whose views were more or less those of the British Labor party but definitely not Communist. This friend was charged with heretical ideas and the hitherto non-political professor came to his support. "The results of my activity," he states, "were (1) loss of employment and all that this means; (2) inability to find

43. In later private correspondence, Russell admitted that he was "guilty of exaggeration as regards the F.B.I. in relation to the colour question." See Feinberg and Kasrils, eds., *Bertrand Russell's America,* Volume II, (South End Press, 1983), p. 96.

any work in any other American educational institution; (3) sale of my house and a fine library at a loss, as I could no longer live in a community where I could not find employment and where my children were being abused by their fellow-students because their father was a 'Red.'"

I do not think that you and those who think as you do have the vaguest idea of the general state of fear which exists in American universities among young professors and instructors and among intelligent students. I have frequent and numerous contacts with men of this kind, and it is pathetic to see their joy in breathing the air of free discussion without the dread that an unguarded remark will be reported by supposed friends to some Authority with power in inflict ruin.

In every violent conflict, party spirit produces a tendency to excuse or cover up the crimes committed by one's own side. I agree with you in deploring this tendency among Communists and their sympathizers. But the tendency exists also on our side. Those English people, of whom I was one, who denounced the Anglo-French attack on Egypt were accused of being unpatriotic, but unjustly. Those who denounce condemnation of reputed Communists on inadequate grounds are accused of being pro-Communist, again unjustly. It is no true service to any cause to support excesses committed in its name, Such support is especially to be deplored when it tends to produce on our side a reflection of the evils against which we are fighting. What the Russians have done in Hungary is an unspeakable atrocity, but that does not justify the condemnation of Americans by American courts for crimes which there is no adequate evidence to show that they committed. All that I ask of you is that you should study the facts more carefully than you seem to have done, and that, while studying them, you should remember that the sins of others are a poor excuse for our own. Loyalty to the facts should always outweigh loyalty to apart, and loyalty to facts entails, in those who make public pronouncements, willingness to ascertain the facts even when they are painful, and especially when care is taken to conceal them.

I also do not think that you have realized a very important matter: If opposition to real evils in the West is undertaken only by Communists, this gives Communists an immense propaganda advantage and makes American talk about a "free world" appear nothing but hypocrisy.

I do not despair of convincing you that I am in the right where we disagree. You and I, throughout our long lives, have been devoted to not dissimilar causes, and it is much to be regretted if differences about this or that make our divergence seem greater than it is.

Yours sincerely, Bertrand Russell.

[175]

## Dr. Pauling's visit

*The Times* (5th September, 1958), p. 11 | C58.46

*Russell relates an account of the mistreatment by British authorities of the distinguished American scientist and anti-nuclear activist, Linus Pauling.*

Sir, —I am writing to report an incident which must bring shame to all who value the fair name of Britain. The incident concerns the dealings of the Home Office with Dr. Linus Pauling, a very distinguished native-born American, Honorary Fellow of the Royal Society, recipient of honorary degrees from the universities of Oxford, Cambridge, and London, Nobel Prizeman,[44] and well known throughout the scientific world as a man of outstanding intellect and integrity. He came to the United Kingdom on August 31 for two main purposes, to deliver an address which he has been invited to give on September 15 at the Kekule Symposium of the Chemical Society of London and to address a meeting organized for the Campaign for Nuclear Disarmament which is to take place on September 22.

On arrival at London Airport he was separated from the other passengers by the immigration authorities, and his son, who had come to meet him, was refused information as to whether he had arrived. He was closely questioned as to the purposes of his visit. When he mentioned the Chemical Society, he was asked whether he had any evidence that they had invited him. He replied that the evidence was in his baggage which was in the customs shed, and asked whether they accused him of lying. At the moment, they did not answer; but at a later stage they made this accusation. At first they said that he must leave the United Kingdom on September 15. He pointed out that this made his address to the Chemical Society impossible, and they reluctantly extended his permit to the next day, September 16. They stated as the ground of their action: "We do not admit people to Great Britain who come principally to take part in public meetings, especially when against Government policy."

This action by the British authorities is shocking. First, for the gross discourtesy of subjecting a man of great intellectual eminence, who has been honoured by many learned bodies in this country, to insult at the hands of ignorant officials. In the United States McCarthyism has lost

44. Pauling had received the Nobel Prize in chemistry in 1954. He would receive the Nobel Peace Prize in 1962 for his work to end atomic testing.

its vigour, but one is compelled to believe that it is being taken up in this country.

Second, if Government policy is as stated to Dr. Pauling, free speech has been abandoned and the only freedom left is that of supporting the Government.

Third, on the particular issue of nuclear weapons the Government have laid themselves open to very damaging criticism. It will be said that they know their policy to be such as no well-informed person could support. Apparently their watchword is: "Democracy, yes, but only ignorant democracy, for our policy is one which no well-informed democracy would tolerate."

Yours, etc., Bertrand Russell
Plas Penrhyn, Penrhyndeudraeth, Merioneth, Sept. 4

••••••••••••• [176] •••••••••••••

## Abundantly Justified

*Peace News* (2nd January, 1959), p. 1 | C59.02

*A year after the creation of the Campaign for Nuclear Disarmament, and two years before the formation of the Committee of 100, Russell realized the importance of civil disobedience in attracting media attention. At this time civil disobedience was largely relegated to the Emergency Committee for Direct Action, a group loosely associated with CND (whose main function was to raise awareness of the danger of nuclear war and to convert the Labour Party to an anti-nuclear agenda).*

To the Editor: My own feeling is that the demonstration at North Pickenham[45] on December 6 was abundantly justified. The Press, with very few exceptions, has boycotted news of peaceful and orderly activities by those who hope to prevent nuclear warfare. For example, a large conference of eminent men, mostly scientists, was held in Austria in September and was entertained by the Austrian Government. It drew up a valuable and important document signed by all but one of the partici-

---

45. About 80 people obstructed a missile base construction site in an action organized by the Direct Action Committee. Thirty people received two-week prison terms. The issue of civil disobedience would later split the CND and lead to the founding of The Committee of 100 by Russell and others.

pants at the Congress. Hardly any newspaper in this country said one word on the subject. On the other hand, the demonstration at North Pickenham secured wide publicity.

Those who think such methods undesirable should tackle the Press. Until the Press pursues a wiser policy, it is only by methods such as those used at North Pickenham that public opinion can be made aware of the fact that our population is being led blindfold towards mass extinction.

—Bertrand Russell,
Merioneth.

[177]

## The Rocket Site Protests—Freedom or Survival?

*The Manchester Guardian* (15th January, 1959), p. 8 | C59.04

*Russell replies to a correspondent pointing out some non-democratic implications of nuclear deterrence for "uncommitted nations."*

Sir,—In your issue of January 12, Mr. A.J. Hanna[46] speaks of "people like myself who prefer freedom to their own (and their enemies') physical survival." This may be a very noble sentiment, but it seems to me not inconceivable that the inhabitants of India, Japan, Africa, and South America, who do not admire either party to the cold war, might think survival preferable to extinction for the satisfaction of Mr. Hanna's morbid death wish. Mr. Hanna no doubt considers himself a believer in democracy, but he does not think that uncommitted nations should have a vote as to their own extinction. Has it occurred to him that in comparison with himself, Caligula was a milk-and-water humanitarian?

—Yours &c., Bertrand Russell
Plas Penrhyn, Penrhyndeudraeth, Merioneth.

---

46. Alfred Jackson Hanna (1893–1978) was an American historian and author. From 1951 to 1970 he was vice president of Rollins College in Florida.

[178]

## "Massive aid" for China

*The Guardian* (11th January, 1961), p. 8 | C61.03

*China's Great Leap Forward in the late 1950s and its ideological split with the Soviet Union produced chaos in Chinese industry and agriculture, with famine conditions in many regions in the early 1960s.*

Sir, —I wish to express my complete agreement with the admirable letter in your issue of January 9 headed "Massive Aid to China." I am sorry that I had no opportunity to sign the letter for publication. I earnestly hope that the British Government will take some action such as is suggested in that letter.

—Yours &c. Bertrand Russell
Plas Penrhyn, Merioneth

[179]

## Bad Habits in Moscow

*The Times* (30th January, 1961), p. 11 | C61.04

*In this remarkably judicious letter, Russell protests the ill treatment of two friends of Boris Pasternak by the Soviet government. Pasternak was awarded the Nobel Prize for literature in 1958. He was denounced as unpatriotic by many Soviet groups. He died in Moscow in 1960.*

Sir, —I have learnt with deep regret that two friends of Pasternak, Mrs. lvinskaya and her daughter have been sentenced to eight years and three years respectively in labour camps and I have read the report of Moscow radio on their case. In common with those who know them in the west, I find the accusations made by Moscow radio for the most part incredible and I find it impossible to resist the conclusion that savage sentences such as were passed on them were passed only because they were friends of Pasternak.

Before the news became public I wrote a private letter to Mr. Khrushchev pointing out that the endeavors made by many in the west including myself to improve east-west relations were gravely hampered by such incidents and that the harm thereby done to the interest of the Soviet Government must outweigh any advantage derivable from the incarceration of two ladies. This letter was not acknowledged. I still hope, however, that second, and more reasoned, thoughts may prevail and that the ladies may be liberated. If they are not, their fate will remain an outstanding argument on the side of those who are striving to keep hostility to Russia alive.

Yours faithfully, Russell
Plas Penrhyn, Penrhyndeudraeth, Merioneth, Jan. 27

[180]

## Civil Disobedience

*Tribune* (3rd February, 1961), p. 8 | C61.07

*In the latter half of 1960, Russell and others in the Campaign for Nuclear Disarmament (CND) came to think that civil disobedience was required to make the campaign more effective, and so the Committee of 100 was formed. The concept of civil disobedience was not acceptable to some CND leaders like its Chairman, Canon Collins, and there was considerable controversy within CND over the idea.*

*In this letter Russell provides the rationale for civil disobedience and announces an action set for 18th February, 1961. A more detailed account appeared in the* New Statesman *for February 17.*

*The action brought out 20,000 people to Trafalgar Square, 5,000 of whom marched to the Ministry of Defence and sat on the surrounding pavement. Russell (assisted by his secretary, Ralph Schoenman, and the Rev. Michael Scott) affixed a statement of purpose to the Ministry door.*

The Committee of 100 and its supporters propose to commit an act of civil disobedience on February 18 in connection with the arrival of the Polaris missiles in the Clyde which creates a special and deadly danger to the inhabitants of that region and to all Britain. The demonstration is to be non-violent, and any individual who allows himself to become violent will be disowned by the Committee.

We have been driven to a policy of civil disobedience by the lack of representation or the misrepresentation of the policy of unilateralists in the organs of public information. Broadcasting and television are practically closed to us. It is difficult, almost impossible, to get articles or even letters into the daily papers. Most of the press has gone over to Authority—possibly in fear of being, otherwise, gobbled up.

The Campaign for Nuclear Disarmament has been, and is, doing splendid work, but its doings are seldom thought by the press to have "news value." In consequence of the barrier put up by almost all organs of public information, the unilateralist point of view is given by the general public no serious hearing.

The public's attention must be called to the weight of reason and the strength of feeling which impel a large body of people in this country to support the policy of unilateralism—a far larger and more intelligent and informed body than it is recognized to be.

All sorts of legal methods are being employed and should continue to be employed to do this. But in order that these methods may carry their full weight, it is obvious that methods also should be adopted that are now considered to have "news value"—methods of civil disobedience hitherto untried on a mass scale. Only by such means can the barrier of ignorance and indifference concerning the unilateralist point of view be broken down.

The danger of present policies is imminent and terrible. At any moment an accident, a drunkard, or a temporary lunatic may lead to an action which will probably destroy the human race. It is now well known to the minority who are aware of the danger that the early-warning observers at Thule failed to distinguish the moon from a flight of Russian bombers. Accidents to Polaris submarines and missiles, to nuclear plants of various sorts, and to planes carrying nuclear missiles are sometimes mentioned, but never stressed, by the press.

The public in general is entirely ignorant of the facts that: 1) present policies make such danger inevitable; 2) the unilateralist policy is the only practicable policy that provides a way of possibly avoiding such danger; 3) the unilateralist policy provides the only practicable first step towards a world at peace; 4) the unilateralist policy is the only practicable policy that will enable Britain to exercise, as an independent nation, her capability of supporting, even leading, other nations in work towards bringing peace and prosperity to all human beings. These things must be made known to the public.

It must be made known to the public that Government and Authority are cajoling people by means of lies and concealment to join ignorantly in a march towards death. The civil disobedience demonstration of February 18 is a valiant attempt to break down the barrier against the facts becoming known.

Further information concerning this demonstration may be obtained from the Secretary of the Committee of 100, 13 Goodwin Street, London, N.4. Any man or woman who is willing to take part in this demonstration should send their name and address to the Secretary. Every fresh recruit increases the possibility that there may be life in Britain ten years hence.

—Bertrand Russell.
Penrhyndeudraeth

[181]

## The Day I Shouted "Murderer" in Moscow

*Daily Mail* (4th March, 1961), p. 8 | C61.12

*On 18th February the Committee of 100 had staged a sit-down demonstration involving over five thousand people, including Russell, outside the Ministry of Defence.* The Daily Mail, *a right-wing Conservative newspaper, tried to embarrass Russell by quoting the British Defence Minister to the effect that Russell should practice his civil disobedience in Moscow (where, presumably, it would be met with much less than British civility). With much humor and no little irony, Russell recounts his personal experience with protest in Russia more than forty years earlier. (See the cartoon on p. 295.)*

Beneath an excellent cartoon [February 28] you quote the Defence Minister as advising me to squat in the Red Square. The advice is sound but somewhat belated.

In 1920 I stood on the steps of the Foreign Office in Moscow and shouted at the Foreign Secretary (who stood a few steps above me): "I shall denounce you to the whole world as a murderer."[47]

He was just as forbearing as Mr. Watkinson.[48]

Bertrand Russell
Penrhyndeudraeth, Merioneth

---

47. When Russell was visiting Russia in 1920, his friend and fellow pacifist, Clifford Allen became seriously ill, but was temporarily prevented from leaving Moscow by the Russian Minister of Defense, Georgi Chicherin. Chicherin had been involved in leftist politics in Britain during the first world war and was imprisoned for a year there in 1917. He had been friends with Russell's uncle Rollo.

48. H.A. Watkinson (1910– ) was Minister of Defence from 1959 to 1964.

[182]

# Exclusive: Text of Lord Bertrand Russell's Open Letter to President Kennedy

*I.F. Stone's Weekly* (19th June, 1961), p. 3 | C61.21

*President Kennedy, after a June 3rd meeting with Khrushchev in Vienna, proceeded to London for talks with the British government. On June 2nd, Russell had written an open letter to the new President pointing out the growing opposition in Britain to an American Polaris submarine base. The letter is signed by Russell on behalf of the Committee of 100.*

*I.F. Stone notes that Russell's letter was released to the British press and to the U.S. Embassy in London where it was received by a Mr. Campbell of the F.B.I. But only the* Guardian *and the* London Daily Worker *(the Communist Party paper) published it, along with the Committee's announced plans for massive demonstrations in September. The letter was ignored by U.S. correspondents. Similarly, several events coinciding with Kennedy's arrival—a press conference, a march of 8,000 led by American marchers and a Trafalgar Square rally featuring A.J. Muste and Bradford Lyttle—went virtually unreported.*

*Excerpts from Russell's letter were published in the* Guardian *(6th June, 1961).*

To the President of the United States of America:

In your visit to Great Britain on June 5, which we must all hope will prove fruitful, it is important that you should take cognizance, not only of governmental opinion, but also of that very large and rapidly growing section which is opposed to the establishment of a Polaris base, whether at Holy Loch or elsewhere on British territory. There have already, as you know, been preliminary protests, but very much larger protests are to be expected and are being planned. So far as present plans are concerned, these will culminate in nationwide action in September. I have been asked by the Committee of 100, of which I am President, to put before you the reasons for such action.

There are, it seems to me, three kinds of reasons that justify our protests and such as should carry weight with the United States Government.

The first of these reasons is the importance of preserving the hitherto cordial relations between the United States and Great Britain, not only in Government circles, but in public opinion. It is inevitable, though profoundly regrettable, that agitation against a Polaris base in Great Britain should generate some antagonism, not only to the policy of the British

Government, but also to that of the United States. We must all wish that such antagonism should not increase.

## Doubts As to British Safety

A second reason is concerned with doubts as to the safety of the population of Great Britain. Experience has shown that there is uncertainty as to where missiles will land and, in a time of crisis, it would probably be impossible for the British authorities to exercise any degree of control over the station of Polaris submarines. There is a distinct possibility, which has been emphasized by your most authoritative writer Herman Kahn, that, so long as there is a Polaris base in Britain, Russia might retaliate against Britain alone. Such retaliation might, and probably would, destroy the whole population of Britain in the course of, at most an hour, without (again I quote Herman Kahn) provoking American retaliation. It is very questionable whether British membership of NATO, and British permission of American bases on our territory, add anything to the strength of America, while, on the contrary, they impose upon America an onerous obligation which it may prove impossible to fulfill.

Third, the supreme interest of the whole world—East and West and uncommitted nations alike—is the prevention of nuclear war. A rapidly growing body of opinion in this country believes that Britain could be more effective in preventing a nuclear war as a neutral by helping to suggest agreements which could be accepted by both East and West. Hitherto proposals by either East or West have been unacceptable to the other side for reasons, partly of prestige, and partly of suspicion. Proposals by neutrals would obviate these difficulties. Such a policy would not imply that Britain should withdraw from the search for the solution of world problems, but, on the contrary, should seek such solution in ways promising more hope of success than those which have hitherto been pursued in East-West negotiations.

The danger of a nuclear holocaust is the most terrible of all those that face the world at the present time, and those for whom I speak are persuaded that what Britain can do to diminish this danger can best be done by the adoption of a radically new policy by the British Government—a policy devoted to the presentation of world peace rather than to the entirely illusory hope of the victory of one side. It is in the hope that such a change of policy could be carried out without diminution of friendly relations with the United States that I am sending you this open Letter.

Yours faithfully,
Bertrand Russell

••••••••••••• [183] •••••••••••••

# Lord Russell and the CND

*The Guardian* (2nd October, 1961), p. 8 | C61.36

*In September Russell—and his fourth wife, Edith—spent a week in prison for a "Hiroshima Day" (6th August) action with the Committee of 100. While in prison he released a message highly critical of "a few brutal but powerful men" (including Macmillan and Gaitskell) who were "pursuing a common aim: the ending of human life." Here Russell defends himself against Sir Richard Acland's charges of making "unbridled statements."*

Sir,—I am grieved that Sir Richard Acland,[49] whom I have long admired, has stated in an article in your issue of September 27 that I have destroyed any long-term hope of success for the Ban-the-Bomb Campaign and also that he brands as a lie the statement that Mr. Macmillan and Mr. Gaitskell are among "the few brutal and powerful men" who are pursuing policies which are almost certain to end in nuclear war. I mention in the same context Kennedy and Khrushchev, Adenauer and de Gaulle—but of this Sir Richard takes no note.

As for Mr. Macmillan, I will give two illustrations. He has said that "our precautions are amply sufficient to prevent nuclear war starting as a result of accident on the part of the West" (reported in your issue of November 30, 1960, under the heading: "No Nuclear War by Accident"), but all expert opinion holds that, while present policies continue, a nuclear war by accident sooner or later is almost certain. We are thus faced with the dilemma: either Mr. Macmillan is ignorant of the facts which it is his duty to know, or he is deliberately misleading the British people in a matter involving the life and death of us all. Either alternative is sufficient to justify my condemnation.

There is another example of the Prime Minister's real or simulated ignorance. Speaking a few months ago at Ottawa about the signs of neutralism in Britain he said: "If ever the call comes to them, the young will go straight from the ranks of the neutralists into the ranks of her Majesty's forces, as they have so often done in the past." He ignores what his own officials have told us: that they will only have four minutes in which to show their change of heart. Possibly a few who happen to live

49. Sir Richard Acland had been a member of Parliament from 1945 to 1955, when he resigned his seat as Labour M.P. in protest over Britain's decision to manufacture the H-bomb—an act for which he was highly praised at the time by Russell. See above, document [123].

very near to a recruiting station my reach it in three minutes and spend the last minute of life in proclaiming willingness for the inevitable patriotic death.

Mr. Macmillan does not say how this would benefit anyone and in fact, as his allusion to the past shows, he has not grasped or at any rate has not acknowledged the profound difference between a nuclear war and all former war. I include Mr. Gaitskell in my condemnation because his differences from Mr. Macmillan seem insignificant.

My first statement as to the wickedness of the leading statesmen of East and West was made at the end of a long speech providing the evidence for the statement.[50] The Guardian criticised this speech in a leading article on April 17, but I was unable to reply at the time as I was seriously ill and for some weeks incapacitated. In this article you argued that "since Lord Russell does not advocate American unilateralism he must recognise some validity in the American deterrent." The only validity that I recognise in it is that it can be used in an argument with Russia in favour of the general abandonment of nuclear weapons, which should be the common aim of all sane men. Agreed nuclear disarmament between America and Russia is what must be sought as a first step toward peace. I advocate British neutralism as an aid towards this end. The crime committed by the statesmen of East and West consists either through ignorance of what they should know or through deliberate intention to misguide, in encouraging the people of their countries to run the risk of exterminating the human race. To run such a risk is a greater crime than anybody at any earlier time could have committed.

Sir Richard accuses me of making unbridled statements. They are not unbridled, but are based upon both facts and reasons which I and others have stated again and again but which the press rarely choose to notice. I have discovered that only when my statements appear to be unbridled do they command attention. Only then am I and others sometimes permitted to publish in rebuttal our reasons for our point of view.

As for Sir Richard Acland's contention that I have killed the Ban-the-Bomb Campaign, I think this is sufficiently refuted by the immense national and international response elicited by the recent actions of the Committee of 100 which far surpasses anything achieved by former opposition to the bomb and gives evidence of far greater determination than could have been even hoped for on the part of far more people

---

50. In an *ex tempore* remark at the end of the speech, Russell said that Kennedy, Khruschev and Macmillan were "more wicked than Hitler" because they were willing to commit to a policy which would likely lead to the "massacre of the whole of mankind" (*Autobiography*, Volume 3, p. 204).

throughout the world to demand that their Governments take this first step towards peace.

Yours faithfully, Bertrand Russell
Penrhyndeudraeth

[184]

## Cultural Freedom

*The New Statesman and Nation* (20th October, 1961), p. 552 | C61.38

*Russell protests the actions of the Chairman of the British Committee for Cultural Freedom, a national affiliate of the (international) Congress of Cultural Freedom. He also protests the actions of the Congress for dissolving its British affiliate.*

Sir, —In my preoccupation with other matters during August and September I missed the paragraph by Critic in the London Diary of your issue of 18 August concerning the dissolution of the British Committee for Cultural Freedom. My attention has now been called to it and I cannot forbear, however belatedly, registering my vigorous protest, if you will be kind enough to print it at this late date, to the action of the chairman of the British Committee, of which I was a sponsor, in objecting to a symposium in which Professor Bernal[51] was to write with others about C.P. Snow's[52] lecture on the "Responsibilities of Scientists in the Nuclear Age". What Critic said in his paragraph is entirely just. But I wish to protest with equal vigour against the dissolution of the British Committee by the Congress of Cultural Freedom—a body from which I resigned my position of honorary chairman early in 1957,[53] as I had discovered that freedom to the Congress meant freedom only to express their point of view. One wonders what those who chatter about "the Free World" mean by that phrase.

Bertrand Russell
Penrhyndeudraeth

---

51. J.D. Bernal (1901–71) was a British atomic scientist and Communist. See above, document [99].

52. C. P. Snow (1905–80) was an English novelist, scientist, and advisor to the British government. In his *Two Cultures* (1959) he warned of a growing cultural divide between scientists and non-scientists. He also warned of the dangers of nuclear technology and believed that nuclear war was imminent. See above, document [134].

53. See above, document [172].

[185]

## The Committee of 100

*The Guardian* (7th April, 1962), p. 6 | C62.13

*The Committee of 100 was having difficulties at this time despite much popular success in 1961, and the split with CND was growing. In December the British authorities cracked down on the Committee and sentenced many of its most important leaders to harsh prison terms. The press also seemed to withdraw some of the interest it had shown.*

*Russell and the Committee of 100 were continuously frustrated by an unfriendly and inaccurate press, as this letter, and the next, reveal.*

Sir, —The "reporter" who gave an account in the "Guardian" today (April 4) of the meeting of the London Committee of 100 has a curious view of facts and their meaning. The Committee has found that its support, named and on file, is so extensive that regional committees are required to accommodate this strength. There are now 13 Committees of 100.

Certainly the Committee of 100 has a debt. Our expenditure on the fight against nuclear weapons is so great, and our activity is so continuous, that we are always hard-pressed. This is a sign of a militant movement.

The "Guardian" "reporter" uninvited and unannounced, reports our private meetings without permission. We have always informed the press of our plans when they have been formulated. Is the "Guardian" prepared to justify journalistic standards such as these? It is a matter of public responsibility.

Yours faithfully, Bertrand Russell
43 Hasker Street, London SW 3.

[186]

## [The Nuclear Peril]

*The Bradford and District Chartered Accountant Students' Society Newsletter* (March, 1962), p. 16| C62.10

*Russell likens the mutual threat of the U.S.-Soviet nuclear arms race to an "extreme form of religious persecution."*

Sir, —I have arranged for some copies of the Committee of 100 leaflets to be sent up to you by rail from London, and I am most encouraged by the interest that your paper is taking in the problem of nuclear disarmament.

It is my conviction that unless we can avert it, nuclear war is inevitable. Rockets cover the planet on a hair trigger. The radar on which they rely cannot tell a goose from a missile. Only a mass resistance movement on a world wide basis can prevent a war that will mean mass extermination. We must make clear to the criminal lunatics of the Pentagon and the Kremlin that we are not prepared to see the human race destroyed to satisfy the demands of their dogma and their intolerance. I find it hard to refute by abstract argument the view that no world is better than a Communist world or that no world is better than a capitalist world, but I think that those who hold this view should question their right to impose it upon those of us who do not hold it. They are resorting to a more extreme form of religious persecution than has ever been seen in the long history of intolerance. There is a lot of agitation by humane people against the death penalty for murderers; a far more serious problem is the danger of the application of the death penalty for non-murderers. We are, after all, in the majority.

To prevent the final catastrophe demands determination and courage. We must tell the leaders of the two blocs that we can no longer stand aside while they prepare to destroy us. We shall immobilise their bases. We shall refuse to serve in their forces. We shall attempt to make impossible the whole technology of mass extermination. I do not know if we shall succeed: we are bound to make the attempt.

I should be quite willing for you to publish this letter in your paper, which I wish the greatest success.

Yours faithfully, Bertrand Russell

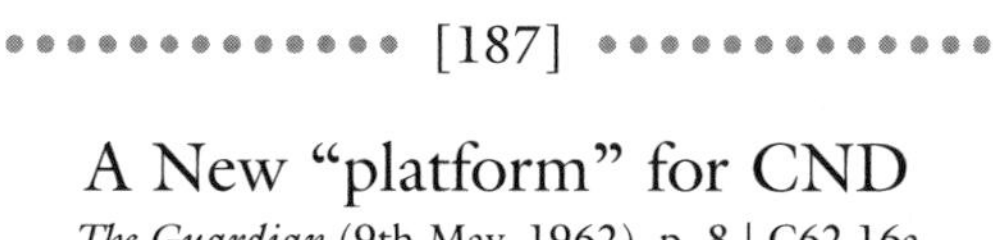

[187]

## A New “platform” for CND

*The Guardian* (9th May, 1962), p. 8 | C62.16a

Sir, —In the “Guardian’s” London Letter of May 2 there is a passage which, as far as my recollection serves, is unrivaled for impudent misrepresentation. This passage says that a quarterly is to be published by the CND “as a platform for its arguments for unilateral disarmament,” in which “the arguments will be on the highest plane”: “It appears that the CND committee has at last realised that there are many people ready to think about the problem at this level, who are most unwilling to involve themselves with marching or sitting down."

The writer of your London Letter cannot be unaware that both the CND and the Committee of 100 have published and are publishing a quantity of pamphlets and leaflets containing the serious arguments which he deems desirable. They have published them at their own expense—often at the expense of individuals—and have distributed them as widely as possible in various parts of the world, both East and West. They have done this because it has proved almost impossible to persuade the press of this country to publish such serious argumentation.

Moreover, part of our reason for marching and sitting down is that such demonstrations are the only things about us which the press appears to be willing to publish, and we are sometimes able to slip into the reports some of the reasons for our beliefs, in spite of the fact that the press is quite obviously bent upon trying to make us appear only hysterical or subversive or both.

I am glad that there is to be this new quarterly, although it cannot be expected that its circulation will be comparable to that of a daily newspaper. Meanwhile, it ill becomes the "Guardian" to complain that we do not "publish argument on the highest plane."

Yours faithfully, Bertrand Russell
Penrhyndeudraeth

••••••••••••• [188] •••••••••••••

## Russell Pleads for Pacifist

*The New York Times* (30th August, 1962), p. 28 | C62.36

*Russell's letter on behalf of Don Martin is one of many pleas for Americans in prison or facing trial because of their peace activities. Martin, in the course of a civil disobedience demonstration, had entered a restricted government area. Russell also wrote to President Kennedy on Martin's behalf, describing him as "a man of conscience who believes, with me, that hydrogen missiles are weapons of genocide and cannot be acquiesced in." He asked Kennedy to consider "the meaning of six years' imprisonment for a person aged twenty and to consider the nature of civil liberty if such a sentence is possible for such an offence."*[54]

54. See Feinberg and Kasrils, *Bertrand Russell's America*, 1945–1970 (South End Press, 1983), pp. 142–43.

To the Editor of *The New York Times:*

I am often told that Americans have a high opinion of my attempts to arouse people to an awareness of the imminent danger of nuclear annihilation. If this is in fact the case, then perhaps Americans will join me in condemning the sentence of six years' imprisonment imposed on a 21-year-old student because of his participation in a demonstration of civil disobedience in your country. I should like to remind you that if I were an American I should only do exactly as he had done and I should do it often.

If freedom, as you understand it, means freedom for those who agree with you and six years for those who do not, then perhaps you will begin to understand why we who are not possessed of fanatical interest in a conflict which could only lead to nuclear annihilation find your behavior almost on a par with the Russians.

I hope that Don Martin will be released, having served one year, and that you will find another way of saving conscience if not face.

Bertrand Russell
Penrhyndeudraeth, Wales, Aug. 23, 1962

# Philosophy and Religion

••••••••••••• [189] •••••••••••••

## Christian Ethics

*The Observer* (13th October, 1957), p. 8 | C57.24

*In the next five letters, Russell responds to reviews of his very popular* Why I Am Not a Christian. *In this letter to the* Observer, *Russell responds to Philip Toynbee's "very kind" review and explains an "appalling" passage on reproduction as prophecy not advocacy. He also points out some items in which he anticipated Huxley's* Brave New World.

Sir, —The very kind review of my *Why I am not a Christian,* by Philip Toynbee, in your issue of October 6, calls for explanation on one point. Mr. Toynbee quotes what he calls "one appalling passage"[55] and does not realize (though for this the fault is mine) that the passage horrifies me as much as it does him. I was engaged, not in advocacy, but in prophecy in the style of Cassandra,[56] but I am to blame for not having made this clear.

A few months before publication of Aldous Huxley's *Brave New World,* I published a book called *The Scientific Outlook,* in the last four chapters of which I developed prophecies very closely similar to Huxley's, in which I made it quite clear that the kind of suggestions which horrify Mr. Toynbee are abhorrent to me. At the end of the chapter called "Scientific Reproduction," I say: "In the end such a system must break down either in an orgy of bloodshed or in the rediscovery of joy. Such, at least, is the only ray of hope to lighten the darkness of these visions of Cassandra, but perhaps in permitting this ray of hope we have allowed ourselves to yield to a foolish optimism. Perhaps by means of injections and drugs and chemicals the population could be induced to bear whatever its scientific masters may decide to be for its good. New forms of drunkenness involving no subsequent headache may be discovered, and new forms of intoxication may be invented so delicious that for their sakes

---

55. Toynbee had referred to a passage from Russell's 1930 essay 'The New Generation', where he speaks of possible "rationally conducted" state functions for regulating childbearing for women "who would have to pass tests as to their fitness from a stock-breeding point of view." See *Why I Am Not a Christian* (Simon and Schuster, 1957), p. 165. See below, document [273].

56. In Greek legend, Cassandra was a Trojan princess who had learned the art of prophecy from Apollo but was never believed.

men are willing to pass their sober hours in misery. All these are possibilities in a world governed by knowledge without love, and power without delight. The man drunk with power is destitute of wisdom, and so long as he rules the world, the world will be a place devoid of beauty and joy."

I agree with Christian ethics in thinking that values reside in the individual rather than in the State. The dangers that I apprehend arise from substituting worship of the State for respect for the individual.

What Mr. Toynbee says in criticism of my views on ethics has my entire sympathy. I find my own views argumentatively irrefutable, but nevertheless incredible. I do not know the solution.

Bertrand Russell
Merioneth

[190]

## Why I am not a Christian

*The Times* (15th October, 1957), p. 11 | C57.25

*In the* Times *review of Russell's* Why I Am Not a Christian, *the reviewer had charged Russell with attacking a form of Christianity no longer in vogue and thereby removing his book from "any applicability to the real problems" of the world. Russell claims relevance and reminds the editor of his own troubles at City College New York.*

Sir, —The review of my *Why I Am Not a Christian* in your issue of October 10 is tolerant and urbane, and for this I am grateful. But it shows in some surprising ways such an ignorance of the world we live in that I doubt whether the reviewer can have read the account of my New York trouble at the end of the volume.

Your reviewer says—and in this I am entirely at one with him—that many Christians exhibit what are called Christian virtues, but what I was concerned with was not individual merit but Christianity as a social force. New York is the largest city in the world and the cultural and intellectual metropolis of the most powerful of western countries. In New York Christian churches, Episcopalian and Roman Catholic, accused me of offences of which I was not guilty and, when their libels were repeated in a law court, succeeded in preventing me from denying the accusations on oath on the technical ground that I was not an interested party. Your reviewer thinks that the kind of Christianity which I criticize ended with the end of the Regency, but George IV had been dead some time in

1940. The title of the review, "A Rationalist in Search of an Adversary," shows that the reviewer does not know how Christians with whom he is not acquainted behave. He might as well have called his review "A Fox in Search of the Hounds."

Yours faithfully, Russell
Plas Penrhyn, Penrhyndeudraeth, Merioneth.

[191]

## Christian Ethics

*The Observer* (20th October, 1957), p. 15 | C57.26

*Russell's second reply to Toynbee's review appeared alongside a response from A.J. Ayer, the Oxford logical positivist, who criticized Toynbee's defense of "absolute" values and their implications for the existence of God. Here Russell expresses dissatisfaction with his own subjectivist/emotivist theory of ethics.*

Sir, —The juxtaposition of Professor Ayer's letter and mine in your issue of October 13 might give the impression that he and I were not in agreement in relation to Mr. Philip Toynbee on absolute ethical values.

I expressed agreement with Mr. Toynbee on one point, viz., that my own ethics are unsatisfactory. I cannot meet the arguments against absolute ethical values, and yet I cannot believe that a dislike of wanton cruelty is merely a matter of taste, like a dislike of oysters. But I am in complete agreement with Professor Ayer in thinking that the question whether ethical values are absolute has no bearing whatever on the question of the existence of God. This is the view of orthodox theology, and was the view of philosophers until Kant was seduced by Rousseau.

Bertrand Russell
Merioneth.

[192]

# Earl Russell Replies

*Time and Tide* (23rd November, 1957), p. 1463 | C57.32

*Russell says that Gerard Irvine's review of his* Why I am Not A Christian *is "full of misrepresentations," and ignores the account of the CCNY case.*

Sir: I have only just come across a review of me by Gerard Irvine[57] in your issue of 26 October. This review is full of misrepresentations. To save your space, I will mention only one: he asserts that I say that I 'once knew a fashionable vicar who had nine children, for which inhuman conduct he was iniquitously rewarded with a fat living'.

I do not know whether Mr. Irvine read the book he is reviewing, but if he did, this statement shows him to be guilty of just the kind of moral lapse which I consider characteristic of many conventional Christians. I did not criticize the clergyman for having nine children, but for having a tenth after the doctors had informed him that a tenth would probably kill his wife. She duly died, but he incurred no odium. For the benefit of those who think that she was a myth invented by me, I will add that she was a god-daughter of Queen Victoria.

In supposing that he has not read the book he is reviewing, I am displaying that Christian charity in which he appears to be lacking. If he had read the concluding portion of the book about my troubles in New York in 1940, he could not have thought that my Christian priests were imaginary. His statement that it is possible to be sceptical about Professor Edwards's account of this episode, suggest that he did not read the account, the worst features of which are quotations from official documents. I shall be glad to know whether he acknowledges the crime of deliberate misrepresentation or the lesser crime of reviewing a book he has not read.

I am, etc., Bertrand Russell
Plas Penrhyn, Penrhyndeudraeth, Merioneth.

57. Gerard Irvine was a writer and scholar who later edited *Christianity in Its Social Context* (1967).

[193]

## Why I am not a Christian

*The Times* (26th November, 1957), p. 11 | C57.34

*A correspondent, S.N. Warren, wrote in* The Times *(23rd November), in response to Russell's letter of 15th October, that Russell's problems in the City College case were not due to intolerant Christians, but to his own legal and moral failings.*

Sir, —In your issue of November 23 you publish a letter from Mr. Schuyler N. Warren which shows complete ignorance of the facts. I shall answer his points one by one.

First as to "libels". I wrote publicly at the time: "When grossly untrue statements as to my actions are made in court, I feel that I must give them the lie. I never conducted a nudist colony in England. Neither my wife nor I ever paraded nude in public. I never went in for salacious poetry. Such assertions are deliberate falsehoods which must be known to those who make them to have no foundation in fact. I shall be glad of an opportunity to deny them on oath." This opportunity was denied me on the ground that I was not a party to the suit. The charges that I did these things (which had been made by the prosecuting counsel in court) were not based on my own writings, as Mr. Warren affirms, but on the morbid imaginings of bigots.

I cannot understand Mr. Warren's statement that my counsel submitted a brief on my behalf. No counsel representing me was heard. Nor can I understand his statement that two Courts of Appeal upheld the decision, as New York City refused to appeal when urged to do so. The suggestion that I could have brought an action for libel could only be made honestly by a person ignorant of the atmosphere of hysteria which surrounded the case at that time. The atmosphere is illustrated by the general acceptance of the prosecuting counsel's description in court of me as: "lecherous, libidinous, lustful, venerous, erotomaniac, aphrodisiac, irreverent, narrow-minded, untruthful, and bereft of moral fiber."

Yours truly, Russell
Plas Penrhyn, Penrhyndeudraeth, Merioneth.

●●●●●●●●●●●●● [194] ●●●●●●●●●●●●●

# The World and the Observer

*The Listener* (13th March, 1958), p. 451 | C58.18

*During the 1950s Russell's brand of philosophy (what he called 'logical atomism') was largely up-staged by the 'ordinary language' school of philosophy at Oxford which had been strongly influenced by the later work of Russell's former pupil, Ludwig Wittgenstein.*

*Russell reminds a* Listener *correspondent that his critics have not gone unanswered.*

Sir, —In *The Listener* of February 27 Mr. Kenneth Stern informs Mr. Purcell about recent literature criticising my philosophy. I think your other readers should be informed of what Mr. Purcell undoubtedly knows, that I have published various articles meeting many of these criticisms.

The articles in question are: 'Philosophical Analysis' in the *Hibbert Journal* of July 1956; 'Mr. Strawson on Referring' in *Mind* of July 1957; 'Logic and Ontology' in the *Journal of Philosophy* of April 25, 1957; and 'What is Mind?' in the *Journal of Philosophy* of January 2, 1958. Some years earlier I published an article on 'The Cult of Common Usage' in the *British Journal for the Philosophy of Science,* Vol. III, No. 12, 1953. None of these articles has, so far, been answered by any of my critics.[58]

—Yours, etc., Bertrand Russell
Penrhyndeudraeth

●●●●●●●●●●●●● [195] ●●●●●●●●●●●●●

# Philosopher's Corner

*Look* (16th September, 1958), p. 14 | C58.49

*In May 1958,* Look *magazine published an article on Russell. He calls attention to some details that require comment.*

I have found a few things that I would have liked to alter.

---

58. All of these articles are reprinted in his *My Philosophical Development* (Simon and Schuster, 1959).

1. To call my wife Lady Edith Finch Russell implies that she is the daughter of a Duke, a Marquis or an Earl, and that I am not a Peer. You must call her either Lady Russell or Countess Russell.

2. It would be more correct to say I drafted my appeal [for scientists to warn against the dangers of H-bomb tests] "with the approval" of Albert Einstein rather than "with the help of Albert Einstein." He wrote that he was too ill to do any drafting himself.

3. Your quotation in the last sentence [" the root of the matter. . . is love—Christian love or compassion"] is entirely correct, but I would have preferred that the adjective "Christian" be omitted. My reason is that since I used it in one of my books, Christians have falsely claimed that I was becoming a Christian, and I have got rather tired of denying it.

I am grateful to you for reporting my views on nuclear matters so accurately.

Bertrand Russell
Plas Penrhyn, Penrhyndeudraeth, Merionethshire, Wales

••••••••••••• [196] •••••••••••••

## A Reply by Bertrand Russell

*Encounter* (March, 1959), p. 84 | C59.10

*Few of Russell's letters dealt with his technical philosophy. He responds here to a critical letter (in the same issue) by Charles Davy, a writer interested in the nature of meaning and consciousness. Russell's response elaborates the main ideas of his theory of mind known as neutral monism.*

Mr. Charles Davy's[59] "Mind and World" shows me once more that I have failed to make my opinions clear. I am accused by Communists of being an idealist, and it seems that Mr. Davy and those who think as he does consider me a materialist. I do not, in fact, think that either mind or matter is part of the stuff of the world. I think that minds and bits of matter are convenient aggregations, like cricket clubs or football clubs. Mr. Davy, in the last paragraph of his discussion, says: "I know it is unfashionable to suppose that mind has any existence apart from brain." My

59. John Charles Davy (1927–1984), an English journalist and science writer for the London *Observer*. In his later years he became absorbed in the mystical writings of Austrian philosopher Rudolf Steiner.

own view is that a brain is composed of thoughts; in fact, of the very thoughts of which we become aware by self-observation as well as of other thoughts that we do not notice. I think that the objects dealt with by physics are assemblages of brief interrelated events which cannot be known to be very different in character from thoughts. The change from sound-waves to sounds that we experience is not, in reality, anything like so great a change as it seems to those who are misled by Cartesian dualism.

I am taken to task by Mr. Davy for speaking of "the transformation by the radio of electro-magnetic waves into sounds." I should have done better, as he points out, to have said "sound-waves," rather than "sounds", but, when he goes on to say that the transformation of electro-magnectic waves into sound-waves is understood in a sense in which the transformation of sound-waves into sounds is not understood, he says something with which I cannot agree. We know the laws of the transformation in each case. If we did not, we could not make machines that would generate intended sounds in hearers. As regards the intrinsic character of the events concerned, we know this in the case of heard sounds, but not in the case of the waves that give rise to them. Our ignorance of the intrinsic character of everything non-mental is not usually realised because people think that what they see is physical, whereas, in fact, is it mental. On this point, I agree with Berkeley, though I disagree with him in that I think we have reason to believe in the existence of things that are probably not mental.

My definition of a mind by means of memory chains appears to Mr. Davy objectionable. He seems to think that I mean to say there is nothing else in a mind. This is not my meaning. I am concerned only to explain what makes some mental events belong to one biography, and others, to another. For those who believe in an ego or soul, this problem does not arise; but if the ego as a subsistent entity is rejected, it becomes necessary to find some other characteristic by which to define the unity of one biography.

Mr. Davy says various things about meaning which he seems to consider that I should disagree with. In fact, I disagree little, if at all, with what he says on this subject, as he will see if he consults my discussion of meaning in *An Inquiry into Meaning and Truth.*

I think that Mr. Davy is unduly suspicious of codes, and feels that anything so material and unspiritual cannot give rise to the lofty emotions and thought which are supposed to give dignity to human beings. This seems to me a sheer mistake. You may be stimulated to very elevated thoughts and feelings by reading *Hamlet*, but the stimulus consists entirely of black marks on a white ground. Anything about Shakespeare that cannot be conveyed by such marks must remain unknown to us. And what is true of Shakespeare in this respect is also true, *mutatis mutandis,* of the starry heavens.

Bertrand Russell
Plas Penrhyn, Penrhyndeudraeth, Merioneth

[197]

## Review Refused

*The Times* (5th November, 1959), p. 13 | C59.22

Words and Things *by Ernest Gellner was a critical examination and repudiation of the main tenets of 'ordinary language' philosophy. Russell thought the book important and was indignant when Gilbert Ryle, the editor of* Mind, *refused to review it on grounds that it was "abusive."*

Sir, —Messrs. Gollancz have recently published a book by Ernest Gellner called *Words and Things.* I read this book before it was published and considered it a careful and accurate analysis of a certain school of philosophy, an opinion which I expressed in a preface. I now learn that Professor Ryle, the editor of *Mind*, has written to Messrs. Gollancz refusing to have this book reviewed in *Mind* on the ground that it is abusive and cannot therefore be treated as a contribution to an academic subject.

Such a partisan view of the duties of an editor is deeply shocking. The merit of a work of philosophy is always a matter of opinion and I am not surprised that Professor Ryle disagrees with my estimate of the work, but *Mind* has hitherto, ever since its foundation, offered a forum for the discussion of all serious and competent philosophical work. Mr. Gellner's book is not "abusive" except in the sense of not agreeing with the opinions which he discusses. If all books that do not endorse Professor Ryle's opinions are to be boycotted in the pages of *Mind*, that hitherto respected periodical will sink to the level of the mutual-admiration organ of a coterie. All who care for the repute of British philosophy will regret this.

Yours &c., Russell
Plas Penrhyn, Penrhyndeudraeth, Merioneth, Nov. 3.

CCCP
CCCP
TO SIBERIA
Emmwood
The unilateralists might consider how they would get on squatting in Red Square, instead of outside my Ministry.—Mr. Harold Watkinson, Defence Minister.


This Emmwood cartoon appeared in the *Daily Mail* (28th February, 1961), ten days after Russell's Committee of 100 led a sit-down demonstration involving five thousand people outside the Ministry of Defence in London. The Minister, Mr. Watkinson, commented that the protesters ought to try protesting in Red Square and they would see what happened. In document [181], Russell pointed out that he had already protested in Red Square, some 40 years earlier, when he had denounced the Soviet Defence Minister as a "murderer."

••••••••••••• [198] •••••••••••••

## Review Refused

*The Times* (24th November, 1959), p. 13 | C59.23

Sir, —Mr. Alec Kassman's letter today demands a reply from me. I have seen nothing either in his letter or in any other on the present controversy which induces me to retract anything in my previous letter. There are two different points at issue. First, is anything in Mr. Gellner's book "abusive"? Secondly, should a book containing anything abusive be, on that account alone, refused a review in *Mind*?

As to the first point, "abusive" is not a very precise word. Mr. Kassman speaks of "instances indicated by the editor" and says that Professor Ryle "rebutted the specific charge in some detail," and complains that I have not replied. I cannot "reply," since Professor Ryle has not given a single instance of a single sentence which he considers abusive. It is up to Professor Ryle to quote at least one passage which he considers abusive. This, so far as I know, he has not yet done.

As to the second and much more important point, I do not think that a serious piece of philosophical work should be refused a review even it it does contain passages which everybody would admit to be abusive. Take, for example, Nietzsche's Beyond Good and Evil. In this book he speaks of "that blockhead John Stuart Mill," and after saying "I abhor the man's vulgarity," attributes to him the invention of the Golden Rule, saying: "Such principles would fain establish the whole of human traffic upon mutual services, so that every action would appear to be a cash payment for something done to us. The hypothesis here is ignoble to the last degree." I do not accept these opinions of Nietzsche's but I think a philosophical editor would have been misguided if, on account of them, he had refused a review to *Beyond Good and Evil,* since this was undoubtedly a serious piece of philosophical work. I note that neither Professor Ryle nor anyone else has denied that the same is true of Mr. Gellner's book.

Yours faithfully, Russell
Plas Penrhyn, Penrhyndeudraeth, Merioneth, Nov. 21.

# Miscellaneous

[199]

## Who's Who

*The Times* (28th February, 1959), p. 7 | C59.09

*At Russell's suggestion, he and the well-known author Russell of Liverpool*[60] *published the following humorous letter in the* Times.

Sir, —In order to discourage confusions which have been constantly occurring, we beg herewith to state that neither of us is the other.

Yours & c.,
Russell (Bertrand, Earl Russell)
Russell of Liverpool (Lord Russell of Liverpool)
February 25.

[200]

## Snobbery

*Encounter* (August, 1959), p. 71 | C59.16

*This open letter to C.P. Snow expresses essential agreement with the scientist's thesis regarding "two cultures," and Russell provides some interesting examples of his own.*

Dear Snow, I have been reading your Rede Lecture with very great interest and as much pleasure as the subject-matter permitted. All that you say as to what ought to be done commands my assent. The separation between science and culture is very much greater than it used to be. In the time of Charles II it did not exist, and in the early nineteenth century there were still many bridges from one territory to the other.

60. Russell of Liverpool, widely known for his best-selling works about Nazi atrocities, was no relation to Bertrand, but he did claim to have been mistaken for an Earl Russell on two occasions—for Russell's elder brother in 1927 and for Russell in 1954. See *The Autobiography of Bertrand Russell,* Volume 3, p. 177.

Cartwright, who invented the power-loom, was my grandfather's tutor and taught him to construe the odes of Horace. So far as I have been able to discover, his invention of the power-loom remained unknown to my grandfather. Mrs. Gaskell's *North and South* and Charlotte Bronte's *Shirley* allow an intrusion of the world of industry into the world of culture. I live just above a causeway constructed by Shelley's friend Maddox with Shelley's enthusiastic support. The early Romantics had a completely romantic admiration for science on the lines of Mary Shelley's *Frankenstein*. Do you remember Peacock's account of Robert Owen's co-operative parallelograms with a steam engine in the middle as maid-of-all-work? The corresponding modern ideas are known only to children in the form of science comics. I wish you all success, but I fear that as a nation we would rather lose all than sacrifice one particle of snobbery.

Bertrand Russell

[201]

## A Man's World

*The New Statesman and Nation* (10th February, 1961), p. 218 | C61.08

Sir, —I observe that Charon, in the last issue of the NEW STATESMAN, repeats the myth that it was Lord Curzon[61] who said 'Ladies don't move'. It was not. It was Lucretius.[62]

Bertrand Russell.
Plas Penrhyn, Penrhyndeudaeth, Merioneth

61. George Curzon (1859–1925) was a British statesman, Viceroy to India and Foreign Secretary.

62. Lucretius (99 B.C.–55 B.C.) was a Roman poet and philosopher.

PART VI

# The Cold War and American Militarism

(1963–1969)

# Bertrand Russell

Most of the controversy surrounding the Cuban Missile Crisis carried over into 1963, and we find six letters dealing with the Crisis. Generally, nuclear weapons and the threat of nuclear war were issues that continued to be of grave concern to Russell, especially in 1963. The Bertrand Russell Peace Foundation was established to work on behalf of peace and human rights, and we find many letters in this period, not only explaining the role of the Foundation in the cause of world peace, but personally appealing to public conscience in cases of government abuse of individual citizens. With the help of the Foundation, Russell took notice of, and wrote public letters concerning, civil rights abuses in Germany, Greece, Poland, Russia, Spain, the United States, and Africa. As one of its earliest tasks, the Foundation took on the investigation of the assassination of President Kennedy, for which it formed an investigative committee ('The British Who Killed Kennedy? Committee'). In several letters Russell explains the Committees's role and reasons for doubting the conclusions of the Warren Commission.

In the mid-1960s, the Foundation, under the direction of Russell's radical American secretary, Ralph Schoenman, apparently went beyond its initial peace function to include support for third world nationalist insurrections on the models of Cuba and Vietnam. The extent to which Russell was aware of this, or approved, is unclear, though some of his writings at the time make it not unreasonable to think he would have been sympathetic to such an expanded role.[1] What the public letters make clear is Russell's growing sympathy for Cuba after the Bay of Pigs invasion (1961) and the Missile Crisis (1962), and his growing conviction that U.S. behavior towards Cuba and Vietnam—and the third world generally—was unjust and a danger to international peace.

But Russell's main concern in this period, as evidenced by the great number of his public letters on the subject, was the war in Vietnam, which he characterized as one of "imperialist aggression" on the part of the U.S. As his letters reveal, he engaged a wide range of citizens, including newspaper editors, university professors and heads of state, and challenged Cold War assumptions and "facts" regarding the nature of the American intervention. In 1967, at the age of 95, with the help of his Foundation, he initiated the International War Crimes Tribunal to expose and condemn U.S. war crimes in Vietnam in accordance with the principles set

1. See for instance his 1966 essay, 'Peace Though Resistance to US Imperialism', reprinted in *War Crimes in Vietnam* (Monthly Review Press, 1967), pp. 94–100.

down at Nuremberg at the end of World War II. There are eight letters concerning the nature and function of this Tribunal.

I think the casual reader will be struck by the extraordinary amount of detail at Russell's command—even into his nineties—in many of these letters, especially those concerning the Missile Crisis, nuclear deterrence, and U.S. actions in Vietnam. He exhibits an intimate knowledge of the western press, and he uses it skillfully to cast doubt on official government propaganda.

Russell turned unequivocally against American foreign policy during these years, but although his criticisms of U.S. international conduct were harsh and many accused him of extreme anti-Americanism, he was never blind to Soviet transgressions, domestic or foreign, and he vociferously condemned the 1968 Soviet invasion of Czechoslovakia, as we can see from the four letters reprinted in this section. These letters have not been reprinted before, nor have they been discussed by any of Russell's biographers. They are especially important because they were written after Schoenman had fallen out of favor with Russell and had been deported from the United Kingdom. So there can be little question that they reflect Russell's own thinking at the time. And what one finds is his characteristic impartial condemnation of injustice.

# Human Rights and Civil Liberties

## *Greece*

[202]

### Prisoners in Greece

*The Guardian* (26th January, 1963), p. 6 | C63.06

*Post-war Greece was politically unstable for many years. The West aided anti-Communist and monarchist forces in Greece's civil war from 1944 to 1949. The issue of political prisoners—pro-Communists and antimonarchists jailed during the civil war—continued to foment the ongoing political crises of the early 1960s. The treatment of these political prisoners—"over a thousand," according to Russell—is the focus of several of his letters to the British press in 1963. This letter, and the next, are representative.*

Sir, —Only official apologists for the Greek Government will fail to be grateful for your editorial last Wednesday. Of all the degradation and misery in the post-war world, the imprisonment of hundreds of Greeks for year after year is outstanding in its calculated cruelty.

The "Guardian's" call for an amnesty comes none too soon. I have received from Athens a further cable from Tassia Glezou, on behalf of the Organization of Families of Political Prisoners and Exiles, which states that the death of Georges Erythriadis on January 21 was the third death among political prisoners within a month. His widow, Elli, is also in prison, their three children in exile. When one recalls that the parents were held for five years before even being brought to trial, the enormity of the Government's vengeance becomes apparent.

Although there are over a thousand political prisoner in Greece, 150 of them—including elderly women—are very gravely ill. How many more deaths must we await before the Greek Government abandons what the "Guardian" rightly describes as undiminished persecution?

Yours faithfully, Bertrand Russell
Plas Penrhyn, Penrhyndeudraeth, Merioneth

••••••••••••• [203] •••••••••••••

# Committee of 100 and Greece

*The Manchester Guardian Weekly* (18th June, 1963), p. 8 | C63.49

*Russell writes in support of ongoing anti-nuclear demonstrations in Greece organized largely under the leadership of the Bertrand Russell Youth Committee for Nuclear Disarmament that flourished in Greece in the mid-1960s. These demonstrations, modeled on those in Britain, were among the largest in the world and played an important role in bringing about a period of reform in 1963. In 1967 a military junta seized power.*

Sir, —Recently I and my secretary and colleague Mr. Pottle[2] have been attacked for our sympathetic support of those Greeks who are opposing the flagrant injustices and dangerous policies imposed by their Government and backed by ours.

It is true that we have supported their valiant opposition to their Government's nuclear policy. The Government banned their anti-nuclear, non-violent march. The police beat up many of those (including Mr. Pottle) who attempted to make the march. The Government refused police protection to the Liberal (not Communist) MPs, Mr. Lambrakis[3] and his colleague, at a peaceful anti-nuclear meeting in Salonika. The latter was severely wounded and Mr. Lambrakis was murdered —with, it is believed, the connivance of the Government.

We gladly support anti-nuclear activities, but to do so is not to abrogate our right to protest against flagrant injustice. The Government of Greece has held over 1,000 prisoners, some for 14 or 15 years, without trial or specific charges beyond being called "Communists" or "criminals." Many of these prisoners were Communists, many are not, and the "crimes" which they are said to have committed were those condoned by us during the war, for it is to them, in the first instance, that Greece owes

2. Pat Pottle was an active member of the Committee of 100. A printer by trade, he served as a secretary for Russell and sometimes represented Russell on assignments abroad. The Bertrand Russell Youth Committee for Nuclear Disarmament in Greece organized a march in April 1963 in which two thousand people were arrested and several hundred, including Pottle, were injured.

3. Grigoris Lambrakis was a Member of Parliament in Greece. A doctor and famous Olympic athlete, he had marched with CND to Aldermaston (a British atomic weapons research facility) in April 1963. He was murdered at an anti-nuclear event in Salonika. His funeral in May erupted into one of the largest peace demonstrations in world history and brought Athens to a stand-still. See L. Wittner, *Resisting the Bomb* (Stanford University Press, 1997), pp. 238–39.

its "liberation." All attempts to persuade the Greek Government to free these prisoners—including the gentle attempt by the wife of one of them to hand a letter concerning them to the Greek Queen in London, which was blown up in Britain into a "Communist-inspired incident"—is to be supported. The pressure has already secured freedom for a few, though to date no civil disobedience has had to be employed.

The King and Queen of Greece are absolute rulers; the elections to the Government were rigged; the majority of the Greek people were against the Karamanlis Government and oppose the policies of the King and Queen. All this is brought into high relief by the resignation of Karamanlis. The King and Queen are now pursuing a policy unsupported by any form of popular approval.

Our Government, in supporting them, particularly in their proposed royal visit, are playing a dangerous game with far-reaching and possibly disastrous results, just as they are in upholding the Governments of South Vietnam, Portugal, Spain, etc.—all unpopular and cruel dictatorships. Far from eliciting violence, we, like the Greek populace, are doing what we can to avoid it. Civil war, especially in a country where the Great Powers in the cold war are deeply implicated, as Britain and America are in Greece, is too likely to result in nuclear war.

Our activities must therefore still be directed towards the avoidance of nuclear war, and are based upon a considerable amount of fact-finding and thought.

Yours faithfully, Bertrand Russell
Plas Penrhyn, Penrhyndeudraeth, Merioneth

[204]

## Royal Visitors from Greece

*The Times* (12th July, 1963), p. 11 | C63.59

*The Committee of 100, placing blame on the Greek monarchy for recent repressive events in Greece—including the murder of anti-nuclear activist, Gregoris Lambrakis—mounted protests against the Greek royal family's visit to London in July 1963. Some rioting occurred and "Tyranny" was scrawled on walls.*

*Woodrow Wyatt was an M.P. and junior minister in the Labour government (1945–51). In 1960 he interviewed Russell for a series of television programs which also appeared as the book* Bertrand Russell Speaks His Mind *(1960).*

Sir, —Mr. Woodrow Wyatt asks of those involved in the demonstrations during the Greek Royal Visit three questions which I welcome the opportunity to answer.

Some of the demonstrators proclaimed adherence to non-violence. They have been joined by some who do not, in the same way that during the world war against fascism Mr. Wyatt was joined by many who did not believe in democracy. I might add that I regret Mr. Wyatt's apparent utter indifference to political prisoners in Greece.

There have been very large demonstrations in London against the worst recent crime of the Soviet Union, the testing of nuclear weapons. They would have been larger if Mr. Wyatt had joined them, but that was not possible this side of hypocrisy because he supported a similar policy by western governments.

The next demonstrations will be held when the circumstances demand them. In the case of Greece, they will continue until political prisoners are released and honest elections permitted.

Mr. Wyatt's attempt to imply that this week's demonstrations are selective in their concern for justice comes strangely from a man who has no difficulty in tolerating injustice perpetrated in the name of the Free World. I invite Mr. Wyatt to consider issues on their merits.

Yours faithfully, Bertrand Russell
Plas Penrhyn, Penrhyndeudraeth, Merioneth, July 11

## *Germany*

[205]

### West Germany

*The Observer* (6th October, 1963), p. 2 | C63.84

*In the next two letters, Russell writes in support of the journal* Blinkfuer *(and its editor, Ernst Aust) against persecution by the West German government.*

Sir, —I am most disturbed by developments in Western Germany. I think the British public is insufficiently aware of the rapid advent of totalitarianism there. Ernst Aust, a courageous journalist, is now charged with "imperilment of the State" and the independent journal he edits, *Blinkfuer*, is to be silenced by Adenauer's regime.

The crime of Ernst Aust and *Blinkfuer* is that they have demanded the resignation of the Secretary of State and an author of the Nazi race laws, Herr Globke. They are further accused of publishing declarations of the resistance fighters to the Nazis, for criticising the German armament programme, for criticising price increases and the practice of providing lectures for school youth by former war criminal Donitz.

*Blinkfuer* is a non-party journal which has opposed the appointment of leading Nazis to important positions in State Justice and industry. It has opposed the prevalence of allowing leading S.S. officers to assume commanding positions in the police force.

An example of the sort of individual whom Aust has sought to expose is Gehlen, currently the director of German political intelligence. He was also head of this structure under Hitler. He switched allegiance to the Pentagon on the day of the allied occupation and conducted intelligence work for them. Gehlen is now so sacrosanct that it is against the law in West Germany to photograph him.

One of the main charges against *Blinkfuer* is that it opposes the Emergency Legislation for which the Adenauer regime is pressing. This legislation will enable all public meetings to be suspended and all constitutional rights to be removed should the Government consider it advisable.

The Germany of Speidel, Heusinger, Globke, Oberlander, Strauss, Gehlen and Schroeder is crushing the few isolated voices of opposition to the chauvinist and neo-Nazi permeation of Western German public life.

I consider it a duty to protest against these developments in West Germany. They affront the memory of the victims of the concentration camps and of the entire Nazi era.

Bertrand Russell
Merioneth

[206]

## West Germany

*The Observer* (20th October, 1963), p. 30 | C63.85

Sir, —The letter from Sarah Gainham which *The Observer* featured last Sunday as "Germany: A Reply to Russell," accused me of being misled about facts and dates and of intending my letter as a spoof. Miss Gainham's reply is a tissue of distortion and oblique suggestion that the letter to which she replies said things which it patently did not.

She suggests by implication that I am unaware of the offices held by Speidel, Heusinger, Globke, Oberlander, Strauss, Gehlen, and Schroeder, by detailing offices they hold and when they retired from those held formerly. My letter made no reference whatsoever to the offices held by these men. I merely stated that the Germany of these men is crushing the isolated voices of opposition to neo-Nazi permeation of West German life.

The second accusation with regard to supposed misinformation on my part concerns the spelling of "Globke" and "Oberlander." I do not know the extent to which Miss Gainham is familiar with German. "E" is placed after an "a" or an "o" only if those two letters possess an Umlaut and one intends to Anglicize the name.

I did not say it was illegal to oppose the Emergency Powers Law; I said that Ernst Aust's journal is being charged with imperilment of the State for propagating opposition to those laws. I should point out that the *Daily Telegraph* carried very long and informative articles concerning the power of Herr Gehlen. He has been described by conservative sources as a man whom even Adenauer fears. As for Schroeder, it is patent nonsense to say that he has never shown attachment to Nazi ideology. Quite the contrary is true.

With regard to the "facts" put forward by Miss Gainham, it should be pointed out that *Blinkfuer* is not a weekly mimeographed news sheet but a very well designed published and printed newspaper with a substantial circulation in Hamburg. The crime of its editor is not that of attacking the constitution of his country but of attacking those who have no regard for constitutions or human liberty.

Finally, I should point out that when it was recently asked why so many of Himmler's former administrative directors were involved in West German Intelligence, it was said to be because the Americans preferred them. I hope I need not say more than this.

Bertrand Russell
Merioneth

[207]

## Letters to Dr. Richard Weyl

*The Observer* (8th December, 1963), p. 14 | C63.98

*Russell publicizes the case of Richard Weyl and exposes lingering Nazi sympathies within the West German legal system.*

Sir, —May I bring to the attention of your readers the case of Dr. Richard Weyl, an Israeli advocate who returned to Germany and applied for admission to the West German Bar for the sole purpose of pursuing compensation and restitution claims.

Dr. Weyl discovered not only members of the Nazi Party throughout the West German Judiciary, but members of the S.A. or S.S. serving on the highest German Compensation Court—the Compensation Senate of the Bundesgerichtshof in Karlsruhe. One of these former members of the S.A. is a man who was highly commended for his "diligence, efficiency, excellent conduct and impeccable conviction" as a Nazi judge and stormtrooper in 1936.

Upon stating publicly these facts and pointing out that the law which excludes such people from this responsibility is entirely ignored in West Germany, Dr. Weyl was recommended for disbarment by that very court, in the following terms: "Dr. Weyl should be eliminated from the German administration of justice as quickly as possible."

It is not only that such people should be excluded from membership of a Board passing upon the claims of those who were victimised in concentration camps or deprived of their possessions, but it is an affront to human sensibility that these evil criminals should sit in judgment over their victims' claims for compensation. Now Dr. Weyl is to be disbarred for seeking to make known these facts. The German complacence which enabled the era of the gas chamber to take place is with us again.

Bertrand Russell
Penrhyndeudraeth, Merioneth

[208]

## War Criminals

*The Daily Telegraph* (1st December, 1964), p. 14 | C64.92

*Russell, writing under the auspices of the Bertrand Russell Peace Foundation, expresses concern over the revival of neo-Nazi groups and the West German government's alleged lax policy towards Nazi war criminals.*

Sir, —Dr. Kempner, the former United States deputy prosecutor at Nuremburg, estimates that there are 10,000 Nazi war criminals living under assumed names.

If the West German Government waives the liability to prosecution for war criminals, these people are likely to return to political life. This is in violation of the London Agreement[4] of August, 1945, which is international law.

I am disturbed at the revival of neo-Nazi groups in Germany as reported from Brussels by the International Union of Resistance Fighters. It seems ironic that the West German authorities permit former SS and Gestapo societies to hold rallies in favour of the Waffen SS although meetings of the committee in support of victims of Nazi persecution are banned under the constitution. Members of this committee were even prevented from laying wreaths on the graves of Nazi victims.

I believe the London Agreement should be supported by the British Government, and I should wish to urge the German authorities to reconsider their decision to waive the time limit on war crimes by Nazis.

Yours faithfully, Bertrand Russell
Bertrand Russell Peace Foundation, S.W. 1.

## *Poland*

[209]

### Polish Professors

*The Times* (6th April, 1968), p. 9 | C68.08

*Russell was even-handed in his defense of civil liberty, and leftist regimes were not infrequent targets. In this letter, Russell, who at times described himself as a humanist and a socialist, rebukes the Polish Government's dismissal of seven Warsaw professors as "a grave disservice to socialist humanism."*

Sir, —I write to support Professor Robert McKenzie's letter (March 28) concerning the dismissal of the seven Warsaw professors. All these men are distinguished academics and their only crime, to judge from Polish newspaper criticisms of them, is their independence of mind. The Polish Government's intolerance and crude pressure will not curtail dis-

4. The London Agreement (August 8, 1945) provided for the establishment of the International Military Tribunal to try war criminals and served as the legal basis for the Nuremberg Trials.

cussion. The pretence that the views of the seven professors are somehow detrimental to socialism is a grave disservice to socialist humanism.

I hope that they will be reinstated at once.

Yours faithfully, Bertrand Russell
Plas Penrhyn, Penrhyndeudraeth, Merionethshire, April 4.

## *Spain*

[210]

### Political asylum

*The Guardian* (9th December, 1969), p. 12 | C69.20

*Russell died seven weeks after the publication of this letter. It was apparently his last letter to the editor, although it was not his last public statement. It seems that Russell felt that no denial of liberty—no matter how seemingly insignificant—was unworthy of his attention.*

Sir, —Edouardo Cruzeiro is serving an 18 months' prison sentence in Spain and awaiting extradition to Portugal on December 24. His crime is that he is a deserter on grounds of conscience from the Portuguese army in Guinea and, as such, he faces a possible death sentence.

Why will Spain not allow Mr. Cruzeiro to seek political asylum abroad, instead of sending him to an infamous sentence in Portugal?

Yours faithfully, Bertrand Russell
Merioneth

## *Bulgaria*

[211]

### Bulgaria and Balkans

*The Times* (22nd October, 1968), p. 9 | C68.29

*The Bulgarians had long laid claim to portions of Yugoslavia populated by Macedonians. In the wake of the Soviet invasion of Czechoslovakia (with Bulgarian co-operation as a member of the Warsaw Pact), Russell caustically comments on Bulgaria's Orwellian "reassurance" of restraint.*

Sir, —It is some reassurance to have from the Bulgarian Ambassador (October 19) the categorical denial that his Government is planning any further aggression. Your readers may remember that for a month before the invasion of Czechoslovakia I tried in vain to obtain such a denial from Mr. Kosygin.

The Ambassador's references to "the peace-loving policy of the Bulgarian People's Republic and the Soviet Union" need no comment from me two months after the occupation of Czechoslovakia and 19 years after the publication of *Nineteen-Eighty-four.*

Yours faithfully, Bertrand Russell
Plas Penrhyn, Penrhyndeudraeth, Merioneth, Oct. 20

## *Bolivia*

[212]

### Debray Plight

*The New York Herald Tribune* (15th June, 1967), p. 4 | C67.14

*Russell speaks out on the wrongful treatment of a French journalist, Regis Debray, by Bolivian authorities. Boliva, one of the poorest countries in Latin America, underwent a series of military coups between 1964 and 1980.*

*Ralph Schoenman went to Bolivia in August and October, ostensibly on behalf of the Bertrand Russell Peace Foundation, to protest the trial of*

*Debray. While waiting for Debray's trial Schoenman attempted to find and aid Che Guevara's guerrillas for whom the Peace Foundation had declared "solidarity" of support. Schoenman was arrested, temporarily imprisoned and finally expelled from the country.*[5] *His relationship with Russell and the Peace Foundation declined significantly after this, and he was officially removed from the Foundation and repudiated by Russell in 1969.*

To the Herald Tribune:

No information is more vital to us in the West than intimate knowledge of the struggles in the Third World. Since the Second World War, the unfolding of these struggles in the arduous process of decolonization has singularly transformed social, economic and political realities on a world scale. One Western journalist who has made an important contribution to our understanding of revolutionary change is now in serious danger because of his courageous attempt to observe at first hand the current resistance movement in Bolivia. I speak of Prof. Regis Debray, author of "Revolucion en la Revolucion" and accredited representative of the Mexican periodical "Sucesos."

Prof. Debray entered Bolivia in the usual manner, traveling on his French passport and showing his credentials as a journalist. He has been captured by the Bolivian armed forces and charged with an improper "association" with the guerrilla forces which oppose the Barrientos dictatorship. Prof. Debray's whereabouts are, at present, undisclosed by his captors. His mother has been denied access to him; he has so far been refused legal counsel. Formal inquiries from the French government, including those from Gen. de Gaulle, have elicited nothing. The commander-in-chief of the Bolivian army, Gen. Alfred Ovando, has stated that Prof. Debray will receive a fair trial, in accordance with the Bolivian constitution. Vice-president Siles Salinas has given the solemn assurance that capital punishment has long been abolished in Bolivia. These words are intended to conceal the arbitrary and harsh treatment which Prof. Debray has received to date. They are, likewise, a feeble contradiction of President Barrientos's own frank and cynical statement that Prof. Debray is "an adventurer who came to Bolivia to bring grief to Bolivian families. His adventures will end in Bolivia."

When we defend Prof. Debray's right to discover the grim reality of oppression among the peasant guerrillas of Latin America, we are doing nothing more than protecting our own interest. We must uphold our right to learn the truth. Our support for Regis Debray is a minimum con-

---

5. See *Bertrand Russell: The Ghost of Madness*, pp. 473–75

tribution toward the preservation of "unmanaged" news and an informed world opinion.

Bertrand Russell
London

## *United States*

[213]

# Lord Russell's Contempt

*The Washington Post* (5th February, 1963), p. A12 | C63.10

*Russell condemns the United States for its hypocrisy regarding its espoused love of freedom and draws a connection between individual civil liberty and U.S. nuclear policy.*

What kind of society is it which claims to be concerned about freedom and individual liberty, yet declares itself fully ready to exterminate several hundred million human beings? The kind of society which calmly contemplates such carnage is exactly that society which has contempt for individual liberty and for human dignity. It is no accident and no surprise that such a society attacks those who oppose mass murder and seeks to discredit and destroy them.

I am speaking about the United States of America, and I am writing this letter to register my disgust at the unmitigated persecution of organizations such as the Fair Play for Cuba Committee, the Women's Strike for Peace and Pacifica Foundation—a subscription radio station dedicated to serious music and serious discussion.

You who prate so often about the Free World might consider whether a secret police, a stable of paid informers, a subversive organizations list, political investigation committees and a general atmosphere of hysterical intolerance are compatible with such a pretense.

Bertrand Russell
Penrhyndeudraeth, Wales

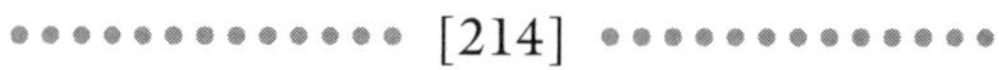

[214]

## Word From Russell

*The New York Times* (5th May, 1963), Magazine Section, p. 12 | C63.36

*Russell's* Marriage and Morals *(1929) was a provocative discussion of sex and marriage which was widely quoted in the City College case in 1940 as the basis of the court's conclusion that Russell was morally unfit to teach. Here Russell retracts a statement about Negro ability, a change which was reflected in later editions.*

To the Editor:

In reply to Leonard Josephson's letter which you published in your issue of April 21, quoting a statement from "Of Marriage and Morals" [the passage quoted from Lord Russell's book included the sentence: "It seems on the whole fair to regard Negroes as on the average inferior to white men ***.—Ed.], I should like to say that subsequent research has led me to consider this unfavorable statement concerning Negro ability unfounded and I regret having made it. I have made efforts to have it corrected in reprints of this book.

Bertrand Russell
London

[215]

## U.S. "Freedom"

*The Sunday Times* (6th October, 1963), p. 18 | C63.83

*Russell took serious interest in the American civil rights movement in the 1960s, writing several influential articles documenting injustices against blacks and making connections to United States domestic and foreign violence.*[6] *As a result of an appeal from an American civil rights group—the Emergency Civil Liberties Committee—Russell wrote several statements and letters on behalf of the Reverend Ashton Jones, a white civil rights advocate. The appeal was successful and Jones was released in early 1964.*

6. See *Bertrand Russell's America: 1945–1970*, ed. by B. Feinberg and R. Kasrils (South End Press, 1983).

Sir, —In the State of Georgia in the United States, the Rev. Ashton Jones has been sentenced to eighteen months' imprisonment—six months of which is hard labour on a chain gang—for the crime of accompanying a Negro boy and girl to an all-white church. Mr. Jones has been beaten and maltreated for an act which is the minimum moral duty of every American.

At this moment, a group of young American students are being charged with conspiracy to commit an illegal act and with being "foreign agents" for the sole "crime" of traveling to Cuba. They face a possible sentence of five years' imprisonment. Are these the circumstances of a free country?

Bertrand Russell
Penrhyndeudraeth, Merioneth

[216]

## Harsh Sentence

*The Times* (1st November, 1963), p. 13 | C63.83

Sir, —The sentence of Reverend Ashton Jones to 18 months imprisonment—six months of which is hard labour on a chain gain—for the crime of accompanying a Negro boy and girl to an all-white church is a monstrous injustice which ought to be universally condemned.

It is appalling that this good man who has been beaten and imprisoned several times in the course of his struggle for Negro rights should now be sentenced for an act which is the minimum moral duty of every American.

I hope the British press will express itself on this barbaric sentence.

Your faithfully, Bertrand Russell
Plas Penrhyn, Penrhyndeudraeth, Merioneth

[217]

## Real Grievances Behind the Harlem Unrest

*The Daily Telegraph and Morning Post* (3rd August, 1964), p. 9 | C64.54

*In this letter, written under the auspices of the Peace Foundation, Russell equates the status of black America to that of "a colonial people."*

Sir, —The unrest in Harlem, Bedford Stuyvesant and Rochester in New York among Negroes, while set off by the killing of a 15-year-old boy by an armed police lieutenant, results from long-standing and genuine grievances.

The nation-wide effort in America for equal rights for Negro citizens is not restricted to securing a cup of coffee at all-white luncheon-counters or the right to attend all white schools. For the entire American Negro population it is often a matter of life or death.

Thirty-five years ago the infant mortality rate was twice as high for Negroes as it was for Whites. Today it remains twice as high. Thirty-five years ago twice as many American Negroes died from pneumonia as did Whites. Today twice as many still die.

The Negro in America must observe that, while thousands of Africans are securing freedom, his own modest efforts for some fair share of that which he has helped to produce in America are denied. To these efforts live ammunition, night sticks, steel-helmeted white police officers, many of them bigots of the worst order, are no answer.

The request for an impartial civilian Review Board to investigate police brutality is sound, and one wonders why New York City has resisted this. The insistence of the City Administration that the Review Board should be composed only of police officers indicates a refusal to understand the purpose of such an agency.

It is a sad comment upon justice in New York that there is need for such a Review Board. If the courts were fair and impartial in evaluating the testimony of police officers and those charging them with brutality, there would be no need for this agency. But it is generally recognised, even by the City administration, that the courts are notoriously prejudiced in favour of the police and that those seeking redress are denied justice.

The violence in the Negro communities of New York, in response to police violence, is a demand by Negroes for an end to subservience, brutality, economic misery—in short the status of a colonial people. American wealth should be directed to the tearing down of all America's Harlems and to the provision of decent living conditions. Only when the Negro rebellion is met by justice and by the prospect of effective political expression can the race problem end and America regain world respect.

Yours faithfully, Bertrand Russell
Bertrand Russell Peace Foundation, S.W. 1

## *Soviet Union*

[218]

# Bertrand Russell vs. Reds On Jews

*New York Herald Tribune* (26th June, 1963), p. 6 | C63.50/63.72

*Russell writes in response to Khrushchev's critical comments on an earlier letter to him from Russell regarding the treatment of Jews in the Soviet Union. Russell's letter to the editor of* Izvestia, *an official newspaper of the Soviet government, is a lesson in humanitarian statecraft. Although some of the earlier Russell-Khrushchev correspondence had been published in the Soviet press, this letter was not.*

*The letter also appeared, with analysis of the plight of Soviet Jewry, in* Jews In Europe *(September 1963) with the editor's introduction claiming: "It is now clear that an important new phase in public discussion of the position of Soviet Jews has resulted from the exchange of letters on the subject between Earl Russell and Primier Khrushchev. This is partly because of Bertrand Russell's unique authority as an advocate of peace and moral responsibility in international affairs, but also because there is a clear common identity between the views he has expressed and those held by . . . Soviet intellectuals who stand in the vanguard of de-Stalinisation."*

To the Editor of *Izvestia*:

Dear Sir, I am pleased to see that the letter written by Premier Khrushchev to me concerning the condition of Soviet Jews was published in *Izvestia* along with one of the letters I have written on this subject to Mr. Khrushchev. I have also read with genuine interest the readers' letters which comment on our correspondence. I am sympathetic to what they say of the achievements of the Soviet Union with regard to the abolition of legal disabilities imposed on Jews during Czarist days. This is a matter of special interest to me because my grandfather was responsible for the elimination of legal discrimination against Jews in Great Britain.

I am a friend of the Soviet Union, of her people and of her desire to improve and advance the conditions under which her citizens live. I am an ardent campaigner for close and genuinely co-operative relations between the people and Governments of Western countries and the Soviet Union. I am a passionate opponent of the Cold War and of all attempt to increase hostility, exploit differences and add to the terrible dangers facing mankind today. I know that no Soviet citizen will misunderstand me or think that when I speak frankly I wish to harm the Soviet Union or co-operate with those who promote the Cold War.

One of the tests of true friendship is the ability to speak frankly without fear of being taken for an enemy or of being misunderstood. I hope, therefore, that you will appreciate the spirit in which I am now writing—one of concern for the Soviet people and not a spirit of condemnation.

The Jews have been subjected to a long and continuous persecution in the history of Europe. The culmination of this cruelty was the wholesale extermination of millions of Jews during our lifetimes, one of the most barbaric crimes in all human history. If ever a people were deserving of understanding and sympathetic treatment after harsh suffering, it is the Jews of Europe.

I should hope, therefore, that the Jews would be permitted full cultural lives, religious freedom and the rights of a national group, in practice as well as in law.

During the last years of Stalin's life, Soviet Jews were totally deprived of their national culture and the means of expressing it. Leading intellectuals were imprisoned or executed by extra-legal practices which have since been condemned.

I am a lifelong non-believer in any religion. I have written and campaigned against superstition. Nonetheless, I believe that the freedom to practise religious views should be allowed Jews of the Soviet Union in the same manner that such freedom is granted people of other religious persuasions. I am concerned that the process of restitution of much smaller groups are more plentiful and the closure of synagogues and shortage of religious facilities have impaired Jews in the pursuit of their beliefs. I am troubled that there should be articles in Soviet journals of many Republics expressing hostility to Jewish people as such.

I understand the objections to economic offences such as were expressed in the letter to me by Premier Khrushchev. I feel, however, that the death penalty upon citizens accused of these crimes harms the Soviet Union and allows those hostile to her to unjustly malign her. I consider the fact that sixty percent of those executed are Jews to be gravely disturbing. I fervently hope that nothing will take place which obliges us to believe that Jews are receiving unjust treatment in contradiction to the law, and that those who break Soviet laws concerning economic offences will be rehabilitated instead of being put to death. I cannot too strongly appeal for understanding of the difficulty experienced by those in the West who are working dedicatedly to ease tension, promote peaceful co-existence, and to end the Cold War. These objects are harmed by events which those who desire the Cold War can exploit and which trouble us who wish peace and good relations. I write as a friend, but one whose friendship requires honesty.

Yours sincerely, Bertrand Russell

••••••••••••• [219] •••••••••••••

## Soviet Jew Writes to Russell

*Jews In Eastern Europe* (November, 1964), pp. 98–99 | C64.59

*In the November 1964 issue of* Jews in Eastern Europe, *the editor published a letter from Russell to a Soviet journal (which did not publish the letter) on behalf of Soviet Jews. The editor provides the following introduction:*

On July 22, 1964 Bertrand Russell released to the press a letter he had sent to the editor of *Sovietish Heimland* in Moscow, enclosing an appeal he had received from a Soviet Jew, writing "on behalf of a great number of people". The writer of the appeal said he was a member of the Soviet Communist Party and a war-veteran holding several military decorations. Earl Russell withheld his name. The correspondence [Russell's letter] is given below:

The Editor,
Sovietish Heimland,
Kirov Street,
Moscow, U.S.S.R.

Dear Sir, I am writing to you to make known the feelings of several Soviet citizens, including members of the Communist party in the Soviet Union, who have addressed letters to me recently. These Soviet citizens wish to enjoy the right to a full cultural life in the Soviet Union. They are Jews and they feel that they are denied the means of living a complete and satisfying life in the Soviet Union because they are denied the cultural facilities made available to all other national and minority groups in the U.S.S.R. I consider this an important and an urgent problem and I should be glad if you would kindly publish the letter I enclose, as well as my own letter.

I write because I am concerned for justice and for the good name of the Soviet Union. Unless people who are concerned for both raise their voices, the cause of peaceful co-existence and the pursuit of peace and general understanding between peoples and nations will be harmed by silence.

Yours sincerely, Bertrand Russell

# *Africa*

············· [220] ·············

## Britain's Support of South Africa

*The Daily Telegraph* (19th September, 1963), p. 14 | C63.73

*The cause of human rights in South Africa was one of many human rights campaigns that Russell championed in the 1960s. It was also at this time that he decided that such work could best be carried out with the help of the Bertrand Russell Peace Foundation, the plans for which were announced in late September.*

Sir, —A nightmare of terror is underway in South Africa. People are imprisoned and subjected to solitary confinement for unlimited periods. One woman, Mrs. Hazel Goldreich, has been so confined, although ill, and has not eaten for six days.

The condition of Africans so imprisoned is even more grave. Twenty-three people have been sentenced to death.

The British Government has sold arms to the Government of South Africa, supported it in the United Nations and allowed its secret police to abduct people from British-administered territories. They are party to the tyranny in South Africa, and stand condemned before world opinion.

I hope an international movement of popular protest will force an immediate change in this disgraceful British support of the South African police state.

Yours faithfully, Bertrand Russell
Penrhyndeudraeth, Merioneth.

············· [221] ·············

## Abuse of South Africa

*The Daily Telegraph* (25th September, 1963), p. 14 | C63.76

Sir, —Further to my letter which *The Daily Telegraph* kindly printed regarding conditions in South Africa, I should wish to call to the attention of the British public the content of a recently received letter:

"I wish there were some way to make known the condition under which those detained without trial are being held. They are all in solitary confinement completely cut off from any contact with other human beings. They are not allowed any books, writing material or anything whatsoever to do . . . shut in all day except for two ten minute periods. The denial of books and all contact is mental torture far worse than physical assault. Thirty days solitary confinement was all that was supposed to be permitted prisoners of war as punishment. The 90 day people who have finished 90 days in solitary have been re-arrested. Some of these will emerge mental wrecks and others find themselves prepared to talk, to implicate anyone to bring an end to their own unbearable isolation . . ."

Is such treatment beyond the concern of established opinion in Great Britain?

Yours faithfully, Bertrand Russell
Penrhyndeudraeth, Merioneth.

[222]

## US in the Congo

*The Guardian* (22nd August, 1964), p. 6 | C64.63

*The Congo (Zaire since 1971) had experienced great civil unrest since its independence from Belgium in 1960. UN troops left the Congo in June 1964. But leftist rebels resisted the central government under Tshombe and set up a "People's Republic" in Stanleyville. Later in the year Belgium paratroops were dropped from American aircraft to rescue Americans and Europeans trapped in Stanleyville.*

*Here Russell draws similarities between American intervention in the Congo and in Vietnam—both of which he characterizes as "brazen economic and political imperialism."*

Sir, —Your leading article on the Congo (August 18) does well to show the relation between American intervention in Vietnam and present American activity in the Congo. The United States is assuming the arrogant right to intrude militarily wherever her economic interests are endangered. These interests reflect the power of private industry and what Fred Cook has rightly called "the Warfare State." The "Warfare State" is controlled by industry in alliance with the military from which so much of its profit derives.

American intervention in the Congo, as in Vietnam, comes to brazen economic and political imperialism, masqueraded as opposition to communism. The United States must be made to cease its perpetual intervention in countries that are so wicked as to use their resources for their own advance, as opposed to American and Western aggrandisement. Rebels do not worry the United States, as we know from their efforts with regard to Cuba. The real concern is neither absence of freedom, instability in a given country, nor the peace of the world. It is time a spade was called a spade where American policy is concerned.

Yours faithfully, Bertrand Russell
Plas Penrhyn, Penrhyndeudraeth, Merioneth

# War and Peace

## *Cuba and the Missile Crisis*

*These letters are important because they help to clarify Russell's role in the Missile Crisis and put into rational context his enhanced support for Cuba after the Crisis. They also reveal a Russell concerned to answer his critics' charges that he was unreasonably moving away from what had been a 'neutral' perspective on superpower rivalry. See also documents [169–170].*

•••••••••••••• [223] ••••••••••••••

### Labour and the Intellectuals

*The New Statesmen and Nation* (1st March, 1963), p. 304–05 | C63.13

*Russell played an active role during the Cuban Missile Crisis. The press, frequently quoting Russell's statements out of context, gave the misleading impression that he favored Soviet missiles in Cuba. In this letter and the next, he addresses Paul Johnson's critical statements about the CND and the Committee of 100 and missiles in Cuba.*

Sir, —In your issue of 22 February there is an article by Paul Johnson[7] called "Labour and the Intellectuals". In the course of this article, he makes statements which are completely untrue as to the attitude in the Cuban crisis of the movement to which I belong. I will assume, charitably, that he believes these statements to be true. If so, I should advise him in future to make some slight effort to ascertain facts before pontificating.

The passage to which I object is:

> Pledged to halt the spread of nuclear weapons, they found themselves, last October, doing exactly the opposite—demonstrating hysterically for Russia's right to open a system of outdoor nuclear relief in Latin America.

In fact, we never defended the placing of nuclear weapons in Cuba. On the contrary, we urged Khrushchev to avoid provocative action. He agreed, and first withdrew his ships and then consented to remove nuclear weapons. At the same time, we urged Kennedy to withdraw

---

7. Paul Johnson (1928– ) is a British writer and historian. His best-selling book *Intellectuals* (Harper and Row, 1988), has a chapter devoted to Russell.

nuclear weapons from places near the frontiers of the USSR. Kennedy did not agree, although Russian dislike of American nuclear weapons in Turkey is precisely as reasonable as American dislike of Russian nuclear weapons in Cuba. All unilateralists, so far as I have been able to ascertain, are glad there are to be no Russian nuclear weapons in Cuba. We think, moreover, that the method we adopted to persuade Khrushchev was more effective than American bluster.

The objection to our action as regards Cuba is that it employed persuasion, not force. To this I plead guilty, but I do not feel inclined to apologize for having helped to keep us all alive. Apparently Mr. Johnson considers that our plea to Mr. Khrushchev was "hysterical" and that nuclear war would have been preferable.

Bertrand Russell
Plas Penrhyn, Penrhyndeudraeth, Merioneth

[224]

## Labour and the Intellectuals

*The New Statesman and Nation* (8th March, 1963), p. 336 | C63.15

*Paul Johnson had replied to Russell's letter of 1st March, 1963. Russell here responds to Johnson's reply.*

Sir, —Mr. Paul Johnson's note in reply to my letter published in your issue of 1 March calls for a few words of reply as it appears that he suffers from what theologians call "invincible ignorance." Not only did I urge moderation upon Khrushchev when his ships were approaching the blockading American ships, but, when the question of Soviet nuclear weapons in Cuba came to the fore, I urged that they should be withdrawn. In the small hours of 26 October I cabled to Castro: "I beg you for the sake of humanity to accept dismantling of any missiles, even if only defensive, in exchange for a solemn pledge that Cuba will not be invaded." At the same time I cabled Khrushchev in the same sense, but at greater length. As to the general charge that unilateralists only demonstrate against America, unilateralists—members of the CND and of the Committee of 100—demonstrated against the governments of both the US and the USSR during the Cuban crisis. On earlier occasions, many unilateralists have been arrested for demonstrating outside the Soviet embassy.

Bertrand Russell

[225]

## Labour and the Intellectuals

*The New Statesman and Nation* (15th March, 1963), pp. 374, 376 | C63.17

*Russell defends his actions in the Missile Crisis, and explains that he was neither pro-American nor pro-Soviet, but pro-peace. Many of Russell's critics at the time, and since, have been angered by Russell's doubts concerning the American version of events.*[8] *In this letter, and in the next, he also reveals the nature and source of some of his doubts about official United States claims regarding 'offensive' missiles.*

Sir, —I have been bewildered by the reaction to my activities in the Cuban crisis. Given the situation as it then existed, I implored, in my letters and cable to Kennedy, Khrushchev, and Castro, heads of the three governments implicated, to exercise caution and to do nothing to risk war which would inevitably escalate into nuclear war and, further, into global nuclear war. When I wrote to one head of state, I wrote to the others. All these messages were given to the press, though the press did not always print them and often printed them in misleading bits. What I asked Khrushchev to do, and what he did do, was exactly what the US government professed to want. I have never been an adherent of communism. I have made my attitude towards it clear and public since 1896. That does not mean that I think that a communist never can or does do the desirable thing. The charge that I am anti-communist or anti-American rests upon inability of those who make the charge to understand that I am neither pro-Soviet nor pro-American, but solely pro-peace and pro as much freedom as it is possible to achieve. Everything that I did in the Cuban crisis had the sole aim of preventing war. There was no trace of ambiguity.

Your correspondent Mr. Frood accuses me of 'ingrained anti-Americanism' and defends the American case against the establishment of Soviet missiles in Cuba. He bases both accusation and defence upon ignorance. If he wishes to take count of my statements and actions against American and against Soviet deeds, he will find that I have condemned those of the Soviet considerably more often than those of the US. As to the Cuban situation, I deplored the spread of nuclear missiles involved in their establishment in Cuba—I equally should deplore their establishment in Canada, though none of those who cry most loudly against their

8. Monk expresses puzzlement as to Russell's doubts. See *The Ghost of Madness,* p. 448.

spread to Cuba seem to mind their spread to Canada, since the former are Soviet and the latter, western. I deplore the spread of all nuclear weapons.

Mr. Frood accuses the Soviet government of 'fraud, deception and outright lying.' The only basis for this charge is Zorin's mistaken statement to the UN which was almost immediately repudiated by Khrushchev, whose repudiation was followed by the removal of Zorin from his post as Russian Envoy to the UN (see the *Guardian*, 24 December). The Soviet installations were never hidden and were known by the Russians to be observable by American planes. Mr. Frood is on very shaky ground when he makes the above accusation. The Assistant Secretary of Defence, Mr. Arthur Sylvester, said that 'news "generated" by the American government was used successfully in the Cuba crisis and that the government would continue to use "news" to further its foreign policy.' He added, 'I think the inherent right of the government to lie to save itself when faced with nuclear disaster is basic.' (See *The Times,* 12 December.) When reprimanded, he remarked that what he had said was true and should have been said by his official superiors. An example of the kind of 'lies' of which he may have been thinking was that of the official US estimates concerning the range of Soviet missiles in Cuba (see the report of Leonard Beaton in the *Guardian*, 15 November, in this connection), or of the fact that the Soviet missiles in Cuba are dubbed 'aggressive', whereas those on the borders of Russia and in Great Britain are dubbed purely 'defensive.' In reply to the second point of defence made by Mr. Frood, I should like to call his attention to the range and number of missiles and installations in Cuba and to compare them with the range of the missiles that the US alleged to be in Cuba.

I entirely agree with Mr. Frood that the situation should have been the subject of negotiation but not during the crisis, since there was no time then. I differ from him in thinking that it should have been the subject of negotiation before drastic provocative action was taken and the world was brought to the brink of nuclear war—a matter of timing upon which he does not touch. I do not think that this point of view on my part is the result of either anti-Americanism or pro-communism. I should like to call attention to the facts—facts, not opinions of mine—that the Soviet missiles were in Cuba at the invitation of the Cubans, and, more important, that the Soviet has carried out all that it said it would do; the Americans are still threatening invasion of Cuba in spite of having given an understanding, though never a clear proclamation, that they would not invade Cuba.

Mr. Frood accuses me of "childish anger" because I say that in Mr. Johnson's opinion nuclear war would have been preferable to my plea and that of others to Khrushchev (and to Kennedy and Castro) to commit no provocative act and to negotiate. Neither Mr. Frood nor Mr. Johnson has suggested any line other than the one that I, and others, took that would have been more likely than ours to prevent nuclear war.

Bertrand Russell
Plas Penrhyn, Penrhyndeudraeth

••••••••••••• [226] •••••••••••••

## Unarmed Victory

*The Spectator* (28th June, 1963), pp. 834–35 | C63.52

*Russell's book* Unarmed Victory *(1963) dealt with the avoidance of war in the negotiated settlement of two international disputes in which Russell had some personal involvement—the Cuban missile crisis of 1962 and the India-China border dispute of 1963. Russell responds to a review by the western scholar of Soviet affairs, Robert Conquest, and he attempts to correct some of the review's "factual inaccuracies."*

Sir, —My attention has been drawn to an article by Mr. Robert Conquest[9] in the *Spectator* of April 5, referring to my book *Unarmed Victory.*

The article is characterised by quotations out of context juxtaposed in such a manner as to create an impression often opposite to that of the intention of the statement. The factual inaccuracies, which are extreme, are as follows:

1. Mr. Conquest invents a meeting between Senor Haya de la Torre[10] and myself during the Cuban crisis. He says, in addition to there having been a meeting, that Senor de la Torre was staying with me at the time. Both these statements are false.

2. Mr. Conquest further claims that I stated to Senor de la Torre that I knew the Americans to be lying about the presence of Soviet missiles in Cuba. This is entirely invented, both with respect to Senor de la Torre and with respect to my having stated this to anyone.

---

9. Robert Conquest was a writer and a scholar of Soviet affairs, who would later document Stalin's crimes in such works as *Harvest of Sorrow: Soviet Colectivisation and the Terror-Famine* (Oxford, 1986).

10. Victor Haya de la Torre (1895–1979) was a Peruvian leader and founder of the APRA (Alianza Popular Revolutionario Americana) party, which advocated the overthrow of the Peruvian oligarchy.

3. Mr. Conquest further states in the article that in my view the Americans would use any means to bring down Castro, and from this it followed that they had faked the evidence of missiles. This again is completely untrue. The closest it is possible for Mr. Conquest to come to justify these statements is that I quoted the *Guardian* report on a statement by the Editor of *Aviation Week*, Mr. Robert Hale, that the range of the missiles was purposely exaggerated so as to include States from which votes were required. This was my quotation of an American authority and not my own surmise.

4. Mr. Conquest further alleges that Dr. Corliss Lamont follows the Communist line. Dr. Lamont is a non-Communist and Mr. Conquest is indulging in a gratuitous smear.

5. Mr. Conquest is also factually inaccurate about what he calls the main theme of Dr. Lamont's book on *Freedom Is As Freedom Does.* Norman Thomas barely figures in the book, and the main theme can hardly be claimed to be an attack on Norman Thomas.

6. The statement that I accepted without check a book on the Rosenberg case shot through with error and misrepresentation is a further misstatement of fact and pure invention. Einstein and I were involved in details of the Rosenberg and Sobell cases well before the publication of any book and my statements on the Rosenberg case depended on no other author. Which book Mr. Conquest had in mind, if any, in this allegation, one is left to guess.

I should be pleased if you would bring these facts to the attention of your readers.

Bertrand Russell
Plas Penrhyn, Penrhyndeudraeth, Merioneth

••••••••••••• [227] •••••••••••••

## The New Doctrine of Aggression

*The Guardian* (20th August, 1963), p. 8 | C63.68

*Writing ten months after the Cuban missile crisis and three months after the signing of the Partial Test Ban Treaty, Russell turns the U.S. logic in the Cuban crisis against U.S. nuclear deployment abroad.*

Sir, —Adlai Stevenson, on behalf of the United States government, justified the blockade of Cuba which launched the Cuban crisis by declaring in the United Nations a new doctrine. He said that it was not necessary to have an open declaration of war. The mere presence of "aggressive weapons" was a sufficient act of hostility to justify measures such as were taken by the U.S.

At the time I sought to make known the radical implications of this position. It was the basis of the American claim of danger from Cuba and of the claim to a right of invasion.

After the test-ban treaty a major issue to be settled is the spread of these very weapons. Their mere presence, according to Mr. Stevenson, constitutes an act of aggression. The Soviet Union has refused to allow its weapons of nuclear or nuclear-rocket character to come into the possession of China or other Communist states.

The U.S. is now giving nuclear warheads to Canada, negotiating with France with a view to giving her a nuclear device, flirting with West Germany along these lines, establishing new nuclear rocket bases in Turkey and placing nuclear submarines in Japan.

I agree with Mr. Stevenson that the justification for his government's reckless blockade of Cuba outlaws such appearance of these weapons in new countries and renders those already in existence sufficient acts of hostility as to constitute a threat of war. I doubt that the U.S. government realized the implications of its representative's arguments in the UN. Today, however, it is urgently needed for those who defended the Cuban blockade on the ground that nuclear weapons were introduced into a new area to forthrightly condemn American plans for Canada, France, West Germany, Turkey and Japan.

The anti-nuclear movement has always contended that nuclear weapons are themselves an imminent threat to the peace and a hostile act. They are instruments of total annihilation which depend on hairtrigger control and on warning systems measured in moments. Such weapons completely transform the nature of relationships between nation states. They do not permit formal declarations of hostilities or elaborate consideration of alternative policies.

Those who condemned their spread to Cuba must now prove the sincerity and consistency of their declared position.

Bertrand Russell
Penrhyndeudraeth, Wales, Great Britain

[228]

# Nuclear Weapons and the "Free World"

*The Guardian* (28th August, 1963) | C63.69

*Russell's letter of 20th August had provoked a response from Professor K.H.W. Hilborn, who distinguished between permissible nuclear weapons (those of the "free world") and impermissible ones (those of the Soviet Union).*

*In this letter, Russell exposes the double standard regarding American missiles as well as some "free world" hypocrisy.*

Sir, —The letter of Professor K.H.W. Hilborn[11] (August 23) is nicely instructive, for it makes explicit the premises which underlie both American policy and the views of those who are its apologists.

I shall leave, for the moment, the matter of nuclear rocket bases in Turkey, nuclear submarines in Japan, nuclear devices for France and West Germany, etc. for, as all these are anti-Communist States, they are part of what Professor Hilborn calls the "free world."

I should be most interested to know what Professor Hilborn means by freedom apart from the joy in preparing for genocide which places those who do so on a higher "moral level," again according to the professor.

Those who are in the "free world" include Thailand, South Vietnam, Taiwan, Pakistan, Turkey, Greece, Spain, Portugal, South Africa, Iran and France. The amount of individual liberty and civic freedom enjoyed in these countries is minuscule. Most are as well, feudal dictatorships in which mass starvation is prevalent. The Latin American satellite States have much the same to be said for their political and social institutions.

The individual freedom to be found in West Germany (and France), in Jordan and Malaya, in Iraq or Afghanistan is not such as can be supported by those committed to such values in the "free world." Buddhist monks are free to burn themselves to death. The same freedom exists in the Communist world but, I understand, is more rarely exercised.

The truth is that the non-Communist world has neither a monopoly nor a greater portion of freedom than does the Communist world. The "free world" is a propagandist's fiction.

Professor Hilborn is also incorrect in his statement of Mr. Stevenson's position as Mr. Stevenson expressed it in the United Nations. The blockade was defended because, it was said, the mere presence of such missiles

11. Kenneth H.W. Hilborn was a history professor, specializing in international relations, at the University of Western Ontario from 1961 to 1997, where he is currently Professor Emeritus of History.

was of such dire danger that nothing less than a blockade was consistent with American safety. The dire danger is imposed by American missiles to the same degree that it is imposed by those of the Soviet Union. The danger is to the survival of man "free" or "unfree."

—Yours faithfully, Bertrand Russell
Plas Penrhyn Penrhyndeudraeth, Merioneth

[229]

## World Needs Free Access to News

*The Herald Tribune* (29th September, 1963) | C63.78

*Russell writes in support of journalist William Worthy and the importance of freedom of information to "publicly challenge the assumptions and policies of governments," especially as regards Cuba.*

To *The Herald Tribune:*

One of the most terrifying facts about our world is the utter dependence of its inhabitants upon the whims of a handful of men concerned with the technology of imminent annihilation. To many people, however, the willingness to engage in the wholesale extermination of populations, in the name of "security" is not part of a decent way to live. To a large extent, the likelihood of life or death through the insanity of nuclear war will follow from the freedom or lack of freedom to question and publicly challenge the assumptions and policies of governments.

The United States has systematically bullied a smaller nation, namely Cuba, and has stuck at nothing to undermine, intimidate and destroy its government. One of the consequences of so unjustifiably aggressive a policy is the hiding of the truth about the government of Cuba, its policies, its philosophy and its popularity.

William Worthy[12] is a spokesman for the right to question authority and the right to unbiased knowledge about political events. Despite every intimidation he has risked his freedom by traveling to Cuba and by reporting fairly on Cuba and world opinion.

---

12. William Worthy (1923– ), a journalist and opponent of racial injustice, defied U.S. bans on travel to Communist countries. In 1963 his federal conviction for travel to Cuba was overturned by the U.S. Court of Appeals.

I am appalled that for exercising his elementary democratic rights and for fulfilling his moral duty as a citizen and journalist, he now faces a sentence of up to five years' imprisonment, in the course of appealing his sentence of three months. On the right to inform Americans accurately and to use liberty to challenge orthodoxy will rest the prospect for survival in this dark age.

Bertrand Russell
Penrhyndeudraeth, Wales, Great Britain

[230]

## The Assassination

*The Minority of One* (February, 1964), p. 22 | C64.10

*Most of this document, here omitted, deals with Cuba a year after the Missile Crisis. Russell praises* The Minority of One *for its analysis of the JFK assassination, and includes a letter to President Johnson regarding an alleged Nicaraguan connection in an alleged U.S. plan to overthrow the Castro regime in Cuba.*

I have read your article and that of Mr. Norden[13] regarding the assassination of President Kennedy with great interest. The facts set out demolish the "case" advanced by the authorities and lend credence to the theory of a high level plot.

The *Texas Observer* has also published information regarding the trajectory of the bullets and the possible place from which they were fired. It is an appalling thought that the conspirators may reside in Washington.

I am enclosing for your interest a copy of a letter I have sent to President Johnson which, I hope, may make such plans as may be in store for Cuba more difficult to carry through.

I admire your good work immensely.

Bertrand Russell
Merioneth, Wales, U.K.

---

13. Eric Norden was a freelance writer whose long article 'The Death of a President' appeared in the January issue of *The Minority of One* along with the editor's (M.S. Arnoni) 'Who Killed Whom and Why?' Norden's article brilliantly anticipated weaknesses of the forthcoming Warren Commission. Arnoni suggests a right-wing conspiracy.

President Lyndon B. Johnson,
The White House,
Washington, D.C.
U.S.A.

Dear President Johnson, I am much disturbed by certain reports in *The New York Times* and *New York Herald Tribune,* respectively for September 24, 1963 and September 30, 1963.

These reports comprise an interview with Mr. Luis Somoza,[14] a powerful figure in Nicaragua and refer to a joint U.S.-Nicaraguan plan leading to an American invasion of Cuba. The alleged facts in these troubling reports entail a three-phased programme.

The first phase consists of smuggling weapons into Cuba for the purpose of harassing the Castro Government. This was to have occurred during the past two months. The second phase consists of an invasion of former Cubans now in the United States armed forces who would be released from these forces for the purpose. They would seek to capture any town with the assistance of those who were prepared in Cuba by the first phase. Any such captured town would be declared the seat of an insurgent Government. The third phase would consist in the recognition of the insurgent Government by certain Central and South American nations who would send troops to support the insurgents at the invitation of the insurgents. The completion of this phase would bring American troops to Cuba in the summer of 1964, shortly before the Presidential election.

I hope you will appreciate the motives which induce me to write you about this. Luis Somoza has enjoyed American support and claims to be in contact with Attorney General Robert Kennedy and the leader of the Bay of Pigs invasion, Manuel Artime. The President of Nicaragua, Rene Schick, confirmed to the reporter from the *New York Herald Tribune* that such a plan existed and that his government would join multilateral action against Cuba with the armed forces of Venezuela, Colombia and possibly Argentina.

I hope you will agree that these authoritative reports are most damaging to the United States and should be repudiated in the interest of the good name of the government of the United States.

I shall seek to bring these facts to the attention of people in the hope that their falsity may be demonstrated and the hopes of mankind for a detente in the Cold War may be strengthened.

---

14. Luis Somoza (1922–1967) succeeded his father, Anastasio Somoza, as dictator of Nicaragua after Anastasio's assassination in 1956.

I look to your office for reassurance in this important matter.
With my respect,

Yours sincerely, Bertrand Russell

[231]

## The U.S. and Cuba

*The Scotsman* (12th May, 1964), p. 8 | C64.34

*Russell appeals for the normalization of relations with Cuba.*

Sir, —The attempts on the part of the United States to improve relations with the U.S.S.R. deserve support. In particular, the statement by President Johnson that he will meet the Soviet Union more than half-way in the matter of Germany is very encouraging.

In this situation, it is difficult to understand the alarming attitude of the U.S. towards Cuba. A tolerant policy towards the U.S.S.R. and the pursuit of good relations with the Soviets can hardly be compatible with so hostile a policy toward Cuba. The only hope for peace lies in the diminution of hostilities in troubled areas of the world. It is hard to see why Cuba should not receive similar consideration.

The flight of American craft over Cuba is in utter violation of Cuban sovereignty and would be unacceptable to any state in the world. The U.S. possesses missiles on her territory but would not permit Soviet or Cuban aircraft to violate her air space on that account. This sort of action on the part of a large country towards a smaller one must be deplored the world over and the maintenance of an unwanted base at Guantanamo Bay by force is sheer imperialism.

I wish to appeal for the establishment of normal relations with Cuba and for an end to plans for flights over her territory. The blind spot America displays over Cuba threatens to dash the hopes of peace so arduously built. I am certain that respecting the rights of Cuba is in the vital interests of the U.S. and is a prerequisite of peace in the world. Such action on the part of America will win her worldwide approval and cannot conceivably be opposed by anyone who wishes an end to the Cold War and the danger of nuclear war.

I am &c. Bertrand Russell
Plas Penrhyn, Penrhyndeudraeth, Merioneth, May 5.

## *The Bomb and the Cold War*

••••••••••••• [232] •••••••••••••

# The Unthinkable

*The Observer* (3rd October, 1963), p. 11 | C63.16

*Russell takes Herman Kahn and his reviewer, John Strachey, to task for dangerously minimizing the destructiveness of a nuclear war.*

Sir, —Mr. John Strachey's[15] review of Herman Kahn's "Thinking About the Unthinkable" is very interesting. According to Mr. Strachey, Herman Kahn advances three theses, with which Mr. Strachey is in agreement:

1. There will probably be a thermonuclear war;
2. It will not be the end of civilisation;
3. After it, but not before, a world government will be created which will prevent further thermonuclear war.

Very reluctantly, I am compelled to agree with the first of these theses to the extent of thinking that the occurrence of a thermonuclear war is slightly more probable than its non-occurrence. The other two theses strike me as absurd.

Herman Kahn, whom Mr. Strachey praises for realism, suggests that there may be as many as tens of millions of deaths. As he is intelligent and well informed he must know, and Mr. Strachey ought to know, that this is a ridiculous underestimate. Who can doubt, in spite of the advocates of "no-cities strategy," that Moscow, London and New York would be obliterated in the first day of the war, and what sane man can imagine that these three cities will be the only targets? Yet they alone make up the tens of millions, and what man with any power of psychological imagination can believe that the maddened and diseased survivors will be capable of an act of statesmanship which the present world cannot achieve?

Mr. Strachey maintains that he and Herman Kahn deplore the prospect of a nuclear war. This may be so, but they are, doubtless unintentionally, doing as much as their abilities permit to bring it about by

15. John Strachey (1901–63) was a socialist political writer who had been a Labour M.P. and War Minister in the post-war Attlee government.

making the prospect familiar and, ignorantly or dishonestly, minimising its destructiveness.

Bertrand Russell
Merioneth

[233]

## The Press as a Weapon

*The Saturday Review* (16th March, 1963), p. 31 | C63.18

*Russell was very much aware of the power of the mass media and its tendencies to aid in the dissemination of government policy and propaganda. Here Russell criticizes Lester Markel—the* New York Times *associate editor—for using the press as a Cold War weapon.*

Should the American Government decide to sterilize "subversives," "liberals" would be concerned to see that there was a proper right of appeal.

Lester Markel's[16] article "The 'Management' of News" (*SR*, Feb. 9) is most astonishing for its lack of self-consciousness. The "news" is now acknowledged as that information which suits governmental convenience. Orwell would have admired Mr. Markel's subtlety of mind. Most American apologists for nuclear genocide are less frank than Mr. Markel. It would be well to examine what it is he assumes and asserts.

He assumes that the function of the press is to criticize the efficiency of governmental operations in the Cold War, which, he declares, is as crucial as any hot war and in which the press is a vital weapon.

The American government systematically lies about the consequences of nuclear fallout. It pursues policies the consequence of which can only be nuclear annihilation. The Cuban crisis is a primary example. Mr. Markel, however, would have us accept the totalitarian function of the press for simple reasons. He assumes that the Cold War is desirable, that the government should lie and suppress truth in the pursuit of it, and that

16. Lester Markel (1894–1977), an American journalist, was *New York Times* Sunday editor (1923–65); and then that paper's associate editor (1965–69). He was also the editor and moderator of the T.V. program *News in Perspective* (1963–69). He wrote *Public Opinion and Foreign Policy* (Harper, 1958).

criticism should never begin with the criminal assumptions of American policy.

I submit that the eager readiness to exterminate several hundred million human beings, the sublime conviction that American rockets are permissible but other rockets are wicked, the refusal to allow that sane men (including journalists) have a duty to tell the truth about the danger to mankind, establish once again the shameful betrayal of America by "liberals" who embrace the conception of the world prepared for the American public in the Pentagon and the exploitative centers of corporate capitalism.

Bertrand Russell
Merioneth, Wales

[234]

## Stop Testing Now!

*The Washington Post* (25th March, 1963), p. A14 | C63.21

*The dangers of atomic testing had not been widely understood in the early 1950s. In the late 1950s the appearance of several scientific studies convinced Russell and others that atmospheric testing of atomic weapons must be stopped "on grounds of humanity." The following letter was written about three months before the signing of the Partial Test Ban Treaty outlawing atmospheric testing.*

All friends of peace are deeply disturbed at the delays and difficulties now taking place in Geneva with regard to the banning of nuclear tests. Nuclear testing as a part of national policy is one of the most unforgivable aspects of the cold war. Every major series of tests results in the death of millions of human beings over many generations.[17] These deaths are due to blood cancer, bone cancer, monstrous births and general genetic and somatic damage. Moreover, the germ plasm of future generations is irreparably damaged by every test series.

The horror of nuclear testing is comparable to the cutting of throats of one million infants under the age of five before the eyes of their mothers.

17. In his book *No More War* (1958), which helped him earn the Nobel Peace Prize in 1962, Linus Pauling estimated (p. 75) that each year of testing causes 230,000 serious birth defects and 420,000 embryonic and neo-natal deaths.

This was the manner in which warfare might have been conducted under Herod or Genghis Khan. We are not sufficiently aware of the barbarous consequences of nuclear testing because the effects are less visible.

They are still dying in Hiroshima and Nagasaki. Victims each year are dying because of the damage done by the fallout over those two cities. What right does any government have to poison the atmosphere, which is the atmosphere of all the peoples of the world? What would governments say if Pakistanis and Indians in their dispute over Kashmir or Arabs and Israelis in their dispute poisoned the atmosphere of the planet in the course of it? What right do governments anywhere have to make the peoples of the world hostage to every petty squabble they might entertain? I appeal for a halt to nuclear testing, irrespective of what the other side is prepared to do, on grounds of humanity and in the interest of human survival on this planet.

Bertrand Russell
Penrhyndeudraeth, Wales

[235]

## Sense and Sensibility

*The Times* (24th April, 1963), p. 13 | C63.31

*In this letter Russell expresses partial agreement with the editor of the* Times *on nuclear disarmament, and he remarks on the place of emotion and violence in politics.*

Sir, —Your leader "Sense and Sensibility" in your issue of April 20 is very interesting to me, especially because I am in agreement with the greater part of it.

You point out that nuclear disarmament, even if general, would not of itself prevent nuclear warfare in the future. I have stated this over and over again with every possible emphasis. In my broadcast "Man's Peril" (reprinted in *Portraits from Memory*) I said: "Here then is the problem which I present to you, stark and dreadful and inescapable: shall we put an end to the human race, or shall mankind renounce war? . . . Some hope that perhaps war may be allowed to continue provided modern weapons are prohibited. I am afraid this hope is illusory. Whatever agreements not to use hydrogen bombs had been reached in time of peace, they would no longer be considered binding in time of war and both sides would set to work to manufacture hydrogen bombs as soon as war broke out." This has always been my opinion.

You go on to say that we must deal with "the roots of international mistrust". This also, has always been my opinion. You continue by conceding that nuclear disarmament would be a great achievement and that there may already be sound and cogent reasons for Britain to stop making nuclear weapons. It is comforting to find that in these immensely important matters you agree with those of us whose campaign you nevertheless deplore.

You accuse us of "applying largely emotional criteria to what is primarily a matter of common sense". To this, there are two answers, or perhaps three. In the first place, nuclear war is a matter about which I should have thought it obviously right to feel emotion. If you can contemplate without emotion the destruction of the human race or even of all the inhabitants of Britain, I can only congratulate you, without envy, on your stoicism.

In the second place, most of us have tried the appeal to reason for a number of years with notable lack of impact. I wrote a book called *Common Sense and Nuclear Warfare*—just such a book as you recommend. I was told that "of course this was common sense, but that it is not by common sense that people are moved," and that I was altogether too coldly rational. Experience has shown that to get a hearing in the newspapers it is necessary to act in ways that you deplore. You say truly that many thousands who do not march are working patiently for a climate in which armed force will no longer be employed. Most of us who believe in more forcible methods have been reluctantly driven to this belief by the failure of what would be considered "rational"methods. There is a long record of the breakdown of disarmament conferences and of the insincerity of Governments which put forward proposals for disarmament. The most noteworthy example was the admirable proposals put forward by the West in 1955 which, to the horror of those who had made them, Russia accepted—whereupon the West withdrew them. The present failure to reach agreement for a test ban is another example of the impossibility of agreement while the will to peace is absent.

You put forward an objection to mob violence in such general terms that it would seem (though, of course, mistakenly) as if you thought an assault on one policeman a worse disaster than nuclear war. Hardly any great reforms have ever been carried without mob violence and, in the present case, experience has shown that the beliefs of opponents of nuclear weapons receive hardly any notice in the press unless they are accompanied by actions such as you think undesirable. And even then a great many newspapers report only incidents which they think likely to throw discredit on the movement, and fail to report sober statements of our aims. For these various reasons, we have been driven, however reluctantly, to forms of demonstration which involve some risk of disorder, though we have never approved of illegal violence whether perpetrated by the demonstrators or by the police.

Yours faithfully, Russell
Plas Penrhyn, Penrhyndeudraeth, Merioneth, April 20.

[236]

## Bertrand Russell on The Sinful Americans

*Harper's Magazine* (June, 1963), pp. 21–22, 24, 26, 28–30 | C63.45

*In March 1963, Russell exchanged several letters with John Fischer, editor of* Harper's Magazine, *concerning a controversy growing out of a January article in* Harper's *by Fischer accusing Russell and others of an "oversimplified" view of the problems of disarmament. Their correspondence was published in the June issue.*

*This fascinating exchange reveals the depth of Russell's understanding of the arcane logic of nuclear deterrence as well as his command of the facts concerning the risks of accidental nuclear war. (This exchange was also reprinted in Feinberg and Kasrils,* Bertrand Russell's America 1945–1970 *(South End Press, 1983), pp. 162–175.)*

March 4, 1963

Sirs, You published an article in your January issue by a Mr. J. Fischer. This article is not sufficiently serious to warrant the time necessary to examine it, but it may be worthwhile to mention that the views attributed to me by Mr. J. Fischer bear no relation to what I have advocated, and it seems clear from the context of his article that he has attributed these false views to me with foreknowledge. I shall charitably assume that this was due to oversight and I shall, therefore, seek to explain briefly what it is I am saying, in sufficiently simple language such as to enable J. Fischer to understand more clearly.

I am contending that human beings live, at the moment, in immediate danger of total annihilation. I do not say this rhetorically, but base the statement upon the fact that rocket bases and nuclear missiles cover our planet and rest upon warning systems of a few minutes. This entire apparatus of global butchery depends upon radar, which is incapable of distinguishing natural phenomena from missiles. Many of *Harper's* readers will be familiar with the kinds of statements made by insurance companies concerning the possibility and likelihood of accidents with regard to airplane flights and automobile transport. We know there will be a mean number of accidents each year, although we cannot say which cars will crash or planes fall. So it is a simple problem of mathematical statistics that with each day the possibility of total annihilation through accident increases to a point of near certainty.

In the Cold War, the two giants competing for power ruthlessly extirpate every semblance of human decency wherever they are able to do so in pursuit of their mad struggle. The United States, for example, imposes intolerable regimes upon Asian, Latin-American, and Middle Eastern countries, and economically exploits the great majority of mankind who live at below-subsistence level to support American profit. Similar things can be said of the Soviet Union, but Americans need reminding of the nature of the society they inhabit. Devil theory, fanaticism, such as was practiced in the Thirty Years' War and evident in the conflicts between Catholics and Protestants, Christians and Moslems, will eliminate life from our planet. The Russians are not devils. Their record is comparable to that of any other nation State, no better, little worse. The American government pursues a policy of genocide. This is a plain statement of fact. You, like Eichmann, acquiesce in this policy and you, like him, have the imperative moral responsibility to demand and end to such a policy. It can be done, if cowardice is put aside for clarity.

Yours faithfully, Bertrand Russell

*In his reply of 10th March, Fischer denied Russell's claim that American missiles "rest upon warning systems of a few minutes" and insisted that the system had "elaborate safeguards" which made it "virtually inconceivable" that a missile could be fired by accident. Russell's long reply of 15th March provides ample evidence that he was a serious student of nuclear weapons and nuclear war.*

March 15, 1963

Dear Mr. Fischer, You suffer from what the theologians call "invincible ignorance." You also lack acquaintance with elementary logic. *Ad hominem* comment is no help to argument. Even if the absurd contention were made that men of particular intelligence are less well equipped to comment on public affairs than men of practiced ignorance, it would still be necessary to examine the remarks of the former on their merits in order to refute their claims. It will not help you to call scientists names.

To complain of their training as a means of coping with their contentions is not an argument but a prejudice.

I shall examine the facts since you show so unbelievable an ignorance of them. You assert unabashedly:

> It is a simple, easily verifiable matter of fact that the American nuclear missile system does not "rest upon warning systems of a few minutes"; nor does its apparatus "depend upon radar, which is incapable of distinguishing natural phenomena from missiles."

And I thought that the Americans were telling the truth when they justified their blockade of sovereign Cuba by invoking the danger provided by wicked Russian missiles. These missiles were dangerous because of the reduced warning time, said Mr. Kennedy. But perhaps he was following the procedure announced by Mr. Sylvester[18] and "lied in the national interest."

The DEW-Line system and NORAD are a fantasy, I suppose.[19] This radar network is designed to detect oncoming missiles, and the firing of American missiles is said to depend upon the information provided by DEW-Line and NORAD. The warning system upon which SAC[20] works is fifteen minutes. The warning system in Britain is four minutes. All of the rocket bases are primed according to signals expected on radar registering missile attack. Would you claim that SAC and rocket bases abroad are not part of the American nuclear missile and bomber system?

So much for that contention. With regard to the reliability of radar, Sir Robert Watson-Watt, who is the inventor of radar, has declared unequivocally that radar can not distinguish natural phenomena from missiles. The Director of Jodrell Bank, Sir Bernard Lovell, has stated that it would not be possible to distinguish on radar between meteorites and missiles. There have been a large number of accidents due to the faultiness of radar. NORAD interpreted the rising of the moon as an invading Russian armada and on the basis of this error the signal to attack was

18. Arthur Sylvester was an assistant Secretary of Defense during the Cuban missile crisis who allegedly lied to further national goals and claimed an inherent right to do so. See above, Russell's reply to Mr. Frood in document [225].

19. The DEW (Distant Early Warning) Line was a radar warning system in Alaska and Canada in the late 1950s and early 1960s against Soviet bombers. NORAD (North American Aerospace Defense Command) was established in the late 1950s, originally as a combined Canadian-U.S. command, against aerospace attack.

20. SAC (Strategic Air Command) was established in 1946 and was until its abolition in 1992, the U.S. Air Force's long-range strike force composed of bombers and ICBMs. Its command depended largely on threat assessments from NORAD.

given; only the freak occurrence of an iceberg cutting an underwater cable delayed it sufficiently to cause doubt in the mind of a Canadian commander.

The Mershon National Security Report, published on June 28, 1960, itemizes fifty accidents involving nuclear weapons including twelve major accidents. It predicted accidental nuclear war during the 1960s as a matter of statistical probability. It lists the accidents caused by radar and confirms the statements concerning its faulty character made by Watson-Watt and Lovell. So much for the infallibility of radar.

You say categorically that the safeguards taken make it inconceivable that a missile could be fired by accident. In 1958 twelve Nike missiles were fired because of an electrical short circuit. Twenty-four warheads were scattered less than a day before the missiles were to be fitted with hydrogen warheads. The Mershon report lists comparable examples.

As regards the Minuteman missile, Professor Ralph Lapp states: "It might go by accident, it might be tampered with by saboteurs, or fired by fanatics."

After discussing safety precautions concerning ICBMs, President Kennedy stated: "All the safety factors leave a serious loophole in the control of ICBMs."

Lloyd V. Berkner, organizer of the International Geophysical Year, stated:

> As large numbers of fast-flying missiles come into the possession of both sides, ready for use, critical command will tend to devolve to lower and lower echelons. To some extent this is already occurring. If we are going to be able to retaliate effectively, it will become less and less practicable to assemble Congress or to call together the Cabinet or even for the President to be consulted when missiles with the ultimate destructive power are seen flying toward us.

As Professor Lapp put it, "In the era of missile warfare, the control of nuclear weapons steadily becomes more diffuse and the danger of war through accident, miscalculation, or madness must rise accordingly."

The President of the American Psychological Association, Dr. Charles E. Osgood, stated: "The maintenance of peace depends upon rational behavior by those in control; yet in the present era of great danger we are more than ever at the mercy of 'the unpredictability of human behavior under stress.'" On the same subject, Professor Lapp stated: "This unpredictability applies equally to chiefs of state and to lower echelons. But with the diffusion of control of nuclear weapons to more and more hands, the chances of someone breaking under the stress are multiplied."

Stockpiles of nuclear warheads are available at bases of the West German Air Force and may, according to President Kennedy, be turned over to the Germans in emergency! When a B-52 bomber had to jettison a 24-megaton bomb over North Carolina, five of the six "safety" mechanisms had been triggered. One switch separated us from the obliteration of a vast area. So it is that the following men had stated the danger:

> Accidental nuclear warfare is extremely likely.
> —*Lord Hailsham*[21]

> Future generations will look back with amazement if war is averted.
> —*John Foster Dulles*[22]

> These modern weapons are simply too hot to handle and as time goes on, the curve of probability that they will go off will steadily rise.
> —*Thomas K. Finletter*[23]

> If developments continue as they have during the last fifteen years, I believe all-out nuclear war is, in the long run, inevitable.
> —*Harrison Brown*[24]

> Every year, every month lost is not just marking time . . . but a lightning fast slide to the line separating peace from the blast of rocket nuclear war.
> —*Andrei Gromyko*[25]

As for genocide, this is a simple matter of definition. The utilization of the nuclear rockets will entail the murder of hundreds of millions. This is genocide.

I shall list the intolerable regimes supported solely by American capital and American guns: Vietnam, South Korea, Thailand, Paraguay, Peru, Chile, Ecuador, Bolivia, Guatemala, Haiti, Formosa, and Spain. There are others. There are even more who are tolerated for just as long as they do not challenge American economic exploitation. Greece, Portugal, and France are tyrannies and all three maintain camps for political prisoners.

---

21. Quintin Hogg, Lord Hailsham (1907– ), a British statesman and Lord Chancellor (1970–82).

22. John Foster Dulles (1888–1959), U.S. Secretary of State, 1953–59.

23. Thomas Finletter (1893–1980) was U.S. Secretary of the Air Force (1950–53) and NATO Ambassador (1961–65).

24. Harrison Brown was an American atomic scientist who worked with Einstein and others in the early post-war period to alert the public to the dangers of nuclear weapons.

25. Andrei Gromyko (1909–1989) was Soviet Foreign Minister (1957–85).

I enclose a copy of my article in the *Bulletin of Atomic Scientists* in which I once again repeat my position as stated in *Common Sense and Nuclear Warfare* and in *Has Man a Future?* It can be found in countless articles and interviews. It is perfectly clear you have never read my writing on the subject and I challenge you to provide the source for the view you attribute to me in your article.

It amuses me to have you suggest that I am unfamiliar with the issues about which I write, and that questions of war and peace are not my province. I have written on social issues since 1896 and on matters of peace and war and international politics for over fifty years.

I can not say whether your ignorance on these matters is real or whether you suppress the facts which alarm you. I can say that it is abominable for a man who edits a journal to be both so ill-informed and so prepared to write on the subjects of which he has no knowledge. This practice spreads ignorance and untruth.

I should wish you to publish this letter along with yours of 10 March.

Yours faithfully, Bertrand Russell

*In his March 24th reply to Russell's letter of March 15th, Fischer claims that Russell has confused warning time and reaction time, and that although ballistic missiles shrink the former, they extend the latter since our Minuteman missiles are safe in hardened silos thereby obviating any need to launch before enemy missiles had actually landed.*[26] *He also charges Russell with a factual error, insisting that the Nike missile was a "short-range anti-aircraft weapon . . . not fitted with a hydrogen warhead." Russell replied the same day.*

March 24, 1963

Dear Mr. Fischer: Our controversy has centered on the issue of accidental war and the nature of American policy. You are unable to refute the overwhelming evidence of specific and statistical kind. You are unable to "unwrite" the Mershon Report, the work of the Pugwash scientists whose competence in their fields is real, the statements of Kennedy, Dulles, Gromyko, Hailsham, and scores of others. And you are unwilling to grasp what you would never deny with regard to the data of insurance

26. The idea that the U.S. would 'launch on warning' has been officially denied by U.S. authorities. However, some experts have insisted that both the U.S. and the Soviet Union did have such a policy. See the interview with Bruce Blair in Jonathan Schell's *The Gift of Time* (Holt, 1998), pp. 72–81.

companies on the accidents in many spheres. Insofar as hundreds of millions of lives are involved, I have no compunction in saying to you that you enhance the prospect of annihilation by your journalism.

The electrical failure which detonated Nike missiles in 1958, the instance of total mental breakdown such as has been recently recorded for American missile officers, the occurrence of a mad first-strike act by a rebellious commander are all part of the data concerning accidental nuclear war. Kennedy's remarks were directed to "hardened" ICBMs.

The "invulnerability" to hydrogen attack from 100-megaton weapons may delude you but its absurdity deludes few other than military propagandists. The errors on radar which give false evidence of massive attack will provoke reply. The Institute for Strategic Studies assesses the strategic strength for early 1963 on the part of the United States to include over 1,600 medium-range bombers, 600 long-range bombers, 250 medium-range missiles, and 500 long-range missiles. If you think that this arsenal will not come into use would radar show a massive attack, I leave you to your delusion. If the missiles which detonated in 1958 are now said to have been anti-aircraft weapons, the claims of the time were lies. The danger is in no way lessened.[27]

Finally, Polaris submarines are increasingly detectable and sinkable. So much so that there is serious consideration of going over to surface vessels. As the day approaches that radar is not felt to give "warning" or "reaction time," the likelihood that either side will feel compelled to strike first will increase. There are many crises brewing in this world, many of them because of the American exploitative policy I have specified, and in each the probability of an error of judgment is high.

Any claim that "accidental war is impossible," any statement that rational acts are guaranteed and American judgment is infallible, are lunatic. I note in this discussion your insensitivity to the issues couched in such grand and pseudo-technical jargon. The issues concern vast suffering and agony, mass murder and devastation. How extraordinary that men so diminished as those who can discuss this without awareness of what they do should escape universal opprobrium. In a long life during which I have often observed the vanity and cruelty of men I can not cite a more cold-blooded parallel.

I should be grateful for your permission to publish this correspondence.

Yours faithfully, Bertrand Russell

---

27. They were anti-aircraft weapons and they did not carry hydrogen (fusion) warheads. But the danger is not diminished because as tactical-theater nuclear weapons in Europe they doubled as surface-to-surface missiles, and they carried Hiroshima-size nuclear (fission) warheads.

[237]

## Does The Warfare State Exist?

*The Minority of One* (June, 1963), p. 14 | C63.46

*Despite its left wing connections, Russell thought well of* The Minority of One, *an independent alternative American monthly edited by M.S. Arnoni. Russell had joined its Board of Sponsors in 1962.*

*In this letter he defends Fred Cook's* The Warfare State—*which he calls "one of the most important documents published since the end of the last World War"—against Julian Critchley's negative review in the London Observer.*

The May, 1963 issue of TMO included a brief article, "Book Unreview", which discussed M.P. Julian Critchley's review of Fred J. Cook's *The Warfare State* in *The Observer* of London. Lord Russell challenged the fairness of Mr. Critchley's review in a letter to the editor of *The Observer.* Lord Russell's letter, published below, was refused publication by the *Observer's* editors. —Ed.

In your issue of March 31 you published a review of Mr. Fred Cook's recent book by Julian Critchley, M.P., whom you call "an authority of defense".

He manages to write about everything except the book he had been requested to review. Mr. Critchley claims that the thesis advanced by Mr. Cook is without merit because of exaggeration and overstatement. He offers no evidence of this. Merely to assert it is not enough.

Mr. Cook documents with precision the overwhelming character of the military-industrial complex in the United States and makes clear the extent to which the institutional life of the country and the weight of organized power are driving mankind to nuclear death.

The Cordiner Report of 1958 placed the value of property owned outright by the American Department of Defense at 160 billion dollars. This does not include property leased to the Department or dependent upon buildings of the Department for its value. Outright ownership of this kind has reached thirty-two million acres within the United States.

Kennedy's budget for 1962 called for seventy-seven cents out of every one hundred to be spent on past wars, the Cold War and preparations for future war. Military assets are three times as great as the combined assets of U.S. Steel, American Telephone and Telegraph (the largest U.S. corporation), Metropolitan Life Insurance, General Motors and Standard Oil. The personnel of the Department of Defense is triple the number of all the above mentioned corporations and their subsidiaries.

LONDON EXPRESS SERVICE

"ALL RIGHT! FOR THE LAST TIME. WHO'S THE BRAINS BEHIND THIS?"

This JAK cartoon appeared in the *Evening Standard* in September 1961. The 89-year-old Russell and his wife Edith had been sentenced to two months in prison for inciting the public to civil disobedience. At the time, Indian Prime Minister Nehru remarked to John Kenneth Galbraith (then U.S. ambassador to India) that in prison Russell was "freer than any of us." See document [183].

Military power and the power of big industry are joined through the interchangeability of their personnel and the billions of dollars provided by the one and fulfilled by the other in military and quasi-military contracts. In 1960, 21 billion dollars were spent on military goods alone and this was only a part of the military budget for that year. General Electric and North American Aviation secure over 900 million dollars.

These awards are conferred at the discretion of public men recently executives in the very industries receiving such contracts. Military officers who champion a weapon produced by one corporation retire to its board of directors. There are over 1,000 such retired officers above the rank of major in the one hundred vast corporations which divided among them sixteen billion dollars. This list includes 261 generals and flag-rank officer. General Dynamics has on its payroll 187 retired officers, 27 generals and admirals and a former Secretary of the Army. The 16 billion were secured in one year.

Sub-contracts from major war contractors spread to every part of the American economy and society. The Defense Department alone hires over three and one-half million people; and four million people work directly in defense industries.

In many cities, missile production provides over fifty percent of all manufacturing jobs. In San Diego, California, it is over eighty-two percent. In eight states, one out of three jobs are directly in defense industry. In Los Angeles more than fifty percent of all jobs depend on defense expenditures. Finally, in the United States of America as a whole, between one-quarter and one third of all economic activity hinges upon military expenditure, and it is predicted that this will soon reach 50% of all economic activity.

The psychological, political and economic involvement in preparations for mass murder affect every food store and petrol station proprietor, every industrial worker, every politician —in fact the entire nation. This is the Warfare State of which Fred J. Cook writes and for which Julian Critchley apologizes. I have described it in barest outline. Why has Mr. Critchley ignored it?

Mr. Critchley maintains that the movement against nuclear war in Britain, which is unilateralist, is similar to the American radical right. Apart from the fact that the American radical right is racist, neo-fascist, and violent, it urges nuclear conflict. We urge its avoidance. This difference is of small interest to Mr. Critchley, which is why he has failed to face the issues raised in the book he was called upon to review and which is one of the most important documents published since the end of the last World War.

[238]

# Russell for Third Parties

*The Texas Observer* (12th July, 1963), p. 14 | C63.58

*Russell reaffirms the role of neutral nations in defusing the Cold War, and he underscores the idea of world government as part of a permanent solution to the problem of war.*

Thank you for your letter of June 27 and the enclosed cheque [for his *Observer* article last issue, "The Doctrine of Extermination" —Ed.], which I have put towards my work for peace.

I have read with interest your comments in the *Texas Observer* of June 28. I believe that unilateral disarmament by either the United States of the U.S.S.R. is extremely unlikely, if only because each nation is controlled by people who have been taught for a lifetime and have gained office on the assumption that military preparations bring security, and that this security is threatened by the other major power. The choice does not appear to me necessarily to be that of invasion or nuclear destruction. The United States would be very considerably safer today and would enjoy much greater liberty than it claims to defend if the massive erosion of the very foundations of political freedom was halted. Insistence on conformity in political thought is quite inconsistent with a free society. If the United States were able to abandon its demand for monolithic conformity and the more hysterical appeals to anti-communism, it would be far less a threat to the rest of the world, and this would certainly meet some response.

Although the most we can reasonably hope for in the United States and the U.S.S.R. is certainly unilateral initiatives, I look to other countries, and particularly those likely soon to acquire nuclear weapons of their own, to abandon entirely dependence upon the threat of such destruction and to join with neutral nations in a last desperate attempt to inculcate a little reason into the chief belligerents. I believe that third parties have a role to play which could be vital in saving man from his own folly, and it is for this reason that for many years I have been associated with the demand for world government. It is difficult to imagine how the Cold War could be successfully terminated without the creation of a world authority of which neither the communist nor anti-communist blocs was unduly suspicious. Such an authority, in order to be effective, would have to maintain a monopoly of the major weapons of war until such time as men had come to look back in history on war as the folly which it is.

Bertrand Russell
London, England

[239]

# Prelude to Another Cold War

*The Times* (15th August, 1963), p. 9 | C63.67

*Russell was aware of China's perception of the recent thaw in US-Soviet relations and saw in it the makings of new nuclear worries for the prospects of world peace.*

Sir, —Those who wish for peace in the countries of NATO and the Warsaw Pact must be glad of the test ban treaty as a first step towards the ending of the Cold War, and must hope that it will be followed by such further measures of conciliation as have been suggested on either side. Unfortunately, though not surprisingly, this is not the view of the treaty which is taken in China.

The Chinese Government, I hope quite mistakenly, regards the rapprochement between Russia and the West as directed against China, and as long as China retains this view it will remain an increasingly dangerous obstacle to world peace. It can hardly be hoped that the mood of China will change while China continues to be treated as a pariah. The Chinese mood will change only when Russia and the West become less hostile to China. If they remain hostile, China is sure to have nuclear weapons very soon. As happened in the case of Russia, the Chinese acquisition of nuclear weapons, if present policies persist, is almost certain to be much sooner than is officially expected in the West.

China is the most populous state in the world and has shown itself immensely tenacious, but its present hostility towards the West is still hypothetical.

The Chinese Government, as announced in *The Peking Review* of August 2, has made certain proposals to the effect that all countries of the world should renounce nuclear weapons "completely, thoroughly, totally and resolutely", and that, in order to carry out this renunciation, they should "step by step" dismantle all bases on foreign soil, establish nuclear-free zones effectively covering the whole world, and agree to those measures at a conference of the Heads of Government of all the countries of the world. This proposal should be treated seriously and not dismissed as Utopian.

If accepted, it would solve the whole nuclear problem. While the Chinese Government makes this proposal, and other powers ignore it, it is mere hypocrisy to suggest that China is more bellicose than the powers of NATO and the Warsaw Pact. World problems cannot be solved by measures to which China is not a party. The West has consistently pretended that China does not exist, and it is hardly surprising that the

Chinese Government has adopted somewhat emphatic measures to remind the world that such a county as China cannot be ignored. The present hostility of China is an echo of the hostile noises that have come from the West. It will cease when those noises cease, but not before.

It will be a profound tragedy if the ending of the Cold War between Russia and the West, if achieved, is nothing but the prelude to another Cold War, which may be just as dangerous and have an outcome just as disastrous as was to be feared by the continuance of the present Cold War.

Yours faithfully, Bertrand Russell
Plas Penrhyn, Penrhyndeudraeth, Merioneth.

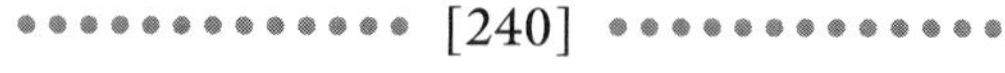

## Friends of Peace

*The Times* (1st June, 1964), p. 11 | C64.44

*As we have seen, Russell had been openly critical of the policies of the Labour Party regarding nuclear policy since the late 1950s. In this letter he raises several questions about the Party's Cold War posture. A little more than a year after this letter was written, differences over Vietnam would cause him to publicly resign from the Labour Party and to tear up his Party card.*

Sir, —Can friends of peace remain in the Labour Party? It is not clear that, at present, there is any appreciable difference between the policy on international affairs of the Labour Party and that of the Conservatives.

The following questions are those as to which I feel most in doubt:

1. Would the Labour Party abandon the British bomb?

2. Would a British Labour Government throw its weight in favour of general and complete disarmament at a disarmament conference, even if this involved agreement on some point or points with Russia rather than America?

3. Would the Labour Government cease to support colonial wars such as that in Aden or to back the United States in wars such as that in Vietnam?

4. Would the Labour Government resist the restoration to power of ex-Nazis in Germany?

5. Would the Labour Government abandon sycophancy toward America and realize that, in addition to the official Government of that country, there is another entrenched in the Pentagon and CIA capable (as

it showed at the time of the Summit Conference at Paris)[28] of giving orders to the official Government?

6. Would the Labour Government not support the United States in its hostility towards Cuba?

7. Would the Labour Government insist upon the admission of China to the United Nations and upon her participation in any disarmament conference?

8. If the leaders of the Labour Party realize that avoidance of nuclear war is more important than any other issue, then how do they show it?

I do not see how any friend of peace can fail to raise these questions.

Yours faithfully, Bertrand Russell
Plas Penrhyn, Penrhyndeudraeth, Merioneth, May 29.

[241]

## For Inspection

*The Sunday Times* (26th July, 1964), p. 15 | C64.53

*Russell sets the record straight on the Soviet Union's position on disarmament and on-site inspection.*

Sir, —During the Commonwealth debate Sir Alec Douglas-Home[29] stated that no sign of a breakthrough in disarmament is possible because the Soviet Union refuses to agree to international inspection. This distortion is frequently repeated by Western statesmen and newspapers. It is important to correct it. The Soviet Union has not opposed inspection. On the contrary, the Soviet Union has stated the following in its draft treaty of General and Complete Disarmament of March 19, 1962, and elsewhere:

---

28. Russell here refers to the Paris Summit in May 1960 between Khruschchev and Kennedy. This Summit was cut short by tensions concerning the American U-2 spy flights over the U.S.S.R. which had come to light earlier that month. Russell's view was not unique. Even some U.S. notables—e.g. Harold Stassen, Eisenhower's former disarmament advisor—charged that "some of our military officers" had deliberately sabotaged the summit. See D. Wise and T. Ross, *The U-2 Affair* (Random House, 1962), p. 103.

29. Sir Alec Douglas-Home (1903– ) was a British Conservative Statesman and Prime Minister from October 1963 to October 1964. Until 1963 he was known as Lord Home or the Earl of Home. In all three cases, 'Home' is pronounced 'Hume'. The great eighteenth-century Scottish philosopher David Hume expressed irritation at the pretentious gesture of a branch of his family in spelling the family name 'Home'.

> If the west agrees to the principle of general disarmament the Russians will call for internationally recruited inspection teams to be placed in every country before any measures of disarmament are begun. If general disarmament were agreed to, the Soviets have stated that they would permit thousands of United Nations Inspectors on Soviet soil before any reduction of armaments is started. These inspectors could control, on the spot, the disbanding of 60 percent of Russian manpower and 100 percent of the means of delivery of missiles.

If Sir Alec is sincere about his desire for disarmament, then why does he pretend that the Soviet Union refuses international inspection when he knows very well that the opposite is the case?[30]

Bertrand Russell
Penrhyndeudraeth, Merioneth

[242]

## An Open Letter to President Johnson

*The St. Louis Post-Dispatch* (25th October, 1964), p. 2b | C64.76

*Russell implores President Johnson to pursue international agreements to reduce the dangers of nuclear war. Johnson did meet with Kosygin in 1967 and set the stage for a number of strategic weapons agreements, including the Nuclear Non-Proliferation Treaty (1968) and the Strategic Arms Limitation Talks (SALT) treaties (1972, 1979).*

Dear Mr. President, I am appealing to you to make use of an opportunity such as has never come before to any human being. You are engaged in a contest with an opponent who is ignorant and bellicose. Your victory would be evidence of the American people's desire for peace. The world hopes confidently for your victory. But if you win, your victory may remain incomplete.

While present policies continue, the danger of a nuclear war not merely remains but increases. Present wars—which risk escalation into larger conflicts—should be halted and negotiations should be instituted for peaceful resolution of the issues involved.

30. Indeed, the Soviet Union had acceded to the idea of on-site inspection as early as 1955. See P. Noel-Baker, *The Arms Race* (Oceana Publications, 1959), pp. 21–22.

Everybody knows and proclaims that the spread of nuclear weapons to new powers will be a disaster. But nothing effective is done to prevent it. France and China already possess such weapons. Germany will soon follow suit. And within a few years every important country will possess the means of exterminating the human race. It is open to you to prevent this disaster.

One essential step will have to be the recognition of the Chinese government by the United States and its admission to the United Nations. The hostile feelings which have been generated will have to be mitigated and we shall all have to recognize that our supposed enemies are also human beings and that the universal wickedness we attribute to them is a myth.

China and Russia call for an international Congress of which the purpose should be to abolish all nuclear weapons. We are told by many in the West that such a proposal is premature. This means only that those who advance this argument have not yet thought out plausible ways to bring about the failure of such a conference.

It is open to you, if you so choose, to add your immense power to the influence of those who advocate such a Congress, in the sincere hope that it may remove the imminent peril of universal destruction.

If you do this you will lift the burden of fear from all the millions of human beings who watch with paralyzed terror the march of mankind toward the abyss.

You will be hailed in every country and in every continent as a saviour, as one who in a mad world has shown the road to sanity; and you will have the satisfaction of knowing that you have performed a service to humanity more noteworthy and more immense than has been performed by even the greatest of your predecessors.

In the name of mercy, in the name of humanity, I implore you not to let this opportunity pass unused.

Yours faithfully, Bertrand Russell
London

## *The Bertrand Russell Peace Foundation*

*The Bertrand Russell Peace Foundation established a global reach in the last years of Russell's life and it received the support of several heads of state including Nehru of India, Kaunda of Zambia, Nkrumah of Ghana, Ayub*

*Khan of Pakistan, Nyerere of Tanzania, and Senghor of Senegal. Under the direction of Russell's impetuous radical secretary, Ralph Schoenman, it seems that the Foundation was for a while, possibly with Russell's knowledge, supporting indigenous rebellions in Africa and Latin America.*[31]

[243]

## Averting War

*The Times* (4th May, 1964), p. 15 | C64.32

*In September of 1963, Russell had publicly announced his plans to form the Bertrand Russell Peace Foundation. In this letter he clarifies its role with respect to the threat of nuclear war.*

Sir, —In your very brief report of my speech in Manchester, you gave the impression that I held that the danger of nuclear war no longer exists and that the task of averting it has been accomplished. This was the exact opposite of my purpose, and I should be grateful if you would allow me to make this clear to your readers, who would otherwise be misled.

Governments and populations, through years of campaigning by those hostile to the cold war, have come, by and large, to grasp that a nuclear war would be a calamity. There remains the second and more difficult task of setting out particular solutions to the many conflicts which rack our planet and which may, at any moment, erupt into war and even nuclear war. Unless extensive research is undertaken into the sorts of solutions which may commend themselves to the disputants, and unless a massive public opinion is obtained in support of these solutions, the prospects of peace are not good, and it is to these essential aims that the Foundation which we have formed is dedicated. The meeting in Manchester was held to set out these aims and to explain why we consider them so important.

Yours faithfully, Bertrand Russell
Plas Penrhyn, Penrhyndeudraeth, Merioneth

31. See Monk, *Bertrand Russell: The Ghost of Madness*, Chapter 13.

[244]

## Peace Foundation

*The Times of India* (2nd December, 1964) | C64.94

*The outreach of the Bertrand Russell Peace Foundation was indeed global. Here he mentions its work in India and invites support. Prime Minister Nehru, who had died earlier in the year, was an original sponsor of the Foundation.*

Sir, —I write to bring to the attention of your readers the efforts of the Bertrand Russell Peace Foundation to overcome the drift to war. The current world expenditure on armaments is more than the total annual income of all the developing countries together, greater than the annual income of Africa, Asia and Latin America. The expenditure is 140,000 million dollars annually or 16 million dollars an hour. As long as the cold war continues, world poverty will remain.

It is clear, therefore, that the armament race and the cold war menace mankind not only because they threaten us with complete destruction but because they prevent the great ills of the world from being remedied. Poverty, disease, illiteracy and over-population cannot be redressed until the world directs its resources towards constructive aims. The Bertrand Russell Peace Foundation is establishing branches in different parts of the world to promote the work for peace and for development.

We are immensely grateful to President Radhakrishnan and to Vice-President Zakir Hussain who are the patrons and sponsors of the Indian branch of the Bertrand Russell Peace Foundation. Our work in India is conducted through our office at P.O. Box 308, New Delhi: the secretary is Mrs. Triska Sundra, wife of the Punjabi industrialist, and the treasurer is Mr. G.L. Dhingra. I urge all who desire peace and the wellbeing of mankind to assist our work, and to follow the great example of President Radhakrishnan and Vice-President Zakir Hussain by contacting Mrs. Triska Sundra.

Bertrand Russell
London, November 27.

[245]

# Brev Fran Bertrand Russell

*Aftonbladet* (26th March, 1968) | C68.07

*Russell requests Swedish support for his Foundation's work. Here he summarizes some of the Foundation's initiatives to date.*

*This letter originally appeared in Swedish. I am grateful for the following translation kindly provided by Stefan Andersson.*

Letter from Bertrand Russell:

I am asking for financial support for the Bertrand Russell Peace Foundation. The work that is being done by our representatives in many countries has been impeded due to the lack of the necessary means to support our extensive and radical activities.

During its short duration,The Bertrand Russell Peace Foundation has taken on a number of important initiatives. We have published books and documents about the current cold war and imperialism, oppressive circumstances in many different countries of the third world, new weapons and their resultant hazards, and other such problems. We have worked energetically and with apparent success on behalf of political prisoners in forty countries. We recently sent five representatives to Bolivia[32] to observe "the trial" against Regis Debray, and thus were able to report on the threats upon his life. We have carried out investigations in Southeast Asia and the Middle East in order to be able to deliver eyewitness reports from the wars there. We have made contributions to other investigations, such as that regarding the assassination of President Kennedy, and we have created committees in Western Europe in order to make public the results of those investigations. We have also participated in the production of a film that has refuted the Warren Commission's report. But most of all, we have worked for five years to reveal the aggression of the United States in Vietnam. We have sent observers, published documents and created the International War Crimes Tribunal.

This work continues and is being expanded. I appeal to all those in Sweden who support our efforts to give as generously as possible to our cause.

Bertrand Russell
Plas Penrhyn. March 15, 1968

---

32. The visit to Bolivia was under the direction of Ralph Schoenman, who was refused re-entry into Britain in March of 1968. See document [212].

## *Vietnam*

*Russell's overview of the historical background of the U.S. intervention in Vietnam is succinctly and insightfully presented in the introduction to his* War Crimes in Vietnam *(1967).*

*He saw the United States involvement as an extension of the French colonial domination in Southeast Asia and as a suppression of a broadly based popular struggle for national and political independence.*

•••••••••••••• [246] ••••••••••••••

# Vietnam Policy Protested

*The New York Times* (8th April, 1963), p. 46 | C63.26

*This is Russell's first letter of protest regarding Vietnam and the American involvement. It's remarkable for its insight at a time when few people knew of the nature of U.S. intervention there. This was sixteen months before the Gulf of Tonkin Resolution, which many take as the mark of the beginning of serious U.S. military involvement.*

*This letter was the subject of a* New York Times *editorial ("Lord Russell's Letter") on the same day, which gave rise to a series of heated exchanges between Russell and the* New York Times *over the next several months. Russell's battle with the* New York Times, *as well as many of his articles on the war in Vietnam, is reprinted in his* War Crimes in Vietnam.

To the Editor of *The New York Times:*

The United States Government is conducting a war of annihilation in Vietnam. The sole purpose of this war is to retain a brutal and feudal regime in the South and to exterminate all those who resist the dictatorship of the South. A further purpose is an invasion of the North, which is in Communist hands.

The real concern which brings the United States to pursue the brutal policy abandoned by France in Indochina is the protection of economic interests and the prevention of far-reaching social reforms in that part of the world.

I raise my voice, however, not only because I am in profound disagreement with American objections to social change in Indochina, but because the war which is being conducted is an atrocity. Napalm jelly gasoline is being used against whole villages, without warning. Chemical warfare is employed for the purpose of destroying crops and livestock and to starve the population.

The American Government has suppressed the truth about the conduct of this war, the fact that it violates the Geneva agreements concerning Indochina, that it involves large numbers of American troops, and that it is being conducted in a manner reminiscent of warfare as practiced by the Germans in Eastern Europe and the Japanese in Southeast Asia. How long will Americans lend themselves to this sort of barbarism?

Bertrand Russell
Penrhyndeudraeth, Wales, March 28, 1963

[247]

## Aid for Vietnam Assailed

*The New York Times* (4th May, 1963), p. 24 | C63.35

*Russell responds to an editorial of 8th April attacking him and his letter of the same date (see above) protesting United States conduct in Vietnam. In this long and detailed letter, Russell reveals that his charges are not "transparent Communist propaganda," but are derived mainly from reports in the Western press. Russell was angered and shocked when* The New York Times *published his letter without his evidence supporting his chemical weapons charge and without any mention that that portion of his letter had been excised. See his* War Crimes in Vietnam, *pp. 32–41. In Russell's letter below, the portion excised by* The New York Times *is placed in brackets.*

To the Editor of *The New York Times:*

Your editorial of April 8 "Lord Russell's Letter" calls for a reply from me on various counts.

You accuse me of an "unthinking receptivity to most transparent Communist propaganda." In fact, I base my remarks about the war in South Vietnam upon careful scrutiny of reports in Western newspapers and in publications of the British and American Vietnam committees. My belief derived from this study is that United States support of Diem is driving more and more of the inhabitants of South Vietnam into the arms of the Communists—a result to be deplored.

You accuse me of distorting the truth or of speaking only half truths. This is a charge which may be turned against you. I agree with the point of view that you express in your second paragraph. But in my letter I give reasons for my point of view. It is, I suppose, these reasons to which you take exception. They are that the purpose of the war is to retain "a brutal and feudal regime in South Vietnam and to exterminate all who resist Diem's dictatorship"; that the United States is pursuing a brutal policy (abandoned by France in Indochina) in order to protect economic interests and to prevent far-reaching social reforms in South Vietnam; and that the war is an atrocity.

It is an atrocity because such things as napalm bombs are being used—bombs which do not simply kill, but which burn and torture—and that chemical warfare is employed to destroy crops and livestock and so to starve the people of South Vietnam. I did not mention innumerable appalling atrocities carried out by Diem's Government, because for these America has only the indirect responsibility involved in the continued support of Diem.

You say in your fifth paragraph that napalm bombs have been used, but only against "real or imagined havens of Vietcong guerrillas" and have "certainly killed innocent people." You say, however, that "American advisors" have opposed the use of these bombs. This may be true, but it is less than a half-truth. You have said in your fourth paragraph that Americans are in Vietnam only as advisers and trainers. This is not true, and invalidates your explanation concerning the napalm bombs.

I suggest that you read the report of Richard Hughes on conditions in Vietnam in the [London] *Sunday Times* of Jan. 13, 1963—a journal by no means pro-Communist, anti-American or even very liberal—in the course of which Mr. Hughes speaks of "the Washington fiction that no United States troops are involved in combat and that United States officers and 'trainers' are on the scene merely to 'advise, observe, support and assist'." He says, also: "The Americans are now operating more than 200 helicopters and scores of reconnaissance and troop transport planes in the combat areas. Probably half of all bombing and strafing missions by the South Vietnam air force are undertaken by Americans serving as pilots and co-pilots."

[In your fifth paragraph you also endeavour to minimize the effect of "defoliation chemicals" by calling them "common weedkillers." If sprayed, as they must be to achieve the end for which you say they are intended, certain common weedkillers would destroy many crops and animals. But, in fact, chemicals other than common weedkillers have been used (some of these were once used as "common weedkillers," but were found to be too dangerous). The US Government has been charged by the South Vietnam Liberation Red Cross, after a year's study by them of the chemicals sprayed in South Vietnam and their effect upon the health of human beings, animals and crops, with using weedkillers which, in the large dosages used, are harmful; with using white arsenic, various kinds of arsenite sodium and arsenite calcium, lead manganese arsenates, DNP and DNC (which inflame and eat into human flesh); and calcic cyanamide (which has "caused leaves, flowers and fruit to fall, killed big cattle like buffaloes and cows, and seriously affected thousands" of the inhabitants of South Vietnam); with having spread these poisonous chemicals on large and densely populated areas of South Vietnam. Admittedly, the South Vietnam Liberation Red Cross is, as its name suggests, allied with those opposing the US-supported Diem regime, but its published findings cannot be ignored since it has urged international investigation of the situation. The use of these weapons, napalm bombs and chemicals, constitutes and results in atrocities and points to the fact that this is "a war of annihilation."]

I criticize "atrocities" where I find them. I was considered too anti-Communist by the liberals of the United States in Stalin's day for objecting to the atrocities that occurred in Russia at that time. I have recently been carrying on a correspondence concerning the hardships suffered by Jews in Communist countries. I see no reason to suppose that atrocities are to be condoned when committed by Western governments.

It is not I, but you, who in attempting to whitewash United States action in South Vietnam, are speaking half-truths and thereby, doing the very thing of which you accuse me: ignoring the Communist push for domination.

Two other accusations you make against me. You say that "to call the United States the aggressor and to say nothing about the Communist push for domination against the will of the inhabitants in Vietnam is to make a travesty of justice and a mockery of history." The latter is a fine peroration. But I would call to your attention the fact that you yourself had already said (paragraph 2) that you have criticized the United States Government's "support of the autocratic Diem regime, which has insufficient popular backing."

I would also call your attention to the following bit of history: The Geneva Conference of 1954 proposed compromise concerning Vietnam, which was admirable and which would have solved the problems of that country if it had been observed. The signatories were Molotov and Selwyn Lloyd, who signed as co-chairmen representing East and West respectively. The agreement reached by the conference was, with the backing of the United States, not observed by South Vietnam. A new regime was established in South Vietnam under a dictator named Diem of whom *Time* says (Nov. 21, 1960): "Diem has ruled with rigged elections, a muzzled press, and political re-education camps that now hold 30,000."

I can only deduce that in your failure to face the facts and to publicize them concerning the war in South Vietnam you are, to use your own phraseology, indulging in "arrant nonsense as even you in your heart must know."

Bertrand Russell
Penrhyndeudraeth, Wales, April 12, 1963.

[248]

## Russell Protests

*New Generation* (July–August, 1963), p. 2 | C63.53a

*This article in* New Generation *publishes three of Russell's letters to the mass media (*The New York Times, The Guardian, *and* The Washington Post*) dealing with Vietnam which these newspapers declined to publish. These letters are mainly concerned to make known the details regarding United States use of chemicals in Vietnam—essentially those details which* The New York Times *excised from Russell's letter which was published on 4th May (see the previous letter). The following is Russell's reply to the editor of* The New York Times *regarding his 4th May letter from which the details regarding chemical weapons had been omitted.*

*The end of the following letter has been omitted. It reiterates the information contained in the bracketed paragraph in the May 4th letter.*

May 9, 1963
To the Editor of *The New York Times:*

Sir, I am profoundly shocked by the journalistic standards of *The New York Times.* I have been engaged in a public controversy with *The New York Times* concerning a matter of international importance, namely, the atrocities presently being carried out by the Government of the United States in Vietnam. You attacked me in an editorial, accusing me of arrant nonsense and of stating things without evidence to substantiate them. In my reply to that attack, I presented the evidence in the course of a long letter. You published my letter, omitting my evidence and without even an indication by means of dots to suggest that the letter had been cut or shortened. I have had correspondence and controversy in the pages of *Izvestia* and *Pravda* and I wish to point out to you that never have I been so shabbily treated, never have *Izvestia* and *Pravda* behaved in a manner comparably dishonest. . . .

Yours faithfully, Bertrand Russell

[249]

## War in Vietnam

*The Observer* (9th February, 1964), p. 30 | C64.13

*This letter begins a series of three letters on the subject of United States use of chemical weapons in Vietnam with the London* Observer's *Far Eastern Correspondent, Dennis Bloodworth. Thirteen months later Russell writes two more (see below, C65.15 and C65.22.) Bloodworth's responses (to all but the third letter, C64.19) were printed as footnotes to Russell's letters in* The Observer.

Sir, —I wish to bring to the attention of people facts which I have before me concerning the use of chemical poisons by American and South Vietnamese Governmental forces in Vietnam. In the area along the Ong-Doc River, in the province of Ca-Mau, toxic chemicals were used, causing nearly 1,000 people, over half of whom were children, severe illness. The illnesses were characterised by vomiting, bleeding, paralysis and loss of sight and consciousness. Fruit trees, vegetables, cattle and domestic animals died from the effects.

Similar atrocities occurred in My-Tho province, Go-Cong province and the provinces of Can-Tho, Gia-Dihn, Ma-Lam, Bai-Lap, Kon-Tum and Dar-Lac.

In early December, 1963, American and South Vietnamese forces used toxic gas on densely populated areas. Thousands of tons of arsenic and arsenic derivative (D.N.P. and D.N.C.) have been in use with ghastly consequences.

The source of this evidence is the Foreign Minister of the Democratic Republic of Vietnam. I found the evidence carefully documented and particularised, and I wish to bring to the attention of people in this country the strong indication that the United States is indulging in chemical and gas warfare of an atrocious kind in Vietnam. I consider it essential that an international agency, such as the Geneva Conference on Indo-China, impartially investigate this evidence.

Bertrand Russell
Merioneth

[250]

# Earl Russell and Vietnam

*The Observer* (16th February, 1964), p. 30 | C64.15

*Bloodworth's response to Russell's February 9 letter was published on the same page. Russell replies.*

Sir, —In his reply to my letter on Vietnam, Mr. Dennis Bloodworth repeats the State Department contention that the chemicals employed in South Vietnam by the American authorities were no more than weed-killers. It is true that common weedkillers were used. The chemicals to which I referred were not said to have been weedkillers but killers of human beings and animals. (Remember Madame Nhu's delightful remark: "If they don't like the effect of our chemicals why don't they get out of our jungles?")

I shall name the chemicals and the effects for which evidence has been provided: white arsenic, arsenite sodium and arsenite calcium, lead manganese arsenates, D.N.P. and D.N.C. These chemicals inflame and eat into human flesh. They are poisons and they have been used on large and densely populated areas in South Vietnam. In addition, calcic cyanamide has had the effect of killing large cattle such as buffaloes and cows, rotting crops and causing lingering and ultimately fatal disease in the population. I have the facts before me and the photographs.

I criticise atrocities where I find them. I do not indulge in spreading the propaganda campaigns of Communists or of the State Department. I do not recommend to Mr. Bloodworth and his editor that they either drink the chemicals to which I refer above or spread them on their hands and arms, before submitting them to an impartial investigatory body. I suggest that the effects would be different than those they claim were observed when some chemicals were so used by South Vietnamese officials for the entertainment of Western correspondents. What I ask is that international scientists should be allowed to examine the evidence impartially.

I do not see how Mr. Bloodworth and his editor can take exception to this, particularly as they seem to be ignorant of the chemicals which have been used in South Vietnam. I should mention that these chemicals have been used as recently as December of last year and January, 1964.

Finally, I should point out that euphemisms employed in Vietnam, such as "strategic hamlet" for concentration camp, "defoliation campaign" for the use of arsenic on people, and "pacification" for the use of napalm and chemicals on 1,400 villages (as stated in *The New York Times* of January 19, 1962), do not inspire in me the relief they seem to bring to *The Observer.*

Bertrand Russell
Merioneth

••••••••••••• [251] •••••••••••••

## [The Vietnam War]

*Tribune* (28th February, 1964), p. 3 | C64.19

*Bloodworth answered Russell's February 16th letter in* The Observer *on the same page. Russell's reply was rejected by* The Observer *but published in* Tribune *(a publication representing the left wing of the Labour Party), with the following introduction by the editor:*

Bertrand Russell opened a controversy in *The Observer* this month, when he accused the United States authorities in Vietnam of using chemical warfare methods against their Vietcong enemies. An *Observer* correspondent, Dennis Bloodworth, replied to Russell's two letters, throwing doubt on this claim and adding (February 16th) that it was misleading to refer to the "strategic hamlets" (within which many of the population have been restricted) as concentration camps. Bertrand Russell's third letter has been rejected by *The Observer,* and is therefore published here. (All dates mentioned in his references are of 1963).

"I am pleased that Mr. Bloodworth finds my proposal for an impartial international inquiry into the use of chemicals in Vietnam "unexceptionable". I accept his suggestion that I should initiate one.

"It is noteworthy that defoliants and pesticides used in the United States and Great Britain were found to be so harmful that Dr. Weisner, the chief science advisor to President Kennedy, declared them "more dangerous than radioactive fallout" (*The Guardian,* May 17). *The Times* (May 16) disclosed the death by pesticide of birds of 58 species and described 50 pesticides in widespread use as responsible for "acute poisoning" of animals and human beings. President Kennedy found it necessary to halt their use and began a formal investigation. I hope it is now clear that chemicals kill human beings and even "weedkillers" have consequences.

"This atrocious war, which has been conducted in Vietnam since the ceasefire of 1954, is in brazen violation of international agreements.

These agreements called for elections in South Vietnam which were never held.

"Mr. Bloodworth fails to mention that the population which was not permitted to vote freely was uprooted, deprived and ruthlessly regimented in 'strategic hamlets' by force. Sixty-five percent of the total population, or 7,800,000, were moved to these camps, surrounded by barbed wire and moats (*Observer*, November 3).

"Napalm, which destroyed 1,400 villages is a chemical which burns unremittingly and cannot be extinguished. The victims suppurate before terrified observers. The United States has spent over one million dollars daily on this war; four thousand have been killed or wounded each month (*Observer*, September 8). Private armies have been financed by the CIA at a cost of £250,000 monthly (*The Times*, September 10).

"All this has taken place against an 'enemy' which now controls nearly 70 percent of South Vietnam. The majority of the Vietcong was described as non-Communist in the *Observer* by former Premier Tran Van Huu, The Vietcong official policy demands a neutral and disengaged South Vietnam. A popular front which has fought an appalling tyranny in South Vietnam has been opposed by the United States at an incalculable cost to the population. Even the Communist North has declared through Ho Chi Minh that it wishes to be unified with the South on terms of neutrality in the cold war and independence from 'Russia, China, and the West' (*The Times,* November 5).

The truth is that America has waged a war of conquest against a popular uprising which claims the support of the vast majority. The war is in violation of international agreements, uses techniques employed by the Japanese in the Second World War, and has the sole aim of frustrating a neutral and stable Government independent of Western dominance. Will the *Observer* demand its immediate cessation?

Yours faithfully, Bertrand Russell."

••••••••••••• [252] •••••••••••••

## Bertrand Russell calls U.S. Viet Nam policy "disastrous"

*The Toronto Daily Star* (6th March, 1964), p. 6 | C64.22

*Russell reviews the nature of the American intervention in Vietnam and pleads for an end to the war and the establishment of a neutral and independent Vietnam.*

Sir, —The United States is pursuing a policy which is both wrong and disastrous in Southeast Asia. The series of dictatorships in South Viet Nam are cruel and tyrannical. In order to conduct the war there, the United States has rounded up into strategic hamlets 7,800,000 people, some 65 percent of the population, as reported in the London *Observer* (Nov. 3, 1963). These internment camps are surrounded by spikes, moats, barbed wire and police dogs.

I appeal to Americans to consider the following facts:

1. The Viet Cong[33] of South Viet Nam have a non-Communist majority and are a popular front resistance, as was repeatedly stated by former Premier Tran Van Huu[34] in Paris.

2. The policy of the Viet Cong stipulates that Viet Nam should be neutral and independent of East and West in the cold war.

3. Despite statements to the contrary in the United States, Premier Ho Chi Minh of North Viet Nam has categorically asserted that he advocates for both North and South Viet Nam neutrality and independence of Russia, China, and America (London *Times,* Nov. 5. 1963).

These are the facts which lie behind De Gaulle's[35] efforts to bring neutrality and an end to the war in Viet Nam. There is no other means whereby the peace of Southeast Asia may be preserved. American intervention would have no justification, would lead to intense hatred for the United States throughout Asia and would immensely imperil the safety of all mankind.

Bertrand Russell
Penrhyndeudraeth, Wales

---

33. The Viet Cong was a name for the Vietnamese guerilla forces in the South who opposed the Diem regime in the late 1950s and early 1960s. They became the military part of the National Liberation Front (NLF) organized in 1960 for the overthrow of the South Vietnamese government and for the unification of North and South Vietnam. The label 'Viet Cong' ('Vietnamese Communist') was used by Premier Diem to discredit his opponents.

34. Tran Van Huu was Premier of Vietnam, 1950–53, in the French-controlled Vietnamese government led by Bao Dai, a French-picked former Emperor who was replaced by Ngo Dinh Diem in 1955.

35. Charles De Gaulle (1890–1970) was a French soldier, writer, and statesman. A hero of World War I, he formed and led the Free French Forces in World War II, headed two provisional French governments in 1944–46, was elected President in 1958, and created the Fifth French Republic. Although strongly favoring an independent French bomb, he announced France's withdrawal from NATO and used his influence to promote neutralism and exert pressure on the U.S. to withdraw from Vietnam.

[253]

# Bertrand Russell Endorses Aid to S. Vietnam Front

*The Haverford News* (5th June, 1964), p. 2 | C64.44a

*Russell was a keen observer of the American anti-war student movement, and he realized its potential in affecting political attitudes towards the war in Vietnam. In this letter to the Haverford College newspaper (Haverford, Pennsylvania) he applauds the students' humanitarian efforts on behalf of the guerrilla fighters in South Vietnam.*

To the Editor:

I wish to express my whole-hearted support for the action of the Haverford students who are raising money for medical supplies for the National Liberation Front in South Vietnam. I support their action and their call for an end to this war.

The Government of North Vietnam itself has specifically stated that it desires neutrality in the Cold War and independence of China, Russia and the U.S.A.

The Liberation Movement in the south also wishes neutrality and unification.

The American Students who are seeking to gain support for the dispatch of medical supplies to the Viet-cong deserve the widest support for their courage and their point of view. The war in Vietnam is one of atrocity, it has been waged against a popular front which is avowedly neutralist and a national movement, the aim of which is independence and the removal of a brutal dictatorship supported by the U.S.A.

The United States violated international agreements and sabotaged the clear opportunity for a neutral Indo-China by conducting an aggressive war which has involved the use of chemicals, napalm, torture and concentration camps. Sixty-five percent of the rural population of Vietnam has been uprooted and placed in camps surrounded by spikens, moats, barbed wire and patrols with police dogs. The United States in its insistence upon conducting this war poses a threat to world peace and behaves as the Japanese did in their warfare in South East Asia during World War II.

Those Americans who have the courage to speak out against this war and its extension, and to appeal for individual responsibility for the policies conducted in the name of the American people deserve world wide support. The dispatch of medical supplies to the victims of American crimes is the minimum duty incumbent upon Americans whose government has behaved so atrociously.

Bertrand Russell
Penrhyndeudraeth, Wales

[254]

# War in Indo-China

*The Guardian* (27th June, 1964), p. 8 | C64.48

*Russell, joined by fellow peace activist J.D. Bernal, calls for an end to the war in Indochina based on the Geneva Agreements.*

Sir, —Recent events give cause for grave alarm about events in South-East Asia. The war in Vietnam and the resumed hostilities in Laos threaten world peace. It is appalling that this fighting should be extended, since it is perfectly clear that a sane conclusion to military action is within reach through the implementation of the Geneva Agreements[36] of 1954 and 1962.

It is imperative that the fourteen nations who met at Geneva should be reconvened for the purpose of arranging an immediate cease-fire in Laos and the beginning of talks for the neutralisation of the area.

China, the Soviet Union, and the United States should guarantee the absence of interference on the part of the Great Powers, thus allowing the people of Indo-China to decide their future. The renewed activity on the part of the United States in Laos, the dispatch of marines to Siam, the bombing missions from the Philippines and the stepping up of the horrific war in Vietnam are all causes for alarm and must be vigorously opposed. No delay should be tolerated, for we are facing again the prospect of world war, where a perfectly just and humane solution is within direct reach. The recent declaration of the United States of its willingness to extend the war to China opens up disastrous prospects. We appeal to people and to leaders to speak out vigorously for the reconvening of the fourteen Geneva Powers and for a peaceful negotiated settlement of the war in Indo-China.

Yours faithfully,
Bertrand Russell,
J.D. Bernal.[37]
3 and 4 Shavers Place, Haymarket, London SW1

---

36. International conventions in Geneva, Switzerland, which provided for an armistice and political settlement in Indo-China. The 1954 agreement provided for 1956 elections and unification of Vietnam. (The elections were thwarted by U.S. and South Vietnamese intervention and never took place.) The 1962 agreement provided for neutralization and a three-faction coalition government for Laos, which the U.S. had tried to make into an anti-Communist bastion since 1958.

37. J.D. Bernal was a British scientist and a Communist activist. At this time he was president of the World Peace Council. See above, document [99].

[255]

## Vietnam

*The Times* (26th August, 1964), p. 9 | C64.64

*In this letter, and in the next two, Russell engages P.J. Honey, the Vietnam scholar at the University of London, on the nature of United States intervention in Indo-China. A year earlier Honey had met with Robert McNamara, U.S. Secretary of Defense, whom he had impressed with the importance of maintaining the American anti-Communist mission in Vietnam.*[38]

Sir, —Mr. P.J. Honey is guilty of his own charge of factual inaccuracy and distortion which he made in a letter to *The Times* on July 28. If Mr. Honey believes that the absence of their signatures makes the Geneva Declaration the work of other men, who, if not the participants in the conference, prepared the report? Such petty quibbling amounts to distortion.

Mr. Honey's statements that the war is controlled from North Vietnam and could be ended by the recall of North Vietnamese forces are grossly inaccurate and misleading. The Chief of the United States military operation for Vietnam has stated "that the guerrillas are neither reinforced nor supplied from North Vietnam, China or any place else" and depend for weapons on what they capture (*Washington Post,* March 6, 1963.)

The National Liberation Front has a non-communist majority and a programme of neutrality. The United States maintains the only foreign troops in Vietnam, refuses elections provided by the Geneva agreements, has placed nearly eight million people in barbed wire camps with machine gun turrets and patrolled by dogs, conducted 50,000 air attacks on villages in 1962 alone, razed the country with chemicals and napalm, killed 160,000 maimed 700,000, and imprisoned 350,000.

The South Vietnamese Government and Army are American puppets financed by $1,500,000 daily. When the United States ceases its war of atrocity against a popular national movement and accepts the neutrality agreed 10 years ago, the war will end.

The United States should be condemned as an aggressor by the United Nations for its atrocity-ridden war of annihilation in Vietnam.

Yours faithfully, Bertrand Russell
Plas Penrhyn, Penrhyndeudraeth, Merioneth, Aug. 24

---

38. See Robert McNamara, *In Retrospect* (Random House, 1995), p. 74.

[256]

# Vietnam

*The Times* (3rd September, 1964), p. 11 | C64.68

*In his reply to the* The Times *(August 31), Honey insisted that the Final Declaration of the Geneva Conference was not, as Russell had originally claimed, signed by Anthony Eden. And he denounces Russell's charges about the nature of U.S. conduct in Vietnam as "fantasy," and accuses Russell of repeating "Communist propaganda." Russell cites his sources and discusses the meaning of "signed."*

Sir, —The sources of my statements concerning Vietnam to which Mr. P.J. Honey takes exception (August 31) were: Mr. Peyrefitte, the French Foreign Office; *The Washington Post* (6.3.63); *Newsweek* (10.12.62); *Time* Magazine (17.5.63); *The Observer* (3.11.63); *Voice of America* (6.1.63);The White Paper of the Democratic Party of Vietnam, whose motto is "For the Defeat of Communism in the Interest of Free Men EVERYWHERE"; and the *Los Angeles Times* (19.10.62). All the above sources are anti-Communist and unlikely to repeat "some of the wilder excesses of North Vietnamese Communist propaganda". There are many other sources of equal respectability, though merely written in English or translated into English giving the same information which I might have used.

As to Sir Anthony Eden's not having signed the Final Declaration of the 1954 Geneva Conference on Indo-China, I am aware that there were no actual signatories to the Declaration—advisedly, in order that Mr. Dulles might be able to support a Declaration that was also supported by Mr. Chou En-lai. But the word "signed" is commonly used for the support of the representative of a nation upholding such a declaration on the part of that nation. I find distasteful the lack of humanity which in such a case as this believes it necessary to quibble over words for well-known deeds.[39]

Yours faithfully, Bertrand Russell
Plas Penrhyn, Penrhyndeudraeth, Merioneth, Aug. 31.

---

39. In his *Vietnam: History, Documents, and Opinions* (Mentor, 1970), Marvin Gettleman says, regarding the Final Declaration, "This section of the Geneva Agreements was not signed by any nation, but rather agreed to by voice vote" (p. 182).

[257]

## Vietnam

*The Times* (27th October, 1964), p. 11 | C64.77

*P.J. Honey, in his letter to the* Times *of September 19th, had claimed that Russell's citations don't support his allegations of American atrocities in Vietnam and accused Russell of attacking not only him, but the "whole non-Communist press." Russell responds.*

Sir, —Mr. Honey's ignorance of the war in Vietnam passes credibility. He contends (September 19) that the whole of the non-communist press is in contradiction to the quotations I have cited in my previous letters. Is he unaware of the speech of Senator Morse[40] in the United States or the statement by the American Federation of Scientists that "chemical poisons are used by the United States in South Vietnam. The United States is using Vietnam as a battlefield and proving ground for chemical and biological warfare"?

Ninety percent of the data I have compiled on the war in Vietnam derives from western newspapers. Mr. Honey claims not to be able to discover support in my citations for the charge that American atrocities have taken place. To take one of the six I mentioned: "The United States Air Force carried out 50,000 attacks on villages in 1962 and on virtually all of the rural population outside of strategic hamlets."—Voice of America, 6 January, 1963.

My other citations concern the strategic hamlet programme and the forced labour, torture, disembowelment and other atrocities which have occurred in these camps. I do not believe that Mr. Honey is unaware that the strategic hamlets have been set up under the direction of Americans in accordance with the Staley-Taylor Plan.[41]

---

40. Wayne Morse (1900–1975) was professor and dean of of the law school at the University of Oregon (1931–1944) and U.S. Senator from Oregon (1944–1968). He was one of two members of Congress to vote against the Tonkin Gulf Resolution (1964) which authorized President Johnson to escalate U.S. military involvement in Vietnam.

41. The Staley-Taylor Plan (named for Professor Eugene Staley and General Maxwell Taylor) was a plan to pacify the rural population in the South by separating them from the Vietcong guerillas by means of "strategic hamlets," i.e. concentration camps. The plan was put into effect in 1961 and ended in 1963 with the removal of Diem.

Those who wish to know the nature of the war in Vietnam may obtain material documented from western sources from the office of the Bertrand Russell Peace Foundation.

Yours faithfully, Bertrand Russell
Bertrand Russell Peace Foundation, 3 & 4 Shavers Place, Haymarket, S.W.1

[258]

## Russell and Vietnam

*The Observer* (20th March, 1965), p. 28 | C65.15

*In this letter and the next, Russell resumes his dispute with the* Observer's *Far Eastern Correspondent, Dennis Bloodworth (see above, document [249]).*

*Russell cites Bloodworth's article of the previous month affirming the non-Communist nature of the guerrilla movement in the South and asks why Bloodworth accused him of spreading Communist propaganda.*

Sir, —In the *Observer* of February 21 Mr. Dennis Bloodworth discovers:—

"For the past 11 years the United States has backed a succession of quasi-dictatorial, sometimes oppressive regimes in Saigon that were despised or even hated by the Vietnamese people . . . Most Vietcong guerrilla leaders are not Communists but genuine Nationalists who fought with the Vietminh and against the French colonial forces in the Indochina war solely to win independence for Vietnam. . . .Give them clean, democratic and progressive rulers who worked for the people and not for themselves, and they could be drawn away from the Communists. . . . Sources in the Liberation Front itself have confirmed that only 10 percent of their followers are Communists."

Mr. Bloodworth cites the year 1962, a time when I had been appealing in vain to the Western Press to note the fact that the "Vietcong" were a national movement, representing the whole population, enjoying their support and struggling for the independence of their country. Mr. Bloodworth states:—

"Like most North Vietnamese officials, he [Pham Ngoc Thuan] would accept any progressive Government in Saigon that was thrown up by unrigged nation-wide elections organised during a cease-fire."

Why did Mr. Bloodworth denounce me for spreading Communist

propaganda when I tried to alert Western opinion to the facts about this war of atrocity in Vietnam? If you knew the truth about the Vietcong in 1962, why are you still justifying the American attacks on the Democratic Republic of Vietnam in 1965? The record of the Western Press over the war in Vietnam is a sorry one.

Bertrand Russell
S.W.1.

············· [259] ·············

## Reports from Vietnam

*The Observer* (4th April, 1965), p. 28 | C65.22

*In his response to Russell's previous letter (C65.15), Bloodworth had continued to maintain that Russell's charge of chemical and gas warfare was unsubstantiated, since Russell, by his own admission, had based it on reports from North Vietnam. Also, his characterization of strategic hamlets as "concentration camps," was said to be "grossly misleading." Russell insists that his evidence was originally from the Western press.*

Sir, —Mr. Bloodworth seeks to dismiss my charge that the United States has constructed concentration camps and has used widely poisonous chemicals by suggesting that my source is the Foreign Minister of North Vietnam. He knows this is not the case. My information originally came from Western newspapers to which Mr. Bloodworth has long had access. *Time* magazine stated on May 17, 1963: ". . . 8,000,000 villagers are living in 'hamlets'. . . . The basic element of the plan is to resettle the entire rural population in 'strategic hamlets' with bamboo fences, barbed wire and armed militiamen."

*The Dallas Morning News* stated on June 1, 1963: "Vietnamese farmers are forced at gunpoint into these virtual concentration camps. Their homes, possessions and crops are burned. In the province of Kien Tuong seven villagers had their stomachs slashed and livers extracted and put on display. They were women and children . . . A dozen mothers were decapitated before the eyes of compatriots . . . Expectant mothers had their stomach ripped and unborn babies removed."

Mr. Bloodworth, in his previous reply (February, 1964), stated that the defoliants were drunk from canisters by South Vietnamese officials. Even if the chemicals were restricted to defoliants, all of them are toxic and have been banned in the U.S. and Great Britain. I do not suggest to Mr. Bloodworth that he emulate the procedure of the South Vietnamese officials. I do suggest that he examine the facts and make them known.

The failure of Western intellectuals to expose the atrocities in Vietnam, although they have known of them, is comparable to the silence of Communists during the time of Stalin about which Western liberals prate so much.

Bertrand Russell
S.W.1.

[260]

## Routine

*The Nation* (28th June, 1965), p. 685 | C65.28

*Penetrating the euphemistic use of language by the Pentagon posed a significant challenge to those trying to understand the nature of the war—a point which Russell fully understood.*

Dear Sirs: Reports from Vietnam that napalm is dropped regularly on "Vietcong positions" euphemistically show that the United States is burning alive hundreds of Vietnamese as routine policy. I ask people to try to understand imaginatively what this means.

Bertrand Russell

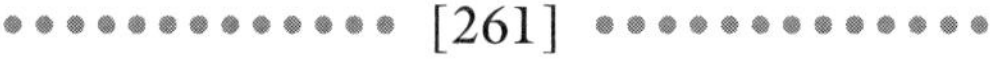
[261]

## Vietnam Teach-in

*The Observer* (11th July, 1965), p. 26 | C65.30

*Russell takes issue with the* Observer*'s account of the British Foreign Secretary's performance during a Vietnam teach-in and debate at Oxford. At this time the U.S. State Department began a campaign to justify American escalation against North Vietnam by characterizing the Vietnam conflict as essentially a matter of aggression from the North.*

Sir, —In your issue of July 4 you state: "Professor Morgenthau[42] . . . suffered. . . the same sort of drubbing which Michael Stewart[43] gave his opponents at Oxford." I am amazed at the insistence of the British Press that the Foreign Secretary answered satisfactorily any of the questions put to him at Oxford. In fact, the speech of the Foreign Secretary was composed of a series of bald terminological inexactitudes regarding the reality of events in Vietnam.

The Foreign Secretary maintained that it was the North which prevented elections from being held, despite the repeated requests of Ho Chi Minh[44] for election under international supervision in both North and South Vietnam and the statements by American officials, such as President Eisenhower, that any election would mean a vote of 80 percent for Ho Chi Minh. The Foreign Secretary maintained that the war was one of aggression from the North and sustained through Northern arms and troops, although General Harkins, the American officer in charge, stated categorically: "The guerrillas are not being reinforced or supplied systematically from North Vietnam, China or any place else. They depend for weapons primarily on whatever they can capture" (*Washington Post*, March 6, 1963); and *The New York Times* (March 6, 1964) has stated: "No capture of North Vietnamese in the South has come to light."

Bertrand Russell
S.W.1.

[262]

## Waiting for Visas

*The Times* (25th August, 1965), p. 9 | C65.33

*Russell, writing under the auspices of the Bertrand Russell Peace Foundation, draws attention to the dilatory actions of the Home Office regarding participation of NLF representatives at British teach-ins on Vietnam.*

42. Hans Morgenthau was a professor of history and political science at the University of Chicago.

43. Michael Stewart (1906–1990) was a British statesman and Foreign Secretary in the Labour Government (1965–66).

44. Ho Chi Minh (1890–1969) was the revered Vietnamese Communist leader in the struggle for independence from France and President of North Vietnam during the height of American military intervention.

Sir, —During the famous Oxford teach-in the Foreign Secretary stated: "It seems to me an excellent thing that students should have the opportunity of having access to news, information, and comment from all over the world, that they should be able, in the light of that, to form their own opinions and to express those opinions freely. I am very glad that we have had and are to have more of these teach-ins in this country."

At none of the many teach-ins in Britain has it been possible to hear the point of view of the representatives of the National Liberation Front or of North Vietnam. If Mr. Cabot Lodge could come to present the point of view of the United States Government on Vietnam it would, surely, be in keeping with the words of the Foreign Secretary that the spokesman on foreign affairs for the Central Committee of the National Liberation Front in South Vietnam should also be allowed to come to Britain to speak at teach-ins.

Three leading members of the National Liberation Front are waiting to visit Britain so that the people of Britain may have an opportunity to hear their views. I have made application on their behalf for visas to the Home Office on July 21. In a matter as important as this, one might expect the Home Office to make a favourable decision quickly. It is now one month that we have been waiting for the Home Office to act.

We have been overwhelmed with enquiries from people throughout Britain anxious to hear the representatives of the National Liberation Front in this country, and we hold that the British Government has a responsibility, in keeping with British traditions, to permit them to present their case.

Yours faithfully, Bertrand Russell.

Bertrand Russell Peace Foundation, 3–4 Shavers Place, Haymarket, S.W.1.

[263]

# Vietnam Manifesto

*The New Statesman and Nation* (24th June, 1966), p. 928 | C66.12

*By the summer of 1966 the U.S. had 285,000 troops in Vietnam and the bombing of the North was intense. Russell believed that any just settlement required U.S. departure, and he calls for support for the "defeat of the United States and the victory of the Vietnamese," and likens their fight to that of the British against Hitler.*

*In June, Russell and his colleagues organized the Vietnam Solidarity Campaign, with Russell as its president, to disseminate throughout the U.K. information about the atrocious nature of the war. About the same time he conceived the idea of a war crimes tribunal to sit in judgment of U.S. conduct. See below, document [267].*

Sir, —Many people who had hopes of opposition at last within the Labour movement will be disappointed by the Vietnam Manifesto. It does not constitute a contribution to the cause of justice and peace in Vietnam, but is a different formulation of Wilson's policy of complicity.

The United States is the blatant aggressor in Vietnam and it is impossible to expect the Vietnamese to permit the aggressor to be the arbiter of a provisional government. It only promotes confusion if we slide over our moral responsibility to stand side by side with the victim against the aggressor. The demand for peace in areas where people are struggling for their economic and political emancipation.

In Vietnam the United States is using gas, chemicals and napalm. They are bombing hospitals and sanatoria. They have no more right to use their occupation of Vietnam as a basis for suggesting terms of a settlement of their own aggression than had the Nazis in Yugoslavia. The issue is as clear as the blitz, but it is more grave. Nazi Germany did not invade Britain, nor did Nazi Germany commit war crimes against Britain involving gas, chemicals, fragmentation bombs or the placing of sixty per cent of the rural population in concentration camps. Yet Churchill declared that Britain would fight on the beaches, fight for decades, if necessary, but would never surrender. Churchill went further, calling for the unconditional surrender of the Nazis and for conquest of Germany. The Vietnamese do not propose occupation of Washington. Their demand is simple: that the aggressor get out.

It is an unwarranted concession to the brute force of imperialism for socialists in the West to bargain with the rights of the oppressed by demanding that the Americans, who perpetrate such terrible war crimes and who have been in occupation of Vietnam for twelve years should set their conditions for an end to their own aggression. All of us have the duty to struggle for the defeat of the United States and the victory of the Vietnamese, just as we had that responsibility in support of those resisting Hitler a quarter of a century earlier.

Bertrand Russell<br>
President, Vietnam Solidarity Campaign<br>
London, SW7

[264]

# Vietnam Manifesto

*The New Statesman and Nation* (8th July, 1966), p. 52 | C66.17

*Here Russell points out the David-and-Goliath nature of the American war in Vietnam and its moral implications.*

Sir, —There is a basic moral and political difference between the Vietnamese resistance and the American aggression. A tiny, physically weak country has been barbarously assaulted by a colossus. Is there no spark of human decency in those who fail to understand the monstrous injustice involved in the use by the United States of its massive power to obliterate a non-industrial and hungry Asian people struggling for the most elementary rights of self-determination and social advance?

A peace movement which is blind to the David and Goliath character of this conflict is unworthy of the name. That the US, with all its air power and destructive force, with poison gas, chemicals and razor bombs, can bombard and torment a small people without evoking an immediate response of solidarity for the beleaguered victim against the savage bully, speaks for itself.

Expulsion of the US from Vietnam can only be effected through the struggle of the Vietnamese and the courage of people in the West to undertake resistance against their governments not unlike that undertaken by those few Germans who did what they could to stop Hitler.

What is called support for the "military victory of one side" is support for the rights of victimised human beings everywhere who ought to be regarded as our brothers and not as the occasion for the unpleasant display of disguised callousness.

The Solidarity Campaign stand with the people of Vietnam. We do them no favour. The barbarism against which they struggle virtually alone is our own and we may yet learn what napalm and torture mean if we do not stop it.

Bertrand Russell
President, Vietnam Solidarity Campaign
8 Roland Gardens, SW7

[265]

## Vietcong Wrong

*The Guardian* (13th July, 1966), p. 10 | C66.18

*Russell, ever sensitive to the role of language in political persuasion, eschews the label "Vietcong" as U.S. propaganda and as untrue to the NLF's "broad alliance."*

Sir, —"Miscellany" (July 6) refers erroneously to the "Victory for the Vietcong" banners of the Vietnam Solidarity Campaign. "Vietcong" is a slang expression meaning "commie" and was invented by the United States Information Service. Our support is for the the National Liberation Front which leads the people of South Vietnam in their 12-year struggle against American aggression. The NLF is a broad alliance ranging from Catholics to Communists and it is important to note that our banners avoid the term "Vietcong".

Yours faithfully, Bertrand Russell
President, Vietnam Solidarity Campaign
Merioneth

[266]

## Bertrand Russell Replies on Vietnam

*Tribune* (2nd September, 1966), p. 7 | C66.26

*Francis Flavius, a political columnist for* Tribune, *had criticized Russell's cable to Premier Kosygin appealing for Soviet military help against American bombardment of North Vietnam, pointing out its apparent inconsistency with his efforts to avoid super-power confrontation during the Cuban Missile Crisis. Russell defends his recent appeal on "grounds of elementary morality" and argues that defensive intervention before "the penultimate moment" is the best way to avoid the imminent danger that we faced in the Cuban crisis.*

Francis Flavius (*Tribune*, August 26) is critical of my cable to Premier Kosygin, which he apparently has not read. I asked the Premier to turn part of the Soviet air force over to the Vietnamese for the purpose of defending the territory of Vietnam against the unrelenting air bombardment of the United States.

The issue which Francis Flavius chooses to raise is that of increasing the dangers of World War III and he compares my appeal to Kosygin with my request to Khrushchev and Kennedy to draw back from confrontation over Cuba.

The fundamental problem in both crises has been how is this world war to be averted without sacrificing the rights of the oppressed people whose social revolution was under such vicious attack by the United States. I am in no doubt that had the Soviet Union made clear at the time of the Bay of Tonkin that the Soviet air force would defend Vietnam against air attack, that air attack would not have occurred. The vast bombardment of a small people without an air force is the supreme atrocity and it is too terrible for supposed allies to allow such destruction to be rained on an heroic people, pitting their revolutionary spirit against the evil and gigantic power of the largest military arsenal possessed by any nation in the history of warfare. Thus, on grounds of elementary morality, there is an absolute obligation incumbent upon the Soviet Union, which has the means to accomplish adequately the defence of Vietnam against air attack.

I should point out to Francis Flavius that every piece of evidence we have about the war in Vietnam shows that the United States tests the water before plunging in. The Bay of Tonkin incident was faked, preparatory to full-scale bombardment of the North. World reaction was observed in between time. An incident involving poison gas took place before the massive and indiscriminate use of the gas was undertaken. Air strikes on the periphery of Hanoi and Haiphong were performed before direct strikes on these cities were risked. In all these instances, the pattern is that of Hitler's in the Rhineland and in Czechoslovakia.

Those who are anxious to prevent world war without betraying the Vietnamese revolution must consider how this is really to be done. It is too easy to say any defence of the Vietnamese is a provocation to the bully and the aggressor. On the contrary, unless the Soviet Union intervenes now with its air force to protect Vietnam, American imperialism will extend the scale of the war outside Vietnam precisely as it has within Vietnam. The Soviet Union will then be obliged to intervene on a massive scale or to permit the United States to carry on in its aggression. The lesson of appeasement is that nothing is gained by delay. In fact, delay makes more likely the larger conflict later.

The Soviet air force over Vietnam is clearly a defensive action restricting the conflict to the borders of Vietnam, but when Laos, Cambodia, Thailand and China are attacked the problem of the Soviet Union will be vastly more serious. It is precisely because that penultimate moment will be more likely to occur that the Soviet Union is asked to act now, the better to avoid having the penultimate moment the only moment when it is possible to intervene.

Francis Flavius advances the official Soviet view regarding China's unwillingness to let Soviet military equipment and personnel pass through its territory. The Russians have been asked to say that an attack on China would be an attack on the Soviet Union. They decline to do this. The implications of such a refusal when combined with the request that Chinese territory should be so used, is clear.

Francis Flavius is late in supporting the Vietnamese, for he has been occupied, in the page of *Tribune*, with pressing on them formulae for negotiations which would ratify the American aggression and the presence of American troops in Vietnam. If a world war is to be avoided, universal defence of the Vietnamese is the first prerequisite. Sitting on one's hands while the Americans do their worst is the surest way to bring the world to the point of no return, the point at which Cuba was in 1962.

Bertrand Russell
London, S.W.1.

## *International War Crimes Tribunal*

••••••••••••• [267] •••••••••••••

### The War Crimes Tribunal: Lord Russell Writes

*The Boston Globe* (4th August, 1966), p. 18 | C66.20

*Here Russell defends the rights of the North Vietnamese to try American pilots for the "supreme atrocity." He also announces the formation of a War Crimes Tribunal to document the criminal nature of the American conduct in Vietnam.*

The recent outcry in the United States about the proposed trial of American pilots is revealing. These pilots have chosen consciously to bomb civilian areas and, in doing so, have killed agonizingly thousands of people. Not only do they know their targets, but they are fully aware of the weapons they employ. These are weapons of sheer evil, including canisters containing ten thousand slivers of razor-sharp steel (the lazy dog), and napalm, which turns the victim into a bubbling mass. The vast bombardment of a small people, unable adequately to defend themselves against 650 sorties a week involving 1500 tons a day, is the supreme atrocity.

Not only are the Vietnamese within their rights to try their tormentors, but the indifference in the United States to the fate of their victims while the trail of pilots who are responsible for definite war crimes is decried, can be nothing other than racism.

The American press and television have carried pictures and reports of the consistent mutilation and torture of Vietnamese prisoners by the puppet regime of Ky, with American connivance and participation. Let it be clear that the Vietnamese are the victims of American aggression and have the sympathy of every decent human being including, I feel certain, increasing numbers of Americans with a conscience.

It is to document the war crimes perpetrated by the United States that our international War Crime Tribunal, whose members include to date Lelio Basso, former President Cardenas, Josue de Castro, Simone de Beauvoir, Vladimir Dedijer, Danilo Dolci, Isaac Deutscher, Jean-Paul Sartre and Peter Weiss is being urgently prepared.

Bertrand Russell
Bertrand Russell Peace Foundation
London, England

[268]

## Bertrand Russell Replies

*The New York Herald Tribune* (14th September, 1966), p. 4 | C66.30

*Russell replies to an editorial critical of him and the planned international war crimes tribunal. He compares the editor's dismissal of the tribunal with "Nazi attempts to laugh off the Nuremberg trials." This is one of several letters defending the concept of such a tribunal.*

To the *Herald Tribune:*

You state editorially (Aug. 4) that the forthcoming international war crimes tribunal to hear evidence of U.S. actions in Vietnam "will look queerly in history"; you describe me as a "now shadowy figure"; and you contend that it is "extremely doubtful" whether the tribunal "can produce any evidence of any acts" in the war in Vietnam "that will come as a surprise to anybody."

These are three serious charges. On the first question I do not fear the verdict of history, which is likely to be far more favourable than on, say, the *Herald Tribune*'s prompt endorsement of the Warren Commission

Report. Your second charge is too silly either for you to be explicit or for me to reply, but I note that you are already agitated by my shadow. Your third comment is enlightening. I understand that evidence will be presented of the destruction of over 30 hospitals, 120 schools and kindergartens, thousands of pupils and hundreds of villages in North Vietnam in 1965 alone.

There are many Americans who will be profoundly surprised and shocked at such news, which is why every day brings me cables, letters, money and offers of assistance for this tribunal from all over the world—not least from U.S. citizens. They know how history will judge the use of napalm, gas, chemicals and razor darts and the vast bombardment by a giant nation of a small agrarian people.

Your attempt to dismiss the Paris tribunal as a "big show" that "might do well on Broadway" is reminiscent of Nazi attempts to laugh off the Nuremberg trails. All that is established is your support for the actions of those accused of war crimes.

Bertrand Russell
London

[269]

## War in Vietnam

*The Times* (21st September, 1966), p. 11 | C66.32

*Russell explains the function of the War Crimes Tribunal and names several of its members. He also quotes American Supreme Court Justice Jackson on the significance of Nuremberg and the rule of law.*

Sir, —Professor Dedijer (September 12) raises several important points concerning the international War Crimes Tribunal which require elaboration. The Tribunal is not conducting a trial entailing an adversary procedure with defence counsel and defence witnesses. We are unable to compel defence witnesses to appear and so could not guarantee a proper court trial.

President Johnson has been asked to appear or to designate official representatives to defend American policy. This, however, does not change the fact that the Tribunal functions as a commission of inquiry, with *prima facie* evidence of crimes, sufficient to induce it to investigate exhaustively the evidence.

There is no suggestion on our part that the esteemed members of the Tribunal, who include: Gunther Anders, Lelio Basso, Simone de

Beauvoir, former President Lazaro Cardenas, Stokely Carmichael, Josue de Castro, Vladimir Dedijer, Isaac Deutscher, Danilo Dolci, Jean-Paul Sartre and Peter Weiss, are impartial in the sense that they have no opinions concerning the occurrence of war crimes in Vietnam.[45] On the contrary, their deep feeling that *prima facie* evidence of such crimes exists is responsible for the convening of this international War Crimes Tribunal.

The Tribunal, nonetheless, will view evidence fairly and draw only such conclusions as the evidence itself will sustain. The data will be publicly available, as will the testimony of witnesses and victims. The proceedings will last approximately 12 weeks.

Large numbers of Vietnamese will testify. Scientific expertise will be fully employed in the assessing of the chemicals, gases, bacteriological poison, and other unique weaponry used widely in Vietnam. Investigative teams are gathering all data, which will be presented to the appropriate commission appointed to prepare evidence in a given area by the Tribunal.

American Supreme Court Justice Robert H. Jackson, Chief Counsel at Nuremberg, stated:—

"The real complaining party at the bar is civilisation. Civilisation is asking whether law is so laggard as to be utterly helpless to deal with crimes of such magnitude as Germany's. . . .

"Civilisation expects this Tribunal to put the forces of international law, its precepts, its prohibitions and most of its sanctions on the side of peace. . . .

"Certainly no future lawyer or nation undertaking to prosecute crimes against the peace of the world will have to face the argument that the effort is unprecedented and, therefore, by inference, improper. . . .

"If certain acts and violation of treaties are crimes, they are crimes whether the United States does them or whether Germany does them. We are not prepared to say down a rule of criminal conduct against others which we would not be willing to have invoked against us."

Yours faithfully, Bertrand Russell
Bertrand Russell Peace Foundation
3 and 4 Shavers Place, Haymarket S.W.1. Sept. 17

---

45. Those listed here plus another 13 eventually comprised the Tribunal. These 24 individuals of international repute included philosophers, scientists, playwrights, legal scholars, social reformers, and national political leaders. Details of the Tribunal may be found in *Against the Crime of Silence: Proceedings of the Russell International War Crimes Tribunal*, ed. John Duffett (O'Hare, 1968).

[270]

# Partisan Defence in Vietnam

*The Daily Telegraph* (30th September, 1966), p. 16 | C66.34

*Russell responds to a correspondent critical of the War Crimes Tribunal.*

Sir, —Mr. Stephen Spingarn[46] (Sept. 21) engages in *ad hominem* abuse as a substitute for consideration of the issues involved in holding a war crimes tribunal for the purpose of assessing the acts of the United States Government in Vietnam.

Mr. Spingarn is extraordinarily ignorant of the Vietnamese war, which undoubtedly accounts for his inability to understand the relevance of such a tribunal. He purports to be unaware of the repeatedly documented fact that the National Liberation Front is an indigenous partisan movement of resistance, enjoying the support of virtually all peasants of the south.

If this were not true, the unparalleled military power of the industrial United States would have achieved its end of exterminating the brave Vietnamese who struggle to liberate their country from American domination and occupation.

I should remind Mr. Spingarn, and those for whom he speaks, that more Vietnamese died between 1954 and 1959 than since 1960, when the National Liberation Front first undertook armed resistance to the unparalleled repression and savagery of Diem, under the aegis of the United States.

There is a guerrilla war being waged now against an occupying power which employs poison gas, chemicals, napalm, razor darts and the relentless bombardment of a small country without an air force. I am not silent about the resistance of the National Liberation Front or the death at its hands of tribal chiefs and large landlords, who serve as Quislings and oppress the people. I am very vocal in my support of the National Liberation Front, which I regard in the same way as I did the resistance in France, Norway, Denmark, and Jugoslavia and the uprising of the Warsaw Ghetto.

The members of the international war crimes tribunal are Gunther Anders, Lelio Basso, Simone de Beauvoir, former President Lazaro Cardenas, Stokely Carmichael, Josue de Castro, Vladimir Dedijer, Danilo Dolci, Isaac Deutscher, Jean-Paul Sartre and Peter Weiss. They

46. Stephen J. Spingarn was a Washington, D.C. writer of letters to the editor.

Russell had written an 'Open Letter to Eisenhower and Khrushchev' in the *New Statesman and Nation* (23rd November, 1957), urging a summit meeting to consider the conditions for peaceful co-existence. Khrushchev responded favorably. Eventually, Secretary of State John Foster Dulles replied for Eisenhower. See document [128]. The cartoon by Duncan Macpherson, depicting Dulles, Khrushchev, and Russell, appeared in the *Toronto Star* (9th January, 1959).

will function as a commission of inquiry, and evidence will be heard in public, after having been examined by the most scientific authorities.

I am confident that public opinion will know how to assess the findings of the tribunal, as well as the ill-informed abuse of American apologists for atrocities, such as your correspondent from Washington.

Yours faithfully, Bertrand Russell,
London, S.W.1.

••••••••••••• [271] •••••••••••••

## War in Vietnam

*The Times* (30th September, 1966), p. 11 | C66.35

*In his response to Peter Kemp, Russell draws a distinction between the violence of aggressors and the defensive violence of innocent victims, and he invokes the model of resistance to Nazi aggression in World War II.*

Sir, —Mr. Kemp[47] (September 26) suffers from the inability to distinguish the violence of an oppressed people from that of the overwhelmingly powerful invader. His letter does not suggest that he is a pacifist. Were he a pacifist, he might, more convincingly, dissociate from the violence to which the National Liberation Front must resort in order to repel the aggressor who occupies their country and inflicts incalculable suffering. The partisans of Yugoslavia and the Jews of the Warsaw Ghetto had the same claim on our allegiance in relation to the Gestapo.

Donald Duncan,[48] a Special Forces officer of the United States Army, has recently revealed, from years of experience, that the guerrillas enjoy the ardent support of the entire rural population, which accounts for their ability to survive and overcome the terrible weaponry and the great power of the United States and its puppet army. Mr. Duncan further makes clear that the executions carried out by the guerrillas have been of those village chiefs and landlords who, in serving the corrupt feudal regime, have tortured, dismembered or in other ways tormented the villagers over whom they had control. The restaurant to which Mr. Kemp

---

47. Peter Kemp was a naval historian and literary editor for the London *Sunday Times.*

48. Donald Duncan was one of many U.S. military personnel who testified before the War Crimes Tribunal.

refers was a place habituated by senior American officers and intelligence personnel. This made it a clear target for the Vietnamese resistance.

The War Crimes Tribunal is concerned with the war of aggression in Vietnam and the unique weaponry employed by the United States as it tries to destroy a national revolution. We do not regard the violence of the resistance as a crime, because we are able to distinguish the victim from the aggressor, as easily as we could distinguish the Jews of the Warsaw Ghetto from the Gestapo. Even a pacifist, abhorring all violence, would be morally obliged to recognize that much.

Yours faithfully, Bertrand Russell
Bertrand Russell Peace Foundation,
3 and 4 Shavers Place, Haymarket, S.W.1. Sept. 28.

[272]

## Russell Defends War Crimes Trial

*The New York Times* (6th October, 1966), p. 46 | C66.39

*Russell defends the Tribunal against criticisms from a* New York Times *editorial. Again, Russell cites Supreme Court Justice Jackson, Chief Counsel at Nuremberg, on justice and the law.*

To the Editor:

*The New York Times* (Sept. 10) reports from Saigon that the United States, "pleased with the effectiveness of chemical defoliation and crop destruction missions. . . is taking steps to triple the capability of those efforts." The Times further reports that in this year alone "1,324,430 gallons" have been sprayed.

Let me state first of all that I possess documentary evidence of the toxic character of these chemicals and of their extraordinary effects on human beings, which include paralysis, blindness, convulsions, hallucination and inability to achieve unconsciousness (to fall asleep).

You have published a letter criticizing our War Crimes Tribunal on the ground that the judges should not also be accusers [July 5]. This criticism rests on a basic misconception of the nature of the tribunal.

We are not establishing an adversary proceeding, because we cannot compel Government witnesses to appear in their own defense, although President Johnson has been invited either to come or to appoint representatives. Rather, the tribunal functions as a commission of inquiry, formed by men who have *prima facie* evidence of crimes and, like a grand jury, have brought an indictment.

We are not stones without feeling, oblivious to the barrage of evidence concerning war crimes in Vietnam. We are people compelled by conscience to form a tribunal because we have witnessed the crimes against the people of Vietnam and wish to examine exhaustively their full meaning, with a view to assessing the responsibility of those who have perpetrated them.

Americans are familiar with the bringing of indictments on the basis of *prima facie* evidence and also with the precedent of the Dewey Commission[49] which, composed of eminent international figures, examined fairly the evidence concerning Stalin's purge trials in the late 1930's.

### Assessing Responsibility

I suggest that those who raise procedural points in objecting to the international War Crimes Tribunal would be better occupied in assessing their own responsibility for the horrendous acts against the people of Vietnam, acts which our tribunal will examine relentlessly and exhaustively.

Justice Robert H. Jackson, Chief Counsel at Nuremberg, stated:

"If certain acts and violation of treaties are crimes, they are crimes whether the United States does them or whether Germany does them. We are not prepared to lay down a rule of criminal conduct against others which we would not be willing to have invoked against us."

Bertrand Russell,
London, Sept. 16, 1966

••••••••••••• [273] •••••••••••••

## Vietnam Guilt

*The New Statesmen and Nation* (21st October, 1966), p. 586 | C66.42

*In this powerful letter, Russell rejects the idea that there is moral equivalence between "two sides" in Vietnam, and he affirms the moral disgrace of those who witness a crime "in silence."*

---

49. John Dewey (1859–1952) was an American philosopher and educator. In 1937 his commission heard evidence in Mexico from Leon Trotsky and others, regarding Stalin's 'show trials' of 1935 and 1936.

Sir, —Mr. Philip Toynbee,[50] in his letter last week, exemplifies the group of intellectuals who gave full support to Stalin during the ugliest and most morally vile period of his rule and, consequently, have occupied themselves ever since with discovering such propensities in others. In one sense, I can sympathise with Mr.Toynbee's fear to identify himself with a cause again as he was so terrifyingly wrong before. But that same insensitivity which led such people to identify the revolution and socialism with Stalinism now permits Mr. Toynbee to decry the unequivocal support given by me to the Vietnamese.

Mr. Toynbee says there must be two sides to this war. Why? Why should we equivocate about the monstrous injustice involved in the US crime against a small people? Why should the Jews shovelled into gas chambers suffer also the disgraceful moral ambivalence of those who sought justification for Nazi barbarism? There are not two sides in Vietnam. Jose Marti[51] said: "He who witnesses a crime in silence, commits it." "We," said Eichmann, [52] "only provided the lorries." Marti and Eichmann man the barricades of a moral divide, and between them such even as Mr. Philip Toynbee must choose. Vietnam is an acid test for this generation of Western intellectuals.

Bertrand Russell
Penrhyndeudraeth, Merioneth

[274]

## Lord Russell's Denial

*Newsweek* (24th April, 1967), p. 4 | C67.09

*In 1967 Russell sold his papers to McMaster University in Hamilton, Ontario, where the Bertrand Russell Archives and Bertrand Russell Research Centre are currently located. Russell denies a* Newsweek *report that proceeds from the sale will go to "Communist forces in Vietnam."*

---

50. Philip Toynbee (1916–1981) was a British editor and writer. He was the son of historian Arnold Toynbee and grandson of Gilbert Murray, the Oxford classicist and long-time friend of Russell. Toynbee was on the editorial staff of *The Observer*. Like many British leftists, but not Russell, he was slow to acknowledge Stalin's crimes before World War II.

51. Jose Marti (1853–1895) was a Cuban poet and leader of the movement for independence.

52. Adolf Eichmann (1906–1962) was the Nazi official in charge of "the final solution." He was extradited from Argentina in 1960 and hanged in 1962.

The item published by *Newsweek* (*The Periscope,* April 17) stating that I intend giving the proceeds of the sale of my private papers to the "Communist forces in Vietnam" is totally false.

Bertrand Russell
Penrhyndeudraeth, Wales

[275]

## Who is "Undesirable"?

*The Observer* (25th June, 1967), p. 14 | C67.15

*Russell relates the British government's immigration practice towards Tribunal members; he reveals an inconsistency between the Home Office and Prime Minister Wilson. The hostility of the British government to the Tribunal is the main reason that the proceedings of the Tribunal were held abroad: the first session in Stockholm, Sweden (2nd–10th May, 1967) and the second session in Copenhagen, Denmark (20th November–1st December, 1967).*

Sir, —On 28 May you published an account of the difficulties experienced by Mr. James Baldwin[53] with immigration officials at Heathrow Airport on his recent visit to London. For more than an hour and a half Mr. Baldwin was denied entry into Britain. He was informed on his arrival that the Home Office had instructed the authorities at the airport not to issue him a visa because of his association with the International War Crimes Tribunal. Mr. Baldwin was ultimately granted a visa after he had made clear that his travel to Britain at that time was in no way connected with his participation in the Tribunal. Your article went on to say: 'The Home Office says there would never be blanket exclusion of a whole category of people (e.g., those connected with the Russell Tribunal), but as to whether there were instructions to exclude Baldwin they will not comment.'

The contention of the Home Office that there would never be 'blanket exclusion of a whole category of people' seemed to be at odds with what the prime Minister had earlier informed me by letter. In a letter dated 14 March, Mr. Wilson wrote:

53. James Baldwin (1924–1987) was a black American writer and a member of the International War Crimes Tribunal.

'. . . I wish to take this opportunity to inform you that Her Majesty's Government have decided in principle to deny facilities to visit Britain to all foreigners who may seek to take part in the "International War Crimes Tribunal."' To clarify the apparent inconsistency between the statement of the Home Office as quoted by you and the position of the Government as indicated by Mr. Wilson, I wrote to Mr. Wilson on 30 May. The Prime Minister replied as follows: "No new instructions have been given to the immigration service, and the position with regard to the admission of people coming here in connection with the Tribunal remains as in my letter of March 14."

However embarrassing it may be to the Home Office, we must assume that Mr. Wilson's statement is the more authoritative. The policy indicated by Mr. Wilson clearly contravenes usual practice. To proscribe visas to such eminent literary figures as Mr. Baldwin, Jean-Paul Sartre and Peter Weiss is a disgrace to Britain or to any civilised nation. Must they be considered 'undesirable aliens' because they cannot be silent about the crimes committed against he people of Vietnam?

Bertrand Russell
Penrhyndeudraeth.

••••••••••••• [276] •••••••••••••

## Tariq Ali

*The Sun* (15th May, 1968), p. 4 | C68.14

*Tariq Ali was a journalist from Pakistan, resident in Britain, who opposed the war in Vietnam. He worked closely with the Bertrand Russell Peace Foundation's Vietnam Solidarity Campaign in 1966. And he accompanied Schoenman on various Foundation projects abroad, including Vietnam and Bolivia. See documents [212] and [245]. A year earlier, he had provided material for the Stockholm session of the International War Crimes Tribunal.*

*The Sun* reports (May 8) that the Home Secretary[54] has told the Minister of Public Building and Works[55] that he has no power to deport Mr. Tariq Ali, a leading demonstrator against the war in Vietnam, unless there is a court order for his deportation.

---

54. James Callaghan.
55. R. Mellish.

The Minister had asked the Home Secretary to send Mr. Ali home to Pakistan.

The Home Secretary's statement that he cannot do so unless there is a court order is an open invitation to the police to seek such an order and is in keeping with our Government's record of dealing with Socialist opposition by administrative fiat. Mr. Ali's demonstrations are made necessary only by the cruelty which the Government support.

Bertrand Russell,
Penrhyndeudraeth, Merioneth.

## *Czechoslovakia and the Russians*

*The following letters (except for the first which Russell signed but did not compose) were written after Russell had officially severed Ralph Schoenman's connections with the Bertrand Russell Peace Foundation. Russell's evenhandedness in his criticisms of the superpowers—a trait which he claimed to exhibit throughout the 1960s—is evident in his condemnations of the Soviet invasion of Czechoslovakia.*

[277]

## Czechoslovakia on the Brink: The Threat of Intervention

*The Times* (24th July, 1968), p. 9 | C68.18a

*Russell signs a letter to* The Times *protesting the imminent invasion of Czechoslovakia by the Soviet Union. The letter appeared as "From Lord Russell, O.M., F.R.S., and others," which caused Russell considerable consternation. See below, document [278].*

Sir, —For the third time in three decades Czechoslovakia is on the brink. In 1938 it was Munich and the German occupation, In 1948 it was the Prague coup and Stalinist rule. In 1968 Czechoslovakia is pushing through a process of reform within a socialist framework, but in line with her own democratic traditions, quietly and unprovocatively. Yet once more she is facing interference and even threats of intervention.

The Czechs are no longer "a far-away people of whom we know nothing". Their situation is being watched with sympathy and anxiety by the public in this and other countries; it has also aroused strong feelings in many communist parties. The outcome of the present crisis will affect the prospects of European, if not world, political development for years to come.

Czechoslovakia is not threatening anyone. She has a right to self-determination, yet she freely admitted military forces of the Warsaw Pact countries to prove her loyalty to them. Should her sovereignty be destroyed again, this would gravely damage any prospect of a genuine detente with the Soviet Union. All men of good will must hope that this does not happen.

Yours, &c., Bertrand Russell
Paul Johnson
Kingsley Amis
Henry Moore
Max Beloff
N.F. Mott
Lennox Berkeley
Soper
Benjamin Britten
Mervyn Southwark
Brigid Brophy
Stephen Spender
David Carver
Philip Toynbee
Hugh Casson
David Watt
Robert Conquest
Arnold Wesker
Stuart Hood
Angus Wilson
Elizabeth Jane Howard
Peregrine Worsthorne
Julian S. Huxley.
July 23

[278]

## Czechoslovakia

*The Times* (13th August 1968), p. 7 | C68.20

*Russell here refers to* The Times *letter of July 24 on Czechoslovakia which had appeared as "From Lord Russell, O.M., F.R.S., and others." According to Paul Johnson who had negotiated its appearance in* The Times, *Russell was annoyed that its appearance gave the false impression that Russell had organized the letter. Johnson says he told Russell by telephone that Russell's name was put first simply to give the letter maximum impact, and he added that since he had signed the letter, he couldn't complain that his name was listed first—"it wasn't logical." According to Johnson, Russell replied "Logical fiddlesticks," and slammed down the receiver. (See Paul Johnson,* Intellectuals *[Harper and Row, 1988], p. 224.)*

Sir, —On July 24 you published prominently a letter from a group of 23 signatories concerning the threat of intervention in Czechoslovakia. Although I agreed to join in signing this letter, I was surprised to find in your columns that, although all the other signatories were listed alphabetically, my name appeared first and also preceded the letter, so that it appeared to have been sent to you on my initiative.

I wish to explain that I did not know who would be asked to sign it. In fact I had severe doubts about some parts of the letter, but signed it because I wish to do anything at all possible to support the Czechoslovak people at this time.

Yours faithfully, Bertrand Russell.
Plas Penrhyn, Penrhyndeudraeth. Merioneth.

[279]

## The Russians in Czechoslovakia

*The Guardian* (26th August, 1968), p. 8 | C68.23

*Russell continues to protest the invasion of Czechoslovakia while exposing the double standard of those who assert the rights of small nations but endorse American action in Vietnam.*

Sir, —Many British people must feel themselves helpless spectators of the Soviet suppression of elementary liberties in Czechoslovakia. What can be done? Parliament has been recalled to debate the situation, and no doubt to repeat at Westminster the condemnations at the United Nations. But how many parliamentarians have clean hands?

Those who temporarily interrupt their applause for the American bombardment of Vietnam to discover and assert the rights of small nations are allies that must embarrass the Czechoslovaks and play into the hands of the Soviet Union. Only the refusal to renew the N.A.T.O. treaty next year would remove the last Soviet alibi for a threat to the East and ensure that the Czechoslovak and other demands for liberty were insuperable.

Such a solution would transfer power from bureaucrats to people, and must terrify governments which wish to divide the world into spheres of influence and control. Those in Britain who wish to see the Soviet Empire fall to pieces, and the nations of Eastern Europe establish an independent socialist humanism, must work for the removal of N.A.T.O. from the heart of British foreign policy.

By committing ourselves to every American invasion and to the division of Europe, we increase enormously the price that independent socialists in Eastern Europe pay for proclaiming basic liberties. And we know the price paid by Imre Nagy.[56]

Yours faithfully, Bertrand Russell
Plas Penrhyn, Penrhyndeudraeth, Merioneth.

## Czechoslovakia

*The Times* (16th September, 1968), p. 9| C68.24

*Russell refers to a cable he sent to Kosygin, a month before the Soviet invasion (20th August, 1968), asking him to affirm a policy of military restraint in Czechoslovakia. In this letter, written a month after the Soviet invasion, Russell warns of forthcoming Stalinist style "show trials" against supporters of the Dubcek reforms.*

Sir, —On July 21 I appealed to Mr. Kosygin to declare publicly that

56. Imre Nagy (1896–1958) was a Hungarian Communist politician and Prime Minister (1953–56) who took some steps to liberalize Hungarian Communism. After the Soviet invasion in 1956, he was deposed and killed.

the Soviet Union had no intention of using military force in Czechoslovakia. I received some criticisms that I was unduly alarmist. A month later Soviet tanks occupied Prague.

I write now to warn that the Soviet Union is preparing new horrors in Czechoslovakia. On September 13 you published an important article by a well known Czechoslovak intellectual. In it the author revealed that the wave of anti-Semitism in Soviet press attacks on Czechoslovakia, and the vicious treatment accorded to Mr. Frantisek Kriegel in Moscow, have been followed by Soviet demands for a show trial, to be staged with Mr. Kriegel and Professor Goldstuecker as the victims.

I have very good reason to confirm, because I have it on excellent authority, that the Soviet Union is still demanding such a trial. There is a grave danger that the Soviet Union, in its determination to stop reforms and to hide its lack of support by diverting the danger of the people both in Czechoslovakia and abroad, is pressing for a trial in the classic Stalinist tradition of the "Doctors' Plot".[57] I appeal with all the gravity at my command to socialists and communists throughout the world resolutely to oppose these Soviet demands for scapegoats.

Yours faithfully, Bertrand Russell
Plas Penrhyn, Penrhyndeudraeth, Merioneth. September 14

[281]

## Czechoslovakia

*The Times* (19th August, 1969), p. 9 | C69.12

*Russell laments the situation in Czechoslovakia on the first anniversary of the Soviet invasion. And he warns against encroachment by both superpowers on the independence of democratic social reform in Europe.*

Sir, —The anniversary of the Soviet invasion of Czechoslovakia must be the occasion for a most sober assessment of its implications. Within a year the Soviet Union has been able to conduct a series of purges in the party, the mass media and other areas of authority or influence which, though not yet complete, have silenced effectively the voices of "social-

57. The Doctors' Plot (1953) was an alleged conspiracy of Moscow physicians, mainly Jews, to murder leading government and party officials; it is widely believed that Stalin intended to use the resulting trials as a pretext for purges reminiscent of the 1930s. Stalin died later that year.

ism with a human face". A further deterioration in the political and economic circumstances of Czechoslovakia can be anticipated with confidence in the coming year.

I hope that the anniversary will be marked throughout the country as a day of mourning, because the invasion destroyed the only hopeful road for the country: the development of democratic and humanistic forms of socialism in place of the former bureaucracy and secret police.

While there has been considerable sympathy for Czechoslovakia from Governments and mass media in the West, most of these are curious and embarrassing would-be allies for those who wish to create a socialist democracy. Perhaps the Russians may be permitted a laugh when a Times leader condemns the harassment of independent-minded Czech trade unionists.

A more valuable service to Czechoslovak socialists would be for socialists everywhere to re-examine their principles in the light of the past year. In particular it is high time for the Left in Europe to reassert its commitment to socialist democracy and internationalism before the leaders of the Soviet Union and the United States further force their will on the spheres of influence in Europe which they respectively claim.

If the Brezhnev doctrine of "limited sovereignty" triumphs, not only are all reforms in Eastern Europe to be subject to the veto of the Kremlin bureaucracy, but no nation in the shadow of a super-power can hope for either independence or social transformation. President Nixon is unlikely to overlook the usefulness of the doctrine in any renewed uprising in France.

Yours faithfully, Bertrand Russell
Plas Penrhyn, Penrhyndeudraeth, Merionethshire, Aug. 17.

[282]

## Coming Czech Trials

*The Times* (25th November, 1969), p. 9 | C69.15

Sir, —The renewed reports of preparations for show trials in Czechoslovakia are highly alarming. It is imperative to defend the lives of those whose crime was the Czechoslovak "Spring" of 1968. If trials are to be staged, the offered evidence must be subjected to the most exhaustive scrutiny, and this task must not be left to cold warriors.

May I, therefore, appeal through your columns to all those who have conducted independent investigations into the character of the war in

Vietnam—and whose work has been so well justified recently—to stand ready to participate in hearings on Czechoslovakia?

Yours faithfully, Bertrand Russell.
Bertrand Russell Peace Foundation Ltd.
3 and 4 Shavers Place, Haymarket, S.W.1.
Nov. 23

# JFK Assassination

*Early press reports of the assassination of President Kennedy in November 1963 caused Russell to doubt the "lone gun-man" theory. In June of 1964, when he met with Mark Lane, the New York lawyer who had been looking into the affair on behalf of Oswald's mother, Russell's suspicions were confirmed by the evidence Lane had gathered. Working closely with the Bertrand Russell Peace Foundation, Russell headed The British Who Killed Kennedy? Committee which challenged the official U.S. explanation as given in the Warren Commission Report.*

*In September, about the same time that the Warren Report was being released, Russell published an article 'Sixteen Questions on the Assassination' in* The Minority of One *which drew the criticism that Russell's criticisms were premature and that he couldn't have known what he was talking about. In his autobiography, Russell says that Mark Lane had in fact sent him an "early copy."*[58] *See also document [230].*

•••••••••••••• [283] ••••••••••••••

## Kennedy Data

*The Sunday Times* (31st May, 1964), p. 18 | C64.42

Sir, —Your report last Sunday concerning the efforts of Mr. Mark Lane to uncover the facts surrounding the murder of President Kennedy was very informative and welcome, except in one respect. Your reporter implies that Mr. Lane is a "Left-winger" and cites as evidence that his material was published in the United States in a Left-wing journal, the "National Guardian."

Mr. Lane is no more a Left-winger than was President Kennedy. He attempted to publish his evidence regarding Oswald and the murder of Kennedy in virtually every established American publication, but was unsuccessful. Only the "National Guardian" was prepared to print his scrupulously documented material. Mr. Lane had not even heard of the "National Guardian" before learning of their willingness to publish it.

I think it is important that no unnecessary prejudice against the valuable work of Mr. Lane should be aroused, so that his data concerning vital events may be viewed with an open mind by people of all political persuasions. I am seeking to organise a committee in Britain for the purpose

58. *Autobiography,* Volume 3, p. 238.

of dissemination the information being gathered by Mr. Lane on the death of the president. I hope that it will be given a fair hearing.

Bertrand Russell
Penrhyndeudraeth, Merioneth

[284]

## A Hearing for Oswald

*The Sunday Times* (20th December, 1964), p. 8 | C64.95

*Russell writes on behalf of the British "Who Killed Kennedy?" Committee in support of* The Sunday Times *for its willingness to publish material critical of the Warren Commission. Russell's committee was made up of a number of prominent people, including Hugh Trevor-Roper, historian; Kingsley Martin, former editor of* The New Statesman; *Lord Boyd-Orr, former UN official and Nobel peace laureate; and Michael Foot, Labour leader and M.P.*

Sir, —*The Sunday Times* is to be congratulated for being the first major British or American newspaper to allow a fair hearing to the overwhelming case against the Warren Report and the official version of the assassination of President Kennedy. In providing Professor Trevor-Roper an opportunity to publish his wholly admirable article, *The Sunday Times* has allowed the wider public to come into contact for the first time with the evidence we have been striving to make known, heretofore against overwhelming odds.

Not one of the basic conclusions of the Warren Commission Report can be sustained, and in all the important areas the actual testimony is at complete variance with the Commissions summary of it in its Report. Key witnesses to the direction of the shots and the murder of Tippit were not allowed to testify. Professor Trevor-Roper deals conclusively with the identification of Oswald by Brennan, the supposed basis for the circulation of Oswald's description in connection with the murder of Tippit. What is even more remarkable is that Oswald's description was circulated in connection with Tippit's murder over thirty minutes before Tippit was shot.

Considering that the rifle alleged to have been used by Oswald is incapable of the necessary performance, that the number of shots admitted by the Commission require President Kennedy to have been struck at an angle which does not correspond to the holes in his jacket and shirt, the Report of the Commission not only fails to establish its conclusion, but succeeds unintentionally in establishing that more than one person was involved in murdering the President.

The measure of the achievement of Mr. Lane (who is investigating the case) is that, despite the weight of organised authority and the hostility of the Press, he has accomplished for Oswald in one year what Zola required twelve to provide for Dreyfus.[59]

The independent investigators working for us in Dallas are turning up new evidence continually. I am hopeful that we shall not have to wait very much longer for the answer to the question: "Who killed Kennedy?"

Bertrand Russell
British "Who killed Kennedy?" Committee

---

59. The Dreyfus Affair (1894–1906) polarized French opinion in the Third Republic. Alfred Dreyfus (1859–1935), a Jewish military officer, was convicted of treason by the French government on flimsy evidence and sentenced to life in prison on Devil's Island. The French writer and anticlerical social reformer Émile Zola (1840–1902) took up Dreyfus's cause and accused the authorities of framing Dreyfus, who was exonerated in 1906.

## Miscellaneous

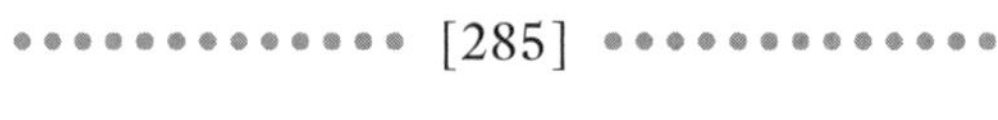

### Only Begetter

*The Times* (12th April, 1963) | C63.96

*Russell speculates on the authorship of Shakespeare's sonnets and tries to clear up a scholarly puzzle.*

Sir, —Your interesting leader of November 29 on Shakespeare's sonnets prompts me to suggest with all due pomp and solemnity another theory about Mr. W.H. I suggest that, like Melchizedek[60] according to *Encyclopedia Biblica,* he owes his existence to a scribe's error—H. for S. Mr. W.S., after all, was certainly the only begetter of these ensuing sonnets.

Yours faithfully, Russell
Plas Penrhyn, Penrhyndeudraeth, Merioneth, Nov. 29

### Savagery

*The Observer* (12th January, 1963), p. 30 | C64.05

*Russell reflects on the nature and root causes of political violence and intolerance around the world.*

Sir, —Most people in this country, and I among them, have been appalled by the savagery displayed last year during the happenings in Dallas, Texas, and by the electrical torture recently accorded peaceful marchers in the American South.

I am, however, constrained to remember the possibly more vicious, but in large measure deliberately hidden, happenings of the past year in Britain: the "Profumo scandal," the events in Aden, the pressure to

60. Melchizedek, a priest-king in the Old Testament who, according to some scholars, foreshadowed Christ.

restore flogging, to preserve capital punishment and to strengthen the laws against homosexuality.

There were many who rejoiced in the assassination of President Diem of South Vietnam, who read avidly of the coups d'etat in Iraq and elsewhere.

Have we all become savage? Why do we turn, inevitably, towards ferocity in dealing with political opponents—towards maiming or killing or sentencing them to disproportionately long imprisonment?

I think it is because we live in an atmosphere of fear bred by present political policies. We have been conditioned to accept cruelty, even the threat of extermination, as the sole means of defending a way of life that seems to prove itself, by such a result, hardly worth defending.

Bertrand Russell
Merioneth

[287]

## Split Infinitive

*The Daily Telegraph* (15th May, 1964), p. 18 | C64.36

*In this letter and in the next, Russell gives a grammar lesson as he points out a split infinitive in Milton's 'Lycidas'.*

Sir, —The aggressive military behaviour of the British Government in Southern Arabia[61] has not lessened my admiration, ironical as it may seem, for the uses to which the English language was put by famous writers.

For instance, Milton, who, apart from his concern for individual freedom, managed to admirably split infinitives. A reading of "Lycidas" might be expected to adequately teach this to Mr. S.P.W. Corbett. Even Fowler could be of help.

Yours faithfully, Bertrand Russell
Penrhyndeudraeth, Merioneth

---

61. Russell no doubt refers to British resistance to South Yemen's rebellion against the 125-year-old British rule—a rebellion which began in 1963 and ended with South Yemen's independence as The People's Republic of Southern Yemen in 1967.

••••••••••••• [288] •••••••••••••

## Split Infinitive

*The Daily Telegraph* (22nd May, 1964), p. 16 | C64.39

*Several* Daily Telegraph *correspondents had been puzzled by Russell's reference in his May 15 letter to a split infinitive in Milton's famous poem. Perhaps Russell had in mind lines 65–66: "To tend the homely slighted shepherd's trade, /And strictly meditate the thankless Muses?"*

Sir —I regret Mr. G. M. Douglas's inability to discover the split infinitive in "Lycidas." I suggest he read it again.

Yours faithfully, Bertrand Russell.
Penrhyndeudraeth, Merioneth.

••••••••••••• [289] •••••••••••••

## Against World War One

*Tribune* (7th August, 1964), p. 7 | C64.60a

*Russell is joined by his friend and pacifist, Fenner Brockway. Brockway was a supporter of the No Conscription Fellowship during World War I and a leader in the CND movement during the 1960s. In this letter they underscore the heroism of the C.O.s during World War I. Brockway, like Russell, was imprisoned for his pacifist politics during the war. At the time of the letter (August 1964), he was a Labour MP.*

Just 50 years ago, on August 4, 1914, World War One began. No doubt we shall now see an intensification of the efforts of writers, editors and publishers to remind us of its heroisms and its stupidities.

One vital part of this story, however, has so far suffered neglect. This is the part dealing with struggle and sometimes heroism, not in the face of the enemy of foreign fields, but in the face of established authority at home: the story of opposition to the war.

In voicing a political or moral objection to the war, 69 men died in Britain alone and 39 were driven insane, according to records complied by the No Conscription Fellowship in 1919. We ourselves had our periods in prison. It is time for the full story to be told.

We are therefore appealing to our fellow objectors to come forward with letters, diaries, photographs, documents and personal reminiscences.

These should be sent to David Boulton, who has been commissioned by Messrs. Macgibbon and Kee to write a book on the subject, at 66 Vandon Court, Petty France, London, S.W.1. Documents will be copied and returned immediately.

We ourselves are offering Mr. Boulton every possible assistance, for it is fitting that the story of resistance to World War One should be told by one who, as a journalist and editor of CND publications, has been active in the resistance to World War Three.[62]

Bertrand Russell
Fenner Brockway
House of Commons, S. W. 1.

•••••••••••••• [290] ••••••••••••••

## False and True

*The Observer Review* (12th March, 1967), p. 33 | C67.04

*Russell corrects a misstatement of a variation of the 'liar paradox' that appeared in his autobiography.[63] This paradox is very similar to the contradiction discovered by Russell in 1902 (Russell's paradox), which dominated his work in the philosophy of mathematics for the next eight years.*

Sir, —Some readers of extracts from my autobiography have questioned—and rightly—the contradiction which I mentioned as being "essentially similar to that of Epimenides."

On a piece of paper is written: "The statement on the other side of this paper is false." The person turns the paper over and finds on the other side: "The statement on the other side of this paper is false." On turning over the paper, the recipient should read: "The statement on the other side of this paper is true." I regret that I made this error.

Bertrand Russell
Penrhyndeudraeth

62. David Boulton's book, *Objection Overruled,* was published in 1967 by MacGibbon and Kee.

63. *Autobiography,* Volume 1, p. 222.

[291]

## Bertrand Russell on the Afterlife

*The Humanist* (September–October 1968), p. 29 | C68.25a

*Although Russell embraced a sort of pantheistic mysticism for a few years around the time of the first world war, he was an agnostic regarding the existence of the Judeo-Christian God for most of his life. He did emphasize the importance of love ("The good life is one inspired by love and guided by knowledge"), and he sometimes even called it "Christian love."*[64]

Thank you for bringing to my attention these continuing rumors of my imminent conversion to Christianity. Evidently there is a lie factory at work on behalf of the afterlife. How often must I continue to deny that I have become religious? There is no basis whatsoever for these rumors.

My views on religion remain those that I acquired at the age of 16. I consider all forms of religion not only false but harmful. My published works record my views.

Bertrand Russell
Merioneth, Great Britain

[292]

## Lord Russell's Last Message

*The Washington Post* (2nd March, 1970), p. A7 | C70.01

*This statement on the Middle East is dated 31st January, 1970, and was read on 3rd February, the day after Russell's death, to an International Conference of Parliamentarians meeting in Cairo.*

The latest phase of the undeclared war in the Middle East is based upon a profound miscalculation. The bombing raids deep into Egyptian territory will not persuade the civilian population to surrender, but will stiffen their resolve to resist. This is the lesson of all aerial bombardment.

64. See above, document [195] where Russell says, in an article about him in *Look* magazine, that what the world needs is more "love—Christian love or compassion." But in his letter to the editor, he says: "I would have preferred that the adjective 'Christian' be omitted. My reason is that since I used it in one of my books, Christians have falsely claimed that I was becoming Christian, and I have got rather tired of denying it."

The Vietnamese who have endured years of American heavy bombing have responded not by capitulation but by shooting down more enemy aircraft. In 1940 my own fellowcountrymen resisted Hitler's bombing raids with unprecedented unity and determination. For this reason, the present Israeli attacks will fail in their essential purpose, but at the same time they must be condemned vigorously throughout the world.

The development of the crisis in the Middle East is both dangerous and instructive. For over 20 years Israel has expanded by force of arms. After every stage in this expansion Israel has appealed to "reason" and has suggested "negotiations". This is the traditional role of the imperial power, because it wishes to consolidate with the least difficulty what it has already taken by violence. Every new conquest becomes the new basis of the proposed negotiation from strength, which ignores the injustice of the previous aggression. The aggression committed by Israel must be condemned, not only because no state has the right to annexe foreign territory, but because every expansion is an experiment to discover how much more aggression the world will tolerate.

The refugees who surround Palestine in their hundreds of thousands were described recently by the Washington journalist I.F. Stone as "the moral millstone around the neck of world Jewry." Many of the refugees are now well into the third decade of their precarious existence in temporary settlements. The tragedy of the people of Palestine is that their country was "given" by a foreign Power to another people for the creation of a new State. The result was that many hundreds of thousands of innocent people were made permanently homeless. With every new conflict their number have increased. How much longer is the world willing to endure this spectacle of wanton cruelty? It is abundantly clear that the refugees have every right to the homeland from which they were driven, and the denial of this right is at the heart of the continuing conflict. No people anywhere in the world would accept being expelled en masse from their own country; how can anyone require the people of Palestine to accept a punishment which nobody else would tolerate? A permanent just settlement of the refugees in their homeland is an essential ingredient of any genuine settlement in the Middle East.

We are frequently told that we must sympathize with Israel because of the suffering of the Jews in Europe at the hands of the Nazis. I see in this suggestion no reason to perpetuate any suffering. What Israel is doing today cannot be condoned, and to invoke the horrors of the past to justify those of the present is gross hypocrisy. Not only does Israel condemn a vast number of refugees to misery; not only are many Arabs under occupation condemned to military rule; but also Israel condemns the Arab nations only recently emerging from colonial status, to continued impoverishment as military demands take precedence over national development.

All who want to see an end to bloodshed in the Middle East must ensure that any settlement does not contain the seeds of future conflict. Justice requires that the first step towards a settlement must be an Israeli withdrawal from all the territories occupied in June, 1967. A new world campaign is needed to help bring justice to the long-suffering people of the Middle East.

# Index